Fodor's

BELIZE

Welcome to Belize

It's easy to become immersed in the natural beauty of Belize. Broadleaf canopies shelter exotic birds, and ancient Mayan ruins are wrapped in vines. Underwater caves and the chute of the Blue Hole offer some of the world's best diving, and the Belize Barrier Reef astounds snorkelers with a lavish medley of coral and fish. Belize's secluded resorts embrace these surroundings: here, you can sleep under a palm-thatched roof in a lush jungle lodge and escape to a dreamy overwater bungalow with turquoise sea views all on the same trip.

TOP REASONS TO GO

★ **Mayan Ruins:** Evidence of the ancient Mayan empire is everywhere in Belize.

★ **Snorkeling:** The Belize Barrier Reef presents amazing underwater vistas.

★ **Diving:** Reefs and atolls provide many of the world's greatest dive sites.

★ **Bird-Watching:** Belize has more than 500 species of birds, many rare or endangered.

★ **Beach Stays:** Often remote or removed, and nearly always right on the water.

★ **Jungle Lodges:** For an unforgettable close-to-nature experience in comfort.

Contents

MAPS

Chapter 1

EXPERIENCE
BELIZE

20 ULTIMATE EXPERIENCES

Belize offers terrific experiences that should be on every traveler's list. Here are Fodor's top picks for a memorable trip.

1 Belize Barrier Reef

Belize's 200-mile (322-km) sector of the Mesoamerican Barrier Reef stretching from Mexico's Yucatán Peninsula to Honduras's Bay Islands makes it one of the world's top diving and snorkeling destinations. It's home to 300 species of fish and 65 kinds of coral. *(Ch. 4)*

2 Ambergris Caye

Ambergris Caye's San Pedro town is so popular it inspired a Madonna song. The Belize Barrier Reef lies less than a mile away and it has Belize's best nightlife. *(Ch. 4)*

3 Hopkins Beach

Enjoy the fun clutter of the friendly town of Hopkins on the southern coast and its 5-mile-long (8-km-long) strand of golden sand lined with coconut trees. *(Ch. 7)*

4 Bird-Watching

Belize's jungles teem with wild birds—nearly 600 species. Endangered beauties such as the scarlet macaw and keel-billed toucan roam freely in the country's interior. *(Ch. 5–8)*

5 Diving the Blue Hole

Diving this spectacular site 45 miles (72 km) off the coast is not for novices—you need to log 24 dives before you tackle this one—but helicopter tours from Belize City let you gaze at it from above. *(Ch. 4)*

6 Private Island Life

Belize's cayes and atolls have many fantasy getaways—some with surprisingly down-to-earth prices and only a handful of guests—including Thatch Caye, Coco Plum Caye, and Bird Island. *(Ch. 4)*

7 Cave Tubing

Underground, you'll find subterranean rivers that provide thrilling passage through spooky caves. The easiest caves to visit are in the Cayo, including Barton Creek Cave and ATM. *(Ch. 6)*

8 Snorkeling at Glover's Reef Atoll

One of Belize's three atolls, Glover's Reef is great for snorkeling and kayaking. Stay at the Isla Marisol or Off the Wall for an unforgettable experience. *(Ch. 4)*

9 Mayan Ruins

For 5,000 years the Maya inhabited this region, leaving 600 archaeological sites behind. Caracol and more than a dozen sites are open to visitors for exploring. *(Ch. 3–9)*

10 Jaguar Trekking

Jaguars are shy and nocturnal, so sightings are rare, but Belize has the highest concentration in the world. Cockscomb Basin Wildlife Sanctuary is your best chance to spot one. *(Ch. 7)*

11 Staying at a Jungle Lodge

In Belize there's a jungle lodge for every budget. The best of the best include the Cayo's Chaa Creek, Chan Chich, and Blancaneaux. They all offer a surprising degree of comfort. *(Ch. 5–8)*

12 Shark-Ray Alley

This site off Ambergris Caye will give you "I dove with the sharks" bragging rights. No one needs to know the nurse sharks at the Hol Chan Marine Reserve are harmless, right? *(Ch. 4)*

13 Exploring Wildlife Sanctuaries

Belize sets aside an impressive 26% of its territory for environmental protection. Crooked Tree, only 30 minutes from the airport, and Cockscomb Basin are the best. *(Ch. 5, 7)*

14 Hummingbird Highway

To experience Belize at its most scenic, drive on this roadway, which winds through limestone hill country, mountains, and citrus groves. *(Ch. 6)*

15 Garifuna Culture

Dance to the drums of Belize's vibrant Garifuna population in the coastal city of Dangriga or down the coast in Punta Gorda. Several drum workshops offer lessons. *(Ch. 7, 8)*

16 Actun Tunichil Muknal

The country's spookiest site is a Mayan underworld filled with eerie chambers where ancient artifacts and human skeletons remain undisturbed. *(Ch. 6)*

17 Placencia Resorts

Belize's up-and-coming beach destination is ready to give the cayes a run for their money with a string of resorts in three communities—Maya Beach, Seine Bight, and Placencia Village. *(Ch. 7)*

18 Historical Belize City

Before you pass through Belize's former capital, take a look around at the early 1900s colonial government buildings, built in tropical style, the Supreme Court and the House of Culture among them. *(Ch. 3)*

19 Ziplining

Whoosh from tree to tree of Belize's rain forest canopy, courtesy of a cable, helmet, gloves, and very secure harness. You'll find the majority of these canopy tours in the Cayo. *(Ch. 6–8)*

20 Bioluminescent Night Snorkeling

One of Belize's great spectacles takes place from February through April on the Anderson Lagoon near Hopkins. The water glows in the dark like a tropical aurora borealis. *(Ch. 7)*

Best Diving and Snorkeling Sites in Belize

TURNEFFE ATOLL

The country's most dived and snorkeled atoll lies closest to the mainland, 15 miles (24 km) east of Belize City. Reef sharks, dolphins, eagle rays, lionfish, and sea turtles thrive in abundance here among the 200 small islands, and there's a dive for every level.

HALF MOON CAYE

At the Lighthouse Reef Atoll's southeastern corner lies this island, which divers know best for the Half Moon Caye Wall's "6,000 feet of vertical abyss." Spotted eagle rays and sea turtles are the main underwater attractions, but the island is a national monument and bird sanctuary to the red-footed booby.

LAUGHING BIRD CAYE

About 11 miles (18 km) from Placencia, Laughing Bird Caye makes an easy half-day trip for family-oriented snorkeling. You'll see stingrays, barracudas, black groupers, and moray eels. The island serves as a bird sanctuary for the laughing gull, which has a distinctive laugh-like call, of course.

THE BLUE HOLE

A marine sinkhole enclosed within the Lighthouse Reef Atoll 45 miles (72 km) off the coast forms Belize's most famous dive site. The dark blue, nearly perfect circle measures 1,000 feet across and 400 feet deep. (The diameter is large enough that the Blue Hole is technically two dive sites—north and south—in one.) You'll need 24 dives in your logbook before you can attempt this one.

GLOVER'S REEF ATOLL

You'll catch sight of nurse sharks, barracudas, and manta rays at the southernmost and remotest of Belize's three atolls. Glover Reef's Emerald Forest site drops only 25 feet, making it a good dive for novices. Long Caye and Southwest Caye entail drops of hundreds of feet and must be expertly done. Two dive resorts—one expensive, one more moderately priced—allow you to base yourself way out here, 30 miles (48 km) east of Hopkins on the mainland.

HOL CHAN MARINE RESERVE

The name translates to "little channel" in modern Mayan. "Hol Chan" aptly describes the split of 25 yards that naturally cuts through the barrier reef off the southern tip of Ambergris Caye. Authorities aggressively protect the environment here at Belize's first national marine park, and you'll encounter nearly pristine conditions. The reserve encompasses three habitats, with the coral reef (Zone A) of most interest to

Blue Hole

divers. Fishing is off-limits, so you can spot squirrelfish, yellowtail snappers, barracudas, and Nassau groupers among the 160 species of fish logged in the reserve. Zones B and C are the lagoon and mangrove, respectively. The popular Shark-Ray Alley (Zone D, also on this list) was a later addition.

SAPODILLA CAYES
Relatively few visitors get out here, 40 miles (64 km) east of Belize's far southern coast. Those that make the trip will find the most beautiful island group in Belize, with spadefish, parrot fish, and dolphins all common sights. Though Guatemala and Honduras also claim the Sapodillas as their own, Belize maintains control of the islands and the dispute need not concern you as a visitor. Outfitters in Punta Gorda can arrange a trip.

SOUTH WATER CAYE
This small island sits directly atop the barrier reef and anchors a protected marine park. Its shallow lagoon is home to nurse sharks, eagle rays, manta rays, and sea turtles. Outfitters in Hopkins and Dangriga can arrange excursions.

GLADDEN SPIT
Get out your calendar for this one. Gladden Spit draws divers for a rare chance to swim with the gentle whale shark, which measures up to 60 feet in length. The sharks are drawn by the spawning of various snappers from March through June.

SHARK-RAY ALLEY
True to its name, Shark-Ray Alley in the Hol Chan Marine Reserve attracts nurse sharks and stingrays. Nurse sharks are considered harmless—most of the time. The site makes for a good intro dive and great snorkeling, although the current can get strong.

Belize's Top Mayan Ruins

ALTUN HA

You've already seen Altun Ha—the name means "rock stone pond"—if you've imbibed Belize's iconic Belikin beer. Its Temple of the Masonry Altar is right there on the label. It's one of the country's most visited Mayan sites and a popular shore excursion with cruise visitors.

CHAN CHICH

The ruins at Chan Chich come complete with a snazzy jungle lodge—it's one of Belize's top places to stay (and one of its most expensive).

ACTUN TUNICHIL MUKNAL

A hike, a wade, and a swim take you to the inner reaches of "ATM," or "Cave of the Crystal Sepulchre," Belize's most haunted sight. The remains of the "Crystal Maiden," a sacrificial victim, sparkle eerily in the darkness.

LUBAANTUN

In one of history's great archaeological hoaxes, British pulp writer F. A. Mitchell-Hedges captured the world's imagination with his claim to have found a mystical crystal skull here.

LAMANAI

One of the few Belizean sites whose original Mayan name is known—it means "submerged crocodile"—Lamanai was inhabited for over 3,200 years and well into the 18th century. A boat ride up the New River Lagoon offers the coolest, most "Indiana Jones" way of getting here, but the site is accessible by road too.

CERROS

Although the name translates as "hills," many of coastal Cerros's 170 structures, including several temples, are partially submerged. The ocean water has seriously eroded the stone on many of the buildings. The site sits across the bay from the town of Corozal and is reached by boat.

BARTON CREEK CAVE

Picture a longer, more rustic, Mayan version of the "It's a Small World" ride at the Disney parks, but without the song. Area tour operators canoe you into, through, and out of this ceremonial cave near San Ignacio. Half-day excursions take you 1 mile (1.5 km) into the cavern, but it is thought to go farther.

Xunantunich

XUNANTUNICH

We suggest you don't dress in white while visiting Xunantunich, lest you be mistaken for the ghost who allegedly haunts this site. (You probably won't have the specter's reputed fiery red eyes, though.) The site's name, pronounced shoon-ahn-TOO-nitch, means "stone woman" and was given by modern archaeologists to honor the legendary specter. The massive El Castillo pyramid dominates the 26 temples here.

SANTA RITA

Belizean couples come from all over the country to get married in Santa Rita's pretty garden on the outskirts of Corozal. Presently one ruin structure, containing two burial chambers inside, is open. Historians continue to debate Santa Rita's significance. The area was a center of cacao, honey, and vanilla production during pre-Columbian times, and Santa Rita may have existed to protect an important trade route. It may also have been the lost Mayan city of Chetumal.

CARACOL

If you visit the Cayo, you must see Belize's largest and most significant archaeological site, which also happens to have the country's tallest structure (Caracol's Caana pyramid). The site measures 75 square miles (194 square km) and is the most remote of all the ruins. Caracol's estimated 35,000 structures—most remain unexcavated—are thought to have made up a city of 200,000 inhabitants. The Belize Defence Force accompanies convoys to and from Caracol.

What to Eat and Drink in Belize

Belikin beer

BELIKIN BEER

Perhaps no international brew has forged a cultural identity with its nation the way Belize's iconic Belikin beer has. The brewery's line consists primarily of a European-style 4.8% lager and a slightly sweet 6.5% stout (it is sugar country, after all). Two specialty stouts (sorrel and chocolate) make limited appearances annually.

RICE AND BEANS

The ultimate Belizean staple is pleasant and unassuming. Red beans are seasoned, often with garlic or onions but always steeped in coconut milk; cooked rice is stirred into the mix. It's usually a side dish, served with grilled meat or fish.

CEVICHE

The key to this Latin America–wide specialty is letting the acidity of lime juice do the "cooking" of raw meat, usually shellfish. Belizean ceviche was traditionally prepared with raw conch, but overfishing makes conch difficult to find. These days, shrimp is placed into lime marinade, usually with chopped cucumbers, tomatoes, onions, and cilantro.

Salbutes

TROPICAL FRUITS
We all know bananas. They account for 16% of Belize's exports. But reliable tropical rain and sunshine mean you'll also encounter all manner of exotic fruits—exotic to us, at least—including the creamy soursop and the yellow craboo (or nance).

BOIL UP
If rice and beans has any competition for the title of "Quintessential Belizean Dish," it's this heavy-on-the-starches Creole specialty from the southern part of the country. A stew of fish, plantains, eggs, potatoes, cassava, bread, and vegetables gets "boiled up" and topped with a glaze of coconut milk.

ESCABECHE
It's the chicken soup of Belize, and it's good for whatever ails you. The chicken and onion soup, made with lime and vinegar, clears the sinuses, especially when you spice it up with some habanero peppers.

CHIMOLE
Fundamental to this hearty Creole soup is black *recado*, a roasted mixture of spices that imparts a smoky flavor to the dish. Stateside Latino groceries sell ready-made recado; Belizean cooks prepare their own in advance, always outdoors.

SALBUTES
Crispy and colorful *salbutes* are the ultimate on-the-go Belizean snack. These fried corn tortillas are topped with chicken, tomatoes, and peppers, and have a signature zing and color from red recado spices. Some add a few pickled onions to give it a final bit of tang.

TAMALES
These Mexico- and Central America–wide treats are made from chicken or pork and beans with veggies, all stuffed into a cornmeal square. Wrap that square into a plantain leaf and tie with string, and you have a *tamal*. Oh, and you don't eat the wrapper.

CARIBBEAN SPINY LOBSTER
The entire country circles June 15 on the calendar—when lobster season starts. The beach town of Placencia celebrates with Lobster Fest in late June.

CHOCOLATE
The ancient Maya revered the cacao bean, which flourishes in southern Belize's Toledo district. Cotton Tree Chocolate and The Belize Chocolate Company sell bars with a complex, earthy flavor.

WHAT'S WHERE

1 Belize City. Depending on your perspective, Belize's commercial, transportation, and cultural hub is either a lively Caribbean port city of raffish charm or a crime-ridden, edgy backwater best seen through the rearview mirror.

2 The Cayes and the Atolls. Hundreds of cayes (pronounced *keys*) dot the Caribbean Sea off Belize, both inside and outside the Barrier Reef. The largest are Ambergris, Belize's most popular visitor destination, and Caulker. Farther out are three South Pacific–style atolls.

3 Northern Belize. This is the land of sugarcane and sweet, off-the-beaten-path places to visit. Corozal Town, up against the Mexican border, has a lovely bayside setting, and Sarteneja is a fishing village just waiting to be discovered.

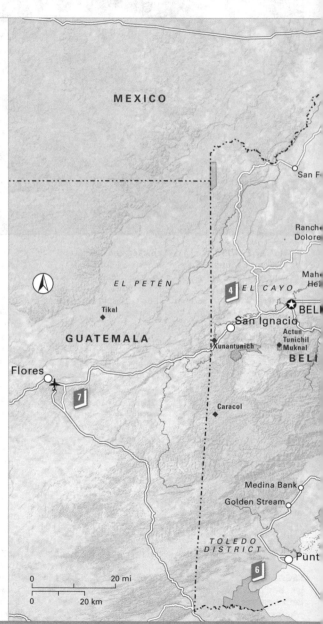

4 The Cayo. The rolling hills of western Belize, anchored by San Ignacio, offer outdoor activities aplenty—caving, canoeing, hiking, horseback riding, and mountain biking. Several remarkable Mayan sites also await, including Caracol, Xunantunich, and Actun Tunichil Muknal.

5 The Southern Coast. Want beaches? The best on the mainland are on the Placencia Peninsula, especially in the Maya Beach area, and in Hopkins.

6 The Deep South. Rainy and lush, beautiful and remote, Punta Gorda in far southern Belize is the jumping-off point for the unspoiled Mayan villages of Toledo District and for onward travel to Guatemala and Honduras.

7 El Petén. This part of Guatemala, easily visited from the Cayo District of Belize, is home to the most spectacular of all Mayan sites, Tikal, and the remains of many other ancient cities.

How to See Wildlife in Belize

One of the defining characteristics of Belize is an almost universal cultural appreciation of local wildlife. And there's a lot to appreciate: jaguars and other big wild cats, colorful parrots like toucans and macaws, and strange creatures from tapir to snake-mimicking caterpillars. Fortunately for visitors, access to witnessing wildlife without disturbing it is easily available, with knowledgeable guides ready to share their knowledge. Just remember—do not feed the wildlife and only go on tours with recommended guides.

TAG ALONG WITH CROCODILE CONSERVATIONISTS

When the sun goes down on La Isla Bonita, the crocodiles come out. For only BZ$50 you can tag along with the American Crocodile Education Sanctuary (ACES) team on a nighttime boat tour through the mangrove lagoons of Ambergris Caye using a flashlight to spot the red-orange reflective eyes of local crocodiles, all while learning about this magnificent dinosaur-like species.

GO WILD IN A JUNGLE LODGE

The great thing about a jungle lodge like Chaa Creek is the ability to be surrounded by Belize's rain forest without sacrificing the benefits of modern luxury. Besides the wild howler monkeys, amphibians, and toucans that call Chaa Creek home, one of the most popular attractions at the resort is the Blue Morpho Butterfly Exhibit, where visitors can interact with the iridescent blue butterflies.

SEE IT ALL AT THE BELIZE ZOO

What started as an impromptu wildlife rescue center logically evolved into a zoo showcasing the vast beauty of Belize's faunal diversity with over 170 animals. The Belize Zoo is home only to native species, including jaguars—both regular and melanistic (black)—the formidable harpy eagle, keel-billed toucans (the country's official bird), tapir, and so much more.

CUDDLE WITH GREEN IGUANAS

The Green Iguana Conservation Project at the San Ignacio Resort Hotel is one of the most popular activities in the city for tourists and locals alike, granting visitors the opportunity to get up close and personal with one of Belize's most intriguing creatures. This highly interactive exhibit puts green iguanas literally in the laps of guests while they learn about the life cycle and conservation efforts in action for this threatened species.

GO BIRDING WITH THE BEST

From seabirds to colorful parrots, Belize is home to a wide range of beautiful birds, making it one of the top birding destinations in the world. The Audubon Society is the world's premier bird-related organization, and the Belize branch is extremely active. Join them for census, seasonal bird counts, and one of their most successful programs, the Urban Bird Watch, which introduces the concept of birding and bird conservation to those living in the bigger cities of Belize.

TRACK JAGUARS IN THE NIGHT

Belize is home to the world's third-largest cat, the jaguar, which is alive and well in all of Belize's protected parks, especially the Cockscomb Basin. This elusive creature is as beautiful as it is mysterious, and the best chance of seeing one is deep in the jungle. The Cockscomb Basin Night Tour with DTOURZ is known for good luck in sighting wild cats, but the three-plus-hour hike through the nighttime rain forest reveals many more species beyond the jaguar.

HORSEBACK RIDE TO MAYAN RUINS

Ruins of Mayan civilization can be found throughout the country, but because the communities were abandoned long before modern society arrived, nature moved back in. This makes visiting ruins like Xunantunich compelling not just for the history but for the natural beauty. A unique way to take in the howler monkeys and birds that call these ruins home is to explore the region by horseback, which can be done from places like San Jose Succotz.

BE RAPT BY RAPTORS

On the western border of the country, a huge forest reserve called Mountain Pine Ridge made up primarily of pine trees (and related plant species) is an excellent place to go looking for raptors, or birds of prey, in the wild. The Belize Raptor Research Institute is a great resource for determining the places to spot raptors.

SEE THE WORLD'S SECOND-LARGEST BARRIER REEF BEFORE IT'S GONE

Coral colonies create some of the most important ecological systems in the world, and Belize happens to be home to the second-largest one in the world, after the Great Barrier Reef in Australia. Snorkel or dive anywhere along the coast to witness the fascinating colors and structures that corals comprise, plus the millions of animals that call the reef system their home, including barracuda, majestic eagle rays, and puffer fish.

SNORKEL WITH SHARKS AND STINGRAYS

From Ambergris Caye and Caye Caulker, relatively small vessels are constantly bringing curious visitors to snorkel in a marine area along the UNESCO Heritage reef that's home to hungry sharks and stingrays. The sharks are nurse sharks, which are often likened to big catfish, but it's not recommended to get close, nor is it advised to touch them.

SAVE THE SCARLET MACAWS

In the Chiquibul Jungle, you have the rare opportunity to be on the front lines of defending an endangered species while simultaneously experiencing the genuine, virgin rain forest and all the wildlife within. Thanks to the ceaseless efforts of Scarlet Six Biomonitoring, the scarlet macaw population has increased from 200 to 300 in the past few years, largely as a result of guarding the nests of fledgling macaws, which are at risk of being poached for pets. Volunteers camp (along with a guide) at nests along the Raspaculo River for up to two weeks at no cost, experiencing the ultimate jungle camping opportunity including up-close interactions with Belize's wildlife.

SWIM WITH WHALE SHARKS

The only thing that could make swimming with the world's largest fish—the 40-foot whale shark—more magical is the fact that in Belize, it can only be done during the days surrounding the full moon. These majestic creatures migrate through southern Belize every spring, and April and May are the ideal months to see them. The fish congregate around Gladden Split. Tours are available out of nearby Placencia during whale shark season.

WITNESS THE MAJESTY OF MANATEES

Playful manatees love the warm waters off the coast of Belize, and they often can be spotted from the beaches in Hopkins or any of the coastal villages. Manatees pop their heads up above the water, and at first glance they look just like humans taking in the view of the beach. While it's illegal to swim with the manatees, watching them frolic in Belize's blue waters is an experience all its own.

How to Do Belize Off the Beaten Path

Belize will forever be linked with diving, snorkeling, and jungle treks. But stray off the beaten tourist path in this Central American country and you'll find eclectic cultural experiences like a chocolate-making class (at a cacao farm, to boot) and a solar-powered private island. Other off-the-beaten-path excursions to weave into your itinerary while in Belize are a tour of a hot-sauce factory and a stay at a jungle lodge owned by one of America's most famous film directors.

LEARN TO MAKE CHOCOLATE

Belize's chocolate industry may date back to ancient Mayan times, and during the 1970s Hershey's ran a plant here, but the country's bean-to-bar movement is still quite new. Taste Belize leads a day-long tour to Ixcacao Chocolate's small certified-organic farm, where you can learn to make chocolate in an intimate setting. Tours of the tiny factory are also offered.

STAY AT A FILM DIRECTOR'S LUXE LODGE

Resorts hugging the waterfront in Belize, from San Pedro to Dangriga, grab all the attention. But for a very different glimpse of the country, travel inland, across remote terrain and small villages, to the jungle. That's where Francis Ford Coppola debuted Blancaneaux Lodge, born out of his family retreat in the Cayo District, in 1993. Each of the chic cabanas sports a thatched roof and modern amenities, with access to a restaurant, pool, horseback riding, and a spa.

DANCE IN DANGRIGA

This community a two-hour drive south of Belize City is flush with Garifuna residents who showcase traditional dance, with lots of hip-shaking and drumming. Dig deeper into Belize's musical roots at the Lebeha Drumming Center in Hopkins, which hosts performances and lessons. For a more modern edge, check out *punta* rock, a music style born out of

this traditional dance that adds electric guitar and synthesizer—many stores in Belize sell albums. In 2006, the center's "Traditional Garifuna Music" album was nominated for a Grammy.

VISIT A SOLAR-POWERED PRIVATE ISLAND

On Bomba Island in Belize, solar power is the main source of electricity. From Ambergris Caye, it's a 70-minute boat ride, the perfect day-trip offered by several tour operators. You can explore the remote island and purchase crafts, wood carvings, and wood bowls from local artisans.

SHOP AT A FISH MARKET

Punta Gorda, in southern Belize's Toledo District, hosts one of the country's best seafood markets, with booths selling spiny lobster, crab, octopus, fish fillets, shrimp, and fresh produce. Mennonite farmers sell their products alongside Mayan farmers every Monday, Wednesday, Friday, and Saturday. If you're renting a villa with a kitchen, consider picking up the daily catch for that night's dinner.

VISIT A HOT-SAUCE FACTORY

While Marie Sharp's hot sauces, jams, and jellies—crafted from farm-grown ingredients within a few miles of the factory—are sold here and there in the United States, when it comes to culinary ingredients, there's nothing better than heading to the source. The factory in Dangriga features a retail store and very informal tour of the factory where you might meet Marie herself.

EXPERIENCE SAN PEDRO'S NIGHTLIFE

The town of San Pedro is truly a hub for after-dark fun. It's on the southern tip of Ambergris Caye, not far from the luxury resorts on the sand. Check out some very local establishments, such as Crazy Canucks Beach Bar, with theme music nights (such as reggae) and hermit-crab races. Nearby Coco Loco's Beach Bar is a great place to soak up the sunset.

TOUR A MENNONITE AND MAYAN COMMUNITY

About 10,000 Mennonites live in Belize, selling poultry, vegetables, and dairy products at farm markets. Only within the past five years have they allowed tours of their village. Book MayaWalk Tours' Maya and Mennonite Cultural Village tour for a sample of two cultures, starting with the Mennonites of Barton Creek and visiting the village of San Antonio to have lunch with the Mayan women who operate a bakery. There are also weavers, clothing designers, artists, and sculptors.

STAY WITH A MAYAN FAMILY

While most come to Belize to stay in upscale jungle lodges and luxe beachside villas, perhaps the best way to experience the culture here is staying in a modern-day Mayan village. Homestay programs in the Deep South, like the Aguacate Homestay Program or the Toledo Ecotourism Association Maya Village Guesthouse Program, offer the chance to live, eat, and do everyday chores with a Mayan family. Living conditions and meals are basic, and there's usually no running water or electricity, but it's an inexpensive way to get an authentic cultural experience, and the money goes to the family and village. Plus, you could pick up a new skill, such as cooking Belizean dishes or processing cacao. It's a once-in-a-lifetime experience.

GO OFF THE GRID IN NORTHERN BELIZE

Most visitors come to northern Belize to see impressive Mayan sites like Altun Ha and Lamanai, but it's worth sticking around to explore some of the smaller towns here. Gallon Jug is home to the most memorable jungle lodge in the

country, Chan Chich, which is beautiful, remote, and literally on top of a Mayan ruin. Sarteneja, close to Corozal Town, is one of the most relaxed beach destinations in the country and is home to the Shipstern Nature Reserve, where you can spot toucans, jaguars, pumas, and more.

DINE ON BELIZEAN-STYLE CHINESE FOOD

Belize's Chinese population—around 1,700 people—lives mostly in Belize City and the Cayo District. Many have opened up restaurants with a unique spin on Chinese cuisine. Fried chicken with sweet ketchup is a must. Lee's Chinese Restaurant in Orange Walk serves Hong Kong–style cuisine, and Chon Saan Palace's Cantonese-style restaurant in Belize City is another popular choice.

SAMPLE FOOD STALLS IN BELMOPAN

Belmopan is the country's capital. With around 16,000 residents, it's Belize's third-largest city. An outdoor market in the city's center is a major hub for locals and sells food items for bargain prices, perfect for grabbing a quick meal with regional flavor. Food and vegetable vendors are also at the market.

Belize Today

BELIZE'S OWN POLITICS OF CHANGE

Belize was long a backwater of the British Empire, used extractively for mahogany harvested by enslaved peoples. Colonialism runs deep: at one point, the British-controlled Belize Estate and Produce Company owned an astonishing one-half of all private lands in British Honduras (now Belize). In fact, the country only became Belize in 1973, declaring independence in 1981. George Price (the heroic "George Washington of Belize") was one of the principal architects of the country's independence, becoming Belize's prime minister. On the global stage, Belize is new, proud, and utterly unique. Since independence—and indeed, before it—the nation has worked to dismantle toxic pieces of its colonial heritage; but Belize also struggles with colonialism's lingering legacy, such as corruption.

One milestone in this journey was the 2008 national election, when Belize, like the United States, elected its first black leader in history. Dean Barrow, a lawyer by profession educated in Jamaica and Miami, became prime minister. His party, the United Democratic Party (UDP), swept into office comfortably. PM Barrow won again the next cycle, and then again in 2016. At first, the UDP government generally took a low-key approach to governing. It followed a reform-oriented agenda, trying to mitigate charges of high-level corruption levied against the former government. Seeking greater diversity in government, the UDP tapped Mayans and Mennonites for high office, in addition to the traditional core of Kriol (or Creole) and mestizo politicians. However, as years passed, Belize's UDP government has faced growing challenges and increasing popular discontent. Rising prices and a slow economy (when the United States sneezes, Belize catches a bad cold) cost PM Barrow some popularity, as did increasing crime, especially in Belize City. The government became mired in new charges of corruption. A new election takes place in 2020.

OLD TENSIONS FLARE

In 2016, old and painful tensions between Guatemala and Belize flared, seeing occasional firefights between the two national forces in the far south and west of Belize. Both countries inherited a territorial dispute from their former colonial powers (Spain in Guatemala, Britain in Belize). Guatemala never completely accepted the boundaries etched in an 1859 border treaty, maintaining that Belize hadn't fulfilled its side of the bargain. By 2019, both nations voted to take their protracted dispute to the United Nations' International Court of Justice in The Hague. Justice can be slow, however, so time will tell what the trials bring. Many hope the vehement flag-waving will give way to a peaceful solution.

TOURISM SIZZLES

Belize is hot. Piping hot. People back home might say, "Come again?" when you mention Belize—and indeed, it's still largely untrodden—but the beautiful country is on the map. In 2018, overnight visitors totaled almost half a million—a number that nearly doubled in just six years—while cruise-ship arrivals neared a whopping 1.2 million. New air service to Belize by a number of carriers has made the country more accessible. There are direct flights from 11 cities in the United States (Atlanta, Charlotte, Chicago, Dallas, Denver, Fort Lauderdale, Houston, Los Angeles, Miami, Minneapolis, Newark) and two in Canada (Toronto and Calgary). Harvest Caye, a US$50 million cruise port on an island off Placencia, while highly controversial and opposed by many Belizeans, has boosted cruise tourism.

BRIGHT SPOTS

The Placencia Peninsula continues to pick up momentum as Belize's next major visitor and vacation-home destination. Peninsula development got a boost from the paving of the main road to Placencia from the Southern Highway. The road to nearby Hopkins also was paved, creating a tourism boomlet in that Garifuna Village. In the Deep South, a new paved road from the Southern Highway to the Guatemala border near Jalacte Village has been completed, but, as with many projects in Belize, has a murky opening date.

Tourism and real estate development also chug along on Ambergris Caye, Belize's leading visitor destination. Myriad restaurants have recently opened on the island, boosting San Pedro's reputation as the dining capital of Belize. New hotel projects also are under way on Ambergris Caye and on nearby islands, including Blackadore Caye where Hollywood star Leonardo DiCaprio is planning a luxury private island eco-resort. Dream Belize and Unscripted Belize are bringing beach-front cabanas and upscale accommodations to Placencia, and a Four Seasons with overwater bungalows is being built on Caye Chapel. For visitors to Belize, the increase in rooms could spell good news, as hotel managers scramble to discount rates to keep their slice of the tourism pie.

RECENT MILESTONES

Good news for nurse sharks and sea turtles: the Hol Chan Marine Reserve, a marine national park near Ambergris Caye, is now seven times bigger. A massive expansion began in 2015, to much applause (human applause, that is).

In 2016, after a lengthy court process, thanks to efforts spearheaded by Caleb Orozco, a modern Belize hero who survived threats and personal attacks,

the Belize Supreme Court at long last laid to rest a homophobic colonial-era law that called for up to 10 years in prison for "unnatural sexual acts." The Belize government declined to appeal, and the anachronistic law is now thankfully erased from the books. Some Belizeans, however, still hold negative views of LGBTQ+ rights.

Retiring in Belize

So you fell in love with the Belize experience, outdoors and indoors, met some expats who bought their beachfront lot for a song, and want to do the same for your retirement years? Here are three options to look into and what you can expect if you decide to follow suit.

The Qualified Retired Persons Incentive Program. It's run by the Belize Tourism Board, and anyone at least 45 years old is eligible to participate in the program. It requires a pension, Social Security, or other provable, reliable income of at least US$2,000 a month. A QRP participant (an individual or couple) must deposit US$24,000 a year in a Belize bank. In return, you (and your spouse and minor children) have the right to import household goods, a car, a boat, and even an airplane free of import duty. Income generated from outside Belize isn't taxed by Belize. Although as a QRP participant you can't work for pay in Belize, you can own a business or rental properties and have employees who work for you. Hundreds of QRP applications have been approved since the program was started in 2001. It's a wonder that more haven't applied: 75 million baby boomers in the United States alone are expected to retire over the next 20 years. Contact the Belize Tourism Board for more information. ⊕ www.travelbelize.org

Official Permanent Residency. For those not ready to retire, it's still possible to move to Belize, although work permits usually are somewhat difficult to obtain, and salaries are a fraction of those in the United States, Canada, or western Europe. The best option may be to invest in or start a business in Belize that employs Belizean workers, thus paving the way for a self-employment work permit and residency.

With official permanent residency, you can work in Belize or operate a business, just like any Belizean. You can bring in household goods duty free. Before you can apply for residency, you need to live in Belize for a year, leaving for no more than two weeks. Permanent residency applications are handled by the Belize Immigration Department and may take a few months to a year for approval. Belize citizenship requires living in Belize for at least five years as a permanent resident.

Regular Tourist Permit. Many expats simply stay in Belize on a tourist permit (actually, it's a stamp in your passport). Upon entry, you receive a free visitor permit, good for up to 30 days. This permit can be renewed at any Immigration Office for BZ$50 a month per person for up to six months. After that, renewals cost BZ$100 a month. With a tourist permit, you can't work in Belize. If caught, you could be fined, jailed, and deported. Renewals are never guaranteed, and the rules could change at any time.

Ambergris Caye, the Corozal Town area, Placencia and Hopkins, and Cayo have attracted the largest number of foreign residents, some full-time and others snowbirds. Ambergris Caye, the number-one choice for expats, has an idyllic Caribbean island atmosphere, but real-estate prices here are high. Corozal Town and its environs have among Belize's lowest living costs.

The best advice for anyone contemplating retiring or relocating: Try before you buy. If possible, rent an apartment or house for a few months. Be cautious about buying property. Real-estate agents generally aren't licensed or regulated, and because the pool of qualified buyers in Belize is small, it's a lot harder to sell than to buy. Bottom line: Belize isn't for everyone. The country, as seen from the perspective of a resident, isn't the same as the Belize that's experienced by vacationers.

Chapter 2

TRAVEL SMART BELIZE

Updated by
Rose Lambert-Sluder

★ **CAPITAL:**
Belmopan

∰ POPULATION:
385,000

$ CURRENCY:
Belize dollar; pegged to U.S.
dollar at BZ$2 to US$1

⌨ LANGUAGE:
English, Spanish, Kriol,
several Mayan languages,
Garifuna, Mandarin, and a
dialect of German

☎ COUNTRY CODE:
501

⚠ EMERGENCIES:
911

🚗 DRIVING:
On the right

⚡ ELECTRICITY:
120v/60 cycle; plugs are
U.S. standard two and
three-prong

⊙ TIME:
Two hours behind EST during
daylight saving time; one
hour behind otherwise

⊕ WEBSITES:
⊕ www.travelbelize.org
⊕ www.ambergriscaye.com

What You Need to Know Before You Go

Can you drink the water? Is it a safe country to visit? Will they accept U.S. dollars? And speak English? You may have a few questions before you head out to Belize. We've got answers and a few tips to help you make the most of your visit, so you can focus on exploring this Caribbean paradise.

U.S. DOLLARS ARE WIDELY ACCEPTED

Fortunately for American travelers, U.S. dollars are accepted everywhere, so there's no need to exchange money. Most hotels, tours, and car-rental prices are quoted in U.S. dollars, while restaurant and store prices are in Belize dollars. Always ask which currency is being used. There are ATMs in most areas, and credit cards are accepted at resorts.

ENGLISH IS THE OFFICIAL LANGUAGE

Spanish is widely spoken especially in northern and western Belize, but English is Belize's official language. Several Mayan dialects and the Garifuna language are also spoken. Some Mennonite communities speak a German dialect. Kriol, or Creole, which uses versions of English words and a West African–influenced grammar and syntax, is spoken as a first language by many Belizeans, especially around Belize City.

DON'T DRINK THE WATER IN REMOTE VILLAGES

You can drink the water in Belize City, Cayo, and Placencia, on Ambergris Caye, and in most other areas you're likely to visit, though you may prefer the taste of bottled water. In remote villages, however, water may come from shallow wells or cisterns and may not be safe to drink. On trips to Tikal or other areas in Guatemala, assume that the water isn't safe to drink.

BELIZE IS (MOSTLY) SAFE

Most visitors say they feel quite safe in Belize (except in some areas of Belize City's South Side, especially after dark). Tourist Police patrol areas of Belize City, Placencia, Ambergris Caye, and elsewhere, and many hotels and jungle lodges have security guards. In the past, the U.S. Embassy in Belize has issued a warning for LGBTQ+ visitors traveling outside of the tourist-friendly cayes, as some incidents of verbal or physical assault have been reported. However, out of the hundreds of thousands of visitors annually, the number who are victims of any kind of crime, mostly petty theft, is perhaps a few hundred. So, while this is still a developing country, enjoy yourself and follow standard travel precautions: don't wander into areas that don't feel safe; avoid deserted beaches and streets after dark; and don't flash expensive jewelry or cash. Be aware that there have been a few carjackings and robberies on remote roads or at little-visited parks and Mayan sites; travel in a group or with a guide to less popular places.

OPENING HOURS CAN BE LIMITED

Few restaurants are open late, and many are closed on Sunday. Remember, though, that small restaurants may open or close at the whim of the owner. Off-season, restaurants may close early if it looks as if there are no more guests coming, and some restaurants close completely for a month or two, usually in September and October. Mealtimes are similar to those in the United States: breakfast is usually served from 7 to 9, lunch from 11 to 2, and dinner from 6 to 9.

BE STRATEGIC ABOUT WHERE YOU STAY

The Belize Barrier Reef is just offshore Ambergris Caye, the country's most popular destination. The caye's largest town, San Pedro, has some of the best selection of restaurants and hotels in the country, making it a little pricier. For a more laid-back and inexpensive area close to the reef, choose Caye Caulker. To stay in Belize's jungle lodges, you'll need to head inland to areas like the Cayo. Although Belize is not an all-inclusive kind of destination, some beach resorts and jungle lodges offer a tweaked version of the sort of all-inclusive you often find in Mexico or Jamaica: optional packages that include nearly everything, such as all meals, guided tours, and sports (fishing, diving, or snorkeling).

YES, YOU SHOULD TIP

Belize restaurants rarely add a service charge, so in better restaurants tip 15%–20% of the total bill. At inexpensive places, leave a roughly 10% tip. Many hotels and resorts add a service charge, usually 10%, to bills, so at these places additional tipping generally isn't necessary. By and large, Belizeans tend not to look for tips, and Belizeans themselves tip sparingly, although with increasing tourism this is changing. It's not customary to tip taxi drivers or service station attendants. Guides at archaeological sites and fishing guides often expect a tip, around 10%–15% of the guide fee. In Guatemala, restaurant bills do not typically include gratuities; 10% is customary.

THERE'S SOME ETIQUETTE YOU SHOULD LEARN

Belizeans generally are incredibly kind and friendly, and they generally shake hands more gently than the assertive handshakes common in the United States. Greet folks with a "Good morning" before asking for directions

or a table in a restaurant, or when entering a store or museum, for example. It will set a positive tone and you'll be received much more warmly for having done so. Don't take pictures inside churches. Do not take pictures of indigenous people without first asking their permission. Offering them a small sum as thanks is customary.

DON'T EXPECT WORLD-CLASS BEACHES

Although there are lovely stretches of beaches, many of them are not as good for swimming or sunbathing as the wide, sandy beaches of the main Caribbean or of Mexico's Yucatán. Recently, a scourge of floating Sargassum seagrass has lashed Belizean shores, making beaches less pleasant—and in some cases downright unpleasant—for weeks at a time throughout the year. Sargassum aside, Belizean beaches are usually narrow ribbons of sand with clear but shallow water, rooted seagrass, and an often-mucky sea floor. The best beaches on the mainland are on the Placencia Peninsula and in the Hopkins area. Ambergris Caye has some beautiful beaches, though swimming isn't always good right off the shore. South Water Caye and Belize's three atolls have excellent (nearly deserted) beaches as well.

YOU CAN SNORKEL FROM SHORE

Belize has world-class snorkeling, but most of it requires a boat ride to the Barrier Reef. There are exceptions—the small islands that are on or near

the reef, such as South Water, Ranguana, and Tobacco Cayes, or the areas around the atolls, especially Glover's. Of course, you can go snorkeling off almost any beach, and see at least a few fish, especially around a pier, even if there's no patch of coral nearby.

THERE ARE MANY NATURE RESERVES

More than 40% of Belize's land is protected as national parks and preserves, meaning you'll find a lot of untouched jungle wilderness here to explore. Head to Crooked Tree or Cockscomb wildlife sanctuaries for a chance to spot the elusive jaguar and other flora and fauna.

FLIGHTS ARE USUALLY EXPENSIVE, BUT THERE ARE WAYS TO SAVE

Belize is not a mass-market tourist destination—and that's what makes it wonderful. Charter flights are rare, so fares tend to stay high. To find the most affordable flights, stay flexible on your dates, check the meta-fare comparison websites such as Kayak. com, and avoid peak holiday travel (around Christmas and Easter). Another option is to fly into Cancún, which usually has good air deals, bus to Chetumal at the Mexico-Belize border, and water taxi or bus from there, or alternatively fly Tropic Air from Cancún International to Belize International. The other option is the ADO Express overnight service from Cancún to Corozal Town, Orange Walk Town, and Belize City.

Getting Here and Around

✈ Air Travel

TO BELIZE

North American flights to Belize can be expensive, but all told it's not a strenuous trip. To Belize City it's roughly 2½–3 hours from Miami and Atlanta; 2½–3½ hours from Dallas, Houston, and Charlotte; 4½ hours from Newark and Denver; and about 6 hours from Los Angeles and Toronto. All international flights to Belize fly into the modern Philip S. W. Goldson International Airport (BZE) in Ladyville about 9 miles (15 km) north of downtown Belize City. The airport runway is capable of handling all but the largest jets. U.S. gateway cities with nonstop service by international airlines to Belize include Atlanta, Charlotte, Chicago, Dallas–Fort Worth, Denver, Houston, Los Angeles, Miami, Fort Lauderdale, and Newark. International cities with nonstop service to Belize on international airlines include Panama City, Panama; San Salvador, El Salvador; and Toronto and Calgary, Canada. Not all cities have daily service, and in some cases service is seasonal, typically during the high season from late November to April or May.

Seven international airlines fly into Belize from U.S. and Central American cities: American Airlines has multiple flights daily from Miami (MIA) and Dallas–Fort Worth (DFW) and nondaily, limited seasonal service from Charlotte (CLT). Avianca Airlines, formerly TACA, has daily service from its hub in San Salvador, El Salvador (SAL). Copa Airlines currently has multiple nonstop flights a week from Panama City, Panama (PTY). Delta Airlines has daily nonstop service from Atlanta (ATL) and some flights from Los Angeles (LAX), although service may be reduced during off-season months. Southwest Airlines has daily service from Houston Hobby (HOU), weekly service from Denver (DEN), and some flights from Fort Lauderdale (FLL). United Airlines has multiple daily flights from Houston's George Bush Intercontinental Airport (IAH) and a weekly flight from Chicago O'Hare (ORD). WestJet, a Canadian airline, and Air Canada have twice-weekly nonstop service from Toronto Pearson International (YYZ) to Belize. Both airlines now fly direct from Calgary (YYC) as well. Currently, there is no nonstop service to Belize from anywhere in Europe, but American has a flight from London connecting in Miami that allows a same-day arrival in Belize without an overnight layover. The Belize Tourism Board and others are campaigning for flights from Europe.

Tropic Air, one of two Belizean airlines and the only one with international flights, offers twice-daily service between Belize City's international airport and Flores, Guatemala, with continuing service (usually on a code-share with TAG, a Guatemalan airline) to and from Guatemala City. It also has service between Belize City and Cancún, Mexico, as well as Roatán, Honduras. Service frequency varies during the year, depending on demand. Maya Island Air, another Belizean airline, currently has domestic service only.

WITHIN BELIZE

Domestic planes are single- or twin-engine island-hoppers and puddle-jumpers, such as Cessna Caravans. They typically carry 4 to 14 passengers. The carriers are Tropic Air and Maya Island Air; both have about 250 domestic flights daily and fly to San Pedro on Ambergris Caye and Caye Caulker as well as to Corozal Town, Dangriga, Placencia, and Punta Gorda. Tropic Air also has domestic service to Orange Walk Town, Belmopan, and San Ignacio. Maya Island Air also has service to Savannah and Kanantik, airstrips near Placencia.

Belize domestic flights on Maya Island and Tropic Air from and to the international airport are between BZ$250 and BZ$500 round-trip and somewhat less, about BZ$150 to BZ$400 round-trip, between the Sir Barry Bowen Municipal Airport (TZA) in Belize City and domestic destinations. A Belize Airports Authority Rider Fee of BZ$5 is added into the cost of tickets, and a BZ$1.50 security fee is added if using the international airport.

Charter services such as Javier Flying Service will take you almost anywhere for around BZ$1,500 per hour and up; Javier specializes in flights to Chan Chich Lodge, Blancaneaux Lodge, and Hidden Valley Inn on the mainland and the Phoenix Resort on Ambergris Caye. Both Maya Island and Tropic Air also offer charter services to remote lodges and resorts with airstrips such as Chan Chich and Blancaneaux. For an unforgettable experience, Astrum Helicopters, based near Belize City, offers transfers, aerial property tours, and custom sightseeing and photography tours anywhere in Belize. Costs for up to six people in the Bell 206 helicopters are around BZ$2,200 an hour, with fixed rates for transfers to specific resorts.

You'll save 10% to 50% on flights within Belize by flying to and from the municipal airport near downtown Belize City, rather than to or from the international airport north of the city in Ladyville. If you're arriving at the international airport, a transfer by taxi to the municipal airport is BZ$50 for two people, plus an additional BZ$10 for each extra person; transferring to the municipal airport sometimes makes more sense for families or groups traveling together. If you need to fly between Belize City and another part of the country, it's always at least a little cheaper to fly to or from municipal airports. Be aware that the municipal

airstrip is short, just 1,825 feet, suitable only for short-takeoff-and-landing aircraft. It sits right beside the sea. Landings and takeoffs can be a thrill.

AIRPORTS

International flights arrive at the Philip S. W. Goldson International Airport (BZE) in Ladyville, north of downtown Belize City. It's the world's first airport with a mahogany ceiling (in the original terminal building). Snack bars, souvenir shops, a Belikin Store, and even a store selling Harley Davidson accessories can all be enjoyed in the main terminal.

In San Pedro (SPR), Tropic Air and Maya Island Air both have spacious modern terminals, Maya having built a luxe new lobby in 2018, complete with crystal chandeliers and granite finishing (and a mahogany ceiling, perhaps the world's second in an airport).

Most other Belize domestic airports are just landing strips with a one-room check-in. These domestic airports include the Sir Barry Bowen Municipal Airport in Belize City (TZA), Belmopan (BCV), Corozal (CZH), Dangriga (DGA), Savannah (SVH), Placencia (PLJ), Punta Gorda (PND), Orange Walk Town (ORZ), and Caye Caulker (CUK). An airstrip near Hopkins has been proposed, but as of this writing it has not received government approval. With the exception of the San Pedro airport, which has nighttime lighting, all the domestic airstrips operate only during daylight hours.

A controversial, privately funded international airport under construction on the Placencia Peninsula culminated in the American investment manager pleading guilty to fraud in 2019. Needless to say, the Placencia international airport (not to be confused with the domestic airstrip) has not opened. The current Belize government has announced plans to build an

Getting Here and Around

international airport on North Ambergris Caye, but no timeline has been given.

Philip S. W. Goldson International Airport has security precautions similar to those in the United States; the domestic airstrips have limited security systems, but there has never been an airline hijacking in Belize. For international flights, arrive at the airport at least two hours before departure; for domestic flights, 30 to 45 minutes ahead. For connections from international flights to domestic flights, allow 45 minutes. In Belize, domestic airlines with more passengers than seats sometimes simply add another flight.

A new visitor identification system including fingerprint scanners was introduced in 2013 by Belize immigration at Philip S. W. Goldson, paid for in part by the United States. The government is expanding this system for use at all land and sea arrival points to Belize; however, the system is not always in use. The system includes computer workstations, webcams, and passport readers. It is managed through a central server at immigration headquarters in Belmopan. U.S. PreCheck status doesn't apply in Belize.

⚙ Boat Travel

Since Belize has about 200 miles (325 km) of mainland coast and as many as 1,000 islands (most just tiny spits of sand, coral, and mangroves) in the Caribbean, water taxis, passenger ferries, and private boats are key to moving around the islands and coastal areas.

If you're staying at a lodge or resort on a remote caye, transfers will (almost always) be arranged for you. Otherwise, to reach the more remote cayes and the atolls, you're basically left to your own devices. The resorts on the atolls run

their own boats, but these usually aren't available to the general public.

FERRIES AND PRIVATE BOATS

A local ferry company, Coastal Xpress, provides scheduled boat transportation up and down the east side of Ambergris Caye. One-way rates start at BZ$10, and daily and weekly passes are available.

Several private boats make daily runs from Dangriga to Tobacco Caye; boats usually leave Dangriga around 9 or 9:30 am and return later in the day. Check at the Riverside Café in Dangriga or ask your hotel on Tobacco Caye, as several of these lodges include transport in the rate. Charter boats to Tobacco Caye also are available from Hopkins. Many hotels on Ambergris Caye and Caye Caulker and in coastal resort areas can arrange boat charters for you with a captain. Visitors cannot pilot a boat unless they have a Belizean captain's license; exceptions include the use of small personal sailboats such as Hobie Cats and bareboat sailing charters of catamarans and monohull sailboats. In the case of bareboat sailing charters, you need to demonstrate you are an experienced sailor to get a boat.

WATER TAXIS

There are two main, reliable water-taxi companies that serve the cayes of Ambergris and Caulker: Ocean Ferry Belize and San Pedro Belize Express. These companies' fast boats, holding up to 110 passengers, embark from Belize City many times day. From Belize City, water taxis make the 45-minute run to Caye Caulker, and then continue on to San Pedro, another 30 minutes away. These water taxis serve Belizean 9-5 workers as much as tourists and are professional and reliable, though occasionally run late. Ocean Ferry boats also do on-demand stops and pickups at Caye Chapel and St. George's Caye. These water taxis also connect San Pedro and Caye Caulker with Chetumal, Mexico. In addition, Thunderbolt connects San Pedro with Corozal Town in northern Belize, with a stop on demand in the village of Sarteneja.

Most scheduled water taxis allow two pieces of luggage per person, along with miscellaneous personal items. Seas, especially in the south between Dangriga/Placencia and Puerto Cortes, Honduras, and also between Punta Gorda and Puerto Barrios, Guatemala, can be rough. Postpone your trip if the weather looks bad, or in the case of private charters, cancel if the boat offered looks unseaworthy or crowded.

Several water-taxi companies, including Requena's, offer daily service from Punta Gorda to Puerto Barrios, Guatemala. D'Express offers weekly service between Placencia and Puerto Cortes, Honduras.

As of 2019, the Belize Port Authority requires passenger manifest, which means that every passenger must present an ID for recording (at present this crime-prevention policy applies to all water taxis to and from Ambergris Caye and Caye Caulker). The Belize water-taxi business is in a state of flux, with companies entering and leaving the business. Schedules and rates are subject to frequent change.

🚌 Bus Travel

Bus service on the Philip Goldson and George Price Highways (sometimes referred to as the Northern and Western Highways) and to southern Belize via the Hummingbird and Southern Highways is frequent and generally dependable. Elsewhere service is spotty. There's limited municipal bus service from point to point

Travel Times from Belize City

To	By Air	By Car, Bus, or Boat
San Pedro	20 minutes	1¼ hours (boat)
Caye Caulker	15 minutes	45 minutes (boat)
Corozal Town	1–2 hours (via San Pedro)	2–3 hours
San Ignacio	30 minutes	2–2½ hours
Placencia	50 minutes	3–3½ hours
Punta Gorda	1 hour	4–6 hours
Cancún, Mexico	1½ hours	8–11 hours

within Belize City on several small local lines.

Buses can get you just about anywhere cheaply (for intertown trips) and quickly. (The trouble is finding a schedule.) Expect to ride on old U.S. school buses or retired Greyhound buses. Buses with restrooms and air-conditioning are rare to nonexistent in Belize. On some routes there are a few express buses that stop only at bus stations. These cost a few dollars more.

■ TIP➜ Be prepared for tight squeezes— this can mean three people in a two-person seat. On some busy routes, seats may be full, and you may have to stand. Drivers and their assistants (in Guatemala, cobradores or ayudantes, fare collectors, who call out the stops) are knowledgeable and helpful. They can direct you to the right bus, and tell you when and where to get off. To be sure you're not forgotten, try to sit near the front of the bus. On most Belize buses, your luggage will be put at the back of the bus, behind the last seats.

Most buses on main routes run according to more-or-less reliable schedules; on

Getting Here and Around

less-traveled routes the schedules may not mean much. Buses operate mostly during daylight hours, but they run until around 9 pm on the western route between Belize City and San Ignacio, and service begins before sunrise on that route and on the northern route between Corozal Town and Belize City. Published bus schedules are rare, and almost no bus line has a website. Some lines have Facebook pages updated with some regularity, while many post handwritten schedules in bus terminals. The Belize Tourism Board sometimes has schedules for popular routes. Be sure to check the Belize Bus Blog, which has generally up-to-date information on Belize bus rates and schedules and also on other types of transportation in Belize. Buses in Belize accept only cash in U.S. or Belize dollars.

Inexpensive public buses, also of the converted school bus variety, crisscross Guatemala, but they can be slow and extremely crowded, with a three-per-seat rule enforced. Popular destinations from Guatemala City, such as Santa Elena/ Flores near Tikal, use first-class Pullman buses. Your hotel or INGUAT office can help you make arrangements. Fares on public buses in both Belize and Guatemala are a bargain.

■ TIP→ In Belize, in cities and towns where there are bus stations, you buy tickets at the station. When boarding elsewhere, you pay the driver's assistant. The same system applies in Guatemala.

Reservations are usually not needed or expected in Belize or Guatemala, even for express departures. Arrive at terminals about a half hour before departure.

Shuttles

Shuttles can be a lower-hassle and cheaper alternative to renting a car in Belize. Belize has a variety of reliable shuttle services catering to tourists, most of which have door-to-door service, dropping you off right at your destination. These operate most commonly between Belize City and San Ignacio, although shuttles also are available to Belmopan; Placencia; Chetumal, Mexico; and elsewhere. Most hotels and lodges in Cayo will arrange round-trip van transfers for guests to and from the international airport in Belize City. Several private shuttle services transport visitors between the airports or water-taxi locations in Belize City to Belmopan and San Ignacio in Cayo District. Rates vary depending on the number of people, whether the service is on demand or prescheduled and what other services, such as a stop at the Belize Zoo, are included. Among the recommended shuttles are William's Shuttle, Discounted Belize Shuttles, Mayan Heart World Adventure Tours, Belize Shuttles and Transfers, and PACZ Tours. In the north, Belize VIP Transfers will whisk you across the border to Chetumal, but the fee does not include the BZ$40 Belize exit fee. Mayan Heart World Adventure Tours has a daily shuttle from San Ignacio to Tikal. A BZ$40 Belize exit fee also is required when going to Tikal from Belize's western border.

Shuttles in Guatemala are private minivans that hold up to eight passengers. Minibus shuttles between Flores and Tikal run frequently, starting at 5 am from Flores.

🚗 Car Travel

GASOLINE

Modern gas stations—Shell, Uno, Puma, and other international or regional brands, some of them with convenience stores and 24-hour service—are in Belize City and most major towns and along major highways in Belize. In more remote areas, especially in the south, fill up the tank whenever you see a station. Unleaded gas costs around BZ$10–BZ$13 for a U.S. gallon. Diesel fuel is around BZ$9–BZ$11. Most stations have attendants who pump gas for you. They don't expect a tip, although they are happy to accept it. Most stations now accept credit cards, along with Belize and U.S. dollars.

Prices at Guatemala's service stations aren't quite as high as in Belize. At most stations an attendant will pump the gas and make change. Plan to use cash, as credit cards sometimes aren't accepted.

PARKING

In Belize City, with its warren of narrow and one-way streets, downtown parking is often at a premium. For security, try to find a guarded, fenced parking lot, and don't leave your car on the street overnight. Elsewhere, except in some areas of San Ignacio and Orange Walk Town, there's plenty of free parking. San Ignacio has a downtown municipal lot with guarded parking at modest rates—the lot is behind the Cayo Welcome Center.

There are no parking meters in Belize. In most cities and towns parking rules are laxly enforced, although cars with license plates from another district of Belize or a foreign country may attract a ticket.

ROAD CONDITIONS

All four main roads in Belize—the George Price Highway (formerly Western Highway), Philip Goldson Highway (formerly Northern Highway), Southern Highway,

From/To	Route	Distance
Belize City–Corozal Town	Philip Goldson Highway	94 miles (160 km)
Belize City–San Ignacio	George Price Highway	72 miles (116 km)
Belize City–Placencia	George Price, Hummingbird, and Southern Highways	147 miles (237 km)
Belize City–Punta Gorda	George Price, Hummingbird, and Southern Highways	200 miles (323 km)
San Ignacio–Placencia	George Price, Hummingbird, and Southern Highways	113 miles (182 km)

and Hummingbird Highway—are completely paved. These two-lane roads are generally in good condition. The once-horrendous Placencia Road is now completely paved, as is the Hopkins Road. The San Antonio Road from the Southern Highway near Punta Gorda to the Guatemala border has been upgraded and paved all the way to Jalcate village near the Guatemala border, although an official border crossing has yet to open at this writing. Signage is good along the main highways; large green signs direct you to major sights. Large speed bumps are ubiquitous, and some of them are unmarked.

Elsewhere in Belize, expect fair to stupendously rough dirt, gravel, and limestone roads. Some unpaved roads, and occasionally stretches of even paved roads, may be impassable at times in the rainy season.

Immense improvements have been made to Guatemala's ravaged roads.

Getting Here and Around

A highway from Río Dulce to Tikal has cut travel time along this popular route significantly. In the Petén, the road from Belize to Tikal and Flores is paved and in good condition. Roads in remote areas are frequently unpaved, rife with potholes, and treacherously muddy in the rainy season. Four-wheel-drive vehicles are recommended for travel off the beaten path. In the town of Flores, expect mostly narrow streets, some paved with cobblestones. Road signs are generally used to indicate large towns; smaller towns may not be so clearly marked. Look for intersections where people seem to be waiting for a bus—that's a good sign that there's an important turnoff nearby.

RULES OF THE ROAD

Driving in Belize and Guatemala is on the right. Seat belts are required, although the law is seldom enforced (but do wear yours—Belizean roads can be dangerous). There are few speed-limit signs, and speed limits are rarely enforced. However, as you approach villages and towns watch out for "sleeping policemen," a local name for speed bumps. The entire country of Belize has only about a dozen traffic lights, and only Belize City, downtown Orange Walk Town, downtown San Ignacio, and downtown San Pedro have anything approaching congestion. In recent years, Belize has been changing many intersections to roundabouts. One unusual aspect of driving in Belize, likely a holdover from British Honduras days when driving was on the left, is that vehicles turning left against traffic are not supposed to hold up cars behind them; instead, they signal a right turn, pull over to the right, and wait for a break in traffic to turn left.

Despite the relatively small number of private cars in Belize, road traffic injuries are among the nation's leading causes of death. Some drivers in Belize are reckless, and drunk drivers can be a problem. Guatemala's narrow roads and highways mean you can be stuck motionless on the road for half an hour while a construction crew stands around a hole in the ground. Always allow extra travel time for such unpredictable events, and bring along snacks and water. In both Belize and Guatemala, be prepared to stop for police traffic and auto insurance checks. Usually tourists in rental cars are checked only cursorily. In Belize, auto liability insurance is mandatory (it's included in the cost of car rentals). In Guatemala, liability insurance isn't required but it's advised. If you observe the rules you follow at home, you'll likely be fine. Just don't expect everyone else to follow them.

 Rental Cars

Belize City and the international airport in Ladyville have most major car-rental agencies as well as several local operators. At the international airport, a line of about 10 rental-car offices is on the far side of the main parking lot across from the airport entrances. There also are car-rental agencies in Corozal Town, San Ignacio, Placencia, and Punta Gorda. Some Belize City car-rental companies will deliver vehicles to other locations in Belize, but there is always a drop fee that varies depending on destination. Prices for car rentals vary, but all are high by U.S. standards, and vehicles are often a few years old with quite a few miles. If renting from an agency at the international airport, there's a BZ$10 airport fee. Off-season, rates are a little lower. Weekly rates usually save you money over daily rates. Make sure you ask the agency what procedures are in place if your car breaks down in a remote area.

Most agencies in Belize send a driver with a replacement vehicle or a mechanic to fix the car.

For serious safaris, a four-wheel-drive vehicle is invaluable. But since unpaved roads, mudslides in rainy season, and a general off-the-beaten-path landscape are status quo here, all drivers will be comforted with a four-wheel-drive vehicle.

Car rental has never really caught on in Guatemala, which, given the narrowness of some roads, is just as well. If you want to rent, several international and local car-rental companies, including Hertz, are based at the Flores airport, serving Tikal. If your car breaks down in Guatemala, your best bet is to call the National or Tourist Police.

In Belize and Guatemala, rental-car companies routinely accept driver's licenses from most other countries without question. Most car-rental agencies require a major credit card for a deposit, and some require you be over 25 but under 70.

Most Belize agencies don't permit their vehicles to be taken into Guatemala or Mexico. Crystal Auto Rental in Belize City does permit its vehicles to be taken into Guatemala, as do a couple of the car-rental companies in San Ignacio, although without any insurance coverage while in Guatemala. There is no place to buy Guatemalan liability insurance at the Belize-Guatemala border.

On Belize's cayes you can't rent a car, but you can rent a golf cart, at prices not much less than renting a car. You'll need a driver's license and a credit card.

CAR-RENTAL INSURANCE
Auto liability insurance is mandatory in Belize, and nearly all rentals include basic liability coverage in the rental rate. However, other damage to the car, such as from hitting a tree or stolen car, is not covered by basic liability insurance. If you own a car, your personal auto insurance may cover a rental to some degree, though not all policies protect you abroad; always read your policy's fine print. If you don't have auto insurance, then consider buying the collision- or loss-damage waiver (CDW or LDW) from the car-rental company, which eliminates some of your responsibility for damage to the car. Many credit cards offer CDW coverage, but it's usually supplemental to your own insurance and rarely covers trucks, minivans, luxury models, and the like. American Express and some other credit/charge card companies offer a premium CDW plan for a flat fee, usually around US$20–$25 per rental, not per day, that has more leeway than regular CDW plans—for example, covering SUVs, trucks, and driving off paved roads. If your insurance coverage is secondary, you may still be liable for loss-of-use costs from the car-rental company. But no credit-card coverage is valid unless you use that card for *all* transactions, from reserving to paying the final bill. All companies exclude car rental in some countries, so be sure to find out about the destination to which you are traveling.

Belize has agents or franchisees of international auto rental companies including Alamo, Avis, Budget, Enterprise, Hertz, and Thrifty along with local companies such as Crystal Auto Rental and AQ Auto Rental. Recommended auto rental agencies in Belize City have kiosks across the main parking lot at Philip S. W. Goldson International Airport in Ladyville as well as locations in Belize City. See individual chapters for vehicle rentals in other locations in Belize and Flores, Guatemala.

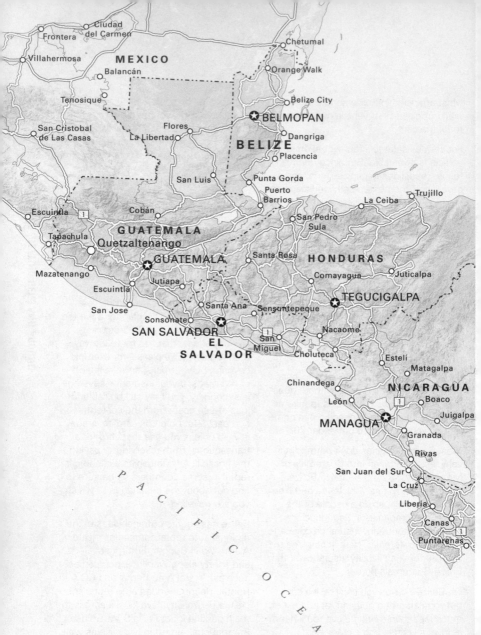

Central America

Montego Bay

JAMAICA
KINGSTON

C a r i b b e a n   S e a

Brus Laguna

Puerto Lempira

Puerto
Cabezas

Bluefields

San Juan de Nicaragua

Quesada
Alajuela
SAN
JOSÉ
Cartago
COSTA
RICA
Sixaola
Puerto Limon
Bocas del Toro
Almirante
Colón
Ciudad Cortes
Golfito
David
PANAMA
Penonome
PANAMA
CITY
La Palma
Puerto
Armuelles
Santiago
Chitré
Las Tablas
Jaqué
Juradó

COLOMBIA

0   100 mi
0   100 km

Before You Go

Passport

A passport is required for citizens of the United States, and it must be valid for three months after the date of your arrival.

Visa

A visa is not required for Americans, Canadians, and European Union citizens, among others; a tourist card (actually a stamp in your passport) good for up to 30 days is issued free upon arrival. You can renew your entry permit at immigration offices for a fee of BZ$50 per month for the first six months; after six months, it costs BZ$100 a month for up to six more months, at which time you may have to leave the country for 72 hours to start the process over (sometimes this rule isn't enforced). Note that renewals aren't guaranteed but normally are granted.

Immunizations

You should be up to date on shots for tetanus and hepatitis A and B. Children traveling to Central America should have current inoculations against measles, mumps, rubella, hepatitis, and polio. If traveling to either Belize or Guatemala from a country with risk of yellow fever transmission, a yellow fever vaccine is required.

When to Go

High Season: The busiest time is from the holidays through New Year's, followed by Easter. Hotel rates spike from mid-November through April. February through May is the best time to visit the coast and cayes.

Low Season: Rainy season is roughly June through October, with fewer crowds and lower prices, but some restaurants close and hotels offer limited facilities.

Value Season: May through November has some of the most bearable temperatures, and the best rates for hotels are in late spring, September, and October.

Safety

Belize City has a bad rep for crime, especially in the poverty-ridden sections of Belize City's South Side, but it rarely involves visitors. If you avoid walking around at night (except in well-lighted parts of the Fort George area), you should have no problems in Belize City. Outside of Belize City, and possibly the rougher parts of Dangriga and Orange Walk Town, you'll find Belize to be safe and friendly. Petty theft, however, is common all over, so don't leave cameras, cell phones, and other valuables unguarded.

Packing

Pack light. Baggage carts are scarce at Central American airports, and international luggage limits are increasingly tight. Tropic Air and Maya Island Air officially have 50-pound (22-kg) weight limits for checked baggage. However, in practice airlines in Belize rarely weigh luggage, and if you're a little over it's usually no problem. Occasionally, if the flight on the small Cessna or other airplane is full and there's a lot of luggage, some bags may be sent on the next flight, usually no more than an hour or two later.

HAND-WASHABLE CLOTHING

Bring casual, comfortable clothing that you can wash by hand—this will come in handy should you be traveling in a jungle location without laundry services. T-shirts and shorts are acceptable near the beach and in tourist areas. More modest attire is appropriate in smaller towns, and long sleeves and long pants will protect your skin from the ferocious sun and mosquitoes.

REEF-SAFE SUNSCREEN

The Belize Barrier Reef is a sensitive, living reef. Do your part in protecting this ecological wonder and bring reef-safe sunscreen without the harmful chemicals that bleach and kill reefs. A few good brands include Babo, Sun Bum, and Badger. Bring a hat for even more protection from harmful rays.

DIVING AND SNORKELING GEAR

Snorkelers should consider bringing their own equipment, especially mask and snorkel, if there's room in the suitcase. Divers will save money—typically BZ$80–BZ$100 or more a day in rentals—by bringing their own equipment.

WATERPROOF GEAR

If traveling in the rainy season, a lightweight rain jacket or waterproof poncho is essential. If you plan to partake of water activites or just to spend a lot of time on the beach, bring a waterproof bag to keep your camera, phone, and wallet dry; it will also come in handy during the rainy season. A waterproof phone case is a good idea, too, if you plan to use your phone's camera when you travel.

LAYERS

If you're heading into the mountains or highlands, especially during the winter months, bring a light cotton sweater, a jacket, and something warm to sleep in, as nights and early mornings can be chilly.

PRACTICAL SHOES

Sturdy sneakers or hiking shoes or lightweight boots with rubber soles for wet or rocky surfaces are essential. A pair of sandals (preferably ones that can be worn in the water) are good, too.

INSECT REPELLENT

Sand flies (also sometimes referred to as no-see-ums, or as sand fleas, which are a different insect) are common on many beaches and cayes and in swampy areas. Use repellent containing at least a 30% concentration of DEET to help deter sand flies. Some say lathering on Avon's Skin So Soft or any oily lotion such as baby oil helps, too, as it drowns the little bugs.

TRUSTED TOILETRIES

Bring your own toothpaste, shampoo, and conditioner, as well as condoms and tampons. You likely won't find them easily, cheaply, or in familiar brands.

EAR PLUGS

Monkeys howling through the night and birds chirping at the crack of dawn are only charming on the first night of your nature excursion.

VPN

If you're planning to work or stay connected while you travel, a portable VPN (virtual private network) will ensure you won't get blocked from accessing certain sites. It also protects your passwords, credit cards, and identity while you travel.

Essentials

Accommodations

Regardless of the kind of lodging, you'll usually stay at a small place, as only a few properties have more than 50 or 75 rooms, and most have fewer than 30. The owners often actively manage the property. Thus, Belize accommodations usually reflect the personalities of their owners, for better or worse.

APARTMENT AND HOUSE RENTALS

You can most easily find vacation home rentals on Ambergris Caye. Airbnb and Vacation Rentals By Owner (VRBO) have scores of rentals on Ambergris Caye and elsewhere in Belize. There also are some vacation rental houses in Placencia and Hopkins and on Caye Caulker.

BEACH HOTELS

Beach lodgings range from a basic seaside cabin on Caye Caulker to a small, deluxe resort such as Victoria House on Ambergris Caye or Hamanasi near Hopkins. On Ambergris Caye many resorts are "condotels"—low-rise condo complexes with individually owned units that are managed like a hotel. An increasing number of properties are "adults only"; some of these hotels accept teenage guests, while some are 18+.

JUNGLE LODGES

Jungle lodges are concentrated in the Cayo District, but they are also in the Toledo, Belize, and Orange Walk Districts and can be found most anywhere except the cayes. Jungle lodges need not be spartan; nearly all have electricity (though the generator may shut down at 10 pm), many have swimming pools, and a number have air-conditioning. The typical lodge has a roof of bay-palm thatch and may remind you of a Mayan house gone upscale.

STAYING ON REMOTE CAYES

Lodging choices on remote cayes appeal to the diving and fishing crowd. Amenity levels vary greatly, from cabins with outdoor bathrooms to simple cottages with composting toilets and comfortable villas with air-conditioning.

TRADITIONAL HOTELS

Traditional hotels, usually found in larger towns, can be basic budget places or international-style hotels such as the Radisson Fort George in Belize City.

CANCELLATIONS

As most hotels have only a few rooms, a last-minute cancellation can have a big impact on the bottom line. Most properties have a sliding scale for cancellations, with full refunds (minus a small administrative fee) if you cancel 60 or 90 days or more in advance, with reduced refund rates for later cancellations, and often no refunds at all for cancellation 30 to 45 days out. Practices vary greatly, so check on them.

HOSTELS AND GUESTHOUSES

Belize has few traditional hostels; however, there are some on Caye Caulker and in San Pedro, San Ignacio, and Belize City, along with at least one in each of the following areas: Corozal Town, Orange Walk Town, Sarteneja, Punta Gorda, Belmopan, Hopkins, and Placencia. Inexpensive guesthouses, common all over · Belize, function much like hostels, albeit generally with less opportunity for guest interaction.

RATES

In the off-season—generally May to November, though dates vary by hotel—most properties discount rates by 20% to 40%. Although hotels have published rates, in the off-season at least you may also be able to negotiate a better rate, especially if you're staying more than one or two nights. ■TIP→ Walk-in rates are usually lower than prebooked rates, and rooms booked direct on the Internet may have lower rates than those booked through agents like Booking.com.

Most hotels allow children under a certain age to stay in their parents' room at no extra charge, but others charge for them as extra adults; find out the cutoff age for discounts.

All prices for Belize accommodations in this guide are in Belize dollars (2 Belize dollars = 1 U.S. dollar) for a standard double room in season with no meals, including service charges if any and 9% hotel tax.

$ Money

There are two ways of looking at the prices in Belize: either it's one of the cheapest countries in the Caribbean or one of the most expensive countries in Central America. A good hotel room for two will cost you upward of BZ$250, and fancy beach resorts and jungle lodges run BZ$600 to BZ$900 or more; a budget one can be as little as BZ$40. A meal in one of the more expensive restaurants will cost BZ$50–BZ$100 for one, but you can eat the classic Creole dish of stew chicken and rice and beans for BZ$8–BZ$10. Prices are highest in Belize City, Ambergris Caye, and the Placencia Peninsula.

Prices throughout this guide are given for adults. Substantially reduced fees are usually available for children and students.

ATMS AND BANKS

Belize has four Belize-based banks: Atlantic Bank; Heritage Bank, which took over some assets of Caribbean International Bank; the new National Bank of Belize, which has only two offices; and

Item	Average Cost in Belize
Cup of Coffee	BZ$2–BZ$4
Glass of Wine	BZ$12–BZ$20
Glass of Beer	BZ$3–BZ$10
Sandwich	BZ$6–BZ$18
One-Mile Taxi Ride in Belize City	BZ$7
Museum Admission	BZ$10–BZ$20

ScotiaBank, which is an independent outpost of the big Canadian bank. Banking hours vary but are typically Monday to Thursday 8–3 and Friday 8–4. There is a branch of Atlantic Bank at the international airport that has longer hours, along with an ATM. Belize Bank has an ATM at the airport. All the banks have ATMs across the country that are open 24/7, although occasionally machines may run out of cash or are out of order.

CREDIT CARDS

In Belize, MasterCard and Visa are widely accepted, American Express less so, and Discover and Diners hardly at all. Remember to inform your credit card company that you'll be traveling internationally, and record your card number in case it's lost or stolen.

■TIP➔ **Hotels, restaurants, shops, and tour operators in Belize occasionally levy a surcharge for credit card use, usually 5% but ranging from 2% to 10%.**

CURRENCY AND EXCHANGE

Because the U.S. dollar (bills only, not coins) is gladly accepted everywhere in Belize, there's no need to exchange it. When paying in U.S. dollars, you may get change in Belize or U.S. currency or in both.

The Belize dollar (BZ$) is pegged to the U.S. dollar at a rate of BZ$2 per US$1, and nearly all shops, stores, hotels,

Essentials

restaurants, and other businesses honor that exchange rate. Note, however, that money changers at Belize's Mexico and Guatemala borders operate on a free-market system and pay a rate depending on the demand for U.S. dollars, sometimes as high as BZ$2.15 to US$1. Banks (and ATMs) generally exchange at BZ$1.98 or less.

The best place to exchange Belize dollars for Mexican pesos is in Corozal, or at the Mexico-Belize border, where the exchange rate is quite good. At the Guatemala border near Benque Viejo del Carmen, you can exchange Belize or U.S. dollars for quetzales—money changers will approach you on the Belize side and also on the Guatemala side. Usually the money changers on the Guatemala side offer better rates.

In Belize most hotel, tour, and car-rental prices are quoted in U.S. dollars, while most restaurant prices, taxi charges, and store prices are in Belize dollars. *In this guide, all Belize prices are quoted in Belize dollars.* Because misunderstandings can happen, if it's not clear, always ask which currency is being used.

Health

According to the U.S. Centers for Disease Control and Prevention, there's a limited risk of malaria, hepatitis A and B, typhoid fever, and rabies in Belize. In most urban or easily accessible areas you need not worry. However, if you plan to spend a lot of time in the jungles, rain forests, or other remote regions, or if you want to stay for more than six weeks, check the CDC website. Guatemala, including El Petén, is a higher-risk area for typhoid fever and malaria.

The mosquito-borne disease dengue fever increased in outbreaks in 2019, especially in northern Belize but in the Cayo and Stann Creek Districts as well. Symtoms are flu-like and include a high fever, aching joints, headaches, and a red skin rash. There is no antiviral treatment at this time. The CDC rates dengue fever in both Belize and Guatemala as frequent/continuous.

The Zika virus, spread by *Aedes aegypti* mosquitoes, has been confirmed in Belize, although as of this writing the number of cases in Belize and in the Petén area of Guatemala is very small. However, pregnant women, and women who may become pregnant, should consult with their physician before visiting Belize or Guatemala, as the virus can cause severe birth defects. Zika can also be transmitted sexually.

Many medicines requiring a doctor's prescription at home don't require one in Belize. Drugstores often sell prescription antibiotics, sleeping aids, and painkillers to anyone who has the money, and a few pharmacies are open 24 hours.

Watch out for common pests including no-see-ums (sand flies) and scorpions, as well as venomous fer-de-lance and coral snakes, bees, and the very unpleasant botfly.

Sargassum seagrass, washing ashore on many beaches in Belize, releases hydrogen sulfide gas and ammonia as it decomposes in the sun. Extended contact with the seagrass or prolonged inhalation of its fumes are associated with respiratory, skin, and neurocognitive symptoms.

FOOD AND DRINK

Belize has a high standard of health and hygiene, so the major health risk is sunburn, not digestive distress. You can drink the water in Belize City, Cayo; and Placencia, on Ambergris Caye, and in most other areas you're likely to visit, though you may prefer the taste of bottled water. In remote villages, however, water may come from shallow wells or cisterns and may not be safe to drink.

On trips to Tikal or other areas in Guatemala, assume that the water isn't safe to drink. Bottled water—*agua mineral* or *agua pura* in Spanish—is available even at the smallest *tiendas* (stores) and is cheaper than in the United States or Canada. Eating contaminated fruit or vegetables or drinking contaminated water (even ice) could result in a case of Montezuma's revenge, or traveler's diarrhea. Also skip uncooked food and unpasteurized milk and milk products.

$ Taxes

The hotel tax in Belize is 9%, and a 12.5% Goods and Services Tax (GST) is charged on meals, tours, and other purchases at the hotel, along with most other purchases in Belize including car rentals, tours, and purchases at stores. The GST is supposed to be included in the cost of meals, goods, and services, but many businesses add on GST like a sales tax instead. Very small shops and street vendors are not required to collect GST.

When departing the country by international air, even on a short hop to Flores, Guatemala, you'll pay US$39.25 departure tax and fees. However, most international airlines include the departure tax in the airline ticket price. Don't pay twice—check your airline to see if the tax is included.

When leaving Belize by land to either Guatemala or Mexico, there's a border exit fee totaling BZ$40 or US$20. This may be paid in either U.S. dollars or Belize dollars but not by credit card.

Some Guatemalan hotels and some tourist restaurants charge a 10% to 22% tourist tax, though others include this Value-Added Tax (V.A.T.) in the price. The Guatemala airport-departure tax is US$30, plus about US$3 security fee, which are typically included in international flight prices. Guatemalan border officials in the past have asked for a Q20 fee (about US$2.50) when entering Guatemala at Melchor de Mencos. There is no exit fee by land from Guatemala.

$ Tipping

Belize restaurants rarely add a service charge, so in better restaurants tip 15%–20% of the total bill. At inexpensive places, leave a roughly 10% tip. Many hotels and resorts add a service charge, usually 10%, to bills, so at these places additional tipping generally isn't necessary. By and large, Belizeans tend not to look for tips, and Belizeans themselves tip sparingly, although with increasing tourism this is changing. It's not customary to tip taxi drivers or service station attendants. Guides at archaeological sites and fishing guides often expect a tip, around 10%–15% of the guide fee.

In Guatemala, restaurant bills do not typically include gratuities; 10% is customary. Bellhops and maids expect tips only in the expensive hotels. Guards who show you around ruins and locals who help you find hotels or give you little tours should also be tipped. Children will often charge a quetzal to let you take their photo.

Tours

ARCHAEOLOGY

In Belize you can participate in a "dig" at a Mayan archaeological site, usually under the direction of a university archaeological team. Sessions run only a few weeks of the year, usually in spring or summer. The Maya Research Program, established in 1992 and affiliated with the University of Texas at Tyler, has two-week volunteer programs in the Blue Creek area of Orange Walk District. Fees for nonstudents start at US$1,850. The Center for Archaeological and Tropical Studies (CATS) at the University of Texas at Austin accepts students and others for summer digs at its field station in the Rio Bravo Conservation area of Orange Walk District, located on Programme for Belize lands. Participants pay a fee (around US$1,050 for two weeks) for a one- to four-week session with room and board. Participants live in a rustic dorm setting and learn the basics of field archaeology through lectures and hands-on experience. Students can gain class credits at the University of Texas. Fees for both programs exclude transportation to Belize.

Road Scholar, a division of Elderhostel, offers an 11-day educational program in Belize, Guatemala, and Honduras on the history of the Maya, with insight into modern-day issues affecting their community, starting at US$2,500. It also offers a 10-day Mystery of the Maya program in Belize and Guatemala that combines snorkeling and visiting Mayan sites. All the Road Scholar programs include accommodations, meals, guides, field trips, and in-country transportation, but not flights to and from Belize.

BIRD-WATCHING

Nearly 600 species of birds have been spotted in Belize, and every year five or more additional species are added to that list. Birders flock to Belize to see exciting species such as the jabiru stork, the largest flying bird in the Western Hemisphere; the harpy eagle; the scarlet macaw; the keel-billed toucan, the national bird of Belize; 21 species of hummingbirds; and endangered or rare species such as the yellow-headed parrot, ocellated turkey, orange-breasted falcon, and chestnut-breasted heron. Birding hot spots in Belize include Crooked Tree Wildlife Sanctuary, the Mountain Pine Ridge, the area around Chan Chich Lodge at Gallon Jug, and the Cockscomb Basin.

When selecting a bird-watching tour, ask questions. What species might be seen? What are the guide's qualifications? Does the operator work to protect natural habitats? How large are the birding groups? What equipment is used? (In addition to binoculars and a birding guidebook, this should include a high-powered telescope, a recorder to record and play back bird calls, and a spotlight for night viewing.) On an à la carte basis, short birding hikes in Belize with a local guide cost from BZ$30 per person. At some jungle lodges such as Chaa Creek, local birding hikes are free.

Victor Emanuel Nature Tours (VENT) has birding tours that combine visits to Chan Chich Lodge and Crooked Tree Wildlife Sanctuary. This tour will set you back about US$5,100 per person, not including airfare to Belize. Wildside Nature Tours has 8-, 10-, and 13-day birding trips (some with an eye toward monkeys, too) that visit Crooked Tree, Cockscomb, and Cayo in Belize and Tikal in Guatemala, from US$2,500 per person, not including airfare. Tours often sell out early.

CULTURE TOURS AND HOMESTAYS

Both unique experiences, homestays and village guesthouse stays in Mayan villages in the Toledo District are offered by Toledo Ecotourism Association and Aguacate Belize Homestay Program, local organizations in the Punta Gorda area. These stays are very inexpensive, typically less than BZ$120 per day including meals and activities, but accommodations are basic.

FISHING

The best-known fishing lodges in Belize are high-end resorts catering to affluent anglers who, after a hard day on the water, expect ice-cold cocktails, equally icy air-conditioning, and Posturepedic mattresses. El Pescador on North Ambergris Caye, two lodges on Turneffe Atoll (Turneffe Flats and Turneffe Island Lodge), and several beach resorts in Placencia and Hopkins offer fishing with a touch of luxury—everything from guides to cold drinks included. Fishing travel companies like Rod and Reel Adventures typically book with fishing lodges.

If you want a less expensive fishing vacation, you can make your own arrangements for lodging and meals and hire your own local fishing guides in San Pedro, Caye Caulker, Placencia, Hopkins, Punta Gorda, and elsewhere. Destinations Belize in Placencia is a compromise between a total package and doing it all yourself. The owner, Mary Toy, an American lawyer from St. Louis, can help you arrange moderate accommodations, some meals, and guides for light-tackle or fly-fishing day-trips (or for longer periods).

HORSEBACK RIDING

Wyoming-based Equitours offers riding tour packages in the Cayo. In addition, several lodges in Belize, including Mountain Equestrian Trails (MET) near San Ignacio and Banana Bank Lodge near Belmopan, specialize in riding vacations.

KAYAKING

There are two types of kayaking trips: base kayaking and expedition kayaking. On a base kayaking trip you have a home base—usually a caye—from which you take day-trips (or longer). On an expedition-style trip you travel from island to island or up mainland rivers. Typically, base kayaking is easier, but expedition kayaking is more adventurous.

Island Expeditions offers a number of complete expedition packages around Glover's Reef, Lighthouse Reef, and South Water Caye Marine Reserve. Several trips combine sea and river kayaking and base and expedition aspects. A six-night kayaking and paddleboarding lodge-to-lodge guided tour in the South Water Caye Marine Reserve is around US$2,000 per person (plus air travel).

MULTISPORT

Many Belize adventure trips include a bunch of different activities. For example, Adventure Life offers a variety of tours, some combining jungle hiking, paddling, snorkeling, and visits to Mayan sites. Island Expeditions' 10-night Ultimate Adventure trip offers kayaking on the southern part of the Belize Barrier Reef, paddling on rivers in Toledo, and caving and other adventures in western Belize. This tour is limited to 13 participants, with up to six guides.

PHOTO SAFARI

Nature Photography Adventure offers occasional photo safaris to Belize and Guatemala, with an emphasis on remote caves; participants must be reasonably physically fit to join this trip.

SPECIAL INTEREST

International Zoological Expeditions has 8- to 10-day trips, usually with an educational component such as ethnobotanical walks or mapping an island. IZE's trips combine time inland at Blue Creek in Toledo and at South Water Caye.

Great Itineraries

Ruins, Rain Forests, and Reef

DAY 1: ARRIVAL

Fly into the international airport near **Belize City** and immediately head out to the **Cayo** in western Belize, about two hours by road from the airport. Stay at one of the superb jungle lodges, such as the Lodge at Chaa Creek, Mystic River Resort, or duPlooy's, or for less money, Black Rock, Table Rock, or Crystal Paradise.

Logistics: The best way to see the mainland is by rental car. Pick up a car at one of the car-rental agencies in kiosks just across the main parking lot at the international airport. If you'd rather not drive, you can arrange a shuttle van, take a bus, or ask your hotel in the Cayo to pick you up. Buses don't come to the international airport—if you're taking one, you have to take a taxi into town (BZ$50 for two people). Tropic Air has service from Belize City to the Maya Flats airstrip between San Ignacio and Benque Viejo.

DAY 2: EXPLORING THE CAYO

On your first full day in Belize, get out and explore San Ignacio and the beautiful hill country around the Cayo. Among the top attractions are the small but interesting Mayan ruins at Xunantunich and Cahal Pech, Green Hills Butterfly Farm, the Rainforest Medicine Trail at Chaa Creek, and the Belize Botanical Gardens at duPlooy's. Save a little time for walking around and shopping in San Ignacio. After a full day of exploring, have cocktails and dinner at your lodge.

Logistics: You can do all the main attractions and San Ignacio in one day if you have a rental car and if you don't dawdle. Sans car, you can hire a taxi for the day, or opt for your hotel's tours.

DAY 3: ACTUN TUNICHIL MUKNAL (ATM)

Prepare to be wowed by the ultimate cave experience. Go into the mysterious and beautiful Mayan underworld and see untouched artifacts dating back thousands of years.

Logistics: You must have a guide for ATM, so book your trip the day before with an authorized tour guide company. It's an all-day event, and you'll get wet—bring a change of clothes and wear walking shoes, not sandals. Also, bring socks for walking through the cave. If you're badly out of shape or have mobility or claustrophobia issues, this isn't a tour for you. You have to hike several miles, swim a little, and clamber through the dark. Photography in the cave is not permitted.

DAY 4: TIKAL

Tikal, very simply, is the most awe-inspiring Mayan site in all of Central America, rivaling the pyramids of Egypt and the ruins of Angkor Wat in Cambodia. It's well worth at least two days and nights, preferably staying in one of the three lodges at the park, but even on a day tour you'll get a sense of the majesty of this Classic-period city.

Logistics: Although you can go on your own, the easiest and most stress-free way to see Tikal is on a tour from San Ignacio—you'll leave around 6:30 am and return in the late afternoon; lunch is usually included. Overnight and multinight tours also are available.

DAY 5: CARACOL AND THE MOUNTAIN PINE RIDGE

A terrific day trip is to Caracol, the most important Mayan site in Belize. The trip there is part of the fun—you bump along winding roads through the Mountain Pine Ridge, past the Macal River, and through broadleaf jungle. If you've seen enough Mayan ruins, skip Caracol and spend the

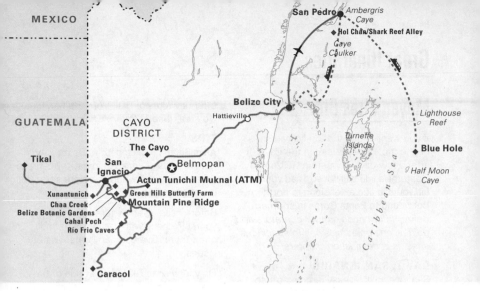

day exploring the Mountain Pine Ridge—
there's the Rio Frio cave and numerous
waterfalls. A bonus: the higher elevation
here means it's cooler and less humid
than in other parts of Belize. If you don't
mind packing and unpacking again, for
your last night in Cayo consider switch-
ing to one of the four lodges in the Pine
Ridge. Our favorites are Blancaneaux and
Hidden Valley Inn.

Logistics: From Blancaneaux or Hidden
Valley it's less than a two-hour drive
to Caracol, and about an hour longer
from most lodges around San Ignacio.
The road can be near-impassable after
heavy rains, and there have been some
incidents with bandits from Guatemala,
so check locally for the latest conditions
and cautions.

DAY 6: SAN PEDRO

Return to Belize City by plane, car, bus,
or shuttle van. Then fly or take a water
taxi to San Pedro (Ambergris Caye) for
fabulous eating (our favorites include
El Fogon, Finn and Martini, Rain, Casa
Picasso, Robin's Kitchen for low-cost
local cooking, and for breakfast with your
feet in the sand, Estel's). Try to arrive
early enough to do a snorkel trip to Hol
Chan/Shark-Ray Alley.

DAY 7: BLUE HOLE

Take a day-trip to dive or snorkel the Blue
Hole at Lighthouse Reef atoll. Dive boats
also stop at Half Moon Caye for other
dives (or snorkeling) besides the Blue
Hole.

Logistics: A trip to the Blue Hole involves
a full day on the water, so bring sea-
sickness medicine, a hat, and plenty of
sunscreen. Dive boats to Lighthouse
leave early, usually before 7 am.

■**TIP→ Some dive organizations recommend a minimum 24-hour interval between a
dive and a flight, so if you're flying out early
the next day consider diving earlier in your
trip, or snorkel instead. Also, the Blue Hole
is a deep dive recommended only for more
experienced divers.**

DAY 8: DEPARTURE

Return to Belize City by plane or water
taxi for your international flight.

Logistics: Plan on arriving at least two
hours ahead of your international flight.
There are often long lines at security.

Great Itineraries

Mayan Sites Blitz

If you want to see the top Mayan sites in one trip, base yourself in the Cayo. If after a few days in western Belize and Guatemala you still haven't had your fill, you can add extensions to northern Belize and to Punta Gorda in southern Belize. *Information on tour operators and guides, and on admissions to specific sites, is in destination chapters.*

DAY 1: SAN IGNACIO

San Ignacio is an easy jumping-off spot for seeing several small but fascinating nearby ruins. If you get an early start, you can take in **Xunantunich, Cahal Pech,** and **El Pilar.** Both Cahal Pech and Xunantunich can be reached by bus (albeit with a short hike after the bus ride in both cases), but a taxi or rental car is needed to get to El Pilar. Guided tours of all these sites can be arranged in San Ignacio or at lodges and hotels in the area. *(See The Cayo, Chapter 6)*

DAY 2: CARACOL

Caracol, the most important Mayan site in Belize, deserves a full day. You can drive yourself—or go on a tour. There is no bus transportation in the Mountain Pine Ridge. Even if you arrive independently, you can hire a guide to show you around once you're at the site, or you can tour it on your own. There's an informative museum and visitor center. Due to a series of bandit incidents, trips to Caracol are being done in convoys, protected by Belize Defence Forces soldiers. Check locally for updates. *(See The Cayo, Chapter 6)*

DAYS 3 AND 4: TIKAL

Tikal is by far the most impressive Mayan site in the region and shouldn't be missed (check in advance about travel warnings to the area). Many operators offer day tours of Tikal from the San Ignacio area. *(See El Petén, Chapter 9)*

TIPS

Altun Ha, the ruin closest to Belize City, gets crowds of cruise-ship day-trippers; try to avoid days when there are several cruise ships in port.

Before heading anywhere remote by yourself, check with the locals to find out if there have been any recent safety issues.

On your visit to Tikal, stay at one of the three lodges at the park—you'll be able to visit the ruins early in the morning or late in the afternoon, when howler monkeys and other animals are active and most day visitors have left. If you can't overnight at Tikal, do a day tour from San Ignacio; there also are daily flights from Belize City to Flores near Tikal.

Bring bug repellent. Mosquitoes are especially bad around **Cerro Maya** in northern Belize, at **Marco Gonzalez** on Ambergris Caye, and at the ruins near Punta Gorda.

On the Calendar

February

Placencia Sidewalk Festival: What was once the world's narrowest street showcases the work of local artisans to the sounds of DJ music and steel drums.

Carnival Festivities: Colorful carnival festivities begin the week prior to Lent, most notably in San Pedro, and extend into March.

March

La Ruta Maya Belize River Challenge: This is a remarkable and strenuous four-day cross-country canoe race over 175 miles (282 km). It's a good thing to watch as you celebrate Belize's holiday of National Heroes. ⊕ www.travelbelize.org/la-ruta-maya-river-challenge

April

Semana Santa (Holy Week): In Benque Viejo del Carmen, this celebration sees streets carpeted in brightly dyed sawdust and a dramatization of Christ's Passion.

May

BTB Love Belize Sea Challenge: A grueling, five-day sea kayaking race stretches over 190 miles (306 km)—that's almost the entire Belize coast. ⊕ www.travelbelize.org/BTB-Love-Belize-sea-Challenge

Toledo's Chocolate Festival: The sweet event is worth the trek south to Punta Gorda.

Crooked Tree Cashew Festival: Farther north, this festival goes all out for the cashew harvest season.

June

Lobster Fest: Wonderful lobster festivals are in San Pedro, Placencia, and Caye Caulker. The annual San Pedro Lobster Fest is the largest lobster festival in Belize, and the week-long festival includes live music, fishing competitions, and all-you-can-eat lobster. Placencia's festival spans three days and includes a beer drinking contest. ⊕ http://www.sanpedrolobsterfest.com

Hopkins Mango Festival: This delicious event celebrates all things mango, serving the fruit up on a stick, sliced, diced—you name it. There's music too, of course. ⊕ www.hopkinsmangofest.bz

July

Taste of Belize: Every two years, the best chefs from around the country come to showcase their best recipes.

November

Garifuna Settlement Day: With spectacular festivals, Garifuna Settlement Day celebrates the Garifuna, or Garinagu, arrival to the country (most notably in Dangriga).

The Taco Festival: This spicy food and music event takes place in Orange Walk Town.

Belize International Film Festival: In Belize City, the festival showcases impressive independent films. ⊕ www.belizefilmfestival.com

Planning Your Adventure

CHOOSING A TRIP

With dozens of options for special-interest and adventure tours in Belize, including do-it-yourself or fully guided package trips, it's helpful to think about certain factors when deciding which company or package will be right for you.

■ **Are you interested in adventure travel on the sea or the mainland or both?** Belize offers two very different adventure environments: the sea and the mainland. The Caribbean, various bays and lagoons, the Barrier Reef that runs 185 miles (303 km) along the eastern coast of the country, and three South Pacific–style atolls are perfect for activities such as fishing, sailing, diving, snorkeling, and windsurfing. Inland, you can rappel hundreds of feet into a limestone sinkhole, explore an underworld labyrinth of caves full of Mayan artifacts, hike the rain forest, ride horses or bikes to remote waterfalls, or tube down underground rivers. Some travelers prefer to concentrate on either water or land activities, but you can combine the two. Just be sure to give yourself enough time.

■ **How strenuous a trip do you want?** Adventure vacations commonly are split into "soft" and "hard" adventures. Hard adventures, such as strenuous jungle treks and extended caving trips, usually require excellent physical conditioning and previous experience. Most hiking, biking, canoeing, kayaking, cave tubing, snorkeling, brief cave tours, and similar soft adventures can be enjoyed by persons of all ages who are in good health and are accustomed to a reasonable amount of exercise. A little honesty goes a long way—recognize your own level of physical fitness and discuss it with the tour operator before signing on. Keep in mind that for most of the year in Belize you'll face hot weather and high humidity, conditions that can take a lot out of you, even if you're in good shape.

■ **Would you like to pick up new skills?** Belize is a great place to pick up new skills, whether it's how to paddle a kayak, how to rappel down a cliff face, or how to dive. For example, you can take a quick resort diving course to see if you like scuba, or you can do a complete open-water certification course, usually in three to four days. Before committing to any program, do some research to confirm that the people running it are qualified. Check to see if the dive shop or resort is certified by one of the well-known international dive organizations, such as the Professional Association of Diving Instructors (PADI), the largest certification agency in the world, or National Association of Underwater Instructors (NAUI), the second largest. Among the other how-to programs or lessons offered in Belize are kayaking, horseback riding, snorkeling, kitesurfing, and windsurfing.

■ **Do you want an "off-the-shelf" tour package or do you prefer to build your own trip?** You can opt to buy a prepackaged adventure or special-interest trip, complete with full-time guides who will do everything from meeting your international flight to cooking your meals, or you can go the more independent route, arranging local guides or tour operators on a daily, or even hourly, basis. Because English is the official language in Belize and most tour operators have email and websites, it's easy to put together an adventure package à la carte. Many package tour operators also offer you the ability to combine two or more trips or to create a custom itinerary. It all comes down to whether you're happier doing it yourself or having someone else take care of all the logistics and details.

■ **How far off the beaten path do you want to go?** As one of the least densely populated countries in the hemisphere—more than two-fifths of the country is devoted to nature reserves and national parks—Belize offers many off-the-beaten-path experiences. Although many trips described here might seem to be headed into uncharted territory, tour operators carefully check each detail before an itinerary goes into a brochure. You won't usually be vying with busloads of tourists for photo ops, but you'll probably run into occasional small groups of like-minded travelers. Journeys into truly remote regions, such as Victoria Peak in the Maya Mountains, typically involve camping or the simplest of accommodations, but they reward with more abundant wildlife and locals who are less accustomed to the clicking of cameras.

■ **What sort of group is best for you?** At its best, group travel offers curious, like-minded companions with which to share the day's experiences. Do you enjoy mixing with people from similar backgrounds, or would you prefer to travel with people of different ages and backgrounds? Inquire about group size; many companies have a maximum of 10 to 16 members, but 30 or more is not unknown. The larger the group, the more time spent (or wasted) at rest stops, meals, and hotel arrivals and departures.

If groups aren't your thing, most companies will customize a trip for you. In fact, this has become a major part of many tour operators' businesses. Your itinerary can be as flexible or as rigid as you choose. Such travel offers all the conveniences of a package tour, but the "group" is composed of only you and those you've chosen as travel companions. Responding to a renewed interest in multigenerational travel, many tour operators also offer family trips, with itineraries carefully crafted to appeal to both children and adults.

MONEY MATTERS

■ **How much are you willing to spend?** Tours in Central America can be found at all price points, and Belize has an adventure for every budget. Local operators are usually the best deal. Tours that are run by as many local people and resources as possible are generally cheaper and also give the greatest monetary benefit to the local economy. These types of tours are not always listed in guidebooks or on the Internet, so often they have to be found in person or by word of mouth. Safety and date specificity can fluctuate. Amenities such as lodging and transportation may be very basic in this category. Some agencies pay attention to the environment, whereas others do not. You really have to do your research on every operator, no matter the cost, to be sure you get what you need. When you find the right match, the payoff in terms of price and quality of experience will be worth it.

On the other end of the spectrum, the large (often international) tour agencies are generally the most expensive; however, they provide the greatest range of itinerary choices and highest quality of services. They use the best transportation, like private tour buses and boats, which rarely break down. First-rate equipment and safe, reliable guides are the norm. Dates and times are set in stone, so you can plan your trip down to the time you step in and out of the airport. Guides are certified and well paid. When food and lodging are provided, they are generally of high quality. If you are a traveler who likes to have every creature comfort provided for, look for tour operators more toward this end of the spectrum.

Contacts

Air Travel

AIRPORTS Sir Barry Bowen Municipal Airport (TZA). ✉ *Marine Parade Harbor Front* ⊹ *On seafront off Princess Margaret Dr.* ☎ *224/5671.* **Philip S. W. Goldson International Airport (BZE).** ⊹ *9 miles (15 km) north of Belize City center, off Philip Goldson Hwy.* ☎ *225/2045* ⊕ *www. pgiabelize.com.*

AIRLINE CONTACTS Avianca Airlines. ✉ *Belize Global Travel Services, 41 Albert St., Commercial District* ☎ *800/284–2622 toll-free in U.S. and Canada,* 227/7363 *reservation in Belize City* ⊕ *www. avianca.com.* **Copa Airlines.** ✉ *Philip S. W. Goldson International Airport, Ladyville* ☎ *800/359–2672 in U.S.* ⊕ *www.copaair. com.* **Maya Island Air.** ✉ *Sir Barry Bowen Municipal Airport, Marine Parade Harbor Front* ☎ *223/1140 reservations in Belize* ⊕ *www.mayaislandair. com.* **Tropic Air.** ✉ *San Pedro Airstrip, San Pedro Town* ☎ *226/2626 reservations in Belize,* 800/422–3435 *reservations in U.S. and Canada* ⊕ *www.tropicair.com.*

⛵ Boat Travel

Coastal Xpress. ✉ *Beachfront, Amigos del Mar Dock, San Pedro Town* ☎ *226/2007.* **D'Express.** ✉ *Placencia Municipal Pier, Main St., Point Placencia, Placencia Village* ⊹ *At south end of Placencia Village, near the Shak restaurant* ☎ *9991/0778 in Honduras.*

🚌 Bus Travel

IN BELIZE James Bus Line. ✉ *Inpendence Rd., Punta Gorda* ☎ *722/0117* ⊕ *www.puntagordabelize. com.* **Zippy Zappy Mayan Travels.** ✉ *Brown Sugar Marketplace, 111 N. Front St., Suite 126, Belize City* ☎ *223/1200* ⊕ *www.travelmundomaya.com.*

IN GUATEMALA Fuente del Norte. ✉ *Terminal de Buses, Santa Elena.* **Marlin Espadas.** ⊕ *www.marlinespadas.net.*

SHUTTLES Belize Shuttles and Transfers. ☎ *637/9922 in Belize* ⊕ *belize-shuttles. trekksoft.com/en.*

🚗 Car Travel

RENTALS AQ Auto Rental. ✉ *Mile 5.5, Goldson Hwy. (main office), Northern Suburbs* ☎ *222/5122 in Belize,* 305/712–5122 *in U.S.* ⊕ *www.aqbelizecarrental.com.* **Crystal Auto Rental.** ✉ *Mile 5, Goldson Hwy., Northern Suburbs* ☎ *223/1600 in Belize,* 936/307–1325 *in U.S.* ⊕ *www.crystal-belize.com.*

Lodging

RENTALS Airbnb. ⊕ *www. airbnb.com/s/Belize.* **Vacation Rentals By Owner (VRBO).** ⊕ *www.vrbo.com.*

HOMESTAYS Aguacate Belize Homestay Program. ✉ *46 Front St., Punta Gorda* ☎ *722/2531 BTIA office in Punta Gorda, 633/9954* ⊕ *www.aguacatebelize. com.* **Toledo Eco-Tourism Association (TEA).** ✉ *TEA office, Punta Gorda* ☎ *637/2101 TEA office in Santa Elena* ⊕ *www. belizemayatourism.org.*

➕ Emergencies

Belize Police. ☎ *911 for police and other emergencies nationwide, 90 for police, fire, and ambulance in Belize City only.* **Guatemalan National Police.** ☎ *120 for emergencies.* **Guatemalan Tourist Police.** ☎ *2421–2810 for 24-hr security info, 1500 for bilingual operator, who will put you in contact with police, fire, or ambulance.*

Chapter 3

BELIZE CITY

Updated by
Jeffrey Van Fleet

⊙ Sights	🍴 Restaurants	🏨 Hotels	💼 Shopping	🍸 Nightlife
★★★★☆	★★★☆☆	★★★☆☆	★★★☆☆	★★☆☆☆

WELCOME TO BELIZE CITY

TOP REASONS TO GO

★ **Great Photo Ops:** Belize City is highly photogenic, full of interesting faces, streets full of color, and charming old colonial houses. In short, Belize City has character.

★ **Colonial Architecture:** Belize City rewards the intrepid traveler with a surprising number of interesting sights and memorable places, among them the everyday colonial-era buildings in the Fort George and Southern Foreshore sections, where people still live and work. Many of the wooden buildings are in need of a bit of repair, but they still have heaps of Caribbean port-of-call atmosphere.

★ **Because You Have To:** As a visitor to Belize, you'll almost certainly have to spend a little time in Belize City, whether you like it or not. The international airport is in Ladyville, at the northern edge of the metropolitan area. Belize City is the transportation hub of the country, and most flights, buses, and car rentals originate here. If you're arriving late or leaving early, you'll probably have to overnight in or near the city.

If you're prepared to go beyond a cursory excursion, Belize City will repay your curiosity. There's an infectious sociability on streets like Albert and Queen, the main shopping strips. The finest British colonial houses—graceful white buildings with wraparound verandas, painted shutters, and fussy Victorian woodwork—are in the Fort George area, near the Radisson Fort George, the most pleasant part of the city for a stroll.

1 Fort George. The "colonial" section of Belize City is notable for its grand, if sometimes dilapidated, old 19th- and early-20th-century homes and buildings with tin roofs.

2 Marine Parade Harbor Front. Along the water near the Ramada Princess Hotel & Casino and BTL Park, there is more open, public space than there are buildings, making this a pleasant escape from the bustle of the city center.

3 The Commercial District. On the South Side, mainly on Albert and Regent Streets, this is the commercial center of the city. Be advised, however, that it is also near some of the worst slums in Belize.

4 The Northern Suburbs. Along the Philip Goldson Highway (formerly the Northern Highway) between the city center and the international airport, this is the fastest-growing part of the metropolitan area, with middle-class residential sections such as Buttonwood Bay and Belama, some of the city's stores and supermarkets, and

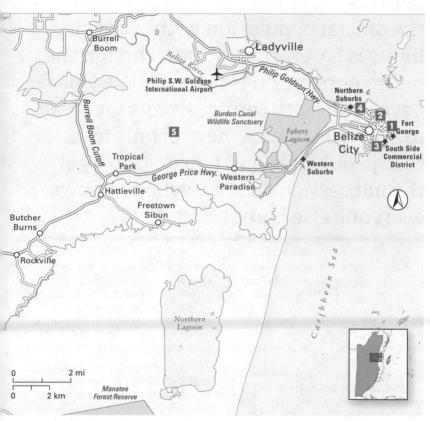

Burrell
Boom

Belize River

Ladyville

Philip Goldson Hwy.

Philip S.W. Goldson
International Airport

Northern
Suburbs

4

2

1 Fort
George

Burdon Canal
Wildlife Sanctuary

Fabers
Lagoon

Belize
City

3

South Side
Commercial
District

Burrell Boom Cutoff

5

Tropical
Park

George Price Hwy.

Western
Paradise

Western
Suburbs

Hattieville

Butcher
Burns

Freetown
Sibun

Rockville

Caribbean Sea

Northern
Lagoon

0   2 mi

0   2 km

Manatee
Forest Reserve

several hotels and bed-and-breakfasts.

5 The Western Suburbs.
A few tourist attractions have popped up here, such as the Old Belize complex. This multiuse commercial and residential area along the George Price Highway, beginning at a potentially confusing series of new roundabouts, is also on the way to the Belize Zoo, Belmopan, and Cayo.

6 Belize Zoo. Small in size, but not in stature, Belize's zoo is one of the best in the Americas, and it lies just southwest of the city.

7 Monkey Bay Wildlife Sanctuary. Beyond the Belize Zoo lies this wildlife sanctuary, staffed by a small army of dedicated volunteers, and you can take part too. Canoeing, hiking, and bird-watching are top activities here.

8 Community Baboon Sanctuary. This wildlife refuge northwest of the city may not actually have baboons, but it is one of the country's best conservation projects. Come to explore the trails and see Belize's black howler monkeys.

Belize City is more big town than city—few of the ramshackle buildings here are taller than a palm tree, and the official population within the city limits is barely over 60,000, though the metro population is near 110,000. Not far beyond the city center, streets give way to two-lane roads where people meet to talk, joke, laugh, and debate. You'll get the impression that everybody knows everyone else here.

On a map Belize City appears to be an ideal base for exploring the central part of the country—it's two hours or less by car to San Ignacio, Corozal Town, and Dangriga, and even less to Altun Ha, Belmopan, and the Belize Zoo. However, many old Belize hands will advise you to get out of Belize City as quickly as you can. They point to the high crime rate and to the relative lack of attractions in the city. Those rain forests, Mayan ruins, and stunning islands out in the rest of the country beckon, after all.

All of that is true enough, and certainly any visitor to Belize City should take the usual precautions for travel in an impoverished urban area, which include always taking a taxi at night (and in rough parts of the city, during the day, too), but Belize City does have an energy and excitement to it. There are good restaurants, a vibrant arts community, and, outside some of the rougher parts of town on the South Side, nice residential areas and a number of pleasant hotels and B&Bs. Belize City offers the most varied shopping in the country, and it's the only place to find sizeable supermarkets, department stores, and the Belizean version of big-box stores. There is always some little treasure to be discovered in a shop with mostly junk. All in all, it's far more interesting than any modern mall.

If you haven't spent time in Belize City, you simply won't understand Belize. It is the commercial, social, sports, and cultural hub of the country. It's even the political hub, despite the fact that the capital, Belmopan, is an hour west. Many government officials and nearly all of the country's movers and shakers still live in or near Belize City, even though the official move to Belmopan took place a half century ago.

Still—and we can't overemphasize this—you do have to be careful, as crime is not limited just to certain areas: when you're in Belize City, bring your street smarts and exercise caution at all times.

Planning

When to Go

The most pleasant time to visit Belize City is in the winter and early spring, December to March or April, when it's cooler and drier. The average high temperature in Belize City is 86°F, and the average low is 73°F. The coolest month is January, and the hottest is May. Hotel rates drop in the off-season, typically from just after Easter to U.S. Thanksgiving. September, a month marked by St. George's Caye Day (September 10) and Belize Independence Day (September 21), sees celebrations and parties; many expatriated Belizeans return home then for a visit to see family and friends. However, September is also peak time for tropical storms and hurricanes in the western Caribbean. September and October are the slowest months for tourism in Belize, and some hotels and restaurants close during this time for maintenance or to allow owners to take their own vacations.

Getting Here and Around

AIR TRAVEL

Philip S. W. Goldson International Airport (BZE) is near Ladyville, 9 miles (14 km) north of the city. The international airport is served from U.S. gateways by American, United, Delta, Southwest, Avianca (via its hub in San Salvador, El Salvador), Copa (via Panama City, Panama), and Canada's Air Canada Rouge and WestJet. Tropic Air has flights between the international airport and Cancún, Mexico; San Pedro Sula and Roatán, Honduras; and Flores, Guatemala, gateway to Tikal. Maya Island Air flies from the international airport to Cancún and San Pedro Sula.

In addition to international flights, a domestic terminal at the international airport has flights on Maya Island Air and

Touring Tip

If you're spending time in downtown Belize City, you are better off without a car. Parking is limited, and leaving a car on the street overnight, especially with any valuables in it, is just asking for trouble. Streets are narrow, and many are closed for repairs, so you could find yourself lost in a maze of unmarked detours.

Tropic Air to Ambergris Caye and Caye Caulker and the coastal towns of Dangriga, Placencia, and Punta Gorda.

Sir Barry Bowen Municipal Airport (TZA), on the seafront about 1 mile (2 km) north of the city center, has domestic flights only; Maya Island Air and Tropic Air serve most of the same domestic destinations from here as from the international airport. Fares from the municipal airport are about 10% to 40% cheaper, depending on the destination, than similar flights departing from the international airport.

CONTACTS Maya Island Air. ✉ *Muncipal Airstrip* ☎ *223/1403* ⊕ *www.mayaislandair.com.* **Tropic Air.** ✉ *San Pedro Airport, San Pedro Town* ☎ *226/2012, 800/422–3435 in U.S.* ⊕ *www.tropicair.com.*

BOAT AND FERRY TRAVEL

You can travel from Belize City on fast boats that hold 50 to 100 passengers or more to San Pedro (Ambergris Caye) and Caye Caulker. The boats also connect San Pedro and Caye Caulker. From Belize City it's a 45-minute ride to Caye Caulker and a 90-minute trip to San Pedro, including a stop at Caye Caulker. Going between Caye Caulker and San Pedro takes about 30 minutes.

Belize Ocean Ferry boats depart from the Marine Terminal at 10 North Front Street near the Swing Bridge; San Pedro Belize Express boats (which also go to

Caulker) leave from the nearby Brown Sugar dock at 111 North Front Street near the Tourism Village. Water taxis also will stop on demand at Caye Chapel and St. George's Caye. Each service has boats departing every couple of hours during daylight hours. Current schedules and prices are on the operators' websites but are subject to frequent change.

There is no scheduled water-taxi service from Belize City to Hopkins, Placencia, or other points on the coast, nor to remote cayes.

Generations of cruise passengers have known Belize City for its exceptionally slow tendering process on arrival and departure. Tenders deposit you at the Fort Street Tourism Village, a self-contained shopping complex for those who don't wish to venture out into the city itself. The construction of an $82 million port at Stake Bank, an island off the coast, will allow for quicker transfer from its deep-water port to fast boats into the city.

CONTACTS Ocean Ferry Belize. ✉ *Marine Terminal, 10 N. Front St.* ✛ *Near Swing Bridge* ☎ *223/0033* ⊕ *www.oceanferrybelize.com.* **San Pedro Belize Express.** ✉ *Brown Sugar Terminal, 111 N. Front St.* ☎ *223/2225 in Belize City* ⊕ *www.belizewatertaxi.com.*

BUS TRAVEL

Belize City is the hub of the country's fairly extensive bus network, so there's service to most regions of Belize and limited service by foreign bus companies to Mexico and Guatemala. The main bus terminal on West Collet Canal Street in Belize City—still locally referred to as Novelo's, though the Novelo bus company is no more—is used by most regional companies on the George Price Highway routes, the Goldson Highway routes, and the Hummingbird and Southern Highways routes. From Belize City, service on the main routes north, west, and south is frequent and inexpensive. Most of these owner-operated buses are old Bluebird school buses from the United States, with cramped seating and no air-conditioning. ⚠ **Take a cab to or from the Belize City bus terminal, day or night, as it is in an unsafe area.**

There is limited bus service within Belize City on a number of small independent lines. Most city buses are old U.S. school buses, but some are more modern minibuses. Ask locally about routes and times, as there are no published schedules. Also, local nonexpress regional buses will stop and drop off most anywhere in or near the city on the standard route.

CONTACTS Belize City Main Bus Terminal. (*Novelo's*) ✉ *W. Collet Canal St.*

CAR TRAVEL

There are only two highways to Belize City: the Philip Goldson Highway, which stretches to the Mexican border, 102 miles (165 km) away, and the George Price Highway, which runs 81 miles (131 km) to Guatemala. Both are paved two-lane roads, in fair-to-good condition. Signs guide you to nearby destinations such as the Belize Zoo.

Finding your way around the city itself can be confusing. With rare exceptions hotels in and near the city center offer mostly on-street parking, and you run the risk of a break-in if you leave the car overnight. Hotels in the suburbs north and west of the city usually have fenced or otherwise secured parking. Give your nerves a break and explore the city by taxi or on foot by day in safer sections like the Fort George area.

If you're driving between western and northern Belize, say from Belmopan to Orange Walk Town, you can take the Burrell Boom bypass around Belize City. The bypass runs between the roundabout on the George Price Highway at Hattieville at Mile 15.5 and and a roundabout at Mile 13 of the Philip Goldson Highway. The bypass, completely paved, is about 11.5 miles (18.5 km) in length; it saves you about 17 miles (28 km) and about a half hour of driving time.

If you are traveling from Belize City to one of the northern cayes and have a car, you won't be able to take your vehicle to the islands, so you'll need a safe place to park. Fenced and guarded parking is available at the international airport lot.

TAXI TRAVEL

Cabs cost BZ$5–BZ$15 for one person between any two points in the city, plus BZ$1 for each additional person. Outside the city, and from downtown to the suburbs, you'll be charged by distance traveled. Traveling between the international airport and any point in the city (including the businesses and hotels along the Goldson Highway north of the city center) is BZ$50 for two people, with BZ$10 for each additional person. There are no meters, so agree on a price before you leave. It's not customary to tip taxi drivers, unless they help you with luggage or perform other services. Most drivers are friendly and are happy to point out interesting sites to visitors. A few are licensed tour guides. Authorized taxis have green license plates. You can find taxis near the Swing Bridge and at the main bus terminal (Novelo's), or hotels will call them for you (this is always preferred, because the hotel staff know the dependable drivers). If you're satisfied with a driver's service, ask him for his card and call him next time.
■TIP➜ Ride-sharing services such as Uber and Lyft do not operate here.

Health and Safety

Belize City has a reputation for street crime. The government has made some progress in cleaning up the problem, despite gang activity and drugs. Crimes against tourists in Belize City are relatively rare. Still, the crime rate in Belize City is comparable to that of a distressed inner-city area in the United States. Take the same precautions you'd take in any

sketchy city—don't wear expensive jewelry or watches, avoid handling money in public, and leave valuables in a safe. Ignore offers to buy drugs. On buses and in crowded areas hold purses and backpacks close to your body. Check with the staff at your hotel before venturing into any unfamiliar areas, particularly after dark. Never walk anywhere at night. Take a taxi: have your hotel call one or have the guard get one for you. When you're ready to call it an evening, have the bar or restaurant get you a taxi rather than flagging one down in the street. Avoid leaving your rental car on the street overnight. Generally the Northern Suburbs are safer than downtown.

Visitor Information

Belize Tourism Board

Belize Tourism Board, a department of the Ministry of Tourism, is the official tourism agency of the government of Belize. ⌂ *64 Regent St., Commercial District* ☎ *227/2423, 800/624–0686 in U.S.* ⊕ *www.travelbelize.org.*

Sights

Belize City is defined by the water around it. The main part of the city is at the end of a small peninsula, jutting out into the Caribbean Sea. Haulover Creek, an extension of the Belize River, running roughly west to east, divides the city into the North Side and the South Side. The North Side is, to generalize, more affluent than the South Side. The venerable Swing Bridge connects the two sides, although in modern times other bridges over Haulover Creek, especially the Belcan Bridge northwest of the city center, carry more traffic. At the mouth of the river, just beyond Swing Bridge, is the Belize Harbor (or Harbour, as it's written locally, in the English style).

If you're staying in the sprawling northern or western suburbs, a car is handy, as there's limited municipal bus service. There are many taxis, however, with affordable rates.

Coming from the north, follow the Goldson Highway through several roundabouts (traffic circles) to Freetown Road and Barracks Road to reach the center. Alternatively, you can swing west on Princess Margaret Drive to Barracks Road, along the seafront. This is the more scenic route. From the west, the George Price Highway, via a new roundabout intersection, takes you to the Goldson Highway, from which you approach the city as described above. The city center itself is a confusing warren of narrow streets, many of them one-way or temporarily closed, with detours that are not well marked or are not marked at all.

Tours

From Belize City you can take day-trips to Crooked Tree Wildlife Sanctuary, the Community Baboon Sanctuary, and the Belize Zoo; to Jaguar Paw for cave tubing; to Altun Ha, Lamanai, and Xunantunich Mayan sites; and to nearby islands, including Caulker and Ambergris Cayes. You can do most of these trips either on your own or with a local tour operator. Your hotel can also arrange day-trips. Keep in mind that most Belize City tour operators focus more on the cruise-ship market than on individual travelers.

★ **Belize Trips**

Belize Trips can organize a custom excursion to almost any place in the country and also to Tikal in Guatemala. ⊠ *Belize City* ☎ *223/0376, 561/210–7015 in U.S.* ⊕ *www.belize-trips.com.*

CAVE TUBING

Several Belize City–based tour operators, including Butts Up and Vital Nature and Mayan Tours, offer cave-tubing trips or cave-tubing and ziplining combo tours, which usually include lunch. These inner tubes are usually bright yellow,

custom-designed tubes with cup holders and head rests. Head lamps or other lights are provided for the dark caves.

Butts Up

ADVENTURE TOURS | Despite the risqué name, the folks here get top marks from cruise passengers for their cave-tubing tours. You can choose from a basic cave-tubing outing (BZ$100 per person) or add a zipline or ATV tour for a total of BZ$150. A separate zipline tour with a visit to the ruins at Altun Ha is also available. Although most of the company's business is with cruise ship passengers, overnight visitors also can do the tours. ⊠ *Near Terminal 1, Tourism Village, Fort George* ☎ *605/1575, 888/637–3351* ⊕ *www.cave-tubing.com* ✉ *From BZ$100.*

Vital Nature and Mayan Tours

ADVENTURE TOURS | Vital Nature and Mayan Tours is based in Corozal Town but does business primarily in Belize City. The company arranges to pick up customers at the cruise ship terminal, at hotels, at the water-taxi terminal or one of the airports, or elsewhere. Besides cave tubing at Jaguar Paw (Nohoch Che'en Caves Branch Archaeological Reserve), the company also does zipline tours and trips to most of the Mayan sites in central and western Belize, as well as to Tikal. ⊠ *Tourism Village* ☎ *602/8975* ⊕ *www.cavetubing.bz* ✉ *From BZ$90.*

HELICOPTER TOURS

Astrum Helicopters

FLYING/SKYDIVING/SOARING | Astrum offers customized aerial tours of the Great Blue Hole, Mayan sites, the Belize Barrier Reef, and other sites, using five-seat Bell helicopters. It also provides helicopter transfers to upscale resorts and lodges on the cayes and inland. ⊠ *Cisco Base, Mile 3.5, George Price Hwy.* ☎ *222/5100, 888/278–7864 in U.S.* ⊕ *www.astrumhelicopters.com.*

MAYAN RUINS

Tour operators based in Belize City, including Butts Up, Vital Nature and Mayan Tours, and S&L Travel and Tours, offer day-trips by road, boat, or air to Lamanai and by road to Altun Ha, and also by road to Xunantunich and Cahal Pech near San Ignacio. The tours to western Belize may be combined with a stop at the Belize Zoo or cave tubing and ziplining at Jaguar Paw.

CONTACTS **Discovery Expeditions.** ⊠ 5916 Manatee Dr., Buttonwood Bay, Northern Suburbs ☎ 671/0748 ⊕ www.discovery-belize.com. **S&L Travel and Tours.** ⊠ 91 N. Front St. ☎ 227/7593 ⊕ www.sltravelbelize.com.

Restaurants

Though most restaurants here cater to locals, their number and quality rival those of tourist magnet San Pedro on Ambergris Caye. The city has inexpensive dives serving "dollah chicken" (fried chicken, a local favorite, though it no longer costs just one Belize dollar), Chinese joints of 1950s vintage specializing in chow mein, and lunch spots for downtown office workers seeking Creole dishes such as cow-foot soup and rice and beans. Belize City also has a few upmarket restaurants serving the city's affluent elite. Only a couple of these are "dressy" (by Belize standards, this means a nice collared shirt for men and perhaps a long tropical dress for women), and reservations are rarely necessary.

A few restaurants around the Tourism Village target cruise-ship passengers, typically for lunch and drinks, but the one thing you won't find here are chain restaurants.

Restaurant reviews have been shortened. For full information, visit Fodors.com.

What It Costs in Belize Dollars

$	$$	$$$	$$$$
AT DINNER			
under BZ$15	BZ$15–BZ$30	BZ$31–BZ$50	over BZ$50

Hotels

Belize City has a limited selection of acceptable accommodation. The Radisson Fort George, Ramada Princess Hotel and Casino, and Best Western Biltmore Plaza are the country's largest hotels and the city's only chain properties. Each has 75 or more rooms, and they strive, not always successfully, for an international standard. The city also has its share of small inns and B&Bs with character, such as the Great House, North Park, D'Nest Inn, and Villa Boscardi. Spend a bit more on a place to stay in Belize City. Cheaper hotels abound, but they have few amenities and present safety risks. Wherever you stay, do a quick check to be sure that doors and windows lock securely and that the entrance is well lit.

Several of the city's best hotels are in the Fort George area, but there are also good choices in the Northern Suburbs between downtown and the international airport. We recommend you don't stay in the Commercial District on the South Side (south of Swing Bridge); safety is always a concern in that neighborhood at night.

Hotel reviews have been shortened. For full information, visit Fodors.com.

What It Costs in Belize Dollars

$	$$	$$$	$$$$
FOR TWO PEOPLE			
under BZ$200	BZ$200–BZ$300	BZ$301–BZ$500	over BZ$500

3

Belize City PLANNING

Nightlife

Although locals love to party, safety concerns keep visitors away from purely local places. The bars at upmarket hotels, such as the Ramada Princess Hotel & Casino and at the Radisson Fort George, are popular (and safe) places to congregate for drinks. The Riverside Tavern is a popular place to have drinks, either indoors in air-conditioned comfort or on the outside patio next to the water, as is the Hour Bar & Grill. After dark, always take a taxi, or, if driving, park in a fenced and secured lot, such as at the Riverside Tavern.

Karaoke is all the rage in Belize. Most hotel bars have karaoke nights once or twice a week. Belizean taste in music is nothing if not eclectic. You'll hear a diverse mix of music, but one uniquely Belizean style of music is *punta* rock. It's based on the traditional punta rhythms of the Garifuna, using drums, turtle shells, and rattles. Punta rock, earthy and sexy, swept Belize and later became popular in other Central American countries.

Shopping

Belize City has the most varied shopping in the country. Most stores in Belize City cater to the local market and those from other parts of the country who need to stock up on supplies at lumberyards, home-building stores, appliance outlets, and supermarkets. Gift shops and handicraft shops are concentrated in the downtown area in and near the Fort Street Tourism Village.

Most stores in the downtown area are open Monday through Saturday from around 8 am to 6 pm. On Sunday, nearly all stores downtown are dark, although some stores in the suburbs are open Sunday afternoon.

Activities

Belize City is a jumping-off spot for trips to the cayes and to inland and coastal areas, but the city itself offers little in the way of sports and outdoor activities. There are no golf courses, public tennis courts, or other sports facilities of note around Belize City, other than a sports stadium named after the now-disgraced Olympic track star Marion Jones, a Belizean-American. Unless you're on a cruise ship or otherwise have only a short time in Belize, you'll be better off going elsewhere for your sporting activities—to the cayes and Southern Coast for snorkeling, diving, and fishing, and inland to the Cayo or Toledo for caving, cave tubing, hiking, horseback riding, canoeing, and other activities. Most of the dive, snorkel, and tour operators in Belize City do cater to the cruise-ship crowd. *See chapters on The Cayo, Southern Coast, The Deep South, and The Cayes and Atolls, and also the Beyond Belize City section below.*

FISHING

If you're a serious angler, you'll likely end up in Placencia, Punta Gorda, or even San Pedro, but you can arrange fishing charters from Belize City. Both the Radisson Fort George and the Princess Hotel & Casino have marinas, and there is also the Cucumber Marina at Old Belize, the city's best. Local fishing-guide services and lodges operate near the city. The oldest continuously operating fishing lodge, Belize River Lodge, is located near Belize City. Fishing licenses are now required for all but pier and shore fishing. Your fishing charter company can arrange them for you.

Belize River Lodge

FISHING | Belize River Lodge is the oldest continuously operating fishing lodge in Belize. The original lodge, basic but with air-conditioning and good food, is on the Belize River near Belize City. It also has an outpost at Long Caye near Caye Chapel for closer access to tarpon, bonefish, jacks, and barracuda inside the reef. Three-night, two-day river fishing trips with lodging, meals, guides, skiff, and transfers start at BZ$1,795 per person, based on four people. Five-night, four-day fishing trips from the Long Caye outpost start at BZ$3,250 per person, based on four people. ⊠ *Belize Old River* ☎ *225/2002, 888/275–4843 in U.S.* ⊕ *www.belizeriverlodge.com.*

SCUBA DIVING AND SNORKELING
Sea Sports Belize
SCUBA DIVING | Sea Sports, with an office downtown near the cruise-ship tender docks, will take you to the Barrier Reef for diving (around BZ$250 to BZ$300). The dive shop also does trips to Turneffe and Lighthouse Atolls. Most of their business is with cruise ships, but they also work with visitors staying in Belize City. ⊠ *83 N. Front St.* ☎ *223/5505* ⊕ *www. seasportsbelize.com.*

Fort George

This is the most pleasant and appealing section of the city, much of it cooled by prevailing breezes from the sea. It has stately if sometimes run-down colonial buildings, a couple of embassies (though the U.S. embassy is now in Belmopan), upmarket restaurants that attract the city's elite, and the city's better hotels, including the Radisson Fort George and the Great House, plus the Museum of Belize, Fort George lighthouse, and the Tourism Village.

 Sights

Fort George Lighthouse and Bliss Memorial
LIGHTHOUSE | Towering 49 feet (15 m) over the entrance to Belize Harbor, the lighthouse stands guard on the tip of Fort George Point. It was designed and funded by one of the country's greatest benefactors, Baron Henry Edward Ernest Victor Bliss. The English nobleman never actually set foot on the

Belizean mainland, though in his yacht he visited the waters offshore. In his will he bequeathed most of his fortune to the people of Belize, and the date of his death, March 9, is celebrated as a national holiday, now officially called National Heroes and Benefactors Day. Bliss is buried here, in a small, low mausoleum perched on the seawall, up a short run of limestone steps. The lighthouse and mausoleum are for photo ops only—you can't enter. ⊠ *Marine Parade, near the Radisson Fort George Hotel, Fort George* ☎ *222/5665 Belize Port Authority* ⊕ *www.portauthority.bz* ⊠ *Free.*

Fort Street Tourism Village
SHOPPING CENTERS/MALLS | Even though this shopping complex is open only when cruise ships are in port, it's a good place to stop, as it has around 30 gift shops, including the MOHO chocolate shop offering free samples of organic, Belize-made chocolates, plus the usual duty-free and jewelry stores you'll find all over the Caribbean. You'll also find clean restrooms, a cybercafé, tour kiosks, restaurants, and other services. Security is tight in the Tourism Village, and you'll feel safe. If you are not here on a cruise excursion, you must show your passport to enter. On cruise-ship days, vendors also set up booths on streets near the Tourism Village. ⊠ *Fort George cruise-ship docks, 8 Fort St., east of Swing Bridge, Fort George* ☎ *223/7789* ⊕ *www. tourismvillage.com* ⊘ *Closed when there are no cruise ships.*

★ Museum of Belize
MUSEUM | FAMILY | This small but fascinating museum, under the aegis of the National Institute of Culture and History (NICH), was the Belize City jail from 1857 to 1993. Permanent displays include ancient jade and other Mayan artifacts; medicinal, ink, and alcoholic-beverage bottles dating from the 17th century; Belize and British Honduran coins and colorful postage stamps; and an actual prison cell. Temporary exhibitions change

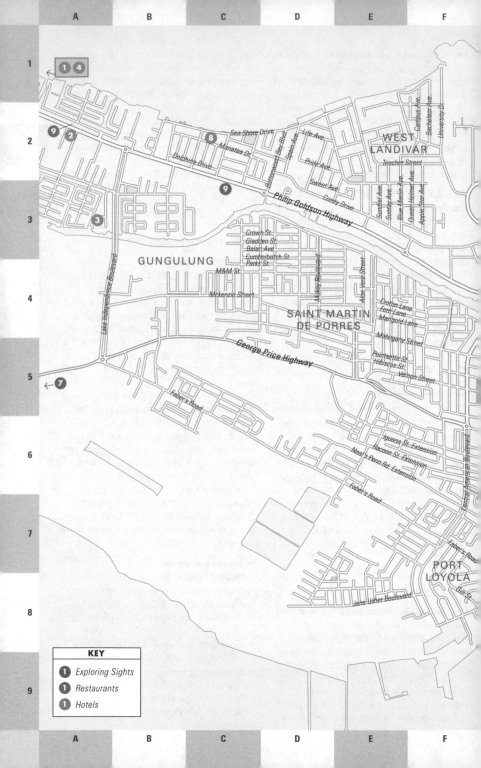

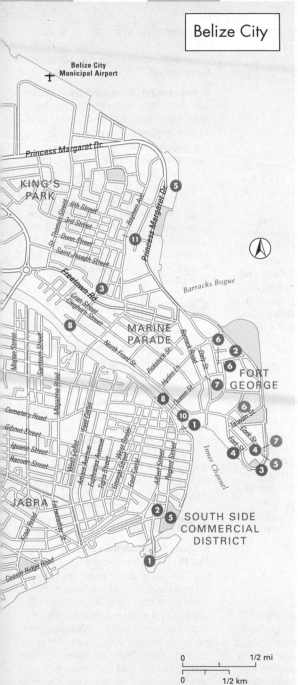

Belize City

Sights ▼

1 Belize Supreme Court............. I6
2 Cathedral of
  St. John the Baptist I7
3 Fort George Lighthouse and
  Bliss Memorial.................... J7
4 Fort Street Tourism Village......... J6
5 Government House/
  House of Culture................... I7
6 Museum of Belize J5
7 Old Belize.......................... A5
8 Swing Bridge...................... I6
9 Travellers Liquors
  Heritage Center................... C3

Restaurants ▼

1 Bird's Isle I8
2 Celebrity Restaurant & Bar........ J5
3 Chon Saan Palace................. H4
4 The 501 Hub J6
5 Hour Bar & Grill................... I3
6 Ice Cream Shoppe................. I5
7 Nerie's I5
8 Riverside Tavern.................. G5
9 Sahara Grill........................ A2
10 Spoonaz Photo Café.............. I6
11 Sumathi........................... H3

Hotels ▼

1 Bamboleo Inn A1
2 Best Western Belize
  Biltmore Plaza.................... A2
3 D'Nest Inn A3
4 Global Village Hotel.............. A1
5 The Great House.................. J6
6 North Park Hotel.................. J6
7 Radisson Fort George
  Hotel and Marina J6
8 Villa Boscardi C2

3

Belize City FORT GEORGE

periodically. ✉ *8 Gabourel La., Belize Central Bank Compound, Fort George* ☎ *227/0518 NICH office at House of Culture* 🌐 *www.nichbelize.org* 🎟 *BZ$10* 🕒 *Closed Sun.*

🍴 Restaurants

★ The 501 Hub

$$ | LATIN AMERICAN | The large dining courtyard here is shaded by breadfruit, mango, and sapodilla trees—you'll see the staff cutting down those fruits to put in your dish—and big turquoise umbrellas. The solid Belizean menu contains dishes with whimsical names like "Not your mamma's waffles, unless she's vegan," which designates plantain waffles with scrambled tofu. **Known for:** good variety, including vegan options; attentive service; pleasant garden setting. [$] *Average main: BZ$18* ✉ *13 Cork St., Fort George* ☎ *639/6949* 🕒 *Closed Tues.*

🛏 Hotels

The Great House

$$$ | B&B/INN | Among Fort George's most appealing sights is the colonial facade of this large wooden 1927 house, converted into a fine inn. **Pros:** lovely old inn; good location in Fort George area; friendly staff. **Cons:** rooms are all upstairs on second and third floors with no elevator; a few rooms get limited light; rooms 1-3 are directly off lobby. [$] *Rooms from: BZ$350* ✉ *13 Cork St., Fort George* ☎ *223/3400, 214/613–9296 in U.S.* 🌐 *www.greathousebelize.com* 🔑 *16 rooms* 🍽 *Free breakfast.*

North Park Hotel

$$$ | B&B/INN | This renovated 1921 wooden house sits just a half block off the ocean promenade, sparkling after its conversion into a boutique hotel in 2019. **Pros:** great rates for what's offered; cool sea breezes on veranda; music offerings many evenings in restaurant. **Cons:** music may disturb your peace and quiet. [$] *Rooms from: BZ$305* ✉ *18 N. Park (Taiwan) St., Fort George* ☎ *223/2607* 🌐 *www.northparkbelize.com* 🔑 *12 rooms* 🍽 *No meals.*

★ Radisson Fort George Hotel and Marina

$$$ | HOTEL | The country's first modern hotel is also the city's best international-style large hotel, and it's located in the historic Fort George district with panoramic views of the sea from the more expensive rooms. **Pros:** Belize City's best large hotel; waterfront location in historic Fort George area; U.S. chain with Belizean touches and decor. **Cons:** some rooms are small; could use updating. [$] *Rooms from: BZ$350* ✉ *2 Marine Parade, Fort George* ☎ *223/3333, 800/333–3333 in U.S.* 🌐 *www.radisson.com* 🔑 *102 rooms* 🍽 *Free breakfast.*

🍸 Nightlife

Baymen's Tavern

BARS/PUBS | This downtown bar at the Radisson Fort George is a comfortable, safe place to sip a rum and tonic, with live entertainment on weekends, usually a singer or a small band. There's also a more casual section of the bar, on an open-air deck, with views of a garden and the sea. On weekends, this bar jumps, with a mostly local crowd. ✉ *Radisson Fort George Hotel, 2 Marine Parade, Fort George* ☎ *223/3333* 🌐 *www.radisson.com.*

🛍 Shopping

Belizean Handicraft Market Place

CRAFTS | This handicraft-market complex has Belizean souvenir items, including hand-carved figurines, handmade furniture, pottery, and woven baskets. The prices are about as good as you'll find anywhere in Belize, and the sales clerks are friendly. It is just a short stroll from the harbor front, the Belize Tourism Village, and many of the hotels in the Fort George area, including the Radisson Fort George and The Great House. ✉ *2 S.*

The boat-lined Haulover Creek runs through the center of Belize City.

Park St., across from Memorial Park, Fort George 🕾 *223/3637* ⊘ *Closed Sun.*

Image Factory
ART GALLERIES | The cutting edge of Belize City's art and hipster scene is at the Image Factory, which holds art and photography shows and publishes books. Its gallery and shop sell books, artwork, and CDs. ✉ *91 N. Front St., Fort George* 🕾 *223/4093* ⊘ *Closed weekends.*

South Side Commercial District

This area, along Albert and Regent Streets, two parallel streets running north–south from Haulover Creek, is the commercial heart of the city. It has many small stores, banks, and budget hotels, along with several places of interest, including the Supreme Court, St. John's Cathedral, and the House of Culture. A third parallel street, the Southern Foreshore, hugs the waterfront along the South Side.

Sights

Belize Supreme Court
BUILDING | Not the oldest building in the city but one of the most striking, the 1926 Belize Supreme Court building is patterned after its wooden predecessor, which had burned in 1918. The current building, painted white, has filigreed iron stair and balcony rails, similar to what you might see in New Orleans (the construction company came from Louisiana), between two arms of the structure, and above the balcony a four-sided clock. This being Belize, the clock faces all seem to show different times. You can't enter the building, but it's worth admiring from the outside. ✉ *Regent St., opposite Battlefield Park, Commercial District* 🕾 *227/4387* ⊕ *www.belizejudiciary.org.*

Cathedral of St. John the Baptist
RELIGIOUS SITE | On Albert Street's south end is the oldest Anglican church in Central America and the only one outside England where kings were invested. From 1815 to 1845, four kings of the

Mosquito Kingdom (a British protectorate along the coast of Honduras and Nicaragua) were crowned here. The cathedral, built of brick brought here to what once was British Honduras as ballast on English ships, is thought to be the oldest surviving building in Belize from the colonial era. Its foundation stone was laid in 1812. Inside, it has whitewashed walls and mahogany pews. The roof is constructed of local sapodilla wood, with mahogany beams. Residents of the city usually refer to the cathedral as simply "St. John's." ■ **TIP→ You can combine a visit to the cathedral with a visit to the House of Culture, as they are just across the street from each other. The street is safe to visit during day; as dusk approaches, take a taxi.** ✉ *Albert St. at Regent St., opposite House of Culture, Commercial District* ☎ *227/3029* 🌐 *www.anglicandioceseofbelize.com* 🎟 *Free.*

★ **Government House/House of Culture**

MUSEUM | FAMILY | The city's finest colonial structure is said to have a design inspired by the illustrious British architect Sir Christopher Wren. Built in 1814, it was once the residence of the governor-general, the British monarchy's representative in Belize. Following Hurricane Hattie in 1961, the decision was made to move the capital inland to Belmopan, and the house became a venue for social functions and a guesthouse for visiting VIPs. (Queen Elizabeth stayed here in 1985, Prince Philip in 1988.) Now it's open to the public. You can peruse its archival records, and art and artifacts from the colonial era, or mingle with the tropical birds that frequent the gardens. Renovations are in the works for the building and gardens. ⚠ **If going here after dark, take a cab, because it's close to some of the city's most crime-ridden areas.** ✉ *Regent St. at Southern Foreshore, opposite Cathedral of St. John the Baptist, Commercial District* ☎ *227/0518* 🌐 *www.nichbelize.org* 🎟 *BZ$10* 🕒 *Closed Sun.*

Swing Bridge

BRIDGE/TUNNEL | As its name suggests, the bridge spanning Haulover Creek in the middle of Belize City actually swings. When needed to allow a boat through or by special request of visiting dignitaries, four men hand-winch the bridge a quarter-revolution so waiting boats can continue upstream (when it was the only bridge in town, this snarled traffic for blocks). The bridge, made in England, opened in 1923; it was renovated and upgraded in 1999. Outsiders' recommendations to automate the swing mechanics or—heaven forbid—rebuild the bridge entirely are always immediately rejected. No one wants to eliminate the city's most unusual landmark. Before the Swing Bridge arrived, cattle were "hauled over" the creek in a barge. The bridge appears in a scene of the 1980 movie *The Dogs of War,* set in a fictitious African country but mostly filmed in Belize. ✉ *Haulover Creek, Queen and Albert Sts., Commercial District.*

🍴 Restaurants

Bird's Isle

$$ | SEAFOOD | This longtime local seafood favorite is an open-air seaside bar and restaurant on the little islet at the south end of Regent Street, also called Bird's Isle. The thatched-roof spot is a great place to sip tropical drinks and eat local seafood (the fried snapper is a favorite) or other dishes at lunch, away from the hustle of downtown. **Known for:** solid seafood offerings; Saturday-afternoon barbecue; cool sea breezes. [$] *Average main: BZ$22* ✉ *9 Albert St., at south end of Regent St., across bridge on Bird's Isle, on South Side, Commercial District* ☎ *207/2179* 🕒 *Closed Sun. No dinner Mon. and Tues.*

Chon Saan Palace

$$ | CHINESE | Locally adored for four decades, Chon Saan Palace is the best Chinese restaurant in Belize City, which is otherwise full of bad Chinese eateries.

It has some 200 dishes on the menu, most Cantonese style, such as sweet-and-sour pork. **Known for:** dizzying menu; Chinese-style crab legs; weekend sushi and sashimi offerings. [$] *Average main: BZ$22* ✉ *1 Kelly St., at Nurse Seay St., Commercial District* ☎ *223/3008.*

★ Ice Cream Shoppe

$ | **AMERICAN** | Belize's abundance of fruit ends up in a variety of flavors scooped up for you at the city's best ice-cream parlor. You'll probably have questions as you gaze at the blackboard menu—what are craboo and sapodilla?—and the good folks here are happy to explain the more exotic flavors. **Known for:** exotic flavors; seasonal offerings; atmosphere of a stateside ice-cream parlor. [$] *Average main: BZ$4* ✉ *17 Eve St., Commercial District* ☎ *223/1965* 💳 *No credit cards.*

Nerie's

$ | **LATIN AMERICAN** | Often packed, Nerie's is the vox populi of dining in Belize City. The many traditional dishes on the menu include fry jacks for breakfast and cow-foot soup for lunch. **Known for:** solid Belizean food; lively local crowd; great prices. [$] *Average main: BZ$14* ✉ *Queen and Daly Sts., Commercial District* ☎ *223/4028* 💳 *No credit cards* ⏲ *Closed Sun.*

★ Riverside Tavern

$$ | **AMERICAN** | One of the city's most popular and agreeable restaurants serves up dependably good food, with friendly service and safe parking. The signature hamburgers, which come in several sizes from 6 oz. to enormous, are arguably the best in Belize. **Known for:** best burgers in the city; Sunday brunches; gated parking lot. [$] *Average main: BZ$28* ✉ *2 Mapp St., off Freetown Rd., Commercial District* ☎ *223/5640* ⏲ *No dinner Sun.*

Spoonaz Photo Café

$ | **CAFÉ** | Duck into this small café near the water-taxi terminal for a sandwich or light fare. The air-conditioning feels heavenly on a hot day, of which there are many here, but seating spills over onto an outside patio, too. **Known for:** terrific bagels and muffins; good selection of coffees, teas, and chocolate drinks; cool black-and-white photos of old Belize. [$] *Average main: BZ$12* ✉ *89 N. Front St., Commercial District* ☎ *223/1043* ⏲ *No dinner Sun.–Wed.*

🍸 Nightlife

★ Riverside Tavern

BARS/PUBS | A longtime favorite among expats, visitors, and locals alike, the Riverside Tavern serves drinks before dinner on the covered patio overlooking Haulover Creek or inside at the bar. Park your car safely in a fenced, guarded lot next to the tavern and restaurant. ✉ *2 Mapp St., off Freetown Rd., Commercial District* ☎ *223/5640.*

🎟 Performing Arts

Bliss Center for the Performing Arts

ARTS CENTERS | **FAMILY** | Overlooking the harbor from the Southern Foreshore near the Supreme Court, this stunning building houses the Institute of Creative Arts and hosts cultural and arts events throughout the year—on a Saturday night you could hear a Mayan singer from Toledo or a marimba band from Benque Viejo del Carmen. Part of the National Institute of Culture and History, the center's 600-seat theater is headquarters for the Belize International Film Festival, usually held in July. Dramas, children's festivals, dance, art displays, and other cultural and musical performances take place at various times. It also houses a small art gallery with a George Gabb sculpture, *Sleeping Giant*, which appears as the watermark on Belize five-dollar bills. Most shows are in English, with Creole often mixed in. Ticket prices typically range from BZ$10 to BZ$40, a bargain compared to what you'd pay for a theatrical performance back home. ✉ *2 Southern Foreshore, between Church* *and Bishop Sts., Commercial District* ☎ *227/2110* 🌐 *www.nichbelize.org.*

Marine Parade Harbor Front

This rather nebulously defined area, which stretches from the Fort George section of Marine Parade to Barracks Road and then to the beginning of Princess Margaret Drive, could eventually be Belize City's equivalent of Havana's Malecón. Only a few years ago it was an unsightly conglomeration of old buildings and vacant lots. With cleaning up and some gentrification, the area now has several good restaurants, condominiums, a hotel-casino, and a park.

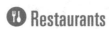

🍴 Restaurants

★ Celebrity Restaurant & Bar

$$$ | **LATIN AMERICAN** | **FAMILY** | Visit at lunch or dinner almost any day and you'll see a cross-section of Belize City's movers and shakers—attorneys, businesspeople, politicians—enjoying the restaurant's large menu of U.S.-inspired seafood, steaks, pasta, and salads, along with Belizean comfort food. If you can get past the flamboyant wallpaper in the main dining room and the fairly basic selection of drinks and wine, you'll enjoy it, too. **Known for:** lobster hollandaise; attentive service; the place to see and be seen in Belize City. [$] *Average main: BZ$40* ✉ *Volta Bldg., Marine Parade Blvd., Marine Parade Harbor Front* ☎ *223/7272* 🌐 *www.celebritybelize.com* 🕒 *No dinner Sun.*

Hour Bar & Grill

$$$ | **SEAFOOD** | You come here for the lively atmosphere more than the food, although the menu of seafood, burgers, salads, and grilled chicken is certainly filling. Locals and expats alike enjoy the breezy, seaside location. **Known for:** lively patrons; cool sea breezes; good drink selection. [$] *Average main: BZ$32* ✉ *1 Princess Margaret Dr., Marine Parade Harbor Front* ☎ *223/3737.*

Sumathi

$$ | **INDIAN** | Tasty northern and southern Indian food is created at Sumathi in its authentic tandoori oven—a large clay oven with intense heat—which cooks meat and seafood quickly, leaving it crispy on the outside and juicy inside. Try the tandoori chicken, with cumin, ginger, and minty yogurt, served with naan. **Known for:** lots of vegan and vegetarian options; generous portions; good value at lunch buffet. [$] *Average main: BZ$24* ✉ *Off Newtown Barracks, 19 Baymen Ave., Marine Parade Harbor Front* ☎ *223/1172* 🕒 *Closed Mon.*

🍸 Nightlife

Casino at Ramada by Wyndham Princess Hotel Belize City

CASINOS | The only serious gambling in town is at the Ramada Princess Hotel, which has live tables for blackjack, roulette, and poker, along with about 400 slots. There are free drinks and a buffet for players, along with dance shows, two movie theaters, and a dance club. It's open 365 days a year until the wee hours of the morning. Gamble here if you like, but we don't recommend staying at the hotel. ✉ *Newton Barracks, Marine Parade Harbor Front* ☎ *223/0638 casino* 🌐 *www.wyndhamhotels.com.*

Western Suburbs

For visitors, this part of the metropolitan area mostly is just a place to pass through on the way to the Cayo. However, local entrepreneurs have opened several businesses targeting cruise-ship passengers, with one that has become one of the area's most popular.

Sights

Old Belize

AMUSEMENT PARK/WATER PARK | FAMILY | Many of the visitors here are on cruise-ship excursions, but you can also visit the museum at Old Belize on your own (it's a BZ$20 taxi ride each way from downtown Belize City). In a large warehouse-style building, exhibits are devoted to the rain forest and the Maya, Garifuna, and Creoles in Belize City, with displays on logging, chicle harvesting, and sugar production. Also at the site of the museum are a large marina; a restaurant where you can get a decent hamburger and other American-style dishes; a gift shop; and Cucumber Beach, a small man-made beach with a 600-foot zipline and a waterslide. ✉ *Mile 5, George Price Hwy. (formerly Western Hwy.), Western Suburbs* ☎ *222/4129* 🌐 *www.oldbelize.com* 🎫 *BZ$10 for museum; BZ$20 for beach and waterslide; BZ$40 for beach, waterslide, and zipline.*

Northern Suburbs

If you're arriving by air at the international airport, you'll pass through the Northern Suburbs on your way to the city, or (unless you take the Burrell Boom bypass) on your way to points south and west.

Sights

Travellers Liquors Heritage Center

MUSEUM | This museum, often just called the rum museum, celebrates Belize's love affair with rum and its oldest distillery, Travellers. Although it's small, the museum is fascinating, with displays of old rum bottles and distillery equipment and the history of rum-making in Belize. You can also look through a window and see rum and other potables being made and bottled at the little factory behind the museum. Best of all, you can get samples of the various rums made by Travellers, including its best-selling One Barrel, along with samples of more exotic drinks such as cashew wino, Rumpope (rum with eggnog), Anise & Peppermint (called A&P, it may remind you of cough syrup and is usually mixed with milk), and Craboo Liquor. Initial samplings are free, with a small charge for further tastings. ✉ *Mile 2.5, Philip Goldson Hwy. (formerly Northern Hwy.), Northern Suburbs* ☎ *223/2855* 🌐 *www.onebarrelrum.com* 🎫 *BZ$2* 🕒 *Closed weekends.*

Restaurants

Sahara Grill

$$ | MEDITERRANEAN | This nondescript Mediterranean/Lebanese restaurant in the Northern Suburbs has good kebabs, *kofta*, falafel, and hummus, with many vegetarian options. Service isn't always perfect, but the food is consistently good. **Known for:** solid Middle Eastern menu; several vegetarian offerings; good variety of kebabs. [$] *Average main: BZ$20* ✉ *Vista Plaza, Mile 3, Philip Goldson Hwy., across from Belize Biltmore Plaza, Northern Suburbs* ☎ *203/3031* 🕒 *Closed Sun.*

Hotels

Bamboleo Inn

$ | B&B/INN | This small inn in a residential area of Ladyville is an appealing option for an overnight stay just five minutes from the international airport. **Pros:** attractive suites with kitchenettes; convenient to international airport; safer residential area on canal. **Cons:** not near good restaurants or other attractions; best to have a car to stay here; can be difficult to find. [$] *Rooms from: BZ$198* ✉ *724 Kingfish Rd., Vista Del Mar, Ladyville* ☎ *600/4954* 🌐 *www.bamboleo-inn.com* 🛏 *7 rooms* 🍴 *No meals.*

Roots Belizean

[👁]

If you spend time talking with Belizeans, sooner or later conversation will turn to "roots." It's not a vegetable, but a term referring to people born in Belize who share a certain set of values. Usually, but not always, it connotes ordinary folk, not wealthy Belizeans. These are Belizeans who ride the bus instead of driving a new Ford Explorer.

"Being roots Belizean is a way of life, a mind-set, and a unique set of values," says Wendy Auxillou, a Belizean who spent much of her life on Caye Caulker. Roots Belizeans enjoy the simple pleasures of life: talking with friends they run into on the streets of Belize City; skipping work or school to swim in the sea, river, or lagoon; sitting on a veranda on a hot afternoon; fishing in an old wooden skiff; raising chickens in the backyard for Sunday dinner.

Roots is also about community involvement. Children are often looked after by aunts and grannies, as well as neighbors. Misbehaving children might find themselves answering to a slew of adults in addition to their parents.

It's going to the market and eating boiled corn, *dukunu* (boiled cornbread), *garnaches* (crispy tortillas topped with beans and rice), and Belizean-style hot dogs, which are wrapped in bacon and grilled with onions. It's buying bananas 10 for a Belizean dollar. It's enjoying the smell and taste of all the local fruits, like *tambran, grocea*, a dozen different kinds of mangoes, sapodilla, mamie, jicama, watermelon, pineapple, guava, and papaya. It's about going to restaurants with local flavor, like Caladium in Belmopan, Nerie's or Dit's in Belize City, and Clarissa Falls in Cayo.

"It's about eating johnnycakes or plucking chickens with your neighbor, just because," says one Belizean.

Some claim that the original, and perhaps only, roots Belizeans are Creoles, descendents of the rough-and-ready Baymen and freed African slaves. Others argue that anybody can be a roots Belizean—that there are roots mestizos, roots Maya, and even roots Mennonites.

—Lan Sluder

Best Western Belize Biltmore Plaza
$$$ | **HOTEL** | This suburban hotel, which mostly gets guests who don't want to stay in the downtown area, has pleasant pool, grounds, and rooms, though it's still a little shy of luxurious. **Pros:** comfortable, secure suburban setting; bar has good happy hour deals; deluxe rooms worth extra cost. **Cons:** not much atmosphere; so-so restaurant; best to have a car to stay here. [$] *Rooms from: BZ$320* ✉ *Mile 3, Goldson Hwy., Northern Suburbs* ☎ *223/2302* 🌐 *www.bestwestern.com* 🛏 *75 rooms* 🍴 *No meals.*

★ D'Nest Inn
$ | **HOTEL** | In a safe, middle-class suburb between the international airport and downtown, D'Nest Inn is run by a couple who impart their charm on their hotel. **Pros:** delightful B&B; delicious breakfasts included; charming and helpful hosts. **Cons:** only a few restaurant choices nearby; rooms could use an update; best to have a car to stay here. [$] *Rooms from: BZ$174* ✉ *475 Cedar St., Northern Suburbs* ✥ *From Goldson Hwy., turn west on Chetumal St. (newly resurfaced and now a divided boulevard), go about 300 yards,*

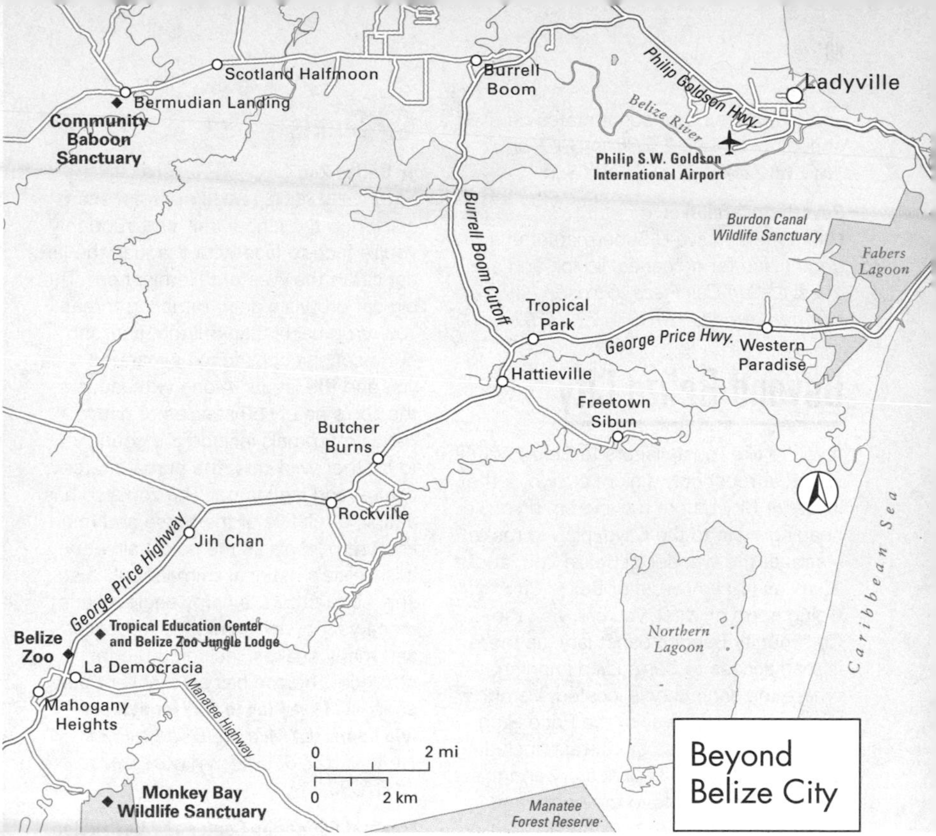

turn right at police station, go 1 short block and turn left, then turn right on Cedar St. ☎ *223/5416* 🌐 *www.dnestinn.com* 🛏 *4 rooms* 🍴 *Free breakfast.*

Global Village Hotel

$ | **HOTEL** | This Chinese-owned motel has no atmosphere and no frills, but it's clean, with modern furniture and fixtures, and a good value. **Pros:** clean, bare-bones motel; free airport pickup and drop-off; secure parking. **Cons:** no atmosphere; mainly for an overnight en route to other locations; few frills. [$] *Rooms from: BZ$110* ✉ *Mile 8.5, Goldson Hwy., just south of turnoff to international airport, Ladyville* ☎ *225/2555* 🌐 *www.globalvillagehotel.com* 🛏 *40 rooms* 🍴 *Free breakfast.*

★ **Villa Boscardi**

$ | **B&B/INN** | If you'd rather not contend with downtown Belize City, this appealing B&B in the Northern Suburbs might be your cup of herbal tea. **Pros:** Belgian-born owner is very helpful; cheerful B&B in safe area; attractive rooms. **Cons:** only a few restaurants nearby. [$] *Rooms from: BZ$178* ✉ *6043 Manatee Dr., Northern Suburbs* ✣ *Turn toward sea off Goldson Hwy. at Golding Ave., then left on second lane to fifth house on right* ☎ *223/1691* 🌐 *www.villaboscardi.com* 🛏 *7 rooms* 🍴 *Free breakfast.*

Shopping

Mirab's

DEPARTMENT STORES | Sparkling, huge department store Mirab's is Belize's largest such institution and worth a look if you're homesick for some stateside-style shopping. ⊠ *Mile 2.5 Philip Goldson Hwy.* ☎ *223/2933* ⊙ *Closed Sun.*

Save-U Supermarket
FOOD/CANDY | Save-U Supermarket is a good place for groceries, liquor, and sundries. ⊠ *San Cas Plaza, Goldson Hwy. at Central American Blvd.* ☎ *223/1291.*

Beyond Belize City

If you're like most visitors to Belize, you'll spend at most only a night or two, if that, in Belize City before moving on. If you're heading west to the Cayo, plan to make a stop at the wonderful Belize Zoo, about 30 miles (49 km) west of Belize City. Going north or west, you can visit the Community Baboon Sanctuary, as there is road access to Bermudian Landing, where the sanctuary is located, via either the Goldson Highway or the Price Highway. For other areas of interest, including Crooked Tree Wildlife Sanctuary and the Altun Ha Mayan site to the north, and Belmopan to the west, within an hour or so of Belize City, *see the Northern Belize and Cayo chapters.*

Belize Zoo

One of the smallest, but arguably one of the best, zoos in the Americas, the Belize Zoo packs a lot into 29 acres. Home to some 200 animals, all native to Belize, the zoo has self-guided tours through several Belizean ecosystems—rain forest, lagoons, and riverine forest. Besides touring the zoo, you can stay overnight at the Belize Zoo Jungle Lodge or Belize Savanna Guest House nearby and hike or canoe the 84-acre Tropical Education Center. Tasty simple meals are offered at a nearby roadside restaurant, Cheers, about 1 mile (2 km) from the zoo.

Sights

★ **Belize Zoo**
NATURE PRESERVE | **FAMILY** | Turn a sharp corner on the jungle trail, and suddenly you're face-to-face with a jaguar, the largest cat in the Western Hemisphere. The big cat growls a deep rumbling threat. You jump back, thankful that a strong but inconspicuous fence separates you and the jaguar. Along with jaguars, the zoo's nearly 50 species of native Belize mammals include the country's four other wild cats: the puma, margay, ocelot, and jaguarundi. The zoo also has a tapir, a relative of the horse and rhino known to locals as the mountain cow; it is Belize's national animal. You'll also see jabiru storks, a harpy eagle, scarlet macaws, howler monkeys, crocodiles, and many snakes, including the fer-de-lance. The zoo has an excellent gift shop. ■ **TIP→ Plan to stay for at least two hours.** ⊠ *Mile 29, George Price Hwy.* ☎ *822/8000* ⊕ *www.belizezoo.org* 💷 *BZ$30.*

Tropical Education Center and Belize Zoo Jungle Lodge
NATURE PRESERVE | **FAMILY** | Across the highway from the Belize Zoo is the 84-acre Tropical Education Center, where you can hike or canoe. There are boardwalk trails through the savanna with wildlife viewing platforms and a deck for bird-watching. Rustic accommodations are available at the Tropical Education Center at the Belize Zoo Jungle Lodge, which include a 30-person dorm and four spartan cabanas. Nighttime tours of the Belize Zoo are offered. ⊠ *Mile 29, George Price Hwy.* ☎ *822/8000* ⊕ *www.belizezoo.org.*

🍴 Restaurants

Cheers Restaurant and Cabañas
$ | **CAFÉ** | Long a fixture on what is now the George Price Highway near the Belize Zoo, Cheers has a surprisingly good open-air restaurant that attracts

local farmers and lots of zoo visitors. You won't go wrong with any of the local dishes, such as stew chicken with rice and beans, but it has good breakfasts and, for lunch, burgers, sandwiches, and daily specials. **Known for:** hearty breakfasts; stew chicken; tasty burgers. $ *Average main: BZ$14* ✉ *Mile 31.25, George Price Hwy.* ✣ *About 2 miles (4 km) west of Belize Zoo* ☎ *822/8014* 🌐 *www.cheers-restaurantbelize.com.*

Monkey Bay Wildlife Sanctuary

Located about 31 miles (51 km) southwest of Belize City, Monkey Bay is a privately owned wildlife reserve on 1,060 acres near the Belize Zoo.

Sights

Monkey Bay Wildlife Sanctuary

NATURE PRESERVE | **FAMILY** | At Monkey Bay you can canoe on the Sibun River, hike a 16-mile (31-km) nature trail along Indian Creek (only partly within Monkey Bay lands), or go bird-watching—some 250 bird species have been identified in the area. It has a natural history library with some 500 books and other reference materials, which visitors can use. The sanctuary also has educational and internship programs. Overnight accommodations for visitors are available if not occupied by students or interns, including tent camping (BZ$24 per person) and a bunkhouse (BZ$60 per person) with 38 beds and shared baths. The nine private cabins and rooms are around BZ$84 to BZ$190. Meals are also available at times, if an educational group is in residence. Otherwise you'll have to make your own meals. Monkey Bay accepts short-term volunteers (minimum stay one week). Internships also are available, usually with a minimum stay of one month. Most of the reserve's facilities demonstrate high ecological awareness. Most programs are geared for overnight or multinight visits, but you can come on a day visit. Call in advance to see what activities or facilities may be available when you want to come. ✉ *Mile 31, George Price Hwy., Belmopan* ✣ *A little over 3 miles (5 km) southeast of Belize Zoo, on opposite side of highway* ☎ *822/8032, 770/877–2648 in U.S.* 🌐 *www.monkeybaybelize.com.*

Community Baboon Sanctuary

One of Belize's most fascinating wildlife conservation projects is the Community Baboon Sanctuary, which is actually a haven for black howler monkeys (*baboon* is Kriol for the howler). No African baboons as we know them are found in Belize.

GETTING HERE

There are two routes to the sanctuary. If heading north on the Goldson Highway, turn west at Mile 13.2 onto the Burrell Boom Road. Go 3 miles (5 km) and turn right just beyond the new bridge over the Belize River. Signs to Bermudian Landing mark the turn. Stay on this road approximately 12 miles (20 km) to Bermudian Landing. If going west on the George Price Highway, turn north on the Burrell Boom Road at a roundabout at Mile 15.5 of the highway, and go 9 miles (15 km) to the new bridge over the Belize River. Just before the bridge, turn left. Signs to Bermudian Landing mark the turn. Stay on this road approximately 12 miles (20 km) to Bermudian Landing. You can also use the Burrell Boom Road as a shortcut between the Philip Goldson and George Price Highways, avoiding Belize City. For this shortcut, stay on the Burrell Boom Road rather than turning toward Bermudian Landing. When on the Burrell Boom Road, you may want to stop at the **Central Prison Gift Shop** at the Central Prison, on the road to Burrell Boom about 3 miles

(5 km) from the Price Highway. Prisoners at the "Hattieville Ramada" make small craft items and sell them at the gift shop.

Sights

Community Baboon Sanctuary

NATURE PRESERVE | **FAMILY** | Spanning a 20-mile (32-km) stretch of the Belize River, the reserve was established in 1985 by a group of local farmers. The black howler monkey (*Alouatta pigra*)—an agile bundle of black fur with a disturbing roar—was then zealously hunted throughout Central America and was facing extinction. (Belizeans refer to the black howler as a "baboon," but baboons are not found in the wild in the Americas.) Today the sanctuary is home, on some 200 private properties, to some 2,000 black howler monkeys, as well as numerous species of birds and mammals. Thanks to ongoing conservation efforts countrywide, you can see the howler monkeys in many other areas of Belize, including at Lamanai in northern Belize; along the Macal, Mopan, and Belize Rivers in western Belize; and near Monkey River and around Punta Gorda in southern Belize. You will also see howlers, along with spider monkeys, at Tikal. Exploring the Community Baboon Sanctuary is easy, thanks to about 3 miles (5 km) of trails that start near a small museum and visitor center. The admission fee includes a 45-minute guided nature tour during which you definitely will see howlers. Some guides may ask you to pay extra to hold or pet the howlers—this isn't appropriate, and don't encourage it. Other themed tours—birding, canoeing, crocodiles—are priced à la carte, although the admission per couple is little more than the per-person rate. ✉ *31 miles (50 km) northwest of Belize City, Bermudian Landing* ✣ *If heading north on Goldson Hwy., turn west at Mile 13.2 onto Burrell Boom Rd. Go 3 miles (5 km) and turn right just beyond new bridge over Belize River. Signs to Bermudian Landing mark the turn. Stay on this road approximately 12 miles (20 km) to Bermudian Landing. If going west on Price Hwy., turn north on Burrell Boom Rd. at roundabout at Mile 15.5 of Price Hwy., and go 9 miles (15 km) to new bridge over Belize River. Just before bridge, turn left. Signs to Bermudian Landing mark the turn. Stay on this road approximately 12 miles (20 km) to Bermudian Landing* ☎ *245/2007* 🎟 *BZ$14; tours from BZ$24.*

Hotels

Black Orchid Resort

$$$ | **RESORT** | This Belizean-owned resort in a pleasant and safe rural setting northwest of Belize City perches at the edge of the Belize River, where you can launch a canoe or kayak from the hotel's dock, or just laze about the riverside swimming pool and thatch-roof palapa bar. **Pros:** most upscale lodging near Baboon Sanctuary; lovely riverside setting; 15 minutes from international airport. **Cons:** not directly in Baboon Sanctuary; some rooms have minimum two-night stay; best to have a car to stay here. [$] *Rooms from: BZ$305* ✉ *2 Dawson La., 12 miles (20 km) from Baboon Sanctuary, Burrell Boom Village* ☎ *225/9158, 866/437–1301 in U.S.* 🌐 *www.blackorchidresort.com* 🛏 *18 rooms* 🍴 *No meals.*

Howler Monkey Resort

$$ | **B&B/INN** | This comfortable family-run cottage colony is the closest lodging to the Community Baboon Sanctuary. **Pros:** close to Community Baboon Sanctuary; free pickup from international airport; family that runs this option is friendly and helpful. **Cons:** older accommodations; far from other sights; best to have a car to stay here. [$] *Rooms from: BZ$215* ✉ *Bermudian Landing* ✣ *Beside Belize River* ☎ *607/1571* 🌐 *www.howlermonkeyresort.bz* 🛏 *7 cabins* 🍴 *Some meals* 💳 *No credit cards.*

Chapter 4

THE CAYES
AND ATOLLS

4

Updated by
Rose Lambert-Sluder

○ Sights   🍽 Restaurants   🛏 Hotels   🛍 Shopping   🍸 Nightlife

★★★★★   ★★★★★   ★★★★★   ★★★☆☆   ★★★★☆

WELCOME TO THE CAYES AND ATOLLS

TOP REASONS TO GO

★ **Scuba Diving:** Dive destinations are often divided into reefs and atolls. Most reef diving is done on Belize's northern section, particularly off Ambergris Caye, but head to the atolls for some of the planet's greatest diving opportunities, such as the Blue Hole.

★ **No Shoes, No Shirt, No Problem:** Unlike some parts of the mainland, the cayes are all about relaxing. "Go Slow" street signs dot the sandy roads (especially on Caye Caulker), and you pass hours lazing in hammocks or sipping beer in a beachside palapa alongside vacationing Belizeans.

★ **Good Eats:** Because they attract so many free-spending tourists, Ambergris Caye and Caye Caulker have more restaurants than anywhere in Belize, and some of the best and most inventive, making the cayes an epicurean excursion.

Belize's two most important cayes, Ambergris and Caulker, are both off the northern end of the country and easily reached from Belize City. Other, smaller cayes dot the Caribbean Sea off the coast all the way south to Punta Gorda. The Belize Barrier Reef runs along most of the coast.

1 St. George's Caye. Not far from Belize City, this caye has great diving and charming colonial homes.

2 Little Frenchman Caye. Tiny caye off Belize City with the family-friendly Royal Palm Island Resort.

3 Ambergris Caye and San Pedro. The Belize Barrier Reef is right off this caye; its biggest and liveliest town is San Pedro.

4 Caye Caulker. Laid-back diver's haven that's less developed and less expensive than sister Ambergris Caye.

5 Tobacco Caye. Popular for diving and fishing, this southern caye is one of Belize's most beautiful.

6 Coco Plum Caye. Just off Dangriga is this caye, home to a private, upscale resort of the same name.

7 Thatch Caye. For a private island feel not far from Dangriga, head to Thatch's all-inclusive resort with cabanas over the water.

8 South Water Caye. Off-the-beaten path diving and snorkeling can be found at this underrated caye.

9 Laughing Bird Caye. Arrange a tour from Placencia to the gorgeous national park here.

10 Bird Island. Off Placencia, this island is an idyllic spot to get away from it all.

11 Ray Caye. A private, luxurious spot off Placencia.

12 Gladden Spit and Silk Cayes. To dive with whale sharks or lounge on the beach, head east of Placencia.

13 Sapodilla Cayes. Small group of cayes off Punta Gorda that is excellent for diving.

14 Turneffe Atoll. Largest of Belize's three atolls, close to Belize City.

15 Lighthouse Reef Atoll, the Blue Hole, and Half Moon Caye. The most famous Belizean dive site.

16 Glover's Reef Atoll. Southernmost atoll with coral reef diving.

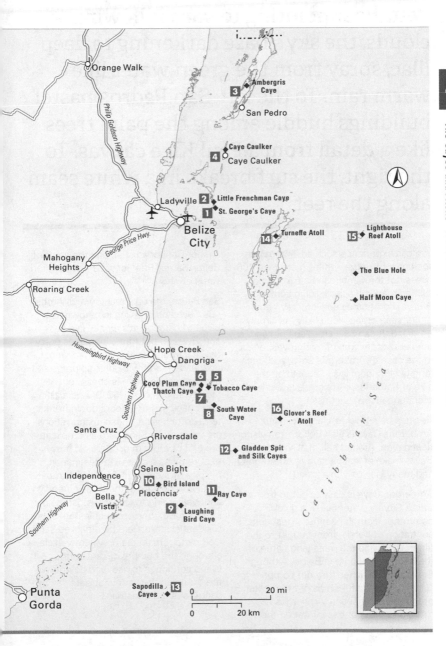

Orange Walk

Philip Goldson Highway

3 Ambergris Caye

San Pedro

4 Caye Caulker
Caye Caulker

Ladyville **2** Little Frenchman Caye
1 St. George's Caye

Belize
City

George Price Hwy.

14 Turneffe Atoll   **15** Lighthouse
Reef Atoll

Mahogany
Heights

The Blue Hole

Roaring Creek

Half Moon Caye

Hummingbird Highway

Hope Creek
Dangriga

6 **5**
Coco Plum Caye **7** Tobacco Caye
Thatch Caye

Southern Highway

8 South Water
Caye

16 Glover's Reef
Atoll

Santa Cruz   Riversdale

12 Gladden Spit
and Silk Cayes

Independence   Seine Bight

10 Bird Island
Placencia

11 Ray Caye

Bella
Vista

9 Laughing
Bird Caye

Southern Highway

Caribbean Sea

Punta
Gorda

Sapodilla **13**
Cayes

0   20 mi

0   20 km

Imagine heading back to shore after a day of snorkeling, the white prow of your boat pointing toward billowing clouds, the sky's base darkening to deep lilac, spray from the green water like warm rain. To the left, San Pedro's pastel buildings huddle among the palm trees like a detail from a Paul Klee canvas. To the right, the surf breaks in a white seam along the reef.

You can experience such adventures off the coast of Belize, where more than 400 cayes dot the Caribbean Sea like punctuation marks in a long, liquid sentence. A caye, sometimes spelled "cay" but in either case pronounced "key," is simply an island. It can be a small spit of sand, a tangled watery web of mangroves, or, as in the case of Ambergris Caye, a 25-mile-long (41-km-long) island about half the size of Barbados. (Ambergris is locally pronounced am- *bur*-griss.)

Besides being Belize's largest island, Ambergris Caye is also Belize's top visitor destination. Around half of all visitors to Belize make at least a stop at Ambergris, and many visit only this island.

Ambergris Caye is easy to get to from Belize City by water taxi or a quick commuter flight. It has the largest concentration of hotels, from budget to the ultradeluxe, and the most (and some of the best) restaurants in Belize. Although the island's beaches may not compare to classically beautiful sands of the Yucatán or the main Caribbean, Ambergris has miles and miles of beachfront on the east or Caribbean side, and the amazing Belize Barrier Reef is just a few hundred yards offshore.

San Pedro, the only real town on Ambergris Caye and growing in renown, is a place of paradox. It's mostly laid-back and low-rise, but traffic increases every day. It's traditionally a fishing town but now has resorts with ionic columns and combed sands. Rum is cheap, but a taco salad can cost US$19. And a zinc-roof shack sits two doors down from a terra-cotta palace. These juxtapositions are what make San Pedro a complicated product of modern economics; however, it remains a charming destination. In spite of the growth in tourism, most San Pedranos are authentically friendly and welcoming to visitors. Most main streets have concrete cobblestones, but residential streets are hard-packed sand. Golf carts remain the prevalent vehicle, although the number of cars on the island continues to rise, and downtown the traffic on the narrow streets can be dangerous to pedestrians.

Since the expanded paving of its single road, or "golf cart path," North Ambergris (above the Boca del Rio bridge) is more accessible and less remote than ever. A celebrated boost in infrastructure, the road means developers can almost be heard shouting "Land ho!" as they envision the area's potential. Currently, this 12-mile stretch has some of the most glamorous resorts in the country.

Caye Caulker is Ambergris Caye's sister island—smaller, less developed, and much cheaper. Caulker, whose name derives from the Spanish word for coco plum, *hicaco,* has the kind of sandy-street, no-rush, low-key Caribbean charm that some travelers pay thousands to experience. Here it can be had almost for peanuts. In recent years more travelers tread its unpaved streets, but Caulker tourism remains far less ambitious than on Ambergris Caye. Less than 10 miles (16 km)—about 30 minutes by boat—from San Pedro, Caye Caulker, sometimes called Caye Corker, is definitely worth a day visit, or, in our opinion, worth a week.

Most of Belize's cayes are inside the Barrier Reef, which allowed them to develop undisturbed by tides and winds that would otherwise have swept them away. The vast majority of them are uninhabited but for pelicans, brown- and red-footed boobies, and some creatures curiously named wish-willies (a kind of iguana). Island names are evocative and often humorous: Wee Caye, Laughing Bird Caye, and—why ask why?—Bread and Butter Caye. Names can suggest the company you should expect: Mosquito Caye, Sandfly Caye, and Crawl Caye, which is supposedly infested with boa constrictors. Several, like Cockney Range or Baker's Rendezvous, simply express the whimsy or nostalgia of early British colonists.

Some cayes have a population of one or two dozen but also have exclusive villas and elegant resorts. One of the hemisphere's most glamorous resorts is Cayo Espanto, while more down-to-earth options like St. George's Caye Resort have rustic lodgings overlooking parcels of paradise. Gossiped about for years, celebrity Leonardo DiCaprio's co-owned island Blackadore Caye is set to open an eco-resort in 2020 (a date that has been revised more than once).

Farther out to sea, between 30 miles and 45 miles (48 km and 74 km) off the coast, are Belize's atolls, Glover's (or Glovers), Lighthouse, and Turneffe, impossibly beautiful when viewed from the air. There are only four true Pacific-style atolls in the Americas, and Belize has three of them (the fourth is Chinchorro, off Mexico). At their center the water is mint green: the white sandy bottom reflects the light upward and is flecked with patches of mangrove and rust-color sediment. Around the atoll's fringe the surf breaks in a white circle before the color changes abruptly to ultramarine as the water plunges to 3,000 feet.

MAJOR REGIONS

The Cayes. Ranging from tiny stretches of sand, mangrove, and palms to large islands like Ambergris and Caulker, Belize's cayes have excellent diving, fishing, and snorkeling. The blight of Sargassum seagrass has worsened swimming conditions off beaches, though swimming off piers is still usually pleasant.

The Atolls. Ovals of coral, majestic and remote, Belize's three atolls—Turneffe, Lighthouse Reef (home to the famous Blue Hole), and Glover's—offer some of the best diving and snorkeling in the Western Hemisphere. The catch? They're difficult and time-consuming to get to, typically requiring a two-hour boat ride on open seas.

4

The Cayes and Atolls

Planning

When to Go

Island weather tends to differ somewhat from that on the mainland. The cayes are generally drier. Storm squalls come up suddenly, but just as quickly they're gone, leaving sunny skies behind. Late summer and early fall is prime tropical-storm season, a time when island residents keep a worried eye out for hurricanes; more than 8 out of 10 hurricanes that hit Belize arrive in either September or October. If a hurricane does threaten, the cayes are evacuated. The Christmas-to-Easter period, when the northern climes are cold and blustery, is the most popular (and most expensive) time to visit the islands. ■TIP→ Many hotels and restaurants on the cayes shut down for part of September and October. This can vary year to year, so verify before your trip.

Getting Here and Around

Island-hopping in the northern cayes is simple, though getting to other cayes and the atolls can be more complicated. Water taxis connect Belize City, Ambergris Caye, and Caye Caulker. There is also frequent air service between Belize City and San Pedro and Caye Caulker. For the other cayes, you're generally stuck with whatever boat transport your hotel provides. Once on the islands, you'll get around by golf cart or bike or on foot.

AIR TRAVEL

Maya Island Airways and Tropic Air operate flights between both the international and municipal airports in Belize City and Ambergris Caye and Caye Caulker. Each airline has roughly hourly service during daylight hours. Aircrafts are puddle-jumpers and people find them either dreadful or delightful, but regardless, aerial views are spectacular. One-way fares on either Tropic and Maya Island to either San

Pedro or Caye Caulker for the 15- to 20-minute flight are roughly BZ$100 (municipal) and BZ$175 (international). You save more than 40% by flying from the municipal airport in Belize City rather than the international airport north of the city. The catch is that if arriving or departing internationally, you have to transfer by cab between the two airports—about a 25-minute ride—and a cab is BZ$50 (for the taxi, not per person), so the extra hassle may not be worth the savings. ■TIP→ Both airlines usually offer a 10% discount, sometimes more, if you pay cash rather than use a credit card. But you'll have to ask for the discount, which only applies in person, not online, and usually not on Saturday.

CONTACTS Maya Island Airways. ✉ Belize City Municipal Airport, Belize City ☎ 223/1140 reservations ⊕ www.mayaislandair.com. Tropic Air. ✉ San Pedro Airstrip, San Pedro Town ☎ 226/2626, 800/422–3435 in U.S. ⊕ www.tropicair.com.

BOAT, FERRY, AND WATER-TAXI TRAVEL

There are no scheduled water-taxi services up and down the coast of Belize, so for example you can't hop a boat in Belize City and go down the coast to Hopkins or Placencia or to one of the southern cayes. Between Belize City and busy Ambergris Caye and Caye Caulker, there's regular boat service; but there is no scheduled boat service to the smaller cayes. There is limited water-taxi service to these northern cayes from Corozal and from Chetumal, Mexico.

Several private boats do make the run from Dangriga to Tobacco Caye for around BZ$35–BZ$50 per person one way. They leave Dangriga around 9:30 am and return from Tobacco Caye in late morning or the afternoon. Inquire with your hotel on Tobacco or at **Riverside Café** in Dangriga about its water-taxi service to Tobacco Caye.

Other than that, you're generally left to your own devices for private boat transportation. You can charter a small boat with driver—typically BZ$600 and up a day—or negotiate a one-way or round-trip price, up to BZ$800–BZ$1,500 or more one way to the atolls. You'll have little luck renting a powerboat on your own, as boat owners are reluctant to risk their crafts, and new laws require that you need a captain's license before you can operate a boat in Belize waters (sailing charters are excepted).

BELIZE CITY TO SAN PEDRO AND CAYE CAULKER

Your cheapest option for travel to the main cayes is by water taxi, really a buslike watercraft. There are two main water-taxi companies—San Pedro Belize Express and Ocean Ferry—with fast, cramped boats that hold 50 to 100 passengers (they've been likened to nautical saunas) connecting Belize City with San Pedro (Ambergris Caye) and Caye Caulker. They also connect San Pedro and Caulker. From Belize City it's a 45-minute ride to Caulker and 75 minutes to San Pedro. There's also a premium water-taxi service, Tropic Ferry, that meets you at the international airport and takes you from its dock near the airport to your resort on Ambergris.

Ocean Ferry Belize

This newer company competes with San Pedro Belize Express, but offers fewer trips (five daily) between Belize City, Caye Caulker, and San Pedro. Ocean Ferry is the cheaper option. Amazingly, it also has free Wi-Fi on board. In Belize City, it departs from the Marine Terminal, then arrives at Caye Caulker's Front Street near Seaside Cabanas, then in San Pedro just north of Fido's. Once you arrive at your destination, it is easy to find your way. ⌧ 10 N. Front St., Belize City ☎ 223/0033 ⊕ www. oceanferrybelize.com.

Riverside Café

This local café on the river in Dangriga is a place to meet local boat owners and arrange transportation to Tobacco Caye. ⌧ Riverside and Oak Sts., west side of North Stann Creek River, Dangriga ☎ 661/6390.

★ San Pedro Belize Express Water Taxi

This company is quite dependable. San Pedro Belize Express water taxis depart from the Brown Sugar terminal on North Front Street. On Caye Caulker, the boats arrive at the pier near the basketball court on Front Street, and in San Pedro they arrive at the pier at Black Coral Street on the east (sea) side of the island. They also provide daily service between the Muelle Fiscal or municipal pier in Chetumal, Mexico, and San Pedro and Caye Caulker. ⌧ 111 N. Front St., Brown Sugar Terminal, Belize City ☎ 223/2225 in Belize City, 226/3535 in San Pedro ⊕ www.belizewatertaxi.com.

Tropic Ferry

The Tropic Ferry provides a premium ferry service between the international airport near Belize City and most resorts on Ambergris Caye. A ferry representative meets you at the airport for a short ride to the dock in Ladyville. It's around a 75-minute trip to your destination on Ambergris Caye. You'll get a complimentary rum punch en route. Rates for this service are somewhat higher than a flight to San Pedro. (This water-taxi service is unrelated to Tropic Air, one of the domestic Belize airlines.) ⌧ 1659 Yellowtail Snapper Dr., Vista del Mar, Ladyville ☎ 631/9253.

COROZAL

Thunderbolt Water Taxi

This small company has round-trip service between Corozal Town and San Pedro Friday to Monday, departing Corozal at 7 am and departing San Pedro at 3 pm. (Off-season service may be reduced or eliminated.) The trip takes 90 minutes to two hours, depending on weather, with stops in Sarteneja on demand. In Corozal, the Thunderbolt arrives and leaves at the Reunion Pier in the center of town; in San Pedro it arrives and leaves at Black Coral Street on the back side of the island near the soccer field. ⊠ *Reunion Pier, Corozal Town* ☎ *610/4475 boat captain's cell, 422/0026 landline in Corozal Town* ☾ *No service Tues.–Thurs.; service may be reduced off-season.*

UP AND DOWN AMBERGRIS CAYE
Coastal Xpress

This is a handy service and efficient, but it demands some preplanning. Coastal Xpress provides scheduled ferry service up and down the island—you stand on a dock and the cozy vessel picks you up at an appointed time. It offers about a dozen daily trips between the Amigos del Mar pier in town and La Beliza Resort in the north, with stops on demand at most hotel and restaurant docks. If you're staying in North Ambergris and want to head to town, have your hotel arrange the ferry and you'll pay when you arrive. At this writing, service starts at 5:30 am and ends around 11 pm. Coastal Xpress also offers charter boat service to other cayes and coastal locations. Ferry schedule and service is subject to change—check locally for updates. Arrive at your dock of departure 15 minutes early. Prices depend on how far you go, starting at BZ$10. ⊠ *Amigos del Mar Pier, Beachfront, San Pedro Town* ☎ *226/2007.*

GOLF CART TRAVEL

There are no car rentals on Ambergris and Caulker; instead, you can rent a golf cart, typically gas powered and so mild they don't have a speedometer. The good news is they're novel, easy, safe, and fun (kids will love them). The bad news is golf cart rentals cost about as much as a car rental in the United States: around BZ$120 a day, or BZ$500–BZ$550 a week, plus 12.5% tax. These rental companies spring up like weeds, and many hotels have a few carts to rent. Compare prices and ask for discounts.

CONTACTS Cholo's Golf Cart Rentals. ⊠ *Jewfish St., behind police and fire stations, San Pedro Town* ☎ *226/2406* ⊕ *www.choloscartrentals.com.* **Island**

Adventures Golf Cart Rentals. ⊠ *Coconut Dr., near airstrip, San Pedro Town* ☎ *226/4343* ⊕ *www.islandgolfcarts. com.* **Moncho's Cart Rentals.** ⊠ *11 Coconut Dr., near airstrip, San Pedro Town* ☎ *226/4490.*

TAXI TRAVEL

Regular taxicabs are available in San Pedro and in the developed area south of town on Ambergris Caye. Most trips in and close to town are BZ$10 for up to four persons (check the price before getting in). For trips north of the bridge over Boca del Rio, it's expensive: cabs charge BZ$25–BZ$50, including the BZ$12 vehicle bridge fee. Have your hotel arrange for a cab, or hail one of the cabs cruising the downtown area. On Caulker there are golf-cart taxis, which charge BZ$5–BZ$10 per person for most trips.

Health and Safety

In San Pedro Town and nearby, the water comes from a municipal water system and is safe to drink, although most people including local residents prefer to drink filtered water. On North Ambergris, water may come from cisterns or wells. On Caye Caulker, there is a village reverse osmosis system, but some buildings may not be on it. If in doubt, drink filtered water. On other remote cayes, the water usually comes from cisterns; stick to the bottled stuff, unless you're assured that the water is potable. To be green, you can buy water in large one- or five-gallon bottles and refill your reusable bottle; you'll save a little money, too. Many hotels also have in-room water coolers.

In terms of crime risk, the cayes are among the safest areas of Belize. However, petty thefts—and sometimes worse—do happen. With at least 20,000 people on Ambergris Caye, if you count tourists and itinerant workers, the island has the same crime problems as any area of similar population. There are drugs, including crack cocaine and opioids, on both Caye Caulker and Ambergris Caye. Although Belize decriminalized the possession and personal use of up to 10 grams of marijuana in 2017, technically it is still illegal to grow, sell, buy, or transport.

Emergencies

The three Ambergris Caye clinics listed below have services just short of a full-scale hospital. The island also has three or four other clinics and private medical practices, four pharmacies, a chiropractic clinic, several dentists, and a hyperbaric chamber (affiliated with many Belize dive shops). In emergencies, patients may be transferred to Karl Heusner Memorial Hospital, the nation's main public referral hospital, in Belize City, or to one of the private hospitals in Belize City, Belize Medical Associates or Belize Healthcare Partners.

On Caye Caulker the Caye Caulker Health Center is usually staffed by a volunteer doctor from Cuba. For dental care or serious ailments you need to go to Belize City. There are no medical facilities on any of the other cayes, but if you have an emergency, call your embassy or contact Karl Heusner Memorial Hospital, Belize Medical Associates, or Belize Healthcare Partners.

Astrum Helicopters provides emergency airlift services. ☎ 222/5100 Triple-R Response (seen as "RRR") is a Texas-based non-profit offering ground ambulance and water rescue services. ☎ 627/1117 ⊕ www.triplerresponse.org

For police emergencies, call 911. On marine radios, channel 16 is the international distress channel.

CONTACTS Ambergris Hopes Medical Clinic. ✉ 23 Pescador Dr., San Pedro Town ☎ 226/2660. **Belize Hyperbaric Chamber.** ⊹ North of airstrip ☎ 226/2851, 615/4288 ⊕ www.sssnetwork.com. **Belize Medical**

Associates. ✉ 2 miles (3 km) north of the Boca del Rio bridge, Ambergris Caye ⊹ at Grand Caribe ☎ 226/2262 ⊕ www.belizemedical.com. **San Pedro Polyclinic II.** ✉ Manta Ray St., San Pedro Town ☎ 226/2536.

Hotels

The more budget-oriented cayes, such as Tobacco and Caulker, have mostly smaller hotels, often built of wood and and without the polish of resorts, though this is changing on Caulker, which is growing more upscale. At the other end, notably on Ambergris Caye, are lavish resorts and deluxe "condotels" (condo developments where individual owners rent their units on a daily basis through a management company) and an increasing number of vacation villas, usually rented by the week. Air-conditioning and swimming pools have become standard on Ambergris; both are increasingly common on Caulker. Regardless of which caye you're staying on, lodgings have several things in common: they're small (usually fewer than 30 or 40 rooms), low-rise (all but a handful are three stories or fewer), and almost always directly on the water. Most actual hotels are boutique, independently owned, or part of a small hotel group: you won't find the hulking all-inclusive resorts of Jamaica or the Dominican Republic here. Belize's moderate scale, however, is giving way to bigger developments, such as Mahogany Bay Village, Grande Caribe, and Alaia. Nonetheless, it's still Belize.

■ TIP→ **Off-season (typically May to around Thanksgiving), most island hotels, especially luxurious ones, reduce rates by around 20% to 40%. However, many hotels shut down for repairs and vacation between September to October; closures can vary year to year.**

Restaurants

Ambergris Caye has the most impressive selection of restaurants in Belize. Restaurants range from barbecue and picnic tables to white linen and candlelight. At the latter type, you can spend BZ$100 a person or more, including a cocktail or wine. You have a wide choice of kinds of food on Ambergris: seafood, of course, but also steak, pizza, sushi, tapas, Chinese, Italian, Thai, and Mexican. Because ingredients are typically fresh and local, dishes pop with flavor.

Caye Caulker has a number of small bistros where fish arrives at your table fresh from the sea, and often you find yourself eating with your feet in the sand. On other islands you're limited to eating at your dive lodge or resort.

On both Caye Caulker and Ambergris Caye street vendors set up barbecue grills along Front Street and on the beachfront, cooking chicken, fish, shrimp, and lobster. Use your own judgment, but we've found in almost all cases the food from these vendors is safe, tasty, and inexpensive.

HOTEL AND RESTAURANT PRICES

Restaurant and hotel reviews have been shortened. For full information, visit Fodors.com.

What It Costs in Belize Dollars			
$	$$	$$$	$$$$
RESTAURANTS			
under BZ$15	BZ$15–BZ$30	BZ$31–BZ$50	over BZ$50
HOTELS			
under BZ$200	BZ$200–BZ$350	BZ$351–BZ$550	over BZ$550

Tours

MAINLAND TOURS

From Ambergris and Caulker, and from smaller cayes with advance planning, you can do day-trips to the mainland to see Mayan ruins, try cave tubing, visit the wonderful Belize Zoo, and have other adventures. However, the cost will be significantly higher than if you did the tour from a closer point.

Tour operators on the cayes run trips to Mayan sites such as **Lamanai** (usually a full-day trip by boat and road) and **Altun Ha** (normally a half-day trip, although it may be longer if it includes lunch and a spa visit at Maruba Spa). If you're up for a real trek, you can visit **Tikal** on an overnight trip by air to Flores, Guatemala, with a change of planes in Belize City. It's also possible to see the small, unexcavated ruins on Ambergris Caye—including **Marco Gonzalez** on the south end of the island, reachable by golf cart or taxi, and **Chac Balam** at Bacalar, reachable by boat.

(See Ambergris Caye "Tour" section.)

SCUBA DIVING AND SNORKELING

Diving near the cayes is world-class; if you prefer to be closer to the surface, snorkeling is also first-rate. Most dive-trip operators (who are usually also snorkel-boat operators) are on Ambergris Caye. Many operators also offer PADI courses. San Pedro has Belize's only two hyperbaric chambers. Many dive shops are attached to hotels, where the quality of dive masters, equipment, and facilities can vary considerably. It's a short boat ride to the spur-and-groove formations along the Barrier Reef and to Hol Chan Marine Reserve. Several San Pedro operators with speedboats can take you to the Blue Hole, the largest ocean sinkhole in the world.

Visitor Information

The best sources of information on the islands are online. Operated by Marty Casado, AmbergrisCaye.com (🌐 *www.ambergriscaye.com*) is the number-one source, with thousands of pages of information on San Pedro and to a lesser extent on Caye Caulker. For intimate insight, see American expat Rebecca Coutant's blog, the San Pedro Scoop (🌐 *www.sanpedroscoop.com*), which also covers Caulker and elsewhere. The Belize Tourism Board has a well-kept website (🌐 *www.travelbelize.org*) with information on the cayes and atolls. The Taco Girl blog (🌐 *www.tacogirl.com*) has timely info on island happenings, though some of it is a little commercial. The *San Pedro Sun* (🌐 *www.sanpedrosun.com*) newspaper publishes a free weekly tabloid-size visitor newspaper, the *San Pedro Sun Visitor Guide. Ambergris Today* (🌐 *www.ambergristoday.com*) is a weekly online newspaper for San Pedro.

St. George's Caye

9 miles (15 km) northeast of Belize City.

Just a stone's throw from Belize City, St. George's Caye is steeped in history. The country of Belize had its origins here, as St. George's Caye held the original British settlement's first capital. In 1798 the island was the site of a decisive battle with the Spanish. As the story goes, British Baymen had only one sloop, while the Spanish had 31 ships. The Baymen's knowledge of the sea, however, helped them to defeat the invaders in two hours. (This history is murky and typically told from the victors' perspective; some maintain that enslaved blacks fought on one or either side, but this, too, is contested.) Today, some affluent Belize City residents weekend in their private cottages with grassy lawns. Although St. George's Caye has great places to dive, many serious scuba enthusiasts choose to head out to the more pristine atolls or to private cayes farther south.

You can take pleasant walks past colonial homes up and down the island of St. George's Caye. At the north end of the island, a local family runs a compact "aquarium" for sick sea life; for BZ$10 you can visit this unusual hole-in-the-wall. Ask your hotel to call ahead.

GETTING HERE AND AROUND

St. George's Caye Resort will meet you at the international airport and handle your 20-minute boat transfer to the islands.

🛏 Hotels

★ St. George's Caye Resort

$$$$ | **RESORT** | In colonial days St. George's Caye was a British favorite for its proximity to Belize City; today visitors can enjoy the beautiful adult-only resort as a rustic venue for adventure. **Pros:** good diving available, though not included in rates; secluded island resort atmosphere; true Belizean flavor. **Cons:** not easy to visit mainland or other islands; paradise comes unplugged (Wi-Fi only in main lodge); group meals can be hard for introverts. [$] *Rooms from: BZ$568* ✉ *St. George's Caye* ☎ *800/813–8498 in U.S. and Canada, 220/4444* 🌐 *www.belizeislandparadise.com* 🛏 *20 rooms* 🍴 *All-inclusive* ☞ *Rate includes meals and boat transfer.*

Little Frenchman Caye

About 9 miles (15 km) from Belize City.

Another option close to Belize City is Royal Palm Island Resort on Little Frenchman Caye. This caye is indeed little, but it offers modern accommodations.

GETTING HERE AND AROUND

Royal Palm Island Resort will meet you at the international airport and handle your 20-minute boat transfer to the islands.

A Crisis in the Caribbean

The Seagrass Mucking Up Belize's Shores

Sargassum is a word you'll hear a lot in the cayes. It refers to the seagrass, a brown, bunchy macroalgae (originating in the Sargasso Sea) washing ashore or clumping in the water, often in incredible masses. Sargassum is ugly, smelly, and devastating to the beaches of Belize. Small waves of Sargassum first came to Belize around 2011; in 2015 and 2018 terrible blooms of Sargassum smothered the beaches. When not cleaned up, it can pile in mountains several feet high. As the seagrass (and the small marine creatures hiding in it) biodegrades on the beach, it releases a rotten-egg stench that can be overwhelming. Worse, decomposing seagrass releases hydrogen sulfide gas and ammonia, which can cause or exacerbate respiratory and other problems. In any case, you won't relish lounging near it or swimming in it. Sargassum comes and goes—by the month, the week, or the hour—so some days are better than others, but many days are bad.

Sadly, this event is affecting all of the Caribbean and beyond. Most scientists chiming in suspect rising ocean temperatures from global warming have given way to a crisis of Sargassum. In certain quantities, Sargassum is a boon to the ecosystem (marine biologist Sylvia Earle calls the seagrass mats a "golden floating rain forest"), but en masse it can harm sea life.

In Belize, hotel and municipal crews work diligently to shovel up Sargassum daily, but the beaches never stay pristine for long. Importantly, Sargassum floats up on the east side of cayes like Ambergris and Caulker, but not on the west (lee) sides. The cayes are still beautiful, and much of the tourism industry has coped with the crisis admirably, but it's important to manage expectations when it comes to Sargassum.

Hotels

Royal Palm Island Resort
$$$$ | **RESORT** | **FAMILY** | For an all-inclusive, family-friendly option, this playful getaway—the only thing on Little Frenchman Caye—is a special experience. **Pros:** relaxing, intimate getaway near Belize City; welcoming staff; good deals can be found. **Cons:** not directly on reef; tiny island; quiet atmosphere isn't for everyone. [$] *Rooms from: BZ$950* ✉ *Little Frenchman Caye, 9 miles (15 km) east of Belize City* ☎ *223/4999, 888/969–7829 in U.S.* 🌐 *www.royalpalmisland.com* 🛏 *5 cottages* 🍴 *All-inclusive* ☞ *Rate includes meals and boat transfer.*

Ambergris Caye and San Pedro

35 miles (56 km) northeast of Belize City.

At 25 miles (40 km) long and 4.5 miles (7 km) wide at its widest point, Ambergris is the queen of the cayes. Here the Northern Barrier Reef is just a few hundred yards from shore, making access to dive sites extremely easy—the journey by boat takes as little as 10 minutes. On early maps it was often referred to as Costa de Ambar, or the Amber Coast, a name supposedly derived from the blackish substance secreted by sperm whales—ambergris—that washes up on the beaches. Having never seen any ambergris in Belize, or a sperm whale, we're not sure we buy this explanation.

In addition to great diving, there's snorkeling, fishing, and kitesurfing, as well as just splashing in the sea or lazing on the beach until it's time to sample one of the dozens of restaurants on the island. Lodging here is bountiful and, by and large, superb. The island's friendly and prosperous population is around 17,000, has one of the country's highest literacy rates, and maintains an admirable level of awareness about the reef's fragility.

GETTING HERE AND AROUND

It's helpful to think of Ambergris Caye in terms of San Pedro. We divide the caye by San Pedro, south of San Pedro, and north of San Pedro.

In San Pedro Town, hard-packed sand streets are giving way to the concrete cobblestones of Barrier Reef Drive, Pescador Street, Coconut Drive, and other island streets, and everyone complains about the worsening car traffic in town. Nonetheless, the most common forms of transportation remain golf cart, bike, and foot.

North Ambergris is far more accessible by golf cart since the expanded paving of the (only) road. This has thinned the crowds in San Pedro and opened up possibility for more construction. When anticipating the future of Ambergris, look north.

For the far north, water taxis remain a common mode of transit to resorts and restaurants.

TIMING

Belize's most popular destination merits a significant chunk of your vacation time. Indeed, many visitors to Belize only experience Ambergris Caye. With its many restaurants, bars, and shops, plus myriad opportunities for water sports, you can easily spend a week or more on the island without beginning to run out of things to do.

Driving Tip

As on most Caribbean islands, downtown San Pedro's main streets are conveniently known as "Front," "Middle" and "Back"—Front Street running along the sea, Back Street running on the lagoon (back) side. However, newer official names have replaced these on maps. When asking for directions, keep in mind that you'll be told the unofficial names. "Front Street" is Barrier Reef Drive, and "Middle Street" is actually Pescador Drive. "Back Street" is known as Angel Coral Drive.

SAFETY

With rapid growth and an influx of workers from other parts of Belize and Central America, Ambergris Caye has seen an increase in all types of crime. However, nearly all visitors to Ambergris Caye say they feel perfectly safe, and most of the larger hotels have full-time security. Use common sense and avoid walking on dark streets and deserted beaches after nightfall. Keep purses on the ground, not the back of your chair, at restaurants. At hotels, take advantage of in-room safes (just don't forget your passport there). Street harassment, especially for women, is the most common problem encountered on the island.

San Pedro

Sights

San Pedro House of Culture

MUSEUM | A small but wonderful cultural center, the House of Culture celebrates the fascinating history and diversity of San Pedro. Past exhibits have explored Garifuna Settlement Day and the village's lobster industry. ⊠ *2101 Almond St., Ambergris Caye* ☎ *226/5100* ☉ *Closed weekends.*

History

Because of their strategic locations on trade routes between the Yucatán in the north and Honduras in the south, the northern cayes, especially Ambergris Caye and Caye Caulker, were long occupied by the Maya. Then, as now, the reef and its abundance of fish provided a valuable source of seafood.

The origin of Belize's atolls remains a mystery, but evidence suggests they grew from the bottom up, as vast pagodas of coral accumulated over millions of years. The Maya were perhaps the first humans to discover the atolls, but by the time the first Spanish explorers arrived in 1508, the Mayan civilization had already mysteriously collapsed and few remained on the islands.

In the 17th century, English pirates used the cayes and atolls as a hideout, plotting their attacks on unwary ships. The most famous battle in Belize history happened on September 10, 1798, when a ragtag band of buccaneers defeated a Spanish armada at the Battle of St. George's Caye.

The economy on the islands has ebbed and flowed, as pirates were replaced by wealthy plantation owners, who were eventually usurped by lobster fishermen. The first hotel on Ambergris Caye, Holiday Hotel, opened in 1965 and soon began attracting divers. Jacques Cousteau visited the Blue Hole in 1971 and helped introduce Belize to the world. Today tourism is by far the top industry on the cayes and atolls.

Restaurants

Ambergris Caye has the largest and most diverse selection of restaurants in the country. Buy cheap tacos, *pupusas*, or grilled chicken from a street vendor, eat barbecued fish on the beach, or, at the other end, dine on lobster, crab claws, and steak at upscale restaurants. Even the most upmarket spots have a casual atmosphere, some with sand floors and screenless windows open to catch the breezes from the sea. The largest concentration of restaurants is in town.

★ Annie's Pastries
$ | BAKERY | Snug as a pink box of pastries, Annie's is open only in the late afternoon and evening and offers empanadas, sandwiches, and mini loaves of banana bread at local prices. Or you can select from the unlabeled display in the window and see what you bite into. **Known for:** savory chicken potpies; coconut tarts; cash only. $ *Average main:*

BZ$4 ⊠ *Laguna Dr., San Pedro Town* ☎ *604/2442* ▭ *No credit cards.*

★ Blue Water Grill
$$$ | FUSION | FAMILY | The jazzy marquee letters reading "I Love Belize" capture the enthusiasm of this well-run restaurant, a long-standing favorite. The beachfront spot serves up colorful options like molé fish with Belizean chocolate and pickled fried okra. **Known for:** watermelon gazpacho; vast wine and cocktail menu; playful atmosphere. $ *Average main: BZ$42* ⊠ *SunBreeze Hotel, Beachfront, Ambergris Caye* ☎ *226/3347* ⊕ *www. bluewatergrillbelize.com.*

Briana's Food Place
$ | CARIBBEAN | If you're hankering for a steaming bowl of cow-foot soup or just a good old plate of stew chicken, join San Pedranos on their lunch break at Briana's. Crunchy eats like *salbutes* and tostadas won't disappoint, but for faithful Belizean cuisine, try whatever is on special that day: think pigtail or curry chicken with

Ambergris Caye is the most popular destination in Belize; the Belize Barrier Reef is just offshore.

coconut rice and beans, plantains, and a scoop of slaw. **Known for:** Belizean comfort food; chimole (also called "black soup" for its black recado spice); local prices (cash only). [$] *Average main: BZ$12* ✉ *Angel Coral St., Ambergris Caye* ✥ *Block south of Waruguma* ☎ *661/2676* ⏲ *Closed Sun.* 💳 *No credit cards.*

Caliente

$$$ | **CARIBBEAN** | **FAMILY** | The red pepper logo and "Eat Love Margarita" signs may remind you of a hokey chain restaurant, and frankly parts of the menu might, too, but the food—Mexican with a Caribbean and Belizean spin—hits all the right notes. The ginger-rum shrimp is brightly flavored, the waterfront patio is airy, and the attitude is unpretentious. **Known for:** tequila-marinated meat; half-price margaritas on Friday; welcoming, tropical scene. [$] *Average main: BZ$38* ✉ *Spindrift Hotel, Barrier Reef Dr., San Pedro Town* ☎ *226/2170* 🌐 *www.calienterestaurantbelize.com* ⏲ *Closed Mon.*

Caramba!

$$$ | **SEAFOOD** | **FAMILY** | You'll quickly sense the frenetic energy of this noisy and often packed restaurant in the middle of town. No view, and there's nothing fancy on the broad menu here—just basics like grilled snapper, fried shrimp, pork chops, and Mexican fajitas, all in American portions—but most everything is well prepared, prices are moderate, and the service is snappy and enthusiastic. **Known for:** fresh seafood; habanero margaritas; a fun dinner. [$] *Average main: BZ$32* ✉ *Pescador Dr., San Pedro Town* ☎ *226/4321* ⏲ *Closed Wed.*

★ DandE's Frozen Custard & Sorbet

$ | **CAFÉ** | **FAMILY** | You'll know from the patchy wallpaper of kids' (and adults') drawings that this parlor is beloved. American expats Dan and Eileen (DandE) Jamison, who used to run the *San Pedro Sun*, have been serving creamy custards and cooling sorbets—so dense they resist quick melting—for almost 15 years. **Known for:** "hand-cranked" ice cream; coconut custard and other tropical

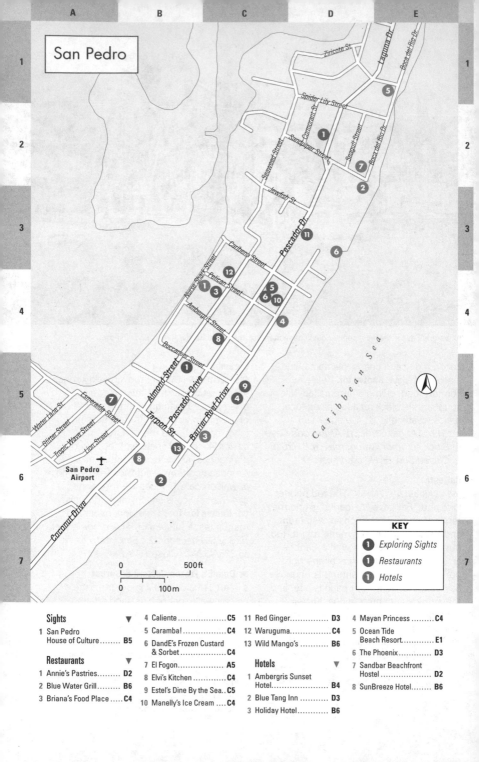

San Pedro

KEY

1 Exploring Sights
1 Restaurants
1 Hotels

Caribbean Sea

San Pedro Airport

flavors; relaxed vibes. $ Average main:
BZ$7 ✉ Pescador Dr., next to Cocina
Caramba, San Pedro Town ☎ 660/5966
⊕ www.dande.bz ▭ No credit cards
⊘ Closed Mon. and Tues.

★ El Fogon

$$ | **CARIBBEAN** | **FAMILY** | Named for the
open wood-fire cooking hearth ("faya
haat" in Kriol), El Fogon serves authentic
down-home Belizean cooking like chaya
tamales, gibnut, and Kriol stews. El
Fogon feels like a hole-in-the-wall, but it's
actually one of the most famous spots
on the island. **Known for:** fish coconut
curry; mango smoothies; off-the-beaten-
path dishes in a well-known restaurant.
$ Average main: BZ$30 ✉ North of
Tropic Air terminal, 2 Trigger Fish St., near
airport, between Esmeralda and Tarpon
St., San Pedro Town ☎ 206/2121 ⊕ www.
elfogonbelize.com ▭ No credit cards
⊘ Closed Sun.

★ Elvi's Kitchen

$$$ | **CARIBBEAN** | **FAMILY** | Here is an island
institution. In the old days, in 1974, Elvi
Staines sold burgers from the window
of her house, soon adding a few tables
on the sand under a tree; today, the
floors are sand, and the tree remains
(lifeless now and cut back to fit inside
the roof), but most else is changed.
Known for: an expansive but quality menu;
Mayan tacos and pulled pork; a classic
San Pedro experience. $ Average main:
BZ$36 ✉ Pescador Dr., near Ambergris
St., San Pedro Town ☎ 226/2404 ⊕ www.
elviskitchen.com ⊘ Closed Sun.

Estel's Dine by the Sea

$$ | **AMERICAN** | **FAMILY** | Build your ideal
breakfast from a mix-and-match chalk-
board menu at San Pedro's most classic
breakfast spot, famous for its fry jacks
served with honey and mango jam.
Estel's even has grits. **Known for:** break-
fast by the beach; sandy floor and port-
hole windows; visitor favorite. $ Average
main: BZ$22 ✉ Beachfront, Buccaneer
St., San Pedro Town ☎ 226/2019.

Manelly's Ice Cream

$ | **CAFÉ** | **FAMILY** | There's nothing glossy
about Manelly's, aside from your ice
cream melting in the cone, and that's
what makes this spot charming. Have a
cheap coconut ice cream or sugarcorn
paleta (popsicle). **Known for:** divey parlor
vibes; old-school video games; tropical
flavors. $ Average main: BZ$4 ✉ Barrier
Reef Dr., San Pedro Town ☎ 206/2285
▭ No credit cards.

★ Red Ginger

$$$$ | **ECLECTIC** | A hip, Los Angeles–style
restaurant of local renown, Red Ginger's
colorful dishes enliven the island. No sea
views here, but the gorgeous teal palm-
leaf motif anchors you in the Caribbean.
Known for: creative dishes using local
ingredients; stylish tropical decor with
a retro flair; half-price wine bottles on
Monday and Friday, half-price bubbles
on Wednesday. $ Average main: BZ$52
✉ The Phoenix, Barrier Reef Dr., at north
end of town, San Pedro Town ☎ 226/4623
⊕ www.redgingerbelize.com.

★ Waruguma

$$ | **CARIBBEAN** | **FAMILY** | This open-air
favorite may be geared toward gringos
(note the giant lobster photo prop),
but the pupusas are steaming and the
ceviche no less stacked high. Handmade
pupusas, from spinach to "crazy," make
a cheap and hearty meal. **Known for:**
vegetarian and meaty pupusas; lobster
burritos; people-watching. $ Average
main: BZ$26 ✉ Almond St., San Pedro
Town ☎ 206/2893 ☞ Credit cards only
accepted for purchases of more than
BZ$100.

Wild Mango's

$$$ | **FUSION** | Noted local chef Amy Knox
has made Wild Mango's one of the most
interesting dining choices in town. She
calls her cooking New Wave Latin—Carib-
bean food infused with spicy flavors from
Cuba, Argentina, and Mexico. **Known for:**
shrimp and fish ceviche; open-air dining;
expanding vegetarian menu. $ Average
main: BZ$32 ✉ Beachfront, 42 Barrier

Reef Dr., San Pedro Town ✥ *South end of town just south of Ruby's Hotel* ☎ *226/2859* ⏲ *Closed Sun.*

Hotels

One of your biggest decisions in Ambergris Caye will be choosing where—which part of the island—to stay. There are three basic options: in or near the town of San Pedro, in the South End area beyond town, or on North Ambergris, beyond the river channel (above the Boca del Rio bridge). Access to restaurants, bars, and other activities is easiest in San Pedro. Accommodations in town are generally simple and more reasonably priced (BZ$100–BZ$300), with a few upscale exceptions such as the deluxe Phoenix; but rooms on the main streets can be noisy from late-night revelers and traffic.

Ambergris Sunset Hotel

$ | **B&B/INN** | **FAMILY** | The island's lagoon side is often underrated; while watching the sun dip into the lagoon from this gentle coral-and-white inn, you might not miss the beach hubbub at all. **Pros:** a stellar bargain; intimate Belizean-owned hotel; a less touristy experience. **Cons:** basic furnishings; a couple blocks from the classic Caribbean side; no restaurant on-site. [$] *Rooms from: BZ$110* ✉ *Nurse Shark St., Ambergris Caye* ☎ *610/4227* 🌐 *www.ambergrissunsethotel.com* 🛏 *9 rooms* 🍴 *No meals.*

★ Blue Tang Inn

$$$ | **B&B/INN** | **FAMILY** | Hibiscus shrubs greet you at the archway of this charming terra-cotta-capped inn, which offers affordable suites just a hop-skip from the bustle of town. **Pros:** long-established hotel with sweet rooms; rooftop sundeck; wallet-friendly option. **Cons:** tiny swimming pool; may hear noise from town; some bathrooms are modest. [$] *Rooms from: US$370* ✉ *Sand Piper St., San Pedro Town* ✥ *North of The Phoenix* ☎ *226/2326* 🌐 *www.bluetanginn.com* 🛏 *14 units* 🍴 *Free breakfast.*

Booking Deals

Booking.com is now the chief reservation platform used on the cayes, but you'll often get better rates booking directly through a hotel. If you're searching for an alternative place to stay that will give you a local perspective, Airbnb is a top choice for San Pedro.

Holiday Hotel

$$$ | **HOTEL** | **FAMILY** | Flat teardrop spindles and icing-like trim give this heart-of-town hotel a modest colonial style; indeed, it's San Pedro's first inn and a dependable place to sleep between the water and the bustle. **Pros:** central location; affordable and clean; island's first hotel. **Cons:** no pool; in-town beach isn't the best for swimming; the hustle and bustle gets noisy. [$] *Rooms from: BZ$325* ✉ *Beachfront, Barrier Reef Dr., San Pedro Town* ☎ *226/2014, 713/893–3825 in U.S.* 🌐 *www.sanpedroholiday.com* 🛏 *16 rooms* 🍴 *No meals.*

Mayan Princess

$$$ | **HOTEL** | **FAMILY** | Sitting pretty and pink in the middle of town, this long-established seafront three-story condo hotel has basic but pleasant efficiencies lacking only a pool to make it a perfect mid-level choice. **Pros:** central in-town location; all apartments have lovely sea views and verandas; near good dive shop. **Cons:** no swimming pool; beach area has heavy boat and pedestrian traffic; not fancy. [$] *Rooms from: BZ$320* ✉ *Beachfront, Barrier Reef Dr., in center of town, San Pedro Town* ☎ *226/2778, 800/850–4101 in U.S.* 🌐 *www.mayanprincesshotel.com* 🛏 *23 suites* 🍴 *No meals.*

Ocean Tide Beach Resort

$$ | **HOTEL** | **FAMILY** | If diving is your reason for being in Belize and you don't want to blow the bank, you couldn't do better than this beachfront inn at the north end

of town, a launchpad for undersea adventures. **Pros:** long-standing beachfront hotel; respected tour operator on-site; good value. **Cons:** rooms aren't huge; beds and furnishings in some rooms need upgrading; no dive shop on-site. [$] *Rooms from: BZ$250* ✉ *Beachfront, Boca del Rio Dr., north end of town, San Pedro Town* ☎ *631/6863* 🌐 *oceantidebeach.com* 🛏 *15 rooms* 🍴 *Free breakfast.*

★ The Phoenix

$$$$ | RESORT | FAMILY | Hard right angles of concrete make this luxury resort a striking study in geometry, though suites are softer: expect cabinets and doors of silky tropical hardwood, greetings lettered in palm leaves on your bed, and covetable kitchenware. **Pros:** stylish condo suites; in-town's most luxurious hotel; complimentary goodies and activities. **Cons:** for some it lacks a get-away-from-it-all feel; the ultrastylish exterior can be a lot; expensive. [$] *Rooms from: BZ$1,150* ✉ *Beachfront, Barrier Reef Dr., at north end of town, San Pedro Town* ☎ *226/2083, 877/822–5512 in U.S. and Canada* 🌐 *www.thephoenixbelize.com* 🛏 *30 suites* 🍴 *No meals.*

Sandbar Beachfront Hostel

$ | B&B/INN | From the seafoam hallways to the cheap rum drinks, everything at this barefoot-easy joint is chill. **Pros:** super value; easy to meet affable folks; the sarong-and-rum-punch atmosphere you crave. **Cons:** earplugs recommended; often booked out; best suits the young or young at heart. [$] *Rooms from: BZ$110* ✉ *7 Boca del Rio Dr., San Pedro Town* ☎ *226/2008* 🌐 *www.sanpedrohostel.com* 🛏 *30 dorm beds; 8 private rooms* 🍴 *No meals.*

SunBreeze Hotel

$$$ | HOTEL | FAMILY | A Spanish arcade makes a pleasant passageway between the rooms and courtyard of this waterfront hotel on the busy southern side of town. **Pros:** comfortable and well-run; great restaurant on-site (under separate management); some rooms handicap-accessible. **Cons:** not much of a beach; not as stylish as newer properties; trafficky area. [$] *Rooms from: BZ$385* ✉ *Coconut Dr., San Pedro Town* ✣ *Across from Tropic Air terminal and airstrip* ☎ *226/2191, 800/688–0191 in U.S. and Canada* 🌐 *www.sunbreeze.net* 🛏 *43 rooms* 🍴 *Some meals.*

South of San Pedro

👁 Sights

★ Belize Barrier Reef

SCUBA DIVING | From the island shore, or from the air, you see the coral reef as an almost unbroken chain of white surf. Get closer and the water is clear and shallow; the reef itself is a beautiful living wall formed by billions of small coral polyps. The Belize Barrier Reef runs along the eastern shore of Ambergris Caye and is one of the most worthy attractions in Belize, accessible by boat and kayak. Just outside the reef, the seabed drops sharply, and gives the water the blue and amethyst tones that astonish. The reef is closest to shore on the far north end of Ambergris Caye. In and around San Pedro Town, the barrier reef is a few hundred yards off the beach. It's widely held that this UNESCO World Heritage site is the second-longest barrier reef in the world, after the Great Barrier Reef in Australia, and it's no less spectacular. At minimum, it's the longest in the Western and Northern Hemispheres. ✉ *Ambergris Caye.*

★ Hol Chan Marine Reserve

SCUBA DIVING | The reef's focal point for diving and snorkeling near Ambergris Caye and Caye Caulker belongs to the spectacular Hol Chan Marine Reserve, a marine national park. The main destinations here—the Hol Chan Cut and Shark-Ray Alley—are a 20-minute boat ride south of San Pedro, or about 30 minutes from Caye Caulker. The Hol Chan Cut (Mayan for "little channel") is a break

How to Help Preserve "the Jewel"

Belizeans are, admirably, dedicated to maintaining their delicate ecological heritage. Anyone in San Pedro will tell you that the Barrier Reef is precious to them; likewise, they are conscious that plastic, such as straws, may end up in the nose of a sea turtle. While climate change and tourism's heavy footprint affect the cayes and atolls, there are a few ways visitors can help Belizeans preserve "the Jewel."

■ Avoid plastic bottles, which often end up in the sea. Carry your own refillable bottle or drink glass-bottled soda water.

■ Ask for drinks without plastic straws, or bring your own metal or bamboo straw.

■ Use biodegradable sunscreen when swimming.

■ Be mindful of electricity usage.

■ Opt for kayaking and paddleboarding rather than gas-powered water sports such as jet-skiing.

■ When possible, walk the beach or bike instead of renting a golf cart.

■ Look for lionfish on the menu, as eating lionfish helps control the invasive species' population.

■ Frequent restaurants that use Belizean-grown vegetables.

■ Don't join other tourists in feeding iguanas or other wild animals.

■ Always object to tour guides touching or feeding sea life.

in the reef about 100 feet wide and 20 to 35 feet deep, through which tremendous volumes of water pass with the tides. Shark-Ray Alley, now a part of the reserve, is famous as a place to swim, snorkel, and dive with sharks (nearly all nurse sharks) and southern stingrays. The park includes a miniature "Blue Hole" and a 12-foot-deep cave whose entrance often attracts the fairy basslet, an iridescent purple-and-yellow fish frequently seen here. The area is also home to a large moray eel population. In 2015, the park began a monumental expansion (with much celebration) to include zones on the west and north of Ambergris, adding 139 square miles (359 square km) of preserved sea, reef, lagoon, and wetlands. Today, the park totals a massive 257 square miles (414 square km).

■TIP➜ When tour guides advertise trips to Hol Chan, they're speaking of the Hol Chan Cut, the most famous part of the national

park. The Hol Chan Marine Reserve itself, however, is much bigger.

Varying in depth from 50 feet to 100 feet, the Hol Chan Cut's canyons lie between buttresses of coral running perpendicular to the reef, separated by white, sandy channels. You may find tunnel-like passageways from one canyon to the next. It's exciting to explore, because as you come over each hill you don't know what you'll see in the "valley." Because fishing generally is off-limits here, divers and snorkelers can see abundant marine life. There are throngs of squirrelfish, butterfly fish, parrotfish, and queen angelfish, as well as Nassau groupers, peppermint bass, barracuda, and large shoals of yellowtail snappers. Unfortunately, also here are lionfish, an invasive Indo-Pacific species that is eating its way—destroying small native fish populations—from Venezuela to the North Carolina coast. Altogether, more than 160 species of fish have been identified in this part of the marine reserve, along with 40 species of coral. Hawksbill, loggerhead, and green turtles have also been found here, as have spotted and common dolphins, West Indian manatees, stingrays, and several species of sharks.

⚠ **The currents through the reef can be strong here at times, so tell your guide if you're not a strong swimmer, and ask for a snorkel vest or float. Also, although nurse sharks are normally docile and very used to humans, they are wild creatures that on rare occasions have bitten snorkelers or divers who disturbed them.** ✉ *Off southern tip of Ambergris Caye, Ambergris Caye* ☎ *526/2247 in San Pedro* 🌐 *www.holchanbelize.org* 🎫 *BZ$20 (normally included in snorkel or dive tour price).*

Shark-Ray Alley

SCUBA DIVING | Shark-Ray Alley is a sandbar within Hol Chan Marine Reserve where you can snorkel alongside nurse sharks (which can bite but rarely do) and stingrays (which gather here to feed) and near even larger numbers of day-trippers from San Pedro and from cruise ships. Sliding into the water is a small feat of personal bravery—the sight of sharks and rays brushing past is spectacular yet daunting. Guides sometimes encourage visitors to pet these sea creatures (object to this behavior, as tourists more than anyone influence the industry's habits). The Hol Chan Marine Reserve office is on Caribena Street in San Pedro. **■TIP→ A night dive at Shark-Ray Alley is a special treat: bioluminescence causes the water to light up, and many nocturnal animals emerge, such as octopus and spider crab. Because of the strong current you'll need above-average swimming skills.** ✉ *Southern tip of Ambergris Caye in Hol Chan Marine Reserve, Ambergris Caye* ☎ *226/2247 Hol Chan office* 🌐 *www.holchanbelize.org* 🎫 *BZ$20 marine reserve fee included as a part of Hol Chan fee.*

🍴 Restaurants

Antojito's San Telmo

$ | LATIN AMERICAN | FAMILY | Step off the tourist trail and have a lunch of stew chicken, stew beans, and coconut rice peppered in Marie Sharp's at this no-frills restaurant known for its down-home Belizean fare and friendly service. Breakfast is a good bet, too, with tacos priced as cheap as gumballs in the States. **Known for:** good lunches; stew chicken with all the fixings; low-key atmosphere. [$] *Average main: BZ$14* ✉ *Coconut Dr., San Pedro Town* ✥ *Across from The Baker* ☎ *226/4575* 💳 *No credit cards.*

The Baker

$ | BAKERY | FAMILY | Warm cinnamon rolls are a favorite at this Irish-owned bakery. You'll also find a cheering bounty of croissants, cookies, and coconut tarts, plus made-to-order egg sandwiches and, at lunch, tuna or ham sandwiches. **Known for:** baked goods with local ingredients; rum cake; irresistible smells. [$] *Average main: BZ$10* ✉ *Coconut Dr. (aka Seagrape Dr.), San Pedro Town* ✥ *Near Marina's grocery* ☎ *206/2036* 💳 *No credit cards* 🕒 *Closed Sun.*

Black Orchid

$$$ | FUSION | Black Orchid is named for the spidery, delicate national flower of Belize, but the gorgeous dishes range from Belizean to global fusion. The island-elegant establishment has thatch accents, a fountain tiered like a Mayan temple, and starched tablecloths. **Known for:** creative cuisine; crusted orange rum grouper; a romantic but not stuffy scene. [$] *Average main: BZ$50* ✉ *S. Coconut Dr., about 2.5 miles (4 km) south of town, San Pedro Town* ☎ *206/2441* 🌐 *www.blackorchidrestaurant.com* 🕒 *Closed Sun. and Mon. No lunch.*

★ Hidden Treasure

$$$$ | CARIBBEAN | Glowing with lamplight, Hidden Treasure brings to mind a treasure chest cracked open, and indeed it's a gem. Tucked away on a residential

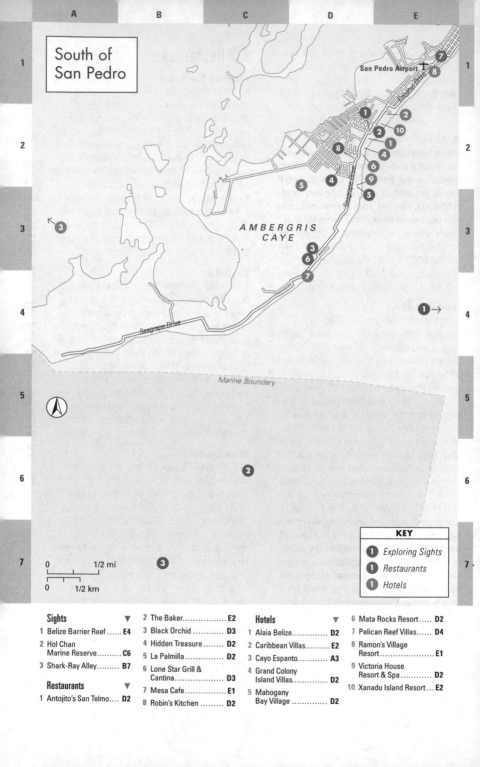

South of San Pedro

San Pedro Airport

AMBERGRIS CAYE

Seagrape Drive

Marine Boundary

0   1/2 mi
0   1/2 km

KEY

- 1 *Exploring Sights*
- 1 *Restaurants*
- 1 *Hotels*

back street, this open-air restaurant offers sophisticated dishes with local flavors. **Known for:** the Seafood Treasure dish; lovely owners; romantic ambience. $ *Average main: BZ$64* ✉ *Escalante Residential Area, 2715 Flamboyant Dr., San Pedro Town* ✛ *About 1.5 miles (2.4 km) south of town; go south on Coconut Dr. past Royal Palm Villas and watch for signs* ☎ *226/4111* ⊕ *www.hiddentreasurebelize. com* ⊙ *Closed Tues. No lunch* ☞ *Complimentary transportation to your hotel.*

La Palmilla
$$$$ | **ECLECTIC** | Even if you're not overnighting at Victoria House, you can still enjoy its sumptuous setting over equally elegant dishes at La Palmilla. The chef does an especially fine job with seafood, notably the grilled lobster. **Known for:** cajun-spiced Belizean pork chop; a complex "caye lime" pie; starched-tablecloth dining. $ *Average main: BZ$58* ✉ *Coconut Dr., at Victoria House resort, San Pedro Town* ☎ *226/2067* ⊕ *www. victoria-house.com.*

Lone Star Grill & Cantina
$$ | **MEXICAN FUSION** | **FAMILY** | If you're in need of a fried steak sandwich or a big screen to watch baseball, here you'll find both. Lone Star Grill & Cantina, run by a couple from the Lone Star State, is an outpost of Texas cooking on the south end of the island. **Known for:** cold beer; margaritas; sports on screen. $ *Average main: BZ$26* ✉ *2.5 miles (4 km) south of town, Coconut Dr., San Pedro Town* ✛ *Past Black Orchid, across from Athens Gate* ☎ *226/4666* ⊕ *www.lonestargrillbelize. com* ⊙ *Closed Tues., and Sept. and Oct.*

Mesa Cafe
$$ | **ECLECTIC** | **FAMILY** | The air-conditioned setting feels more U.S. than Caribbean, but Mesa plates up delicious change-of-pace dishes like churro-spiced pancakes or, for lunch, a tasty pork farmhouse burger. Vegetarians will appreciate the savory bean cake benny, among other options. **Known for:** coconut French toast; vegetarian and vegan options; hip diner

vibes. $ *Average main: BZ$20* ✉ *Vilma Linda Plaza, Tarpon St., San Pedro Town* ☎ *607/1736* ⊙ *Closed Sun. No dinner.*

Robin's Kitchen
$ | **CARIBBEAN** | **FAMILY** | Line up beside the smoking grill for a delicious, no-nonsense plate of jerk chicken with sides. Homemade sauce is dished from a big plastic mixing bowl and Fanta and juices are in the back (but don't expect mixed drinks). **Known for:** jerk chicken and (sometimes) fish; hits-the-spot Caribbean flavors; friendly folks. $ *Average main: BZ$14* ✉ *Coconut Dr., 1.5 miles (2.5 km) south of town, San Pedro Town* ✛ *Across from Banana Beach* ▤ *No credit cards.*

Hotels

For silence and sand, head out of town for resort-style digs. To get more privacy, consider the South End. Though it, too, is developing rapidly, it's still less hectic than in town, and it's only a golf cart or taxi ride away.

Alaia Belize
$$$$ | **RENTAL** | **FAMILY** | This expansive condo complex run by Marriott Autograph Collection features a beach club, a luxe rooftop pool, and a "live" art gallery representing local artists. **Pros:** superb facilities; accommodating to kids; one of the island's best beaches. **Cons:** pricey rates; not the uniquely Belizean experience many are seeking; less personal than peer resorts. $ *Rooms from: BZ$750* ✉ *Beachfront, Seagrape Dr., San Pedro Town* ✛ *1.5 miles (2.5 km) south of town* ☎ *226/3739, 866/352–1163 in U.S.* ⊕ *www.alaiabelize.com* ⇥ *170 units* ⦿ *No meals.*

Caribbean Villas
$$ | **HOTEL** | **FAMILY** | It may not be as modern as the island's newer resorts, but Caribbean Villas, with its gardens, pleasant beachfront, and fun two-story waterslide, is an affordable and low-key alternative to the glitzier developments. **Pros:** reliable hotel with high return rate;

great pier; waterslide and water trampoline are a hit. **Cons:** some units could use updating; not crazy cheap; can attract night revelers. $ *Rooms from: BZ$320* ✉ *Seagrape Dr., 1 mile (1.5 km) south of town, San Pedro Town* ☎ *226/2715, 800/213–8347 in U.S. and Canada* ⊕ *www.caribbeanvillashotel.com* ⇆ *5 rooms, 9 suites* ☉ *No meals.*

★ Cayo Espanto

$$$$ | RESORT | Islanders will tell you that Cayo Espanto, a spectacular private island off Ambergris, is where movie stars stay, and they're not wrong. **Pros:** outrageous luxury and service; you'll feel like a castaway in a utopian scene; intimacy with the natural setting. **Cons:** wildly expensive; island is on the back side of Ambergris Caye, not on the main barrier reef side; privacy can sometimes be oppressive. $ *Rooms from: BZ$3,500* ✉ *3 miles (5 km) west of Ambergris Caye, Cayo Espanto* ☎ *910/323–8355 in U.S.* ⊕ *www.aprivateisland.com* ⇆ *7 units* ☉ *All-inclusive.*

Grand Colony Island Villas

$$$$ | RENTAL | FAMILY | Spacious enough for the whole family, these palatial villas with mahogany details offer plenty of privacy and a distinctly Belizean flair. **Pros:** luxe suites; beautifully finished and furnished; a stellar pool and lounging area. **Cons:** no restaurant on-site; rates run high; lacks the intimate service of some resorts. $ *Rooms from: BZ$650* ✉ *Coconut Dr., 1.5 miles (3 km) south of town, San Pedro Town* ☎ *226/3739, 866/352–1163 in U.S. and Canada* ⊕ *www.grandcolonyvillas.com* ⇆ *16 units* ☉ *No meals.*

Mahogany Bay Village

$$$$ | RESORT | FAMILY | The pulse of south Ambergris is changing with this 60-acre townlet of white, colonial-nostalgic villas by Hilton's Curio brand, complete with boutique shopping, a clubhouse, a taco truck, a spa, and all the trappings of a planned community in the States. **Pros:** stylish and airy rooms; frequent special offers; private beach a boat ride away. **Cons:** on the lagoon and more than a walk to town; can feel impersonal and corporate; accused of environmental irresponsibility. $ *Rooms from: BZ$770* ✉ *2.5 miles (4 km) south of town, San Pedro Town* ☎ *226/4817* ⊕ *www.mahoganybay-village.com* ⇆ *123 rooms* ☉ *No meals.*

Mata Rocks Resort

$$$ | HOTEL | FAMILY | A white building giving the impression of a ship at sea houses an intimate, mid-level hotel on a nice stretch of beach south of town. **Pros:** quiet beachside resort; good value for Ambergris; continental breakfast. **Cons:** no restaurant on-site; "resort" may be a misnomer; a 30-minute walk from the center of town. $ *Rooms from: BZ$360* ✉ *Coconut Dr., 1.5 miles (2.5 km) south of town, San Pedro Town* ☎ *226/2336, 888/628–2757 in U.S. and Canada* ⊕ *www.matarocks.com* ⇆ *17 rooms* ☉ *Free breakfast.*

Pelican Reef Villas

$$$ | RENTAL | FAMILY | While watching the pool's turquoise waterfall, it's easy to believe you've stumbled upon a hidden tropical treasure; however, the faux cave is a swim-up bar, and Pelican Reef is only a couple miles south of San Pedro's bustle. **Pros:** well-run condo colony in quiet south-end location; luxurious digs; lovely breakfast selections included. **Cons:** golf cart rental nearly necessary; a lot of steps to climb to upper-level units; no dinner on-site. $ *Rooms from: BZ$430* ✉ *Coconut Dr., 2.5 miles (4 km) south of town, San Pedro Town* ☎ *226/4352, 281/942–1103 in U.S.* ⊕ *www.pelican-reefvillas.com* ⇆ *24 rooms* ☉ *Free breakfast.*

Ramon's Village Resort

$$$ | RESORT | FAMILY | One of the first and most famous resorts on the island, Ramon's really is a village, with its many buildings paneled in furry palmetto and canopied footpaths that you can get lost in. **Pros:** good in-town beach; classic resort with jungle-like vegetation; island atmosphere many are seeking. **Cons:** busy location across from the airstrip, which is increasingly congested; no sale of liquor means bring-your-own rum; evidence of spotty management. $ *Rooms from: BZ$360* ✉ *Coconut Dr., across from airstrip just south of town, Ambergris Caye* ☎ *226/2071, 800/624–4215 in U.S. and Canada* ⊕ *www.ramons.com* ⇥ *71 rooms* ❍ *No meals.*

★ Victoria House Resort & Spa

$$$ | **RESORT** | This long-standing resort, stately and secluded, wears many laurels for its handsome grounds, seamless service, and Caribbean elegance. **Pros:** quiet and lovely; variety of gorgeous beachside accommodations; idyllic spot for meals overlooking the pool and beach. **Cons:** not a budget place; some will object to the imperialism nostalgia (i.e., "Plantation Suites") and exclusive air. $ *Rooms from: BZ$520* ✉ *Coconut Dr., 2 miles (3 km) south of town, Ambergris Caye* ☎ *226/2067, 800/247–5159 in U.S. and Canada* ⊕ *www.victoria-house.com* ⇥ *29 units* ❍ *Free breakfast.*

★ Xanadu Island Resort

$$$ | **RESORT** | **FAMILY** | A lovely retreat that is eco-minded, relaxed, and just a short walk to town, Xanadu is absent of the pageantry of some upscale resorts. **Pros:** friendly folks; tropical, perfect pool; convenient location. **Cons:** not a postcard-pretty beach; the beachy interiors aren't ultrastylish; rates for many rooms are spendy. $ *Rooms from: BZ$480* ✉ *Seagrape Dr., 1 mile south of town, San Pedro Town* ☎ *226/2814, 866/351–4752 in U.S.* ⊕ *www.xanaduislandresort.com* ⇥ *19 rooms* ❍ *No meals.*

North of San Pedro

Sights

★ Bacalar Chico Marine National Park & Reserve

SCUBA DIVING | Development on Ambergris continues relentlessly, but most of the far north of the island remains unsullied. At the top of the caye, butting up against Mexico, this UNESCO World Heritage Site spans 41 square miles (105 square km) of land, reef, and sea. Here, on 11 miles (18 km) of trails you may cross paths with whitetail deer, ocelots, saltwater crocodiles, and, according to some reports, pumas and jaguars. There are beautiful diving, snorkeling, and fishing opportunities, especially off Rocky Point, and a small visitor center and museum will get you oriented. You'll need a boat and a guide to take you here, where there are at least nine ancient Mayan sites. Walk carefully, as loggerhead and green sea turtles nest here. Be sure to bring insect repellent. An all-day snorkel trip to Bacalar Chico from San Pedro is unforgettable. ✉ *North end of Ambergris Caye, Ambergris Caye* ☎ *226/2833* ▦ *BZ$10 day pass or BZ$30 week pass.*

 Restaurants

The newly (partially) paved golf cart path makes more dining options accessible, but some still are a long trek from town. Fancy spots usually ferry you to them in their own water taxi (ask your hotel to arrange this). Unless you're staying near one of the North Ambergris restaurants listed below, you may want to take a water taxi—the Coastal Xpress—especially after dark. Cabs from town will drive farther north, but the cost is steep (BZ$30–BZ$60 for most destinations, including the BZ$10 vehicle bridge fee). Also up north is the happening Secret

Beach, a lagoon-side destination famous for bars with partially underwater picnic tables and tourist prices.

Mambo
$$$$ | ECLECTIC | A courtesy boat will scoop you up nearly anywhere on the island to whisk you away to this celebrated palm-leaf thatch dining room. The arrival is lovely, but once seated the experience can be spotty: at times, Mambo's flavors underwhelm, but local ingredients like chayote (a sweet squash) and coconut enhance the global cuisine. **Known for:** fresh coconut cream mojitos; lime-marinated snapper; mellow fine-dining ambience. $ *Average main: BZ$56* ⊠ *Matachica, Beachfront 5 miles (8 km) north of bridge, Ambergris Caye* ☎ *223/0002* ⊕ *www.matachica.com/ mambo-restaurant.*

Marbucks Coffee House
$ | CAFÉ | You'll recognize the circular logo from the monolithic coffee chain it references, but vibrant-tiled Marbucks is far more pleasant. The coffee is hit or miss (being sometimes too watery), but it usually beats Belize's Maxwell House standard. **Known for:** Guatemalan coffee; a basic breakfast on your way to town; wine and live music on Thursday. $ *Average main: BZ$12* ⊠ *1.5 miles (2.4 km) north of bridge, Ambergris Caye* ✚ *Right of main road* ☎ *601/3306* ⊕ *www.marbuckscoffeehouse.com.*

O Restaurant
$$$ | FUSION | Dining alfresco under a private, curtain-draped pergola is a dreamy way to pass a starlit evening on North Ambergris. Located at Las Terrazas resort, O Restaurant's detail-oriented Belizean chef animates the menu with playful dishes like porcupine shrimp and a spiky chocolate sea urchin. **Known for:** pineapple-papaya-chicken skewers on a sizzling skillet; Friday night sushi; stylish environs. $ *Average main: BZ$50* ⊠ *Las Terrazas, 3.5 miles (5.5 km) north of the bridge, Ambergris Caye* ☎ *226/4249* ⊕ *www.lasterrazasresort.com.*

Rain Restaurant and Rooftop
$$$$ | FUSION | Simple decor and few walls make space for this rooftop's real ambience: the Caribbean horizon and watercolor sunsets. Good for special occasions, the pricey dishes are worth the cost; noted island chef Chris Aycock has a way with local ingredients and all things seafood. **Known for:** jungle ribs with guava sauce; a winning panorama; quality service. $ *Average main: BZ$60* ⊠ *Grande Caribe, 2 miles (3 km) north of bridge, San Pedro Town* ☎ *226/4000* ⊕ *www.rainbelize.com* ▭ *No credit cards.*

★ Rojo Beach Bar & Lounge
$$$ | CONTEMPORARY | This red-hot beach-front bistro, both stylish and whimsical, is the treasure you didn't know you were looking for. Take your street-food tapas to the splash pool, lounge on sultry day-beds, or catch a game of Belikin pong. **Known for:** customized frozen drinks with fresh fruit; Caribbean ingredients with an Asian-fusion flair; Keppy the pet parrot. $ *Average main: BZ$45* ⊠ *Azul Resort, Beachfront, Ambergris Caye* ✚ *5 miles (8 km) north of bridge* ☎ *226/4012* ⊕ *www.rojolounge.com* ◷ *Closed Sun. and Mon.*

★ The Truck Stop Shipping Container Food Park
$$ | ECLECTIC | FAMILY | Created by American Ben Popik, the hip-to-the-max Truck Stop pulses as the social hub of North Ambergris. Five shipping containers dish up Malaysian and "Nuevo Latino" food, New Haven-style pizza, ice cream, and a host of drinks. **Known for:** happening vibes (think Austin meets the Caribbean); bourbon orange chicken tacos; playful entertainment. $ *Average main: BZ$22* ⊠ *1 mile (1.5 km) north of bridge, Ambergris Caye.*

SECRET BEACH
Right and left, folks in San Pedro will ask you, "Have you been to Secret Beach yet?" Once a lagoon-side hideaway for islanders and reptiles, it's now, well, not so secret. A village of hodgepodge bars

and eateries have cropped up in a mini gold rush. Built for play, you can idle the day away at these clapboard joints, which are all slightly different takes on the same beach-bar-and-seafood vibe. This is solidly a day spot: restaurants close shop right after sunset. An unusual experience, you'll dine inside the expanded Hol Chan Marine Reserve.

Secret Beach is still not the easiest to get to (though it's hard to get lost). Driving up the golf cart path, you'll come to one—and only one—junction, about 4.5 miles (6.5 km) up with signs pointing to Secret Beach. Turn left and follow the bumpy unpaved road, surrounded by mangrove forests, 15–20 minutes, all the way until you hit life-size letters that spell "Secret Beach." You can't miss it.

★ Blue Bayou Bar & Restaurant

$$ | CARIBBEAN | FAMILY | It's not an actual bayou, but the calm, wetland setting does invite a comparison. Set slightly apart from the Secret Beach hubbub, Blue Bayou is your best bet for a less touristy hangout, with partially underwater picnic tables and good prices on local rum. **Known for:** fun underwater seating; wade-up service; frilly frozen drinks. [$] *Average main: BZ$25* ✉ *Secret Beach, Ambergris Caye* ✣ *To the left of main restaurants* ☎ *623/8051* 💳 *No credit cards.*

Pirate's Not-So-Secret Beach Bar & Grill

$$$ | SEAFOOD | Front and center at Secret Beach, Pirate's is always lively. Between the branded koozies, spring-break vibe, and #saltlife Instagram posts, you know you're in tourist territory, but it's a fun spot to spend the day. **Known for:** dragon fruit margaritas; rotating drink specials; a kitschy, day-party atmosphere. [$] *Average main: BZ$35* ✉ *Secret Beach, Ambergris Caye* ☎ *668/2156* 🌐 *www.secretbeachsanpedro.com.*

Hotels

If you really want to get away, choose the more remote North Ambergris, which is reached mainly by water taxis, golf carts, and sometimes regular land cabs. The newer, glitzier hotels mostly populate North Ambergris, the farthest being around 12 miles from the bridge.

Ak'bol Yoga Retreat & Eco-Resort

$$ | RESORT | Get into your yoga flow at this affordable eco-resort, where cabanas seem water forged given their river-rock floors, conch shell faucets, and al fresco showers. **Pros:** artful island-style rooms in a laid-back resort; good value; spectacular setting for yoga studio. **Cons:** you'll feel out of your element if you can't do downward dog; outdoor showers are cabanas' only showers; best suited for outdoorsy folks. [$] *Rooms from: BZ$336* ✉ *Beachfront, Ambergris Caye* ✣ *1.25 miles (2 km) north of bridge* ☎ *626/6296* 🌐 *www.akbol.com* 🛏 *37 rooms* 🍴 *No meals.*

★ Azul Resort (*Casa Azul*)

$$$$ | RESORT | High-profile guests favor Azul for its privacy, luxe amenities, and airy, spacious interiors—each measures around 3,000 square feet, with two bedrooms and soaring ceilings. **Pros:** breathtaking private beachfront villas with every luxury; five-star service; delicious food by Rojo Lounge. **Cons:** expensive; did we mention expensive?; if you go all-inclusive, the wonderful kitchens are a bit of a loss. [$] *Rooms from: BZ$1,500* ✉ *Beachfront, Ambergris Caye* ✣ *5 miles (8 km) north of the bridge* ☎ *226/4012* 🌐 *azulbelize.com/index.php* 🕒 *Closed Sept.* 🛏 *2 villas* 🍴 *No meals.*

★ Cayo Frances Farm and Fly

$$ | B&B/INN | This wonderful, one-of-a-kind fishing camp, with its clapboard cabins that recall an earlier time, makes room for the real star of the show: outstanding flats fishing. **Pros:** incredible fishing conditions; earnest and uncommercial operation; delicious food with a lovely host. **Cons:** very niche and not

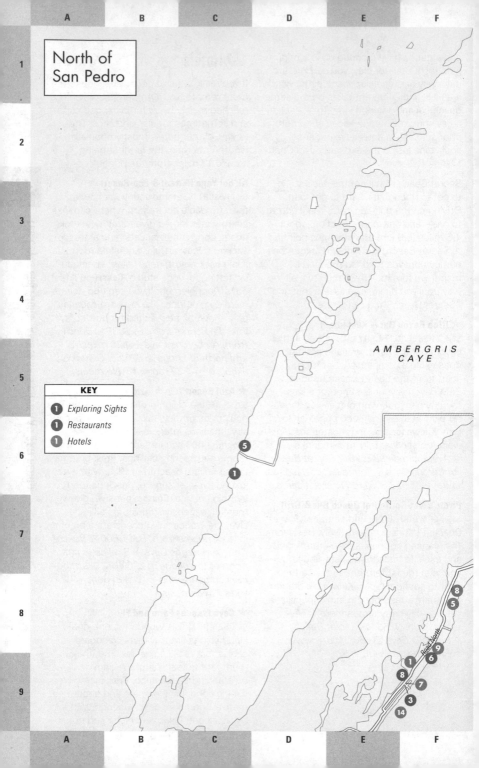

North of
San Pedro

KEY
1 Exploring Sights
1 Restaurants
1 Hotels

*AMBERGRIS
CAYE*

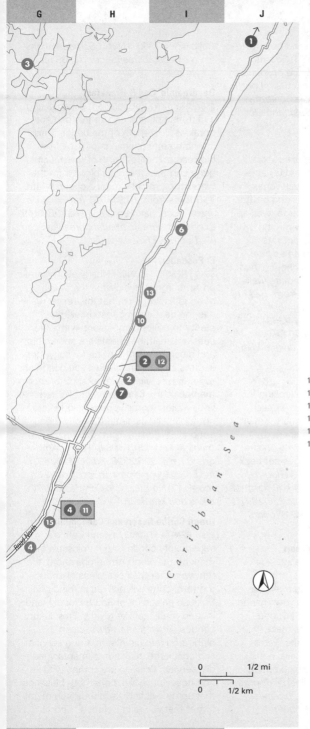

Sights ▼

1 Bacalar Chico Marine
  National Park & Reserve **J1**

Restaurants ▼

1 Blue Bayou Bar & Restaurant.....**C6**

2 Mambo.............................**H5**

3 Marbucks Coffee House...........**F9**

4 O Restaurant **G7**

5 Pirate's Not-So-Secret
  Beach Bar & Grill..................**C6**

6 Rain Restaurant and Rooftop......**F9**

7 Rojo Beach Bar & Lounge........**H5**

8 The Truck Stop Shipping
  Container Food Park...............**F9**

Hotels ▼

1 Ak'bol Yoga Retreat &
  Eco-Resort..........................**F9**

2 Azul Resort **H5**

3 Cayo Frances Farm and Fly.......**G1**

4 Coco Beach Resort................**G7**

5 Cocotal Inn & Cabanas **F8**

6 Costa Blu Dive and
  Beach Resort.......................**I3**

7 Daydreamin' Bed & Breakfast **F9**

8 El Pescador.........................**F8**

9 Grand Caribe Resort and
  Condominiums **F9**

10 La Perla del Caribe **H4**

11 Las Terrazas Resort **G7**

12 Matachica Resort & Spa **H5**

13 Portofino Beach Resort...........**I4**

14 PUR Boutique Cabanas............**E9**

15 Seascape Villas...................**G7**

4

The Cayes and Atolls   AMBERGRIS CAYE AND SAN PEDRO

for everyone; ultra remote and best for short stays; utilitarian digs. [$] *Rooms from: BZ$350* ✉ *Leeward side of island, Ambergris Caye* ✥ *12 miles (19 km) north of bridge* ☎ *610/3841* 🌐 *www.belizefly-fishcamp.com* 🕓 *Closed Sept. and Oct.* 🛏 *2 units* 🍴 *All meals.*

Coco Beach Resort

$$$$ | **RESORT** | **FAMILY** | This luxe resort gives the impression of a Mediterranean palace—or maybe a fun Las Vegas version—with its colonnades and grottos rising from the pools. **Pros:** large, well-appointed suites; gorgeous swimming pools perfect for play; frequent rate specials. **Cons:** not as intimate as peer resorts; decor can be more cheesy than tasteful; upper-level suites require walking a lot of steps. [$] *Rooms from: BZ$710* ✉ *Beachfront, 4 miles (7 km) north of San Pedro, Ambergris Caye* ☎ *844/360–1553 in U.S. and Canada, 226/4840* 🌐 *www.cocobeachbelize.com* 🛏 *54 units* 🍴 *No meals.*

Cocotal Inn & Cabanas

$$ | **RESORT** | **FAMILY** | If you're looking for an unfussy, homey spot on the beach, Cocotal could be it. **Pros:** friendly, small resort on the beach; well managed; affordable rates. **Cons:** no dining on-site; nothing deluxe; some cottages set back from the breeze and beach. [$] *Rooms from: BZ$300* ✉ *2.5 miles (4 km) north of San Pedro, Ambergris Caye* ☎ *226/2097* 🌐 *www.cocotalbelize.com* 🛏 *8 rooms* 🍴 *No meals.*

Costa Blu Dive and Beach Resort

$$$$ | **RESORT** | **FAMILY** | With a seaside beach bar, pool, spa services, and on-site restaurant, Costa Blu makes a great resting place between your marine tours. **Pros:** geared to divers but good for nondivers, too; discounts make rates lower than they look; the warm staff will call you by name. **Cons:** not a huge bargain; uninspired dining options; adults only so not for families. [$] *Rooms from: BZ$600* ✉ *Beachfront, 6.5 miles (10.5 km) north of town, Ambergris Caye* ☎ *844/360–1553 U.S. reservations* 🌐 *www.costablubelize.com* 🛏 *38 rooms* 🍴 *No meals.*

Daydreamin' Bed & Breakfast

$$$ | **B&B/INN** | Four elegant cabanas ring a glittering plunge pool at this bed-and-breakfast just north of the bridge. **Pros:** intimate setting; change of pace from big resorts; not far north of town. **Cons:** quite compact rooms; a block from the waterfront; might expect a cheaper rate. [$] *Rooms from: BZ$430* ✉ *Tropicana Dr., Tres Cocos, San Pedro Town* ☎ *226/4449* 🌐 *www.daydreaminbedandbreakfast.com* 🛏 *4 units* 🍴 *Free breakfast.*

El Pescador

$$$$ | **RESORT** | **FAMILY** | Nearly every hotel on Ambergris Caye claims that it can arrange fishing trips, but this resort really has the best angling resources, plus plenty to do for companions with other passions (half the guests are snorkelers and divers). **Pros:** the place for saltwater anglers, but inviting even if you don't fish; top-notch service; beloved spot for more than 40 years. **Cons:** expect to lighten your wallet; rooms in original lodge are not too spacious; limited nightly menu options. [$] *Rooms from: BZ$700* ✉ *2.5 miles (4 km) north of San Pedro, Ambergris Caye* ☎ *226/2398, 804/661–2259 in U.S.* 🌐 *www.elpescador.com* 🛏 *21 rooms* 🍴 *No meals* ☞ *Complimentary bikes and kayaks.*

Grand Caribe Resort and Condominiums

$$$ | **RENTAL** | **FAMILY** | Grand Caribe's superluxury condos, an unmissable landmark on the North Ambergris shore, are renowned for their seamless glamour: the terra-cotta will put you in mind of a Spanish palace (or of South Florida), and indeed you'll feel like royalty. **Pros:** luxury condos, all with sea views; close to high-rated restaurants; first-rate service and concierge, plus complimentary laundry service. **Cons:** luxury comes with an iron-heavy price tag; behemoth buildings that some will find gratuitous; you might forget that you're in Belize. [$] *Rooms* *from: BZ$520 ✉ Tres Cocos area of North Ambergris, Ambergris Caye ✣ 1.25 miles (2 km) north of bridge ☎ 226/4726, 800/488–5903 in U.S. or Canada 🌐 www.grandcaribebelize.com 🛏 150 suites 🍴 No meals.*

La Perla del Caribe

$$$$ | RENTAL | FAMILY | Expansive villas command the beachfront, all named after precious jewels like Opal and Emerald—and they really do dazzle. **Pros:** bold and textured villas with every amenity; the exotic sensibility that condos lack; peaceful setting. **Cons:** somewhat remote; no on-site restaurant; expensive unless divided in a group. [$] *Rooms from: BZ$850 ✉ Beachfront, 6 miles (10 km) north of San Pedro, Ambergris Caye ☎ 226/4309, 713 /561–5584 U.S. phone 🌐 www.laperladelcaribe.com 🛏 9 villas 🍴 No meals.*

Las Terrazas Resort

$$$$ | RENTAL | FAMILY | The all-white dazzle of Las Terrazas will make you want to don your chicest beachwear—but even if you can't rival the style, this is a welcoming luxury resort. **Pros:** elegant interior design; romantic but also kid friendly; delightful complimentary extras. **Cons:** expensive, especially for larger units; not a central location; lacks a distinct Belizean feel. [$] *Rooms from: BZ$775 ✉ Beachfront, 3.5 miles (5.5 km) north of the bridge, Ambergris Caye ☎ 226/4249, 800/447–1553 in U.S. 🌐 www.lasterrazasresort.com 🛏 39 units 🍴 No meals.*

★ Matachica Resort & Spa

$$$$ | RESORT | Palm-leaf thatch casitas in shades of mango, banana, and melon, offset by brilliant white sand, give this deluxe resort a Gauguin-like quality. **Pros:** a distinctly Belizean experience; stylish and sexy; friendly staff and seasoned management. **Cons:** no kids under 14 allowed; high rates; a/c doesn't always do the trick. [$] *Rooms from: BZ$720 ✉ Beachfront, 5 miles (8 km) north of San Pedro, Ambergris Caye ☎ 226/5010 🌐 www.matachica.com 🛏 31 rooms 🍴 Some meals ☞ Complimentary boat transfers upon arrival and departure.*

Portofino Beach Resort

$$$$ | RESORT | FAMILY | This luxury-meets-adventure resort embodies much of Belize's character: cabanas with ragged crowns of thatch, wonderful staff, imperfect beaches, and exquisite water. **Pros:** beloved by many return guests; naturalistic design style; plenty of services. **Cons:** shows a little wear and tear; faraway from San Pedro's culinary scene; expensive on-site restaurant. [$] *Rooms from: BZ$610 ✉ 6 miles (10 km) north of bridge, Ambergris Caye ☎ 226/5096, 800/813–7880 in U.S. 🌐 www.portofino-belize.com 🛏 17 units 🍴 Free breakfast.*

PUR Boutique Cabanas

$$$ | B&B/INN | If design is important to you but you can do without the spacious grounds of colossal resorts, you might try out one of these six adults-only cabanas, which have made a splash in Ambergris's lodging scene with hip luxury on a small scale. **Pros:** gorgeous beds and bathrooms; Taco Bar on-site; sexy, intimate resort. **Cons:** breakfast not included; tiny pool; you might have trouble keeping up with the style. [$] *Rooms from: BZ$410 ✉ 1 mile (1.5 km) north of the bridge, Tres Cocos neighborhood, Ambergris Caye ☎ 226/2050 🌐 www.purboutiquecabanas.com 🛏 6 cabanas 🍴 No meals.*

Seascape Villas

$$$$ | RENTAL | FAMILY | Organic forms characterize these six exotic villas, whose curved walls echo the slate floors that sweep under cathedral ceilings. **Pros:** inspired textures and design; beautiful free-form pool; stunning sea views. **Cons:** no restaurant on-site; very expensive if not split among a group; lacks the service one receives at condos. [$] *Rooms from: BZ$1,100 ✉ Beachfront, 3.5 miles (6 km) north of San Pedro, Ambergris Caye ☎ 226/2119, 888/753–5164 🌐 www.seascapebelize.com 🛏 6 villas 🍴 No meals.*

ⓨ Nightlife

San Pedro has among the most active nightlife scenes in Belize, but don't expect Miami's South Beach. Several in-town spots such as Fido's have live music. There are plenty of spots just to have a cold one, including some classic beach and pier bars like Crazy Canucks and Palapa Bar. (Be careful going back to your hotel in the middle of the night after sampling rums—take a taxi if possible.) Tonier spots like Rojo Bar can be found on North Ambergris, and there's a small, modern casino at Captain Morgan's. Many hotels have bars that mostly draw their own guests, but anyone is welcome. Among the better resort bars are those at Victoria House, Mata Rocks, Sandbar, and Matachica. Karaoke is big in Belize, and some bars and clubs in San Pedro have karaoke nights, which are as much for locals as visitors. In late January and early February, singer Jerry Jeff Walker holds "Camp Belize," two week-long events in San Pedro during which Walker puts on shows for his loyal fans.
⚠ Don't let your taxi driver pick up an extra passenger at night, a common practice that is unsafe. Don't walk on the beach alone at night—it's unlit and can be dangerous.

Captain Morgan's Retreat Casino
CASINOS | The island's best—albeit the only—casino has over 100 slot and video poker machines, plus live table games, poker tournaments, and a full bar with tapas and courtesy drinks. You can try for jackpot until 4 am. Captain Morgan's offers free evening boat transfer from Fido's dock. ✉ *Captain Morgan's Retreat, 3 miles (5 km) north of bridge, Ambergris Caye* ☎ *226/2207* ⊕ *www.captainmorgans.com.*

Crazy Canucks Beach Bar
BARS/PUBS | A lively beachside bar that rocks out until midnight. The popular Trivioke on Fridays is just what it sounds like (trivia then karaoke). Live music here can be thunderous. ✉ *On the beach, South*

Coconut Dr., at Exotic Caye Resort, San Pedro Town* ☎ *670/8001.*

Fido's Courtyard and Pier
BARS/PUBS | Sooner or later you're sure to end up at Fido's (pronounced fee-dough's), sipping something cold and contemplating the sea views, under what the owners claim is the largest thatch palapa in Belize. If not the largest in Belize, it may at least be the largest on Ambergris Caye. This casual joint serves mediocre burgers, Caesar salad, tacos, and other bar food, but it's a good place to grab a beer and enjoy the near-nightly live music. It can also accommodate large groups. ✉ *Barrier Reef Dr., San Pedro Town* ☎ *226/2056.*

Lola's Pub & Grill
BARS/PUBS | Hunker down at this classic expat pub with a tumbler of scotch or a Moscow mule. You can watch games on the TVs or, some nights, get groovy with a jam band. ✉ *Barrier Reef Dr., Ambergris Caye* ✛ *Across from Belize Bank* ☎ *206/2120.*

★ Palapa Bar and Grill
BARS/PUBS | FAMILY | Bring your swimsuit and dunk into the sea (inner tubes are at the ready) at this end-of-pier San Pedro favorite. The thatch-roof and its salt-water backdrop are what draw crowds (although the pulled pork, fish tacos, and ceviche aren't bad for bar food). Hurricane Earl destroyed the former location in 2016, so Palapa's resurrection was welcome to many. After dark, the colorful lighting lends a festive air. Palapa Bar doesn't rock all night, though—it usually closes around 9, 10 at the latest. ✉ *Beachfront, over the water in front of Sandbar, San Pedro Town* ☎ *226/2528* ⊕ *www.palapabarandgrill.com.*

Paradise Theater
FILM | FAMILY | Here is a Belizean take on an American-style cinema, where you can watch first-run or near-first-run movies in air-conditioned comfort and with Dolby 5.1 sound. It's cheap, though

usually only open on weekends. The theater, which has 300- and 125-seat rooms, is also used for live shows and is a favorite among San Pedranos. If you're thirsty, there's a bar. ■TIP➔ If you're staying in town or south and don't want to pay the BZ$10 fee to take your golf cart across the bridge, you can park it on the south side of the bridge and walk over (no toll for pedestrians), as the theater is just a few hundred feet from the bridge. ⊠ North Ambergris, just across bridge, San Pedro Town ☎ 636/8123 ⚏ BZ$10.

★ Rojo Beach Bar & Lounge

BARS/PUBS | This sizzling beachfront bar on North Ambergris is a sceney but casual place to sip a Shark Bite (light rum, coconut rum, Meyer's rum, mango, and pineapple) or knock back some housemade shots until late evening. Delicious shared plates are generous. ⊠ Beachfront, 5 miles (8 km) north of town, at Azul Resort, Ambergris Caye ☎ 226/4012 ⊕ www.rojolounge.com.

Sandbar Beachfront Restaurant

BARS/PUBS | In daytime you can read under expansive umbrellas and sip something blended, while at night you can join the (sometimes rowdy) crowds and play board or drinking games. Fritters and brick-oven pizza make tasty snacks to share. Fun lasts until midnight, but it's island-flexible. ⊠ 7 Boca del Rio Dr., San Pedro Town ☎ 226/2008.

Wahoo's Lounge

BARS/PUBS | On the odd side of the nightlife spectrum is the Chicken Drop, held on Thursday night at the beachfront Wahoo's Lounge. Bet on a numbered square on a sort of giant bingo board, and if the chicken poops on your square, you win the pot. It's hugely popular. ⊠ Spindrift Hotel, Beachfront, Barrier Reef Dr., San Pedro Town ✛ Near Buccaneer St. ☎ 226/2002.

👜 Shopping

Barrier Reef Drive, formerly sandy Front Street, is San Pedro's Street of Shopping Dreams—it's lined with souvenir shops complemented by restaurants, small hotels, banks, and other anchors of tourist life on the island. Stores with more local appeal are on Pescador Drive (Middle Street) and Angel Coral Street (Back Street), especially at the north end of town. Barrier Reef Drive is closed to golf carts and vehicles on weekends, starting around 6 pm Friday, and local vendors set up shop selling locally made jewelry and wood carvings (they're also out during the week in high season). Except for these items, few are made on the island. Most of the souvenir shops sell crafts from Guatemala and Mexico, along with carved wood and slate from the mainland.

Belizean hot sauces, such as Marie Sharp's and Gallon Jug's Lissette Sauce, along with local rums, make great souvenirs; they're cheaper in grocery stores than in gift shops. To avoid worsening the plight of endangered sea life, avoid buying souvenirs made from black coral or turtle shell. Jewelry made from scales of the invasive lionfish, however, does not put strain on the ecosystem.

Vendors on the beach occasionally try to sell you carvings, jewelry, Guatemalan fabrics, and sometimes drugs. Do not buy drugs as the consequences can be higher for foreigners.

For your daily needs, the dusty supermarkets in San Pedro have standard selections. However, grocery prices generally are 20% to 75% higher than in supermarkets in the United States (a bag of Fritos runs BZ$14), except for a few Belizean-produced items, such as rum.

The Belikin Store

GIFTS/SOUVENIRS | Even if you don't love Belize's signature beer, Belikin merchandise makes a distinctive gift. This shiny store even has a "selfie wall." ✉ *10 Coconut Dr., Ambergris Caye ✛ Across from airstrip* ⊕ *www.belikin.com.*

★ Belize Chocolate Company

FOOD/CANDY | Those who dream in chocolate, this one's for you. Owners Chris Beaumont and Jo Sayer have done marvels with one of Belize's most ancient crops. Here, the famous Belizean cacao bean appears not only in bars (like most of the country's chocolatiers) but as champagne truffles, lip balm, and—get ready—chocolate salami. You can also take your cake and chocolate coconut water to the front porch. Expect U.S. chocolatier prices. ✉ *Barrier Reef Dr., Ambergris Caye ✛ Just north of Wild Mangos* ☎ *226/3015* ⊕ *www.belizechocolatecompany.com.*

Belizean Arts

ART GALLERIES | The country's first art gallery, established more than 30 years ago by Londoner Lyndsey Hackston, Belizean Arts today has the largest selection of art by Belizeans and Belize residents, including paintings by Walter Castillo, Pen Cayetano, Nelson Young, Leo Vasquez, Rene Guerra, and others. The gallery also carries ceramics, jewelry, and other crafts. Even if you don't intend to buy, it's worth a look. ✉ *Fido's Courtyard, Barrier Reef Dr., San Pedro Town* ☎ *226/3019* ⊕ *www.belizeanarts.com.*

D & G Fine Jewelry and Art

JEWELRY/ACCESSORIES | Since 1976, this one-person "factory" has crafted beautiful jewelry. If you don't see a design you like, artist Dimas Guerrero will work with you to create one. We encourage you not to buy items made of black coral, which is highly endangered. ✉ *Boca del Rio Dr., San Pedro Town ✛ 1 block north of high school* ☎ *226/2069* ⊕ *ambergriscaye. com/DandG.*

★ Graniel's Dreamland Construction & Cabinet Shop

HOUSEHOLD ITEMS/FURNITURE | At Graniel's Dreamland, the showroom for Armando Graniel's beautiful carpentry, you can find high-quality woodwork, like clam chairs or checkered cutting boards made from tropical hardwoods. Some pieces the shop will break down and package for shipping or for carrying back on the airplane. ✉ *South end of Pescador Dr., San Pedro Town* ☎ *226/2632* ☽ *Closed Sun.*

The Greenhouse

SPECIALTY STORES | The Greenhouse has a trove of good ingredients that may rival Whole Foods for pricey-ness. ✉ *Pescador St., San Pedro Town* ☎ *226/2084.*

Island Supermarket

CONVENIENCE/GENERAL STORES | Island Supermarket has the largest selection of groceries, liquor, beer, and wine along with hot sauces and other souvenir items, though it's not the cheapest place in San Pedro. ✉ *Coconut Dr., south of town, across from Bowen & Bowen Belikin distributors, San Pedro Town* ☎ *226/2972.*

Man O' War Men's Supplies

CONVENIENCE/GENERAL STORES | What are men's supplies? Apparently they include Sperry's topsiders and Star Wars Lego sets. If you forgot anything from an extension cord to anti-chafing powder, this variety store might carry it. ✉ *Caribena St., San Pedro Town.*

Marina's Store

CONVENIENCE/GENERAL STORES | Marina's Store south of town has good prices for groceries but only a small selection. It has longer and later hours than many stores. ✉ *Seagrape Dr., about 1 mile (1.5 km) south of town, San Pedro Town* ☎ *226/3647.*

Mata Grande Grocery

CONVENIENCE/GENERAL STORES | This dependable little store serves residents and condo guests on North Ambergris.

You can order online and Mata Grande will deliver groceries to your vacation rental north of the Boca del Rio bridge. Expect higher prices than in town. ⊠ *4.5 miles (7.5 km) north of bridge, Ambergris Caye* ☎ *226/4290* ⊕ *www.matagrandegrocery.com.*

San Pedro Supermarket
CONVENIENCE/GENERAL STORES | This reasonably priced store delivers groceries, which can also be ordered online, all over San Pedro Town. ⊠ *Lagoon St., at traffic circle at north end of town off Pescador Dr., San Pedro Town* ☎ *226/3446* ⊕ *www.sanpedrosupermarket.com.*

Super Buy
CONVENIENCE/GENERAL STORES | Many local residents buy their groceries at Super Buy, which has lower prices. ⊠ *Angel Coral St., San Pedro Town* ☎ *226/4667.*

Toucan Gift Shops
GIFTS/SOUVENIRS | For gaudy geegaws and unabashedly touristy souvenirs, the Toucan Gift Shops, including Toucan Too, all sporting the bright green, yellow, and red Toucan logo, are hard to miss. ⊠ *Barrier Reef Dr., San Pedro Town* ☎ *226/2499.*

★ 12 Belize
CRAFTS | Shop for chic clutches and totes handmade in southern Belize with Mayan fabric, as well as cacao body whip, soy candles, and other fashionable gifts. You can even buy lionfish-scale earrings. All products are made in Belize. ⊠ *Tarpon St., in Vilma Linda Plaza, San Pedro Town* ⊹ *Look for signs that point to little alley* ☎ *670/5272* ⊕ *www.12belize.com.*

Wine De Vine
WINE/SPIRITS | Wine De Vine has a curated selection of wines and imported cheeses, at prices (due to import taxes) roughly double the cost in the United States. ⊠ *Coconut Dr., San Pedro Town* ☎ *226/3430* ⊕ *www.winedevine.com* ⊗ *Closed Sun.*

Activities

FISHING
Although southern Belize, especially Placencia, is the main sport-fishing center in Belize, Ambergris Caye also has good opportunities for flats, reef, and deep-sea fishing. May to September is the best time for catching tarpon off Ambergris Caye; April to October is the best time for bonefish; and March through May is best for permit. Reef fishing (which is generally not permitted in marine reserves) for snapper, grouper, barracuda, and others is more expensive than flats fishing. Inquire about the cost of deep-sea fishing outside the reef for billfish, sailfish, wahoo, and tuna; a sport-fishing license is now required for game fishing in Belize waters, except for fishing off piers or from shore. You can buy a license online from the Belize Coastal Zone Management Authority and Institute (⊕ *www.coastalzonebelize.org*), or your fishing guide or hotel may be able to help you get it. El Pescador is the leading fishing lodge on Ambergris Caye and one of the top in Belize.

For fishing that's easier on the pocketbook, you can fish for snapper, barracuda, and others from piers and docks on the island. No license is required. Bring your own gear or buy tackle at local hardware stores and ask local anglers about bait. Small sardines work well. For fly-fishing aficionados, there are multiple shops. You can also wade out in the flats near shore on North Ambergris, north of the river channel on the back (west) side, and try your luck with bonefish. Keep an eye out for the occasional crocodile. You'll catch more with a guide and boat, but fishing on your own is inexpensive fun.

FISHING GUIDES
George Bradley
FISHING | Longtime, reputable local guide George Bradley specializes in fly-fishing for bonefish. ⊠ *San Pedro Town* ☎ *226/2179.*

GoFish Belize

FISHING | Local fishing guide Abbie Marin arranges flats, reef, and deep-sea fishing charters. A full day of fly or spin flats fishing runs BZ$990 for one or two persons. Beginners are welcome. ✉ *Boca Del Rio Dr., San Pedro Town* ☎ *226/3121, 703/646–3474 in U.S.* ⊕ *www.gofishbelize.com.*

★ Lori-Ann Murphy

FISHING | Lori-Ann Murphy is an extremely qualified guide and general resource on fishing in Belize. She also owns the Reel Women Fly Fishing Adventures. ✉ *San Pedro Town* ⊕ *www.loriannmurphy.com.*

JET SKIS

Castaway Caye Water Sports

JET SKIING | **FAMILY** | A reputable outfit which lets you ride Jet Skis, waterski, parasail, kayak, or cruise by catamaran. ✉ *Beachfront, at Palapa Bar, San Pedro Town* ☎ *671/3000* ⊕ *www.castawaycaye.com.*

SCUBA DIVING AND SNORKELING

Dives off Ambergris are usually single tank at depths of 50 to 80 feet, allowing about 35 minutes of bottom time. Diving trips run around BZ$100 for a single-tank dive, BZ$160 for a two-tank dive, and BZ$110 for a single-tank night dive. For longer-distance trips, expect to pay around BZ$650 for a three-tank full-day drive trip to Turneffe atoll and BZ$850 for day-trips with three dives to Lighthouse Reef. Dive gear rental is usually extra—a full package of gear including wet suit, buoyancy compensator, regulator, mask, and fins is around BZ$100.

Snorkeling by boat near Ambergris generally costs BZ$90–BZ$110 per person for two or three hours or BZ$180–BZ$200 for a day-trip, including lunch. If you go to Hol Chan Marine Reserve there's a BZ$20 park fee, but this fee is sometimes included in the quoted rate. A snorkel trip to the Blue Hole is around BZ$450–BZ$480, including the BZ$80 Marine Reserve fee. Snorkel gear rental

may be additional. Prices also may not include 12.5% tax. (Businesses are supposed to include the 12.5% GST in their quoted prices, but not all do.) Most dive shops will pick you up at your hotel or at the nearest pier.

■**TIP→ Be careful when snorkeling off docks and piers on Ambergris Caye. There's heavy boat traffic between the reef and shore, and boat captains may not be able to see snorkelers in the water. Several snorkelers near shore have been killed or seriously injured by boats.**

DIVE SHOPS AND OPERATORS

Ambergris is replete with professional, personable, and safety-conscious diving guides. Many dive shops and resorts offer diving courses, both introductory and refreshers. A half-day basic familiarization course or "resort course" costs around BZ$400. A complete four-day PADI open-water certification course costs BZ$950–BZ$1,150. One popular variant is a referral course, where the academic and pool training is done at home, or online, but not the required dives. The cost for two days in Belize is about BZ$650–BZ$800. Prices for dive courses vary a little from island to island, generally being least expensive on Caye Caulker. However, even prices on Ambergris Caye, which tends to have higher costs for most activities, run a little lower than on the mainland.

If you're staying on Ambergris Caye, Glover's Reef is out of the question for a day-trip by boat. Even in perfect weather—which it often isn't—a trip to Lighthouse Reef takes between two and three hours. Most trips to Lighthouse and the Blue Hole depart at 6 am and return at 5:30 or 6 pm, making for a long day in the sun and water. Turneffe is more accessible, though it's still a long and costly day-trip, and you're unlikely to reach the atoll's southern tip, which has the best diving. Consult your hotel or a dive shop for your best options for your time and budget. Most companies include refreshments like soda and fresh fruit to fortify you during the resurface interval.

★ **Amigos del Mar**

FISHING | Established in 1987, Amigos del Mar is perhaps the island's most consistently recommended dive operation. The SSI/SDI facility has a dozen dive boats, various contracted divemasters, and a range of local dives as well as trips to Turneffe Atoll and Lighthouse Reef in a fast 56-foot dive boat. You can choose from a local two-tank dive or a 12-hour trip to the Blue Hole, with rates including the park entry fee and lunch. In addition to various tours, Amigos del Mar offers an open-water certification course, as well as snorkel and fishing trips. ⊠ On pier off Barrier Reef Dr., near Mayan Princess Hotel, San Pedro Town ☎ 226/2706, 800/882–6159 in U.S. ⊕ www.amigos-divebelize.com.

★ **Chuck and Robbie's Scuba Diving and Instruction**

SNORKELING | Playful, considerate, and professional, these guides can safely accommodate every skill level. With four boats of varying lengths for different water conditions, dive trips depart at 9 am and 2 pm daily. They also do snorkel and fishing tours. Two-tank dives begin at BZ$160 before equipment and other fees. ⊠ Boca del Rio Dr., Beachfront, San Pedro Town ☎ 226/4425 ⊕ www.ambergriscayediving.com.

Ecologic Divers

SCUBA DIVING | This PADI shop has won a good reputation for safety, service, and ecologically sound practices. Local two-tank dives go out daily at 9 and 2 and cost BZ$160, not including any equipment rental or tax. Full-day Turneffe trips, which include breakfast and lunch, run BZ$630. They also offer catamaran cruises. ⊠ On pier at north end of San Pedro, just south of The Phoenix resort, San Pedro Town ☎ 226/4118, 800/244–7774 in U.S. and Canada ⊕ www.ecologicdivers.com.

Lil' Alphonse Tours

FISHING | Specializing in snorkeling, Lil' Alphonse himself usually captains the tours, doing a fabulous job of making snorkelers feel comfortable in the water. ⊠ Coconut Dr., across street from Changes in Latitudes B&B, San Pedro Town ☎ 226/3136 ⊕ www.ambergriscaye.com/alfonso.

SEAduced by Belize

SAILING | This locally run and reputable snorkeling, sailing, and inland tour company does full-day snorkeling trips to Bacalar Chico, Hol Chan, Mexico Rocks, and Robles Point, as well as mainland trips to Mayan sites and cave tubing. They offer sailing cruises as well. A 58-foot "beach house" boat with a water slide goes out on festive cruises. It's easy to confuse with SEArious Adventures, but they are different outfits. ⊠ Vilma Linda Plaza, Tarpon St., San Pedro Town ☎ 226/2254 ⊕ www.seaducedbybelize.com.

SEArious Adventures

SAILING | This long-established snorkeling and sailing shop does day snorkel trips to Caye Caulker at around BZ$100 plus park fees and equipment rental, along with a variety of other snorkel and sail trips. It also offers day sails and mainland tours. ⊠ Beachfront, on dock, Between Tarpon and Black Coral Sts., San Pedro Town ☎ 226/4202 ⊕ www.seariousadventures.com.

★ **White Sands Dive Shop**

SCUBA DIVING | White Sands Dive Shop isn't at White Sands Resort but at Las Terrazas. Never mind, this PADI dive center is run by Elbert Greer, a noted diver and birder who has taught scuba in San Pedro for more than 30 years, getting thousands of divers certified. ⊠ Beachfront at Las Terrazas, Ambergris Caye ☎ 226/2405 ⊕ www.whitesandsdiveshop.com.

How to Choose a Dive Master

Many dive masters in Belize are former anglers who began diving on the side and ended up doing it full time. The best have an intimate knowledge of the reef and a superb eye for coral and marine life.

When choosing a dive master or dive shop, first check the Internet. Participants on forums and newsgroups such as ⊕ www.ambergriscaye.com and ⊕ www.scubaboard.com field many questions on diving and dive shops in Belize. On islands where there are multiple dive shops, spend some time talking to dive masters to see which ones make you feel most comfortable. Find out about their backgrounds and experience, as well as the actual crew that would be going out with you. Are they dive masters, instructors, or just crew? Get a sense of how the dive master feels about reef and sea life conservation.

Besides questions about costs and equipment, ask:

■ How many people, maximum, go out on your dive trips?

■ Is there a minimum number of divers before you'll make the trip?

■ What dive sites are your favorites, and why?

■ What kind of boats do you have, and how long does it take to get where we're going?

■ Who is actually in the water with the divers?

■ What kind of safety and communications equipment is on the boat?

■ What's the procedure for cancellation in case of bad weather?

■ How do you decide if you're going out or not?

If you're not comfortable with the answers, or if the dive shop just doesn't pass your sniff test, move on.

DIVE BOATS

If you want to hit the best dive spots in Belize and dive a lot—up to five or six dives a day—live-aboard dive boats may be your best bet. The *Aggressor* Fleet concentrates on dives around Lighthouse Reef atoll and the Blue Hole. The boats are based at the Radisson Fort George Hotel and Marina in Belize City.

Aggressor Fleet

BOATING | The *Aggressor* Fleet operates two luxurious live-aboard yachts, the *Belize Aggressor III* and *Belize Aggressor IV*. Boats cast off on Saturday from Belize City for beautiful week-long trips to Lighthouse Reef, Half Moon Caye, and the Blue Hole, with unlimited dives each day. The *Aggressor IV*, a 138-foot cruiser, can accommodate up to 20 passengers in 10 staterooms, while the *Aggressor III* is slightly smaller. All staterooms are well appointed and have private bathrooms. Both all-inclusive yachts run about BZ$6,400 per person for the week, exclusive of port fees, equipment, and other fine print matters. ⊠ *Radisson Fort George, 2 Marine Parade, Belize City* ☎ *706/993–2531 U.S. office, 800/348–2628 in U.S. and Canada* ⊕ *www.aggressor.com.*

WINDSURFING AND KITESURFING

Caye Caulker is actually better known than Ambergris Caye as a windsurfing destination, perhaps because it attracts a younger crowd , but the winds are equally good and consistent off Ambergris. February through July sees the windiest conditions, with winds 12 to 20 knots most days. Kitesurfing, combining a windsurfing-type board pulled by a large kite, is also available on Ambergris.

KiteXplorer

WINDSURFING | This company has an office in San Pedro as well as Caye Caulker. These folks know kites, and you can trust them to coordinate a good experience whether you're seasoned or just learned the words *windsurfing* and *kitesurfing*. A three-hour intro to kitesurfing costs BZ$380 including equipment and insurance; a basic course over three or four days is BZ$1,150; and supervised equipment rental is BZ$120 an hour. Windsurfing lessons are given at about BZ$100 an hour. ⊠ *Caribbean Villas, Beachfront, 1 mile (1.5 km) south of town, San Pedro Town* ☎ *635/4769, 368/3874* ⊕ *www. kitexplorer.com.*

MAINLAND TOURS

Mainland tours are pricier from the cayes. If tour prices from San Pedro seem too high, you can take a water taxi to Belize City and rent a car or take a cab for your own DIY tour, though the hassle factor might be too high. Many snorkel and scuba operators, such as SEAduced by Belize, offer a full menu of mainland tours.

Tanisha Eco Tours

ECOTOURISM | One of the top San Pedro tour operators for mainland trips, Tanisha specializes in full-day Lamanai trips where you'll boat up the New River past cohune palms en route to the Mayan ruins. This includes a light breakfast, lunch, beer, rum punch, and soft drinks, and costs around BZ$240. Tanisha also offers cave tubing, ziplining, trips to Altun Ha, and other tours. ⊠ *Beachfront, Boca del Rio Dr., San Pedro Town* ✛ *Inside Hurricane's Restaurant* ☎ *226/2314* ⊕ *tanishatours.com.*

WILDLIFE TOURS

★ American Crocodile Education Sanctuary (*ACES*)

BOAT TOURS | FAMILY | After dark, this remarkable nonprofit takes you on a small skiff, the *Swamp Thing*, where you'll help look for the wily red eyes of crocodiles breaking the water. You might even get up close and personal with the apex predators in the name of environmental research. These Eco Croc tours are BZ$100 per person. ⊠ *Elliot Subdivision, San Pedro Town* ✛ *On lagoon side, at Office Bar and Grill* ☎ *623/7920* ⊕ *www. americancrocodilesanctuary.org.*

FOOD TOURS

Belize Food Tours

GUIDED TOURS | Touristy? Sure. Educational and delicious? Yes, and yes. While sampling authentic dishes around San Pedro, you'll learn about Belizean food, from Mayan maize to colonial plantation sugar. Lunch and dinner tours run between BZ$125–$145 per person; cooking classes are on offer at around BZ$160. This local company is family run. ⊠ *Barrier Reef Dr., Ambergris Caye* ☎ *615/1321* ⊕ *www.belizefoodtours.com.*

Caye Caulker

5 miles (8 km) south of Ambergris Caye, 18 miles (29 km) northeast of Belize City.

A half hour away from San Pedro by water taxi and sharing essentially the same reef and sea ecosystems, Caye Caulker is very different from its big sister island, Ambergris Caye. It's smaller (with a population of around 2,000), less developed, cheaper, and deliciously slow. Flowers outnumber cars 1,000 to 1 (golf carts, bicycles, and bare feet are the preferred means of transportation).

As you might guess from all the "no shirt, no shoes, no problem" signs, the living is relatively easy here. This is the kind of place where people give addresses like "near the football field." Caye Caulker has long been a stop on the Central America backpacker trail, and it remains Belize's most popular budget destination, with a nearly eternal high season.

However, it isn't immune to change. A few four- or five-story buildings now tower over the shore, and prices are creeping up. Some upmarket restaurants now pepper the culinary landscape. In 2020, the microbrewery Caribbean Fusion Brewing Company is slated to open, serving guava or pickled pepper beer from 20 taps. Still, Caulker remains quintessentially laid-back, and as development continues at a feverish pace on neighboring Ambergris Caye, Caulker's simpler charms appeal to those who seek an affordable island experience.

For those used to booking everything online, here's a caution about Caye Caulker: some tour operators and cheaper lodging choices don't have websites. In fact, some tour guides work from a spot on the beach and have only a cell phone. Those that are online often have websites done on the cheap, with poor graphics and servers that are down intermittently. Your best bet is often to Facebook message the company directly, or, in the case of tour guides, ask your hotel to make a call.

GETTING HERE AND AROUND

Other than a few emergency vehicles and several private cars, there are few cars on Caye Caulker. Most locals and visitors get around the island's sand streets on foot, although you can rent a golf cart or bike. (Golf-cart taxis charge around BZ$5–BZ$10 per person to most destinations in the village.) Most hotels listed here have complimentary bikes for guests.

Like Ambergris Caye, Caye Caulker can be used as a base for exploring part of the mainland. It's only about 45 minutes by water taxi or 15 minutes by air to Belize City. Two water-taxi companies now offer daily service between Caye

Caulker and Chetumal, Mexico. Tours run from Caulker to the Mayan ruins at Lamanai and Altun Ha, and other tours go to the Belize Zoo and to the Caves Branch River for cave tubing.

Caye Caulker is a fairly small island, only 5 miles (8 km) long and a little more than 1 mile (2 km) wide at the widest point—most of the island is only a few hundred feet wide. All the streets on the island are hard-packed sand. On the east side you can also walk along the beachfront. Generally, the north end of the village bustles more than the primarily residential south end, which is home to the airstrip. The island itself is divided by "the Split," a small channel of water separating the north area and the south area. The area north of the Split is still chiefly mangroves and lagoons, accessible only by boat, though mangroves are giving way to development. The single village occupies most of the area south of the Split. From the Split to the airstrip, which is at the south end of the island, is about a mile (2 km). When you're told directions, things are either north or south of the main public pier.

TIMING

Caye Caulker's low-key charms take a while to fully appreciate. Stay here a day, and you'll complain that there's nothing to do. Stay a week, and you'll probably tell everyone how much you hate overdeveloped islands like Ambergris.

SAFETY

Several high-profile muggings, rapes, and stabbings of visitors have brought Caulker unwanted attention. Despite these crimes, Caye Caulker remains one of the safest places in Belize. Just don't bring the barfly back to your room or wander around dark alleys at night. Also, keep your camera, wallet, and other possessions close to you, especially in cheaper hotels.

As Caulker grows in popularity, more street vendors aggressively solicit and hawk, which becomes mingled with street harrassment. These encounters can make walking, particularly near the Split, unpleasant. Female tourists are especially likely to be harrassed. When asked to stop, most people are responsive and will cease.

🍴 Restaurants

Once your dining choice on Caulker was fish, fish, or fish, but now you can also enjoy Italian, Mexican, and Chinese, as well as wonderful fresh conch and lobster and, of course, fish. Several restaurants serve wholesome natural foods and vegetarian dishes. Prices for meals here are generally lower than on Ambergris; even a lobster dinner usually sets you back less than BZ$45. The cheapest way to eat on the island is to buy grilled fish, chicken, lobster, and other items from the folks with barbecue grills who set up along the main street and elsewhere. Though you should use good judgment, the food is almost always well prepared and safe to eat. Locals also sell meat pies, tacos, tamales, cakes, and other homemade items at very low prices. Do what local people do and buy your snacks and some of your meals from these street vendors.

The following restaurants are located either in the village of Caye Caulker (south of the Split, where 99% of options are), at the Split, or north of the Split, which currently has only one main option, the newfangled Koko King.

CAYE CAULKER VILLAGE
Amor y Café
$ | CAFÉ | FAMILY | Here is the island's classic spot for a warm smile, coffee (including espresso and lattes), and a morning bite to eat. Sit on the front porch, people-watch on Front Street, and try the homemade yogurt or the yummy fresh breads. **Known for:** waffles with fruit; iced coffee with coffee cubes; Sunday-morning vibes, whatever the day. $ Average

Tip

As on San Pedro, Caye Caulker's main streets are popularly known as "Front," "Middle," and "Back"—Front Street running along the sea and Back Street running on the lagoon (back) side. On maps, however, different names are in use. "Front Street" is Avenida Hicaco (also Playa Asunción). "Middle Street" is Avenida Langosta. "Back Street" is Avenida Mangle.

main: BZ$10 ⊠ Av. Hicaco ✛ Down the street from Hibisca ☎ 610/2397 ☉ No dinner.

★ **Ana's Aladdin Cuisine** (*Ana's Genie Cuisine*)
$$ | MIDDLE EASTERN | FAMILY | Near the tip of the island, this gem is hidden in plain sight. Tuck into a plate of stove-fresh pita, creamy hummus, and skewers of onion-parsley shrimp grilled in a boat of foil, all made by the charming chef Ana. **Known for:** garlic chicken wraps; vegetarian and vegan options; a frill-free setting near the Split. $ Average main: BZ$18 ⊠ Av. Hicaco ✛ By the Split ☎ 605/3305 ☉ Closed Mon. ▤ No credit cards.

Caribbean Colors Arts Café
$ | CAFÉ | FAMILY | For a good cup of coffee and a splash of color, this little café cum art gallery in the heart of Front Street is the place to go. Owner and longtime expat artist Lee Vanderwalker sells her painted canvases and silks here. **Known for:** local art; bagels (rare in Belize); good coffee. $ Average main: BZ$14 ⊠ Av. Hicaco ✛ One block down from Island Magic ☎ 605/9242 ⊕ caribbeancolorsbelize.com ☉ Closed Thurs. No dinner.

★ **Errolyn's House of Fry Jacks**
$ | LATIN AMERICAN | Fry jacks are those puffy pillows of fried dough served at breakfast; here they come stuffed with

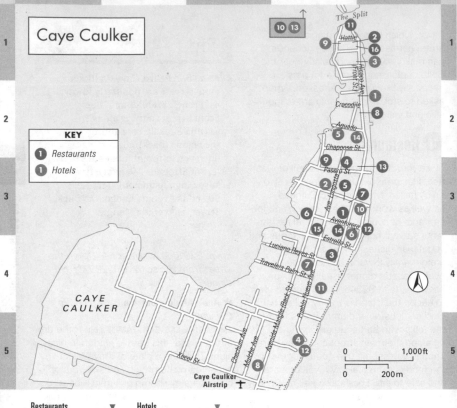

Caye Caulker

KEY
- 🔴 Restaurants
- ⚫ Hotels

a slew of options, from egg and ham to chicken and beans, all for a buck or two. Just one makes a good meal. At the stand next door you can get a liter of fresh watermelon juice (in a repurposed Crystal bottle) for BZ$5. **Known for:** quick counter service; cheap eats; chicken- and cheese-stuffed fry jacks. [$] *Average main: BZ$4* ✉ *Pasero St. at Av. Langosta* ⏲ *Closed Mon. No dinner* 💳 *No credit cards.*

Food Republic

$$ | **SEAFOOD** | **FAMILY** | Dining under fairy lights and a shaggy thatch roof is a wonderful way to conclude your day on Caulker. Seafood is the rage at this remodeled palapa restaurant, and there's an iced display of the catch of the day; choose from snapper, grouper, barracuda, or lobster and have it grilled on the spot. **Known for:** big portions; elaborate fruity cocktails; lovely ambience inland from the water. [$] *Average main: BZ$26* ✉ *Calle del Sol* ✣ *Behind Hibisca* ☎ *206/0600.*

Glenda's Café

$ | **CAFÉ** | **FAMILY** | Glenda's menu is on a chalkboard, short and sweet, and you place your order at the window of a pretty clapboard house. At breakfast, when this café is most popular, you can get a hearty meal of eggs, bacon, beans, johnnycakes, and fresh OJ, all for a pittance. **Known for:** fresh cinnamon buns; a cheap full-order breakfast; homey atmosphere. [$] *Average main: BZ$8* ✉ *Av. Mangle* ✣ *North of post office* ☎ *226/0148* 💳 *No credit cards* ⏲ *Closed Sun. and sometimes other days. No dinner.*

Hibisca by Habanero's

$$$ | **FUSION** | One of the foodie highlights on Caye Caulker, Hibisca (formerly Habanero's) tends to get mixed reactions: one guest goes gaga over the rain-forest snapper and loves the mood lighting, while another sniffs at the cinnamon-spiced pork chop and thinks the restaurant is too dark. But by and large, Hibisca is beloved. **Known for:** delicious marinated meats; big portions; candlelit veranda. [$] *Average main: BZ$46* ✉ *Calle del Sol at Av. Hicaco* ✣ *One block north of Pasta Per Caso* ☎ *626/4911* ⏲ *No lunch. Closed Thurs. and Sept. and Oct.*

Ice n' Beans

$ | **CAFÉ** | **FAMILY** | If you're jonesing for a caffeinated treat—maybe a Nutella frappe or a cappucino—look no further. Ice n' Beans is your quick seafront coffee bar where tasty samples are dished out to anyone who walks up. **Known for:** java chip frappe with organic Belizean beans; friendly faces; beachfront hammocks. [$] *Average main: BZ$8* ✉ *Playa Ascunción* ✣ *Next to Margarita Mike's* ☎ *662/5089.*

Il Pellicano Cucina Italiana

$$$ | **ITALIAN** | Lush palms, lamplight, and blooms of burning love flowers all make for a seductive ambience on an island where you expect picnic tables and sand floors. Il Pellicano features classics like risotto, gnocchi, and margherita pizza (not fresh mozzarella, but better than the island's average), with imported rarities like capers and porcini mushrooms. **Known for:** alfresco dining in a gorgeous, jungle-like garden; live music on a small outdoor stage; rich lasagna. [$] *Average main: BZ$36* ✉ *Back side of island, Pasero St.* ✣ *Past Atlantic Bank on right—enter around corner* ☎ *226/0660* 🌐 *www.ilpellicano.bz* ⏲ *Closed Mon. No lunch.*

The Magic Grill Restaurant & Bar

$$ | **ECLECTIC** | **FAMILY** | Cheesy name aside, Magic Grill is a delightful, breezy perch where you can dine on treehouse-like levels of a palapa overlooking the Caribbean. Okra snapper, sesame-seed shrimp, and Belizean comfort food are on offer, but the real draw is the dreamy setting. **Known for:** creative seafront seating; playful garnishes; cocktails served in fresh coconuts. [$] *Average main: BZ$30* ✉ *Beachfront, Playa Asunción* ✣ *At Island Magic Beach Resort* ☎ *226/0505* 🌐 *www.islandmagicbelize.com/dining.*

★ Namaste Café

$ | **CAFÉ** | After a pineapple-ginger-lime smoothie in this restful thatch café, pop up to the rooftop at 9 am for drop-in yoga. What better way to start your island day? **Known for:** 9 am by-donation yoga classes Monday–Saturday with RandOM Yoga; Belizean drip coffee and homemade kombucha; open-air atmosphere. [$] *Average main: BZ$12* ✉ *Pasero St.* ☎ *637/4109* 🌐 *namastecafebelize.com.*

★ Pasta Per Caso

$$ | **ITALIAN** | From the moment you walk under the leafy trellis, the Milanese hosts of this classic nook will make you feel at home. Choose one of two fabulous nightly pastas (one vegetarian, one meat; you won't go wrong with either), and sip Chianti underneath DIY lampshades made from colanders. **Known for:** gorgeous handmade pasta; panna cotta for dessert; charismatic hosts. [$] *Average main: BZ$28* ✉ *Next block south from Hibisca and Bondi Bar* ☎ *602/6670.*

Reina's

$$ | **CARIBBEAN** | At any given time, two or three generations staff this family-run outdoor eatery, which serves some of the best pineapple shrimp and curry chicken on Caulker. You'll sit under fluorescent lights with feet in the sand, while your dinner sizzles behind you in a tiny kitchenette. **Known for:** mango BBQ chicken; wholesome family dining; local flavor at local prices. [$] *Average main: BZ$18* ✉ *Av. Langosta* ☎ *622/4014.*

THE SPLIT

The Split functions as a type of tropical town plaza on Caye Caulker. Local kids sip Cokes on the seawall and jump into the water while tourists play volleyball in the sand. Until recently the Split's only real option was the Lazy Lizard, but a plethora of businesses have now cropped up, including a pizza joint, a smoothie shop, and a sweets shop, where you can buy a fancy donut for BZ$9. It's shinier than it used to be (and bigger, the backside being filled with sand), but the Split is still the place for gathering with friends.

Lazy Lizard Bar & Grill

$$ | **AMERICAN** | "Sunny place for shady people" is the old-time slogan of the Lazy Lizard, the hangout that still reigns at the ever-happening Split. During the day, wade with some friends into the Caribbean with a icy bucket of Belikins, and at night, jump off the high rickety diving platform. **Known for:** daytime cocktails; spring-break vibes; prime spot for cooling off. [$] *Average main: BZ$28* ✉ *The Split* ☎ *226/0655* 🌐 *www.lazylizardbarandgrill.com.*

Sip n' Dip Beach Bar

$$ | **ECLECTIC** | **FAMILY** | The newer, quieter, more family-friendly competitor of Lazy Lizard, Sip n' Dip is a playful spot to kick it with your feet in the water, rum punch in hand. Though the swimming here is not as good or deep as it is at the Lizard, you're a stone's throw from that area; plus the inner tubes and underwater swings make up for it. **Known for:** a long and pleasant pier; hammocks in the water; cheap-ish beer and rum. [$] *Average main: BZ$22* ✉ *The Split* ☎ *600/0080* 🕒 *Closed Mon. No dinner.*

NORTH OF THE SPLIT

At present, the area north of the Split is reachable only by boat. The only noteworthy hangout thataways is also the island's most buzzing, and definitely worth your time.

★ Koko King

$$$ | **ECLECTIC** | **FAMILY** | Don't come here for an hour, come for the day—and bring friends. Picture paradise with an immaculate beach, "VIP" daybeds for rent, and a bustling restaurant perched over the lagoon. **Known for:** the walk-in beach you've been looking for; "dirty" edamame and garlic shrimp; monthly Full Moon Parties. [$] *Average main: BZ$40* ✉ *North of the Split, on the lagoon side* ✣ *Ferry leaves from the Water Jets dock on the*

west end of Calle del Sol, two blocks west of Plaza Hotel ☎ *661/5656.*

Hotels

Caye Caulker has more than 60 hotels, mostly intimate places with no more than a dozen rooms. Many hotels built in the last decade or so are constructed of concrete, but some, like Yocamatsu and Oasi, are built with quaint clapboard siding, the old style. Almost all properties now have air-conditioning. Lodging options in Caulker are slowly trending more chic and savvy (see Barefoot Hotel, Weezie's, and We'Yu Boutique Hotel). **■ TIP→ Many hotels on the island offer your seventh night free, so be sure to check before you book.**

Barefoot Caye Caulker Hotel

$$$ | HOTEL | If you want to forgo island charm in favor of sleek, modern comfort, this striking hotel right in the heart of town might be for you. **Pros:** modern designs; in the heart of town; Belizean owned. **Cons:** "Barefoot" feels like a misnomer; high rates for Caulker; may need earplugs at night. [$] *Rooms from: BZ$400* ✉ *Playa Asunción* ☎ *671/3668* 🌐 *www.barefoothotelbelize.com* 🛏 *13 rooms* 🍴 *No meals.*

Caye Caulker Plaza Hotel

$ | HOTEL | A practical, recently updated option with decent rates, this classic hotel hosts mainland businesspeople and foreign embassy workers. **Pros:** modern hotel in the center of village; good rates; well managed. **Cons:** not beachfront; no pool; less local flavor. [$] *Rooms from: BZ$185* ✉ *Av. Langosta at Calle del Sol* ☎ *226/0780* 🌐 *www.cayecaulkerplazahotel.com* 🛏 *51 rooms* 🍴 *No meals.*

CayeReef Beachfront Boutique Condo Hotel

$$$ | RENTAL | FAMILY | With private terraces and Belizean artworks, CayeReef is an older condotel gone boutique, right down to the handcrafted soaps. **Pros:** recently updated condo apartments; space to spread out; central location. **Cons:** pricey for Caulker; pool feels towered over by concrete; not especially unique rooms. [$] *Rooms from: BZ$420* ✉ *Playa Asunción at Park St., near Split* ☎ *226/0382* 🌐 *www.cayereef.com* 🛏 *6 units* 🍴 *No meals.*

★ Colinda's Cabañas

$ | B&B/INN | FAMILY | No concrete here, just quaint wooden cabanas with the blue-yellow coloring of a queen angelfish at one of most popular and well-run spots on the island. **Pros:** a hammocked, Caribbean paradise; affable managers and staff; wonderfully affordable. **Cons:** you might miss having a pool; bugs seem to like it; often fully booked. [$] *Rooms from: BZ$160* ✉ *On beach south of town,* ✣ *Near Anchorage Resort* ☎ *226/0383* 🌐 *www.colindacabanas.com* 🛏 *14 rooms* 🍴 *No meals.*

★ Iguana Reef Inn

$$$ | HOTEL | FAMILY | A collection of sturdy, sand-color buildings fanned by mature palms, this is one of Caye Caulker's most upscale lodgings. **Pros:** attractive, well-designed lodging; friendly staff; away from the hubbub of Front Street. **Cons:** on back side of island; expensive for Caulker; heavy on the concrete. [$] *Rooms from: BZ$390* ✉ *Near north end of Av. Langosta* ✣ *Next to soccer field* ☎ *226/0213* 🌐 *www.iguanareefinn.com* 🛏 *15 rooms* 🍴 *Free breakfast.*

Island Magic Beach Resort

$$ | HOTEL | FAMILY | In light seafoam or teal tones, these rooms are dependable; but the more seductive places to spend time are the swinging deck chairs, your private balcony, or the coral-pink loungers beside one of the island's nicest pools. **Pros:** well-run hotel that's good for families; close to everything; Belizean owned. **Cons:** reasonable but not mega bargain rates; uninspired decor; concrete is unappealing. [$] *Rooms from: BZ$260* ✉ *Av. Hicaco* ☎ *226/0505* 🌐 *www.islandmagicbelize.com* 🛏 *20 rooms* 🍴 *No meals.*

★ Maxhapan Cabañas

$ | **B&B/INN** | **FAMILY** | Shaded by breadfruit trees and coconut palms, this sandy spot is away from the water but makes up for it by being neat and clean and a fine value. **Pros:** Belizean owned; darling cabanas have all the amenities you need; such a bargain. **Cons:** not on the water and no pool; somewhat buggy; modest furnishings. [$] *Rooms from: BZ$142* ✉ *55 Av. Pueblo Nuevo* ✣ *In center of village, south of main public pier* ☎ *226/0118* 🛏 *3 units* 🍴 *No meals.*

★ Oasi

$$ | **B&B/INN** | **FAMILY** | Crossing Oasi's picket fence feels like stepping into a jungle garden; just beyond, four lovely studio apartments are calming and exotic. **Pros:** excellent price for the experience; leafy, hibiscus-filled grounds; low-key bar in the evening. **Cons:** not on the water and no sea views; a walk to the action; small kitchens. [$] *Rooms from: BZ$210* ✉ *9 Av. Mangle* ☎ *226/0384* 🌐 *www.oasi-holidaysbelize.com* 🛏 *4 units* 🍴 *No meals; Free breakfast.*

★ Sea Dreams Hotel

$$ | **B&B/INN** | **FAMILY** | Darling rooms surround a venerable banyan tree and courtyard at this Caulker classic, a gem for those seeking a flowered hideaway with a private lagoon pier. **Pros:** convenient location near the Split; ideal for anglers; warm owners and atmosphere. **Cons:** a small walk to the beach; fewer views than beachside hotels; sometimes booked out. [$] *Rooms from: BZ$255* ✉ *Hattie St.* ✣ *Near the Split* ☎ *226/0602* 🌐 *www.seadreamsbelize.com* 🛏 *10 units* 🍴 *Free breakfast.*

★ Seaside Cabanas

$$ | **B&B/INN** | **FAMILY** | Warm in ambience and in attitude, this orange zest-colored inn is arranged snugly around a freshwater pool. **Pros:** sunny decor; feels private despite prime location; good rates for an island that's getting pricier. **Cons:** beach swimming in front of hotel is not good; not actually individual cabanas; bikes and canoes are for rent instead of complimentary. [$] *Rooms from: BZ$280* ✉ *Av. Hicaco, at main public pier* ☎ *226/0498* 🌐 *www.seasidecabanas.com* 🛏 *18 units* 🍴 *Free breakfast.*

Treetops Guesthouse

$ | **B&B/INN** | **FAMILY** | Austrian-born owner Doris Creasey brings an eccentric flair and Teutonic cleanliness to this three-story colonial-style guesthouse, set back a ways from the sea. **Pros:** meticulously clean and well run; affordable rooms; quiet location near the water. **Cons:** some guests complain about fairly strict rules; prices have increased; not in the heart of town. [$] *Rooms from: BZ$175* ✉ *Beachfront, Playa Asunción* ✣ *South of main public pier* ☎ *226/0240* 🌐 *www.treetopsbelize.com* 🛏 *6 units* 🍴 *No meals.*

Weezie's Oceanfront Hotel and Garden Cottages

$$ | **B&B/INN** | **FAMILY** | Framed by coral hibiscus and royal palms, this tranquil inn has shipshape rooms tucked away from the tourists but in the company of green iguanas. **Pros:** decent rates; pool, private pier, and spa by the sea; beautiful, compact grounds. **Cons:** few rooms with sea views; a walk to most restaurants; very limited beach. [$] *Rooms from: BZ$330* ✉ *Playa Asunción* ☎ *226/0603, 970/376–2167 in U.S.* 🌐 *www.weeziescayecaulker.com* 🛏 *13 rooms* 🍴 *No meals.*

We'Yu Boutique Hotel

$$ | **B&B/INN** | **FAMILY** | Attached to Koko King, the rooms at We'Yu—as well composed as a craft daiquiri—are at once off the beaten path and in the heart of Caulker's most buzzing destination. **Pros:** sweetly designed rooms; friendly rates for the superior location; full-time access to the mini-paradise of Koko King. **Cons:** a boat ride to the village and other restaurants; Koko King can get crowded; still-young vegetation makes the waterfront feel sparse. [$] *Rooms from: BZ$275* ✉ *North of the Split, on the lagoon side* ✣ *Ferry leaves from the Water Jets dock on the west end of Calle del Sol, two*

blocks west of Plaza Hotel ☎ *674/1234* 🌐 *www.weyuhotel.com* 🛏 *10 rooms* 🍴 *Free breakfast.*

Yocamatsu Caribbean Bed and Breakfast
$$ | **B&B/INN** | Inland from the sea, this mellow B&B, draped with golden trumpet vines and oleander, offers personal service to a T. The friendly owner and manager make sure you enjoy your trip to Belize, so they'll even lend a hand with logistics and planning your vacation. **Pros:** warm hosts; lush, flowery setting and rooftop views of sea and village; plenty of privacy. **Cons:** not seafront; rooms don't catch sea breezes; shady area keeps some rooms darkish during the day. [$] *Rooms from: BZ$300* ✉ *Chapoose St.* ✣ *Access through football field* ☎ *615/2653* 🌐 *www.yobelize.com* 🛏 *3 rooms* 🍴 *Free breakfast.*

VACATION HOME RENTALS

A large number of privately owned homes are available for rent on the island, either daily or by the week. Rates vary, but hover around BZ$120–BZ$250 a night or BZ$800–BZ$2,000 a week. Airbnb is the most popular booking platform for room and home rentals (🌐 *www.airbnb.com*).

Caye Caulker Vacation Homes (🌐 *www.cayecaulkerrentals.com* ☎ *630/1008*), formerly Caye Caulker Rentals, is the largest vacation-home rental source on the island. It manages a number of cottages from BZ$130 a night, plus 9% tax. Small beachfront houses start at around BZ$1,300 a week.

🍸 Nightlife

You don't come to Caye Caulker for the hot nightlife, but the island does have its share of laid-back bars and late-night gallavanting. The most famous spot is the Lazy Lizard, while a newer complement is the nearby Sip n' Dip (*see Restaurants*). There are also a couple joints away from the water to hang out post-sunset.

Bondi Bar & Bistro
CAFES—NIGHTLIFE | All kinds of hip, this bar pops with texture, from repurposed-tire tables to stamped-tin walls. Killer cocktails, like a mango mojito or raspberry mint lemonade, are a big draw. The dinner menu is as eclectic as the ambience, with Taco Tuesdays and popular Sushi Fridays, plus a smattering of bar food. Monday and Wednesday are movie nights in their little outdoor cinema. On DJ nights the scene gets groovy. ✉ *Av. Hicaco* ✣ *Down the block from Hibisca* ☎ *226/0610.*

I&I Reggae Bar
MUSIC CLUBS | Knock back a *campechana* or two to the beat of reggae jams at this three-story, red-green-yellow mainstay, which has been going strong for more than 30 years. Swings hang from the ceiling in lieu of barstools, and the top floor has hammocks and a thatch roof. The second floor is for dancing, often with a live DJ. This is the kind of joint that gives out prizes of thongs and nail polish on Ladies' Night. ✉ *Av. Langosta at Luciano Reyes St.* ✣ *South of public pier. Go south on Av. Hicaco to dead end, then turn right* ☎ *633/3126* 🎟 *BZ$5 some nights.*

🛍 Shopping

You won't find nearly as many shops here as in San Pedro, but there are a few standout stores to poke around in for some interesting souvenirs. Every day, vendors set up along Front Street north of the main public pier, selling handmade crafts and souvenirs. Some vendors can be pretty aggressive—ignore them and buy from someone else.

Belize Chocolate Company
FOOD/CANDY | A second outpost of the fabulous chocolatier, here you can pick up Belizean coconut milk chocolate for friends—or yourself. The chocolate-covered sponge taffy is an airy yet dense delight. ✉ *Av. Hicaco* ✣ *Next to*

Bambooze ☎ 226/0015 ⊕ www.belize-chocolatecompany.com ☾ Closed Sun.

Caribbean Colors
ART GALLERIES | This gallery sells prints, handpainted silk, and other works by Lee Vanderwalker, as well as handmade jewelry and scarves by local artists. The small café serves tasty coffee and eclectic breakfast and lunch dishes. ✉ *Av. Hicaco ⊹ Down the block from Island Magic ☎ 226/0208 ⊕ caribbeancolorsbelize.com ☾ Closed Thurs.*

Chan's Market
CONVENIENCE/GENERAL STORES | Chan's is a popular supermarket in the village. Pick up your basic groceries and Marie Sharp's hot sauce here. ✉ *Av. Langosta at Calle del Sol ☎ 226/0165.*

Island Sky Supermarket
FOOD/CANDY | Get your boat snacks, Travellers rum, and kitschy magnets at this dependable store, open daily until late. ✉ *Av. Hicaco.*

★ **Little Blue Gift Shop**
CRAFTS | Enter through the blue-picket gate to discover curated goods and crafts all made in Belize. Paintings by Belizean artists can be found here. The owner, Jessie Wigh (who also runs Namaste Café), writes the charming Caye Boy series, children's books about the joys of growing up on Caye Caulker. ✉ *Av. Hicaco ⊹ Next to Anwar Tours ☎ 637/4109.*

 Activities

When you see the waves whiten at the Barrier Reef just a few hundred yards from the shore, boats full of eager snorkelers and divers, and striped sails of windsurfers dashing back and forth, you know you've come to the right place for water play. You can dive, snorkel, and fish the same areas that you can from San Pedro, but usually for a little less dough. However, one area where Caulker suffers by comparison with Ambergris is in the quality of beaches. Caulker's beaches,

though periodically nourished by dredging to replenish the sand, are modest at best, mostly narrow ribbons of sand with shallow water near the shore and, in places, a mucky sea bottom and lots of sea grass. You'll also glimpse the reality of plastic-ridden oceans, getting more and more dire, in the speckles of plastic that appear like seashells in the sand.

You can, however, have a wonderful swim from the end of piers or at the Split, a channel originally cut through the island by Hurricane Hattie in 1961 and expanded over the years, at the north end of the village. The water remains tepid and inviting.

FISHING
Caye Caulker was a fishing village before it was a visitor destination. From Caulker you can fly-fish for bonefish or permit in the grass flats behind the island, troll for barracuda or grouper inside the reef, or charter a boat to take you to blue water outside the reef for deep-sea fishing. Ambergris Caye offers more options for chartering boats for deep-sea fishing than Caye Caulker. If you're a do-it-yourself type, you can fish off the piers or in the flats. Anglers Abroad has a small fly-fishing and tackle shop where you can rent fishing gear if you didn't bring your own. Blue marlin weighing more than 400 pounds have been caught beyond the reef off Caye Caulker, along with big sailfish, pompano, and kingfish. Remember, you now need a fishing license to fish in Belize waters, except from shore or piers. Your guide or hotel can help you get a license.

★ **Anglers Abroad**
FISHING | Haywood Curry, a transplanted Texan, and his crew run all types of fishing trips, starting with half-day trips at around BZ$500 for two persons and, "for the adventurous," two- or three-day camping and fishing expeditions, in which you'll stay on a remote caye. Anglers Abroad, associated with Sea Dreams Hotel, also has a fly-fishing and

tackle shop. ⊠ *At Sea Dreams Hotel near the Split, Hattie St.* ☎ *226/0602* ⊕ *www. anglersabroad.com.*

Tsunami Adventures

FISHING | FAMILY | Tsunami Adventures offers reef and flats fishing trips starting at BZ$500 total for a half day for up to four persons, including boat and guide. Tsunami also offers snorkeling, mainland tours, and a scenic flight over the Blue Hole—the whole shebang (except scuba diving). ⊠ *Playa Asunción* ✛ *Near main public pier* ☎ *226/0462* ⊕ *www.tsunami-adventures.com.*

MANATEE SPOTTING

Several operators do boat trips to see West Indian manatees. The 9,000-acre Swallow Caye Wildlife Sanctuary is home to many of these mammals and is just ten minutes by boat from Caye Caulker. It's illegal in Belize to get into the water with the gentle sea cows, but a few tour operators unfortunately do permit it. Half-day tours typically cost around BZ$100 per person, including the BZ$10 sanctuary admission fee. Some stop at Goff's Caye, which has excellent snorkeling.

Carlos Tours

SNORKELING | Carlos Ayala's outfit Carlos Tours, one of the most recommended tour operators on the island, runs snorkeling trips with stops at some of the best snorkel spots near Caye Caulker, and also at Hol Chan Marine Reserve and elsewhere, along with manatee-spotting tours. Prices vary according to the destination but range from around BZ$80 to BZ$175 per person. ⊠ *Av. Hicaco* ✛ *near Amor Y Café* ☎ *600/1654* ✉ *carlosaya@ gmail.com.*

★ Caveman Snorkeling Tours

SNORKELING | FAMILY | Caveman and staff are known for sensitivity to the marine ecosystem, playful attitudes, and vigilance in giving you the best experience. A day-long manatee-watching tour, combined with snorkeling spots, is about BZ$180 per person, including lunch, gear, and park fees. Caveman has a very navigable website and booking options. ⊠ *Av. Hicaco* ✛ *On water, north of Ice n' Beans.*

SAILING

Touring the aquatic world is certainly made more special by the elegance of sails. A few small sailboats offer sailing and snorkeling trips to nearby areas. One company, Raggamuffin Tours, also offers multiday combination sailing, snorkeling, and camping trips to Placencia.

★ Blackhawk Sailing

FISHING | FAMILY | Captain "Big Steve" offers adventurous snorkeling, overnight camping, and charter trips on a 32-foot vintage sailboat, the *Seahawk*, made in the fishing village of Sarteneja, Belize. ⊠ *Av. Hicaco* ✛ *Next to De Real Macaw* ☎ *607/0323* ⊕ *www.blackhawksailing-tours.com.*

★ Raggamuffin Tours

CAMPING—SPORTS-OUTDOORS | With a fleet of five beautiful sailboats, Raggamuffin offers sunset, moonlight, and day sails, but the winner is a two-night/three-day camping and sailing trip south to Dangriga, with nights at Rendezvous Caye and Raffa Caye, at BZ$900 per person, including meals, reserve fees, gear, and taxes. (On Ragga Caye, guests have the option to upgrade to a cabana.) These normally depart Caulker twice a week, on Tuesday and Friday, weather permitting. Raggamuffin also offers standard snorkeling tours. ⊠ *Av. Hicaco* ✛ *North of main public pier, near the Split* ☎ *226/0348* ⊕ *www.raggamuffintours.com.*

SCUBA DIVING AND SNORKELING

The Hol Chan Cut, part of the enormous Hol Chan Marine Reserve, *(see Ambergris Caye section, above)* is a popular destination for snorkel and dive trips from Caye Caulker. At Hol Chan you can swim with nurse sharks and stingrays and see hundreds of tropical fish, some quite large due to the no-fishing restrictions in the reserve zone. On the way, your boat may be followed by a pod of frolicking dolphins, and you may spot sea turtles or even a manatee. Larger boats from Caulker also go to Lighthouse Reef, including the Blue Hole, and Turneffe atolls.

The Caye Caulker Marine Reserve north and east of Caye Caulker, with its coral canyons, is a favorite of divers, especially for night dives. Caulker has its own mini version of San Pedro's Shark-Ray Alley, called Shark-Ray Village.

A plethora of dive and snorkel operators offer reef tours (some of them are "cowboys"—unaffiliated and unreliable—so make sure you use a reputable company). Plan on spending about BZ$70 for a snorkel trip around the island or BZ$130–BZ$140 for a five-hour snorkel trip to Hol Chan Marine Reserve.

Local two-tank reef dives typically begin at BZ$180, and those to Hol Chan or other nearby areas cost more. If you stop at Half Moon Caye, there's an additional BZ$80 park fee. At Hol Chan, the park fee is BZ$20, and at Caye Caulker Marine Reserve, BZ$10. These park fees, which apply for divers and snorkelers, are sometimes not included in the quoted prices for dive and snorkel trips. The 12.5% Goods and Services Tax (GST) may—or may not—be included in the price you're quoted. There are sometimes fine-print costs. Ask, to be sure.

Anwar Tours

SNORKELING | FAMILY | Anwar Tours, run by brothers Erico and Javier Novelo, offers a variety of snorkel trips starting around BZ$80. A night snorkel tour is BZ$100. Anwar also provides manatee-watching and a slew of mainland Mayan site and adventure tours. ☒ *Av. Hicaco at Pasero St.* ☎ *226/0327* ⊕ *anwartours.page.tl.*

★ Belize Diving Services

SCUBA DIVING | FAMILY | Established in 1978, the reputable Belize Diving Services trains hundreds of divers a year, with a full PADI or SDI open-water course for around BZ$1,250. BDS excels at organization, and they have a complete diving schedule. A two-tank local reef dive is BZ$190, not including gear and tax. A two-tank Turneffe North (not Elbow) trip runs around BZ$340 plus all the fixings. You may pay a slight premium for the service, but their reputation is well-deserved. ☒ *Chapoose St.* ✛ *Near soccer field and Iguana Reef Inn* ☎ *226/0143, 888/869–0233 in U.S.* ⊕ *www.belizedivingservices.com.*

Frenchie's Diving Services

SCUBA DIVING | FAMILY | Frenchie's, a respected local operator, has three experienced instructors and seven divemasters. Their three-dive, full-day trip to the Blue Hole, including gear, breakfast, lunch, BZ$80 park fee, and tax, is BZ$620 per person for divers and BZ$350 for snorkelers. Four-day PADI open-water certification courses run BZ$800. They also offer an overnight at Half Moon Caye, plus a menu of other fantastic sites with professional dive masters. If visiting in high season, book ahead because Frenchie's is popular. ☒ *Beachfront* ✛ *On dock north of main public pier* ☎ *226/0234* ⊕ *www.frenchiesdivingbelize.com.*

★ Raggamuffin Tours

SNORKELING | FAMILY | Take a wonderful three-stop, full-day snorkeling trip off a sailboat to Hol Chan for around BZ$140 including park entrance fee, gear and tax, lunch, and rum and ceviche on the way home. ☒ *Av. Hicaco* ☎ *226/0348* ⊕ *www.raggamuffintours.com.*

WINDSURFING AND KITESURFING

With brisk easterly winds most of the year, Caye Caulker is one of Belize's premier centers for windsurfing. The island gets winds over 12 knots most days from November to July. The best windsurfing is in the morning and afternoon, with lulls around midday. In the late winter and spring, winds frequently hit 20 knots or more.

How Do I Get There?

Not sure which city you should depart from to reach your desired caye? Here's a quick guide.

Cayes off Belize City
- St. George's Caye
- Little Frenchman Caye
- Ambergris Caye and San Pedro
- Caye Caulker

Cayes off Punta Gorda
- Sapodilla Cayes

Cayes off Dangriga
- Tobacco Caye
- Coco Plum Caye
- Thatch Caye
- South Water Caye

Cayes off Placencia
- Laughing Bird Caye
- Bird Island
- Ray Caye
- Gladden Spit and Silk Cayes

KiteXplorer

WINDSURFING | The "wind-addicted" company KiteXplorer offers beginner and advanced kitesurfing lessons as well as windsurfing. A 3.5-hour introduction to kitesurfing costs BZ$360 including equipment and equipment insurance. An intensive "quick basic" course over three days is around BZ$980. If you already are an experienced kitesurfer, equipment rental with assistance runs BZ$120 an hour. Windsurfing lessons are around BZ$100 an hour. KiteXplorer also sells equipment. ⊠ *Playa Asunción ✢ 300 ft south of the Split* ☎ *368/3974* ⊕ *www.kitexplorer.com.*

Southern Cayes

GETTING HERE AND AROUND

The southern cayes are specks of land spread out over hundreds of square miles of sea, and they are spectacular. With their sense of depthlessness, the vistas here make you feel you might fall into the sky. There is no scheduled air or boat service to any of these islands. In the case of Tobacco Caye, private boats leave Dangriga daily around 9 to 9:30 am. If you're lodging at the other cayes and atolls, your resort will help you arrange your boat transfer (usually it is included); if not, you can charter your own boat at high cost.

TIMING

Because of the difficulty and expense of getting to the islands, most resorts have minimum-stay requirements, sometimes as little as three days but often a week. Bring several beach novels, and be prepared to enjoy a quiet vacation filled with salty adventures on and under the sea. Tropical storms are most likely between August and October. If you're unlucky enough to hit a stretch of bad weather, you may run out of things to keep you occupied.

Belize Sailing Vacations

DIVING/SNORKELING | **FAMILY** | These five beautiful catamarans can be chartered crewed for a rare vacation with a personalized itinerary. After few days on one of these yachts it will be hard not to wax rhapsodic about the Caribbean. Rates start around BZ$3,700 a night for two people, inclusive of meals and airport transfer. However, for groups charters can be more affordable than their glamour would suggest. ⊠ *Cucumber Beach Marina, Belize City* ☎ *664/4642,*

866/873–1171 in U.S. ⊕ *www.belizesailingvacations.com.*

Tobacco Caye

11 miles (18 km) southeast of Dangriga.

Tobacco Caye is at the northern tip of the South Water Caye Marine Reserve, a 62-square-mile (160-square-km) reserve that's popular for diving and fishing and has some of the most beautiful islands in Belize. Visitors to the South Water Caye Marine Reserve pay BZ$10 a day for up to three days, or BZ$30 a week, park fee. Rangers typically come around and collect it from guests at the Tobacco Caye hotels.

The island has no shops or restaurants, except those at the hotels, and just a couple of bars, but there is one small dive shop. Boats leave from the Riverside Café in Dangriga for the 40-minute, roughly BZ$50 trip to Tobacco Caye. Get to the Riverside by 9 am; most boats leave around 9:30 (though at busy times such as Easter they come and go all day long). You can get information on the boats, as well as breakfast, at the Riverside Café. ⇨ *See Southern Coast chapter.*

If you don't want to pay a lot for your place in the sun, Tobacco Caye may be for you. It's a tiny island—barely 5 acres, and a walk around the entire caye takes ten minutes—but it's right on the reef, so you can wade in and snorkel all you want. Though the snorkeling off the caye is not as good as in some other areas of Belize (some of the coral is dead and most of the fish are small), you can see spotted eagle rays, moray eels, bat fish, and other residents of the sea.

 ## Hotels

All the accommodations are budget places, simple wood cabins, some not much larger than sheds. Because several hotels vie for space, the islet seems even smaller than it is. Periodically the hotels get blown away by storms but are rebuilt, usually a little better than they were before. Unfortunately, garbage tends to pile up on the island, and the hotels don't always use the most ecologically sound methods for disposing of it.

Though rates have increased, most prices remain affordably low.

Tobacco Caye Paradise Cabins

$ | B&B/INN | FAMILY | Whether it's paradise or not depends on your expectations, but if you seek a gently priced little cabin built partly over the water, backed by coco palms, with snorkeling and adventure right out your door, this could be it. **Pros:** colorful huts on the beach at a great value; snorkeling is 15 feet away; eco-conscious. **Cons:** very basic rooms; no a/c or hot showers; charge for snorkel gear and kayaks. Ⓢ *Rooms from: BZ$175* ✉ *Tobacco Caye Paradise, Tobacco Caye* ☎ *532/2101, 800 /667–1630 in U.S.* ⊕ *www.tobaccocaye.com* ➳ *6 units* ❍*No meals.*

The Windward Lodge

$ | HOTEL | FAMILY | This cluster of turquoise cottages, each with a hammocked porch, is steps from the sea, and while accommodations are simple—just above backpacker level—the Caribbean is your playground. **Pros:** Belize made affordable; a barefoot dream; friendly staff. **Cons:** basic living; trash can wash ashore; too quiet for some tastes. Ⓢ *Rooms from: BZ$150* ✉ *Tobacco Caye* ☎ *532/2033* ⊕ *www.windwardlodgebelize.com* ➳ *6 units* ❍*All meals.*

Coco Plum Caye

Like Thatch Caye, this tiny caye just off the coast of Dangriga is host to a magnificent, upscale resort.

Hotels

★ **Coco Plum Island Resort**

$$$$ | RESORT | FAMILY | It all comes down to this: recline in a hammock on your cottage veranda, sip a cold drink, and contemplate the Caribbean at this luxe, all-inclusive private-island resort off Dangriga. **Pros:** delivers even more than it promises; you'll miss the lovely staff when you leave; package discounts. **Cons:** only fair snorkeling off beach; not on reef; a hefty price tag. $ *Rooms from: BZ$1,500 ⊠ Coco Plum ✛ 8 miles (13 km) from Dangriga ☎ 522/2200, 800/763–7360 in U.S. ⊕ www.cocoplumcay.com ⇌ 13 units ◎ All-inclusive.*

Thatch Caye

Hotels

Thatch Caye

$$$ | RESORT | FAMILY | Thatch Caye is all about you and your private-island vacation; after a day of sea adventures return to lovely rooms, elevated treehouse style, at this well-run adventure lodge. **Pros:** beautiful private island with congenial hosts; plenty of marine activities; attractive cabanas directly on the water. **Cons:** limited snorkeling off beach; not on reef; meal plan is more costly than at other resorts. $ *Rooms from: BZ$475 ⊠ 9 miles (15 km), or about 25 minutes, by boat from Dangriga, Thatch Caye ☎ 800/435–3145 in U.S. ⊕ www.thatchcayebelize.com ⇌ 12 units ◎ No meals.*

South Water Caye

14 miles (23 km) southeast of Dangriga.

This is one of our favorite underrated spots in Belize. The 15-acre South Water Caye has good off-the-beaten-reef diving and snorkeling in a stunning tropical setting, and the beach at the southern end of the island is one of Belize's sandy beauties. The reef is only a short swim from shore. The downside of the small caye? The sand flies here can be a nuisance, and there aren't any facilities other than those at the island's two resorts and the International Zoological Expeditions' student dorm.

Hotels

★ **Pelican Beach Resort South Water Caye**

$$$$ | RESORT | FAMILY | Steps from one of the country's best beaches sits this former convent turned serene island retreat, a pioneer in Belizean eco-tourism since 1971. **Pros:** on great little beach, with snorkeling from shore; tasty, simple Belizean food; comfortable, eco-friendly, no-frills accommodations. **Cons:** you have to make your own entertainment; boat transfer not included; remember: no-frills accommodations. $ *Rooms from: BZ$840 ⊠ South Water Caye ☎ 522/2044 ⊕ www.pelicanbeachbelize.com ⇌ 13 units ◎ All-inclusive.*

Laughing Bird Caye

8–18 miles (13–30 km) east of Placencia.

A few miles off the coast of southern Stann Creek District are several small islands with equally small tourism operations. If Placencia and Hopkins aren't far enough away from civilization for you, consider an overnight or longer visit to one of these quiet little paradises surrounded by fish.

Sights

Laughing Bird Caye National Park

NATURE PRESERVE | This superb little national park lies off the coast of the Placencia Peninsula, and its boosters insist that it, not Belize's northern cayes, has the best beach in the country. The atoll takes its name from the laughing gull (*Larus articilla*), which used to nest extensively here. Visitation by humans has pushed the gulls' nesting to other nearby islets, but you'll still see the birds in abundance here, as well as green herons and brown pelicans. Local boaters in Placencia Village can take you to the park for BZ$80 to BZ$200 round trip. The Friends of Laughing Bird Caye, the park's private administrators, can also help you get here. ✉ *18 km (11 miles) by water southeast of village, Placencia Village* ☎ *523–3565 in Placencia Village* 🌐 *www.laughingbird.org.*

Bird Island

🛏 Hotels

Bird Island

$$$$ | **RENTAL** | **FAMILY** | A patch of coral the shape of a pancake and not much bigger, Bird Island is a self-catering, real-life private island where the solitude and starry skies are exquisite. **Pros:** atoll all to yourself; VIP access to reef; unforgettable adventure launching pad. **Cons:** can get lonely; four-night minimum; self-catering island means planning ahead for meals. [$] *Rooms from: BZ$1,300* ✉ *Placencia Village* ☎ *634/3997* 🌐 *www.birdislandplacenciabz.com* 🕓 *Closed mid-June to mid-July* 🔑 *1 unit* 🍴 *No meals.*

Ray Caye

🛏 Hotels

Ray Caye, an Island Resort

$$$$ | **RESORT** | **FAMILY** | On a private island east of Placencia, Ray Caye offers an unspoiled getaway for honeymooners, divers, or anyone who wants to chase an escape without sacrificing little luxuries. **Pros:** modern, upscale resort with spa; on-site PADI shop; island open to mariners. **Cons:** no shops or choice of restaurants; high rates; you might crave a more rustic island experience. [$] *Rooms from: BZ$1,000* ✉ *Ray Caye, Hatchet Caye* ✥ *17 miles (28 km), or 1-hour boat ride, east of Placencia* ☎ *533/4446* 🌐 *www.raycaye.com* 🕓 *Closed Oct.* 🔑 *9 rooms* 🍴 *No meals.*

Gladden Spit and Silk Cayes

20 miles (31 km) east of Placencia.

👁 Sights

★ Gladden Spit and Silk Cayes

BEACH—SIGHT | If you've always wanted to dive with the gentle, 60-foot-long whale shark, Gladden Spit is the place. But this is the catch: you have an extremely narrow window in which to do so. The spawning of various snappers—cubera, mutton, and dog—draw the whale sharks here, and that takes place from March through June from the full moon to the last quarter. (Even March can be chancy.) If your schedule coincides, all dive outfitters in the village of Placencia can get you here during these mini-seasons. It means needing to reserve far in advance for a popular excursion that can be offered three—four if you're lucky—calendar weeks during the year. The other 48–49 weeks, the two pristine, deserted Silk Cayes offer a chance to picnic on their sugar-white beaches and snorkel in their clear-blue waters. Plan on seeing Goliath and Nassau groupers and various sea turtles, but not the whale sharks. ✉ *Placencia Village.*

Sapodilla Cayes

40 miles (66 km) east of Punta Gorda.

👁 Sights

★ Sapodilla Cayes

BEACH—SIGHT | Few visitors make it to this collection of six sand and mangrove cayes, Belize's southernmost island group. If you're one of those lucky few, you'll come back with tales of Hunting Caye, the largest of the Sapodillas, and its gorgeous

A Guide to Belize's Atolls

What are they?

There are only four atolls in the Western Hemisphere, and three of them are off Belize (the fourth is Chinchorro Reef, off Mexico's Yucatán). Belize's atolls—Turneffe, Lighthouse, and Glover's—are oval-shape masses of coral. A few small islands, some sandy and others mostly mangrove, rise up along the atolls' encircling coral arms. Within the coral walls are central lagoons, with shallow water 10 to 30 feet deep. Outside the walls, the ocean falls off sharply to 1,000 feet or more, deeper than any diver can go.

Unlike the more common Pacific atolls, which were formed from underwater volcanoes, the Caribbean atolls began forming millions of years ago, atop giant tectonic faults. As giant limestone blocks slowly settled, they provided platforms for coral growth.

Because of their remoteness (they're 25 miles [40 km] to 50 miles [80 km] from the mainland) and because most of the islands at the atolls are small, the atolls have remained nearly pristine. Only a few small dive and fishing resorts are here, and the serious divers and anglers who favor the area know that they have some of the best diving and fishing in the Caribbean, if not the world. Of course, paradise has its price: most of the atoll resorts are very, very expensive and have minimum-stay requirements.

How do I get there?

Getting to the atolls usually requires a long boat ride, sometimes rough enough to bring on *mal de mer*. You'll need to take one of the scheduled boats provided by your lodge or ride out on a dive or snorkel boat with a group; otherwise, you'll likely pay BZ$800–BZ$2,000 or more to charter a boat one-way. Remember, there are no commercial services at the atolls, except those associated with an island dive or fishing lodge. To charter a boat, check with a lodge on the atoll where you wish to go, or ask locally at docks in Belize City, San Pedro, Dangriga, Hopkins, or Placencia.

Dive shops and sailing charters in San Pedro, Caye Caulker, Placencia, and Hopkins make regular trips to the atolls.

How long should I spend there?

Because of the difficulty and expense of getting to the atolls, most resorts have minimum-stay requirements of at least three days. There's little to do on the atolls except dive, snorkel, fish, eat, sleep, and drink. If you don't like sea sports, or if you do but hit consecutive days of bad weather, you may be bored.

white-sand beach. Shallow waters immediately off the islands' coasts make for good snorkeling; various dive sites lie farther out. Spadefish, parrot fish, and dolphins are yours for the viewing. The islands' remoteness and official status as a marine reserve ensure a healthy coral reef and diverse underwater life. Camping on Lime Caye is your only option for an overnight stay. Save for a few researchers from the University of Belize, who study the sea turtles here, and Belize Defence Force (BDF) personnel, the islands are otherwise uninhabited. Why the military outpost? Guatemala and Honduras also claim the Sapodillas as their own. Belize maintains control of the islands, with its own military on Hunting Caye to ensure

Thatched-roof bungalows provide the perfect escape at Glover's Reef Atoll.

that status. The dispute need not concern you as a visitor, and, indeed, you might rub shoulders with day visitors from Livingston, Guatemala. They all need to go through passport control with the BDF. You won't. Outfitters in Punta Gorda can fix you up with a trip, either for the day or overnight. ⊠ *Punta Gorda.*

Turneffe Atoll

25 miles (40 km) east of Belize City.

The largest of Belize's three atolls, Turneffe, is the closest to Belize City. It's one of the best spots for diving, thanks to several steep drop-offs. Only an hour from Lighthouse Reef and 45 minutes from the northern edge of Glover's Reef, Turneffe is a good base for exploring all the atolls.

The best-known attraction, and probably Belize's most exciting wall dive, is the **Elbow,** at Turneffe's southernmost tip. You may encounter ethereal eagle rays—as many as 50 might flutter together, forming a rippling herd. Elbow is generally

considered an advanced dive because of the strong currents, which sweep you toward the deep water beyond the reef.

Though it's most famous for its spectacular wall dives, the atoll has dives for every level. The leeward side, where the reef is wide and gently sloping, is good for shallower dives and snorkeling; you'll see large concentrations of tube sponges, soft corals such as forked sea feathers and sea fans, and plenty of fish. Also on the atoll's western side is the wreck of the *Sayonara*. No doubloons to scoop up here—it was a small passenger and cargo boat that sank in 1985—but it's good for wreck dive practice.

Fishing here, as at all of the atolls, is world-class. You can fly-fish for bonefish and permit in the grassy flats, or go after migratory tarpon from May to September in the channels and lagoons of the atoll. Jack, barracuda, and snappers lurk in the mangrove-lined bays and shorelines. Billfish, sailfish, and other big creatures are in the blue water around the atoll.

Hotels

Turneffe Flats

$$$$ | RESORT | The sound of the surf is the only night noise at this smart, red-roofed resort, where you'll commune with others who love fishing and other water activities as much as you do. **Pros:** quality fishing lodge with flats you dream of; special atoll scenery; diving and just plain relaxing available. **Cons:** comes at a price; not the ultra-chic design of some peer resorts; sand fleas get too friendly. *Rooms from: BZ$1,750 ✉ Turneffe Atoll ☎ 671/9022, 888/512–8812 🌐 www.tflats.com ⇨ 10 units 🍴 All-inclusive.*

★ Turneffe Island Resort

$$$$ | RESORT | White-uniformed staff (all lined up for your boat's arrival), the preserved colonial-era buildings, and the oxidized anchor of an 18th-century British warship all set the tone at this upscale, legend-filled resort. **Pros:** breathtaking atoll near great diving and snorkeling; delicious and varied meals; you're sure to be pampered. **Cons:** may need to dive for a treasure chest to pay for this vacation; no alternative dining options; group dinners aren't everyone's cup of tea. *Rooms from: BZ$2,200 ✉ Coco Tree Caye ☎ 800/874–0118 in U.S. 🌐 www.turnefferesort.com ⏲ Closed Sept. and Oct. ⇨ 22 units 🍴 All-inclusive.*

Lighthouse Reef Atoll, the Blue Hole, and Half Moon Caye

50 miles (80 km) east of Belize City.

Lighthouse Reef is about 18 miles (29 km) long and less than 1 mile (2 km) wide and is surrounded by a seemingly endless stretch of coral. Here you'll find two of the country's best dives.

At this writing, visiting Lighthouse Reef is best done as a side trip from Ambergris Caye, Caye Caulker, or another location in northern Belize. The marine reserve fee here is a pricey BZ$80 per person.

Sights

★ Blue Hole

BODY OF WATER | From the air, the Blue Hole, a breathtaking vertical chute that drops several hundred feet through the reef, is a dark blue eye in the center of the shallow lagoon. The Blue Hole was first dived by Jacques Cousteau in 1971 and has since become a diver's pilgrimage site. Just over 1,000 feet wide at the surface and dropping almost vertically to a depth of 412 feet, the Blue Hole is like swimming down a mineshaft, but a mineshaft with hammerhead sharks. This excitement is reflected in the thousands of stickers and T-shirts reading, "I Dived the Blue Hole." ✉ *Lighthouse Reef, Blue Hole.*

Half Moon Caye National Monument

NATURE PRESERVE | Belize's easternmost island offers one of Belize's greatest wildlife encounters, although it's difficult to reach and lacks accommodations other than camping. Part of the Lighthouse Reef system, Half Moon Caye owes its protected status to the presence of the red-footed booby. The bird is here in such numbers that it's hard to believe it has only one other nesting ground in the entire Caribbean (on Tobago Island, off the coast of Venezuela). Thousands of these birds hang their hats on Half Moon Caye, along with iguanas, lizards, and loggerhead turtles. The entire 40-acre island is a nature reserve, so you can explore the beaches or head into the bush on the narrow nature trail. Above the trees at the island's center is a small viewing platform—at the top you're suddenly in a sea of birds that will doubtless remind you of a certain Alfred Hitchcock movie. Several dive operators and resorts arrange day trips and overnight camping trips to Half Moon Caye. Managed by the Belize Audubon Society, the park fee here is a steep BZ$80 per person. ✉ *Half*

Moon Caye National Monument 🌐 *www.belizeaudubon.org* 🎫 *BZ$80.*

Half Moon Caye Wall

NATURE PRESERVE | The best diving on Lighthouse Reef is at Half Moon Caye Wall, a classic wall dive. Half Moon Caye begins at 35 feet and drops almost vertically to blue infinity. Floating out over the edge is a bit like free-fall parachuting. Magnificent spurs of coral jut out to the seaward side, looking like small tunnels; they're fascinating to explore and invariably full of fish. An exceptionally varied marine life hovers around this caye. On the gently sloping sand flats behind the coral spurs, a vast colony of garden eels stirs, their heads protruding from the sand like periscopes. Spotted eagle rays, sea turtles, and other underwater wonders frequent the drop-off. ✉ *Lighthouse Reef, Half Moon Caye* 🌐 *www.belizeaudubon.org* 🎫 *BZ$80.*

Glover's Reef Atoll

70 miles (113 km) southeast of Belize City.

Named after the pirate John Glover, this coral necklace strung around an 80-square-mile (208-square-km) lagoon is the southernmost of Belize's three atolls. There are five islands at the atoll. Visitors to Glover's Reef are charged a BZ$10 daily park fee (BZ$25 per week for fly-fishing).

👁 Sights

Emerald Forest Reef

REEF | Although most of the best dive sites are along the Glover's Atoll's southeastern side, this is the exception, being on the atoll's western arm. It's named for its masses of huge green elkhorn coral. Because the reef's most exciting part is only 25 feet down, it's excellent for novice divers. ✉ *Glover's Reef Atoll.*

Long Caye Wall

NATURE PRESERVE | This is an exciting wall at Glover's Atoll; between its bright coral and dramatic drop-off hundreds of feet down, diving it truly feels like extraterrestrial exploration. It's a good place to spot turtles, rays, and barracuda.

Southwest Caye Wall

BODY OF WATER | Southwest Caye Wall is an underwater cliff that falls quickly to 130 feet. It's briefly interrupted by a narrow shelf, then continues its near-vertical descent to 350 feet. This dive gives you the exhilaration of flying in blue space, so it's easy to lose track of how deep you are going. Both ascent and descent require careful monitoring.

🛏 Hotels

Isla Marisol Resort

$$$$ | **RESORT** | Spend your days here snorkeling in the shallows, doing acrobatics on a water trampoline, and, most dramatically, diving at "The Pinnacles," where coral heads rise 40 feet from the ocean floor. **Pros:** Belizean owned and run; great diving in an unbeatable setting; barracuda and nurse sharks hang around the dock. **Cons:** prices aren't budget; sand flies get troublesome; basic accommodations. [$] *Rooms from: BZ$1,050* ✉ *Southwest Caye, Isla Marisol* ☎ *610/4204* 🌐 *www.islamarisolresort.com* 🛏 *14 units* 🍴 *All-inclusive.*

Off the Wall Dive Center & Resort

$$$$ | **RESORT** | The name doesn't do justice to this intimate lodge on Glover's Atoll, which focuses on diving (sites are a four-minute boat ride away), but snorkeling, fishing, bird-watching, and stargazing aren't to be overlooked. **Pros:** competitive price (for an atoll lodge in Belize); easy access to great diving; very knowledgeable dive staff. **Cons:** modest accommodations; bugs can be a nuisance; "all-inclusive" isn't actually all-inclusive. [$] *Rooms from: BZ$925* ✉ *Long Caye, Glover's Reef Atoll* ☎ *532/2929* 🌐 *www.offthewallbelize.com* 🛏 *5 cabanas* 🍴 *All-inclusive.*

Chapter 5

NORTHERN BELIZE

Updated by
Rachel White

👁 Sights	🍴 Restaurants	🛏 Hotels	🛍 Shopping	🍸 Nightlife
★★★★☆	★★☆☆☆	★★★☆☆	★★☆☆☆	★★☆☆☆

WELCOME TO NORTHERN BELIZE

TOP REASONS TO GO

★ **Mayan Sites:** Several of the most interesting Mayan sites in the region are in northern Belize. These include Altun Ha, Lamanai, Santa Rita, and Cerros. Altun Ha gets the most visitors of any Mayan site in Belize, and Lamanai, on the New River Lagoon, and Cerros, on Corozal Bay, are notable because of their beautiful locations.

★ **Wild, Open Spaces:** This part of Belize has some of the country's wildest tracts of land teeming with wildlife. These include Gallon Jug, 130,000 privately owned acres around Chan Chich Lodge, and Shipstern Reserve, a 22,000-acre expanse of swamps, lagoons, and forests on the Sarteneja peninsula.

★ **Jungle Lodges:** Northern Belize is home to several first-rate lodges, including Chan Chich Lodge, a paradise for birders and the place where you're most likely to spot the jaguar in the wild. Lamanai Outpost, on the New River Lagoon, is a center for crocodile research.

The Philip Goldson Highway, a paved two-lane road, is the transportation spine of the region, running about 95 miles (156 km) from Belize City to the Mexican border at Chetumal, passing the two main towns in northern Belize, Orange Walk and Corozal. A bypass around Orange Walk provides a way to avoid the congested downtown.

1 Crooked Tree Wildlife Sanctuary. A paradise for birders, this wildlife sanctuary is an "inland island" surrounded by a chain of lagoons, in total covering about 3,000 acres. Traveling by canoe among countless birds, you're likely to see iguanas, crocodiles, coatis, and turtles.

2 Altun Ha. Easy to get to from the Northern Cayes or Belize City, Altun Ha is the most visited Mayan ruin in Belize. Cruise ship tours bring hundreds of visitors here daily.

3 Orange Walk Town. Town along the New River that's a jumping off point for visiting Lamanai.

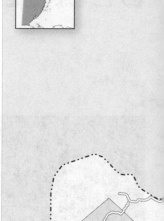

4 Lamanai. This Mayan site, overlooking a lagoon, has a name that means "submerged crocodile."

5 Rio Bravo Conservation and Management Area. Home to a beautiful nature reserve with wildlife and La Milpa Mayan site.

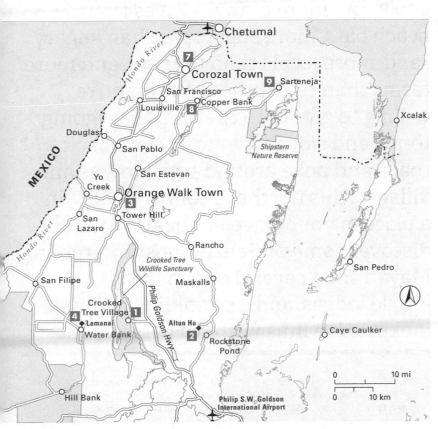

6 Gallon Jug. The big attraction is Chan Chich Lodge, one of the top lodges in all of Central America—and it's set on top of a Mayan ruin.

7 Corozal Town. Near the Mexican border, this expat magnet is low-key, but for relaxation at modest cost you can't find a better spot.

8 Copper Bank. Laid-back, small village near the Cerros Mayan site.

9 Sarteneja. Relaxed, off-the-beaten-path fishing village with a nature reserve.

Northern Belize isn't your average toes-in-the-sand vacation destination. Here you'll find more orange groves than beach bars, more sugarcane than sugary sand, more locals than tourists, and more farms than restaurants. Yet if you're willing to give in to the area's easygoing terms and slow down to explore back roads and poke around small towns and villages, this northern country will win a place in your traveler's heart. You'll discover some of Belize's most interesting Mayan sites, several outstanding jungle lodges, and a sprinkling of small, inexpensive inns with big personalities.

Northern Belize includes the northern part of Belize District and all of Orange Walk and Corozal Districts. Altogether, this area covers about 2,800 square miles (7,250 square km) and has a population of more than 90,000. The landscape is mostly flat, with mangrove swamps on the coast giving way to savanna inland. Scrub bush is much more common than broadleaf jungle, although to the northwest near the Guatemala border are large, wild tracts of land with some of the world's few remaining old-growth mahogany trees. The region has many cattle ranches, citrus groves, sugarcane fields, and, in a few areas, marijuana fields.

The only sizable towns in the region are Orange Walk, about 53 miles (87 km) north of Belize City, with about 14,000 residents, and Corozal Town, which is 85 miles (139 km) north of Belize City, and has a population of around 15,000. Both are on the Philip Goldson Highway, formerly the Northern Highway, a paved two-lane road that runs 95 miles (156 km) from Belize City up the center of the region, ending at the Mexican border.

Northern Belize gets less rain than anywhere else in the country (roughly 50 inches annually in Corozal), a fact that's reflected in the sunny disposition of the local population, mostly Mayan and mestizo. Both Orange Walk and Corozal Towns have a Mexican ambience, with central plazas serving as the focus of the downtown areas. Many locals speak Spanish as a first language, although most also know some English, and many speak both Spanish and English fluently. While several new hotels and restaurants have opened here, Orange Walk Town is mostly a jumping-off point for trips to Lamanai and other Mayan ruins, to Mennonite farmlands, and to several well-regarded jungle lodges in wild, remote areas. Corozal Town, next door to Chetumal, Mexico, is a place to slow down, relax, and enjoy the laid-back atmosphere of a charming small town on the beautiful Corozal Bay (or, as Mexico calls it, Chetumal Bay).

If you tire of small-town pleasures, the Belize side of the Mexican border has three casinos, including one called Las Vegas that claims to be the largest casino in Central America, and a duty-free zone (though the shopping here is mostly for cheap clothing and appliances, with little of interest to international visitors). Corozal has begun to draw foreign expats looking for inexpensive real estate and proximity to Chetumal, the Quintana Roo Mexican state capital, whose metropolitan population is nearly as large as that of the entire country of Belize. Chetumal offers urban conveniences that Belize doesn't, including a modern shopping mall, fast food, a multiplex cinema, and big-box stores including Walmart and Sam's Club. Sarteneja Village, in the far northeastern part of Corozal District, about 35 miles (57 km) from Corozal Town, is a still-undiscovered fishing village at the edge of the sea, near the Shipstern Wildlife Reserve. On the way are several pristine lagoons, including the lovely Progresso Lagoon.

MAJOR REGIONS

Thirty-three miles northwest of Belize City, the **Crooked Tree Wildlife Sanctuary** is one of Belize's top birding destinations and home to jungle lodges. Not far

northwest of the sanctuary is **Altun Ha,** an impressive and popular Mayan site.

Further inland, the **Northwest Orange Walk District** borders both Mexico and Guatemala, and holds four areas well worth the time it takes to visit them: Lamanai Archaeological Reserve, at the edge of the New River Lagoon; the Mennonite communities of Blue Creek and Shipyard; the 260,000-plus acres of the Río Bravo Conservation Area; and Gallon Jug lands, 130,000 acres in which the remarkable Chan Chich Lodge nestles.

To the north, **Corozal Bay,** or Chetumal Bay as it's called on most maps, provides a beautiful waterside setting for Corozal Town and a number of villages along the north side of Corozal District. Tarpon, bonefish, permit, and other game fish are not hard to find. The Belize Barrier Reef is several long hours away by boat; however, the Mexican border and the outskirts of the city of Chetumal are only 9 miles (15 km) away.

Planning

When to Go

Corozal Town and the rest of northern Belize get about the same amount of rain as Atlanta, Georgia, so even the "rainy season" here—generally June to November— is not to be feared. It's hot and humid for much of the year, except in waterfront areas where prevailing breezes mitigate the heat. December to April is usually the most pleasant time, with weather similar to that of southern Florida. In winter, cold fronts from the north occasionally bring rain and chilly weather, and when the temperature drops to the low 60s, locals wear sweaters and sleep under extra blankets.

Getting Here and Around

AIR TRAVEL

Corozal Town has flights only to and from San Pedro (Ambergris Caye). Tropic Air and Maya Island Air each fly four to six times daily between Ambergris Caye and the airstrip at Corozal, about 2 miles (3 km) south of town off the Goldson Highway. The journey takes 20 minutes. From Corozal, there's no direct air service to Belize City or other destinations in Belize. Charter service is available to Chan Chich Lodge and the Indian Church/ Lamanai area.

CONTACTS Maya Island Air. ⊠ *Corozal Air Strip, Ranchito* 🕾 *422/0711 Corozal Airstrip, Ranchito, 223/1403 Belize City* ⊕ *www.mayaislandair.com.* **Tropic Air.** ⊠ *Corozal Air Strip, Ranchito* 🕾 *226/2626 reservations in Belize, 800/422–3435 in U.S.* ⊕ *www.tropicair.com.*

BOAT AND WATER-TAXI TRAVEL

Ferry from Corozal. An old, hand-pulled sugar barge ferries passengers and cars across the New River from just south of Corozal Town to the road to Copper Bank, Cerros, and the Shipstern peninsula. The ferry is free from 6 am to 9 pm daily. To get to the ferry from Corozal, take the Philip Goldson Highway south toward Orange Walk Town and look for the ferry sign just south of town. Turn left and follow the unpaved road to the ferry landing.

Ferry between Copper Bank and Sarteneja. A second, hand-pulled auto ferry is between Copper Bank and Sarteneja, at the mouth of Laguna Seca. From Copper Bank, follow the ferry signs. Near Chunox, at a T intersection, turn left and follow the unpaved road 20 miles (32 km) to Sarteneja.

Water Taxi between Corozal Town and Ambergris Caye. A daily water taxi operates between Corozal Town and Ambergris Caye, with a stop on demand at Sarteneja. The *Thunderbolt* departs from Corozal at the pier near Reunion Park behind Corozal House of Culture at 7 am and also goes from a pier on the back side of San Pedro near the soccer field to Corozal at 3 pm. The trip usually takes nearly two hours but may be longer if there's a stop at Sarteneja, or if the weather is bad. Off-season, service is sometimes reduced and occasionally is discontinued altogether.

Chetumal to San Pedro and Caye Caulker. Two Belize-based water-taxi companies, San Pedro Belize Express and Water Jets International, provide service direct from Chetumal, Mexico, to San Pedro and Caye Caulker. The two companies alternate days of service, so there's only one boat each way daily.

CONTACTS San Pedro Belize Express. 🕾 *223/223–2225 in Belize City, 983/832–1648 in Mexico* ⊕ *www.belizewatertaxi. com.* **Thunderbolt.** ⊠ *Municipal Pier, 1st Ave., Corozal Town* ⊕ *Municipal pier is next to Corozal House of Culture on 1st Ave.* 🕾 *422/0026 in Corozal Town, 610/4475 cell phone* ⊕ *www.ambergriscaye.com/thunderbolt.* **Water Jets International.** ⊠ *Water Jets International, San Pedro Town* 🕾 *226/2194 in San Pedro* ⊕ *www.sanpedrowatertaxi.com.*

BUS TRAVEL AND SHUTTLE SERVICE

Buses between Belize City and Corozal run about every half hour during daylight hours in both directions, and some of these continue on to Chetumal, Mexico. Several small bus lines make the 3- to 3½-hour journey between Belize City and Corozal Town/Chetumal. Northbound buses depart from the Novelo's bus station on West Collet Canal Street in Belize City beginning at 5:30 am, with the last departure around 7:30 pm. Southbound buses begin around 3:45 am, with the last departure at 7:30 pm. Any non-express bus will stop and pick up almost anywhere along the highway.

■TIP→ **Bus service to the villages and other sites off the Goldson Highway is limited, so to reach them you're best off with a rental car or a guided tour.** There is some bus service on the Old Northern Highway and from Orange Walk to Sarteneja. Ask locally for updates on bus lines, routes, and fares.

Two shuttle services based in Corozal Town, Belize VIP Transfers and GetTransfers, and also known as George and Esther Moralez Travel, provide inexpensive and handy transportation across the border between Corozal and Chetumal. These services make crossing the border easy and hassle-free. The transfer services also provide shuttles to and from Cancún and other destinations in the Yucatán and in Belize.

CONTACTS Belize VIP Transfers. ✉ *Caribbean Village, South End, Corozal Town* ☎ *422/2725* ⊕ *www.belizetransfers.com.* **Get Transfers.** ✉ *3 Blue Bird St., Corozal Town* ☎ *422/2485 in Belize* ⊕ *www.gettransfers.com.*

CAR TRAVEL
Corozal is the last stop on the Goldson Highway before you hit Mexico. The 95-mile (153-km) journey from Belize City will probably take about two hours, unless you're slowed by sugarcane trucks. The Goldson Highway is a two-lane paved road in fairly good condition. Other roads, including roads to Lamanai, Río Bravo, and Gallon Jug, and the road to Sarteneja are mostly unpaved. The Old Northern Highway, the route to Altun Ha, has been repaved for the first 12 miles (20 km), with the remaining 9 miles (15 km) a mixture of old broken pavement and dirt. Because tour and long-distance taxi prices are high, especially if you're traveling with family or in a group, you likely will save money by renting a car.

Car-rental agencies in Belize City will usually deliver vehicles to Corozal and Orange Walk, but there will be a drop fee, starting at around BZ$150. Two small local car-rental agencies, Corozal Cars and Belize VIP Service, have a few cars to rent, at rates starting around BZ$140 a day, plus tax.

CONTACTS Belize VIP Transfers. ✉ *Caribbean Village, South End, Corozal Town* ☎ *422/2725* ⊕ *www.belizetransfers.com.* **Corozal Cars.** ✉ *Mile 85, Philip Goldson Hwy. (formerly Northern Hwy.), Corozal Town* ☎ *422/3339* ⊕ *www.corozalcars.com.*

TAXI TRAVEL
It's usually easiest to have your hotel arrange taxi service for you, but if you want to do it yourself, both Corozal and Orange Walk have a Taxi Association. Fares to most destinations in town are low, at BZ$10 or less, but rates to points outside town can be expensive; agree on a price beforehand.

CONTACTS Taxi Association in Corozal. ✉ *1st St. S, Corozal Town* ☎ *422/2035.* **Taxi Association in Orange Walk.** ✉ *Queen Victoria Ave., Orange Walk Town* ✛ *Across from main plaza* ☎ *322/2560* ⊕ *orange-walks-premier-taxi-association. business.site.*

Emergencies

For dental and medical care, many of Corozal's residents go to Chetumal, Mexico. In Corozal, visit Bethesda Medical Centre if you need medical care. The Corozal Hospital, with only limited facilities, is on the Goldson Highway. In Orange Walk, the Northern Regional Hospital doesn't look very appealing, but it provides emergency and other services. Your hotel can provide a list of local doctors and dentists. Consider going to Belize City or Chetumal for medical and dental care, if possible. For police and emergencies, dial 911.

Hotels

Most hotels in northern Belize are small, family-run spots. In Corozal and Orange Walk Towns, hotels are modest affairs costing a fraction of the hotel rates in San Pedro or other more popular parts of Belize. Generally, the hotels are clean and well maintained and offer a homey atmosphere. They have private baths and plenty of hot and cold water, and most also have air-conditioning. Hotels and lodges in Crooked Tree, Sarteneja, and Copper Bank are also small and inexpensive; some have air-conditioning. The jungle lodges near Lamanai, Gallon Jug, and Altun Ha, however, are a different story. Several of these, including Chan Chich Lodge, Maruba Jungle Lodge and Spa, and Lamanai Outpost Lodge, are upscale accommodations, with gorgeous settings in the jungle or on a lagoon and prices to match; meals and tours are extra. These lodges also offer all-inclusive and other package options.

Restaurants

With the exception of dining rooms at upscale jungle lodges, restaurants are almost invariably small, inexpensive, family-run places, serving simple meals such as stew chicken with rice and beans. Here, you'll rarely pay more than BZ$25 for dinner, and frequently much less. If there's a predominant culinary influence, it's Mexican, and many restaurants serve tacos, tamales, *garnaches* (small, fried corn tortillas with beans, cabbage, and cheese piled on them), and soups such as *escabeche* (onion soup with chicken). A few places, mostly in Corozal Town, cater to tourists and expats with burgers, pizza, and steaks. For a quick snack, restaurants on the second floor of the Corozal market sell inexpensive breakfast and lunch items (usually closed Sunday). Likewise, the stalls at the central plaza in the heart of Orange Walk Town sell cheap snacks and food. You can also buy delicious local fruits and vegetables at the Corozal Town market—a huge papaya, two lovely mangoes, and a bunch of bananas cost as little as BZ$3. There is also a fruit and vegetable market in the center of Orange Walk Town.

HOTEL AND RESTAURANT PRICES

Restaurant and hotel reviews have been shortened. For full information, visit Fodors.com.

What It Costs in Belize Dollars			
$	$$	$$$	$$$$
RESTAURANTS			
under BZ$15	BZ$15–BZ$30	BZ$31–BZ$50	over BZ$50
HOTELS			
under BZ$200	BZ$200–BZ$300	BZ$301–BZ$500	over BZ$500

Safety

Corozal is one of Belize's safer areas, but petty theft and burglaries aren't uncommon, so use common sense when traveling through the area. In both Corozal Town and Orange Walk Town, try to avoid anyone standing on the street with a bucket of water trying to earn money by washing car windshields—it could be a scam.

Tours

SEEING THE RUINS

Your hotel in Orange Walk Town or Corozal Town can arrange tours to Lamanai, Cerros, and other sites, starting at around BZ$80 per person. In Orange Walk, Reyes & Sons River Tours, Lamanai Eco Adventures, and J. Avila & Sons run boat trips up the New River to Lamanai. In Corozal Town, Belize VIP Transfers *(see Bus Travel)* can arrange tours of Cerros, Santa Rita, and elsewhere. In Sarteneja, members of the Sarteneja Tour Guide

Association can arrange tours to Shipstern, Cerros, and Bacalar Chica on North Ambergris Caye.

Lamanai Belize Tours
A long-established New River tour operator, Lamanai Belize Tours offers daily boat tours up the New River from Tower Hill to Lamanai. Boats leave around 9 am and cost BZ$80 per person. ✉ *Belize City* ☎ *630/5170* ⊕ *www.lamanaibelizetours. com.*

Lamanai Eco Adventures
Located on the west side of the Philip Goldson Highway at Tower Hill and the New River, Lamanai Eco Adventures has several tours up the New River to Lamanai. Rates are around BZ$100. Depending on the season, there are two to three tours a day, with the first one departing Orange Walk around 8 am. The company does both individual and cruise ship tours. ✉ *Tower Hill, Philip Goldson Hwy., Orange Walk Town* ⊹ *On west side of Goldson Hwy. just south of Tower Hill bridge* ☎ *610/2020* ⊕ *www.lamanaiecoadventures.com.*

★ Reyes & Sons River Tours
Located on the east side of the Philip Goldson Highway just south of the Tower Hill bridge, Reyes & Sons is a veteran boat and tour operator. It offers daily boat trips, leaving around 9 am, up the New River to the New River Lagoon and Lamanai Mayan site. The rate of BZ$80 per person includes the boat ride, admission to Lamanai, and a light lunch. Unlike most other New River/Lamanai operators, Reyes doesn't cater to cruise ship tours and instead takes individual visitors. ✉ *Tower Hill, Philip Goldson Hwy., Orange Walk Town* ☎ *322/3327.*

SNORKELING
From Sarteneja, Sarteneja Adventure Tours can take you to Bacalar Chico Marine Reserve and National Park off North Ambergris Caye. Full-day rates include guide, park admission, snorkeling gear, and lunch.

Sarteneja Tour Guide Association
Members of the Sarteneja Tour Guide Association offer tours to Bacalar Chico Marine Reserve and National Park, Shipstern Nature Reserve, Cerros Maya site, and elsewhere. ✉ *N. Front St., Sarteneja* ☎ *633/0067, 621/6465 Sarteneja Tour Guide Association.*

Visitor Information

An excellent source of general information on northern Belize is the website Northern Belize.

CONTACTS Corozal. ⊕ *corozal.com.* **Northern Belize.** ⊕ *northernbelize.com.*

Crooked Tree Wildlife Sanctuary

33 miles (54 km) northwest of Belize City.

Crooked Tree Wildlife Sanctuary is one of Belize's top birding spots. The 16,400-acre sanctuary includes more than 3,000 acres of lagoons, swamp, and marsh, surrounding what is essentially an inland island. Traveling by canoe, you're likely to see iguanas, crocodiles, coatis, and turtles. The sanctuary's most prestigious visitors, however, are the jabiru storks, which usually visit between November and May. With a wingspan up to 12 feet, the jabiru is the largest flying bird in the Americas. ■TIP→ **For birders the best time to come is in the dry season, roughly from February to late May, when lower water levels cause birds to group together to find water and food, making them easy to spot.** Birding is good year-round, however, and the area is more scenic when the lagoons are full. Snowy egrets, snail kites, ospreys, and black-collared hawks, as well as two types of duck—Muscovy and black-bellied whistling—and all five species of kingfishers native to Belize can be spotted. Even on a short, one- to

Great Itineraries

If You Have 3 to 5 Days in Northern Belize

If you are starting in Belize City, rent a car and drive to Crooked Tree Wildlife Sanctuary, which has great birding and offers the chance to see the jabiru stork, the largest flying bird in the Americas. Spend a few hours here, canoeing on the lagoon and hiking trails. If you have an interest in birding, you'll want to overnight here at one of the simple lagoon-side lodges, such as Bird's Eye View Lodge or Crooked Tree Lodge. Otherwise, you could drive on to Belize Boutique Resort, an upscale jungle lodge and spa. The drive from Crooked Tree takes about 45 minutes. While you're at the Belize Boutique Resort, visit the Altun Ha Mayan site, which you can see in a couple of hours. On the second day, drive to Corozal Town, about 1½ hours from Altun Ha or Crooked Tree. Base here in Corozal Town for two days, at one of the small hotels on Corozal Bay such as Almond Tree Hotel Resort or Tilt-Ta-Dock, making day trips by boat to Lamanai and Cerros ruins (or you can drive). If you have additional days in the north, you can add a visit to Sarteneja or cross the border into Chetumal, Mexico. Alternatively, after the first night in Crooked Tree or at Belize Boutique Resort, drive to the Lamanai Mayan site and spend the night there at Lamanai Outpost Lodge on the New River Lagoon, or, for a different experience, proceed to Blue Creek Village, a Mennonite area, and spend the night at Hillside B&B or at La Milpa Field Station. Then, continue on through Programme for Belize lands to Chan Chich Lodge and spend the rest of your time in northern Belize at this amazing jungle lodge. If money isn't much of an object and you want one of the best jungle lodge experiences in Central America, then ditch the car and fly from Belize City to Chan Chich, where you can spend all your time looking for jaguars and listening to the howler monkeys.

If You Have 1 Day in Northern Belize

With only one day, head to Lamanai, which, with Caracol in the Cayo District, is the most interesting of Belize's Mayan sites. Although you can drive, the most enjoyable way to get to Lamanai is by a 1½-hour boat trip up the New River. Tour boats (BZ$80–BZ$100 per person) leave around 9 am from docks near the Tower Hill bridge over the New River just south of Orange Walk Town, or from a dock in town. If you're staying overnight at Lamanai, your hotel can arrange boat transportation.

three-hour tour, you're likely to see up to 40 species of birds. South of Crooked Tree, on Sapodilla Lagoon and accessible by boat, is a small Mayan site, Chau Hiix.

GETTING HERE AND AROUND

An easy 30-minute drive north from the international airport takes you to the entrance road to Crooked Tree Wildlife Sanctuary at Mile 30.8 of the Goldson Highway. From there it's another 2 miles (3 km) on an unpaved causeway to the sanctuary visitor center and Crooked Tree village. If you don't have a rental car, any of the frequent nonexpress buses going north to Orange Walk or Corozal will drop you at the entrance road, but you'll have to hike across the causeway to the village (or arrange a pickup by your Crooked Tree hotel). Jex buses leave at 10:50

Local Food Festivals

Belizeans love to party, and festivals celebrating lobster, chocolate, cashews, and other local foods give them—and you—the chance to join in the fun. Here are some of the food festivals in Belize. Note that dates can change from year to year.

Cashew Festival, Crooked Tree in early May. Crooked Tree village is named for the cashew tree that often grows in a serpentine fashion, curling and growing sideways as well as up. The yellow cashew fruit, which tastes a little like mango and smells like grapes, ripens in late spring, and the Crooked Tree Festival celebrates the cashew in all its forms: fruit, nut, juice, jam, and wine.

Chocolate Festival of Belize, Toledo in late May. Toledo's increasingly popular tribute to local cacao celebrates the home of chocolate in Belize, with tours of small chocolate factories in Punta Gorda and nearby, visits to organic cacao farms, and local music and dances. Belikin beer even brews a special chocolate stout for the occasion.

Hopkins Mango Festival and Cultural Jam in late May or early June. The Hopkins Mango Fest is devoted to the sweet, juicy mango, spiced by local Garifuna culture. Events include a Garifuna drumming competition, along with bicycle and canoe races.

Placencia LobsterFest in late June. Belize's biggest and best salute to the spiny lobster is held in Placencia village, usually on the last weekend in June. Booths sell local lobster grilled, fried, curried, and in fritters, and there's music, dancing, and lots of Belikin. LobsterFests also are held, typically in late June or early July, in San Pedro and Caye Caulker.

---

am from the corner of Regent Street West and West Canal Street in Belize City and go directly to the village, and another leaves from the Save-U Plaza at the corner of the Goldson Highway and Central American Boulevard at 5:15 pm. Both currently operate daily except Sunday. Another option is a transfer by your Crooked Tree hotel from the international airport in Ladyville or from other points in or near Belize City.

TIMING
One full day is enough to do a canoe trip on the lagoon, hike local trails, and see the small Creole village. But if you're a birder you'll want at least another day.

BUS INFORMATION Jex and Sons Bus Service. ☎ *225/7017.*

◉ Sights

★ Crooked Tree Village
TOWN | One of Belize's oldest inland villages, established some 300 years ago, Crooked Tree is at the center of the Crooked Tree Wildlife Sanctuary. With a population of about 900, most of Creole origin, the community has a church, a school, and one of the surest signs of a former British territory: a cricket pitch. There are many large cashew trees around the village, the serpentine growth pattern of which gave the village its name. The cashews are highly fragrant when in bloom in January and February, and when the cashew fruits ripen to a golden yellow color in May and June, they taste something like mango and smell like sweet grapes. The cashew nuts require roasting to make them

edible. Villagers make and sell cashew wine. A Cashew Festival is held annually in early May. ✉ *Off Philip Goldson Hwy. (formerly Northern Hwy.), Crooked Tree Village* ☎ *223/5004* ⊕ *www.belizeaudubon.org* ☞ *Visits to Crooked Tree village are free, but hiking, boating, and bird-watching in Crooked Tree Sanctuary is BZ$8 per person.*

★ Crooked Tree Wildlife Sanctuary

NATURE PRESERVE | The sanctuary's visitor center is at the end of the causeway. Stop here to pay your admission and arrange a guided tour of the sanctuary or rent a canoe for a do-it-yourself trip. The sanctuary, one of the country's top bird-watching spots, is managed by the Belize Audubon Society. You can also walk through the village and hike birding trails around the area. If you'd prefer to go by horseback, you pay by the hour. The visitor center has a free village and trail map. If you're staying overnight, your hotel can arrange canoe or bike rentals and set up tours and trips. Although tours can run at any time, the best time is early in the morning, when birds are most active. ✉ *Crooked Tree Village* ☎ *223/5004 Belize Audubon Society in Belize City* ⊕ *www.belizeaudubon.org* 💲 *BZ$8.*

🛏 Hotels

Bird's Eye View Lodge

$ | **B&B/INN** | **FAMILY** | Many of the 20 spic-and-span rooms, all with air-conditioning and all recently refurbished, at this modern concrete hotel have expansive views of the lagoon. **Pros:** on shores of Crooked Tree Lagoon; good meals made with local ingredients; breezy second-floor patio with great lagoon views. **Cons:** undistinguished, blocky buildings; no-frills guest rooms; small bathrooms. 💲 *Rooms from: BZ$150* ✉ *On Crooked Tree lagoon, Crooked Tree Village* ☎ *203/2040 at main office, 235/7333 at lodge* ⊕ *birdseyeview-belize.com* � *20 rooms* ⭕ *No meals.*

Crooked Tree Guides

For an introduction to the sanctuary, and for a guide, visit the Crooked Tree Wildlife Sanctuary's visitor center at the end of the causeway. The visitor center can put you in touch with all the best local guides. Expect to pay about BZ$20–BZ$30 an hour for guide services, more if you're going by boat or horseback.

★ Crooked Tree Lodge

$$ | **B&B/INN** | **FAMILY** | Owned by a Belizean-British couple, this small lodge has six comfy hardwood cottages, five with one bedroom and one with two bedrooms, on a gorgeous 11-acre site on the shores of the Crooked Tree Lagoon. **Pros:** perfect lagoon-side location; friendly hosts; good food. **Cons:** no a/c; simple but nice rooms; great spot for birders, but others may find little entertainment. 💲 *Rooms from: BZ$218* ✉ *On Crooked Tree Lagoon, Crooked Tree Village* ☎ *626/3820* ⊕ *www.crookedtreelodgebelize.com* 🚪 *6 rooms* ⭕ *No meals.*

Altun Ha

28 miles (45 km) north of Belize City.

If you've never experienced an ancient Mayan city, make a trip to Altun Ha, which is a modern translation of the Mayan name "Rockstone Pond," a nearby village. It's not Belize's most dramatic site—Caracol and Lamanai vie for that award—but it's one of the most accessible and most thoroughly excavated. The first inhabitants settled before 300 BC, and their descendants finally abandoned the site after AD 1000. At its height during the Classic period the city was home to 10,000 people.

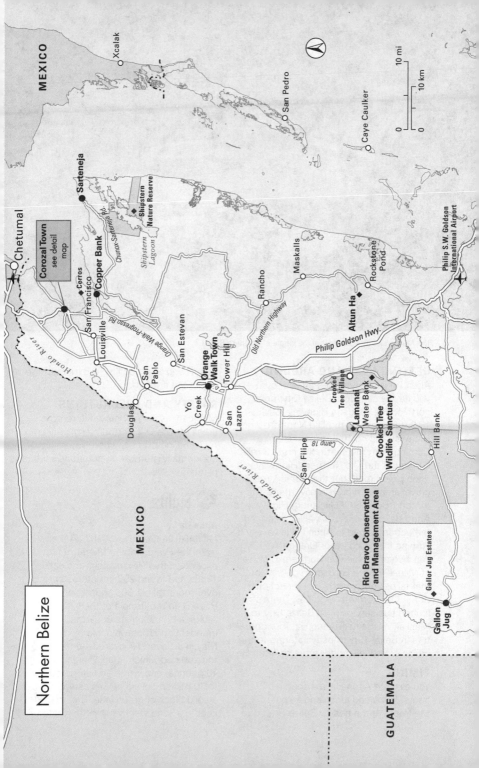

Northern Belize

MEXICO

Chetumal

Xcalak

San Pedro

Caye Caulker

Sarteneja

Shipstern Nature Reserve

Shipstern Lagoon

Corozal Town
see detail map

Copper Bank

Cerros

San Francisco

Chunox-Sarteneja Rd.

Louisville

San Pablo

Orange Walk-Progresso Rd.

San Estevan

Rancho

Maskalls

Rockstone Pond

Philip S.W. Goldson International Airport

Orange Walk Town

Tower Hill

Altun Ha

Philip Goldson Hwy.

Old Northern Highway

Yo Creek

San Lazaro

Crooked Tree Village

Lamanai Water Bank

Crooked Tree Wildlife Sanctuary

San Filipe

Camp 18

Douglas

Hondo River

MEXICO

Hill Bank

Rio Bravo Conservation and Management Area

Gallon Jug Estates

Gallon Jug

GUATEMALA

10 mi

10 km

The Mayan site of Altun Ha is in the jungle of northern Belize.

GETTING HERE AND AROUND

Altun Ha is easily visited on your own—if you have a car. From Belize City, drive north on the Goldson Highway to Mile 18.9; turn right on the Old Northern Highway and go 10.5 miles (17 km). Coming from the south, the first 12 miles (20 km) of the Old Northern Highway is a good paved road, but the rest is a mix of gravel areas and broken pavement. The turnoff from the Old Northern Highway to Altun Ha, on the left, is well marked, and the entrance road to Altun Ha is paved. If coming from Corozal or Orange Walk, you can also enter the Old Northern Highway at Mile 49 of the Goldson Highway, but that takes you over the worst section of the Old Northern Highway. There's limited bus service from Belize City to Maskall Village near Altun Ha. Tour operators in Belize City, mostly catering to the cruise crowd, also offer tours to Altun Ha.

TIMING

You can see Altun Ha in a couple of hours. If you add lunch and a spa treatment at the nearby Belize Boutique Resort and Spa, you'll spend most of the day in the area.

SAFETY AND PRECAUTIONS

Marijuana is illegally grown in remote areas off the Old Northern Highway. Avoid hiking off trail, where you might accidentally stumble on someone's weed plantation.

Sights

Altun Ha

ARCHAEOLOGICAL SITE | FAMILY | A team from the Royal Ontario Museum first excavated the Mayan site in the early 1960s and found 250 structures spread over more than 1,000 square yards. At Plaza B, in the Temple of the Masonry Altars, archaeologists unearthed the grandest and most valuable piece of Mayan art ever discovered—the head of the sun god Kinich Ahau. Weighing nearly 10 pounds, and worth an estimated 5 to 10 million dollars, it was carved from a solid block of green jade. The head is kept in a solid steel vault in the Central

Bank of Belize, though it is occasionally displayed at the Museum of Belize. The jade head appears on all denominations of Belize currency. If the Masonry Altars temple looks familiar to you, it's because an illustration of the Masonry Altars structure appears on Belikin beer bottles. Because the Altun Ha site is small, it's not necessary to have a tour guide, but licensed guides may offer their services when you arrive. Don't skip the visitor center to learn about the Maya before you head in. Try to arrive early to beat the heat and the crowds.

Tours from Belize City, Orange Walk, and Crooked Tree also are options. Altun Ha is a regular stop on cruise ship excursions, and on days when several ships are in port in Belize City (typically midweek), Altun Ha may be crowded. Several tour operators in San Pedro and Caye Caulker also offer day trips to Altun Ha, often combined with lunch at the nearby Maruba Resort Jungle Spa. Most of these tours from the cayes are by boat, landing at Bomba Village. From here, a van makes the short ride to Altun Ha. If traveling independently or on a tour that includes it, call ahead to the Belize Boutique Resort and Spa and book lunch or a spa treatment. ✉ *Rockstone Pond Rd., off Old Northern Hwy., Maskall Village* ✣ *From Belize City, take Goldson Hwy. north to Mile 18.9. Turn right (east) on Old Northern Hwy., which is only partly paved, and go 14 miles (23 km) to signed entrance road at Rockstone Pond Rd. to Altun Ha on left. Follow this paved road 2 miles (3 km) to visitor center* ☎ *822/2106 NICH/Belize Institute of Archeology* 🌐 *www.nichbelize.org* 🎫 *BZ$10.*

🛏 Hotels

Belize Boutique Resort & Spa

$$$ | **RESORT** | This fun and funky tropical boutique resort has a remote location but offers everything you could ask for: beautiful pools, jungle chic ambience, and a laid-back vibe. **Pros:** remote jungle location near Altun Ha Maya site; hospitality and warm ambience; from-scratch upscale cuisine. **Cons:** some decor not "luxury"; can be buggy; long, bumpy road to get there. [$] *Rooms from: BZ$460* ✉ *Mile 40.5, Old Northern Hwy., 10 miles (17 km) north of Altun Ha, Maskall Village* ☎ *225/5555, 800/861–7001 reservations in U.S. and Canada* 🌐 *belizeresortandspa.com* 🛏 *21 rooms* 🍴 *Some meals.*

Orange Walk Town

52 miles (85 km) north of Belize City.

Orange Walk Town is barely on the radar of most visitors, except as a jumping-off point for boat trips to Lamanai and road trips to Gallon Jug and Río Bravo, or as a place to gas up en route from Corozal to Belize City. Though its population of around 14,000, mostly mestizos, makes it the sixth-largest urban center in Belize (after Belize City, San Pedro, Belmopan City, San Ignacio, and Corozal Town), it's more like a "county seat" in an agricultural area than a city. In this case, it's county seat of Belize's sugarcane region, and you'll see big tractors and trucks hauling sugarcane to the Tower Hill refinery. Happily, a bypass around Orange Walk Town has reduced through traffic.

The town's atmosphere will remind you a little of Mexico, with signs in Spanish, a central plaza, and sun-baked stores set close to the streets. The plaza, near the Orange Walk Town Hall, has a small market (daily except Sunday and holidays) with fruits, vegetables, and inexpensive local foods for sale. This was once the site of Fort Cairns, which dates to the Caste Wars of the 19th century, when Mayan attacks drove mestizo residents of Mexico down into northern Belize.

GETTING HERE AND AROUND

Orange Walk Town is about midway between Belize City and Corozal Town, a drive of an hour or so from either

Northern Belize History

The Maya settled this area thousands of years before the time of Christ. Cuello, near Orange Walk Town, dates from 2500 BC, making it one of the earliest known Mayan sites in all of Mesoamerica (the region between central Mexico and northwest Costa Rica). In the pre-Classic period (2500 BC–AD 300) the Maya expanded across northern Belize, establishing important communities and trading posts at Santa Rita, Cerros, Lamanai, and elsewhere.

During the Classic period (AD 300–AD 900), Santa Rita, Lamanai, Altun Ha, and other cities flourished. To feed large populations, perhaps totaling several hundred thousand, the Maya developed sophisticated agricultural systems, with raised, irrigated fields along the New River and other river bottoms. After the mysterious collapse of the Mayan civilization by the 10th century AD, the region's cities went into decline, but the Maya continued to live in smaller communities and rural areas around the many lagoons in northern Belize, trading with other settlements in Belize and in Mexico. Lamanai, perched at the edge of the New River Lagoon, was continuously occupied for almost three millennia, until late in the 17th century.

The Spanish first set foot in these parts in the early 1500s, and Spanish missionaries made their way up the New River to establish churches in Mayan settlements in the 16th and 17th centuries. You can see the remains of a Spanish church at the entrance of Lamanai near Indian Church Village. About this same time, small groups of shipwrecked British sailors established settlements in Belize, but the Battle of St. George's Caye in 1789 effectively put an end to Spanish control in Belize.

In the second half of the 19th century, the so-called Caste Wars (1847–1904), pitting Mayan insurgents against mestizo and European settlers in Mexico's Yucatán, had an important impact on northern Belize. Refugees from the bloody wars moved south from Mexico, settling in Corozal Town, Orange Walk Town, Sarteneja, and also on Ambergris Caye and Caye Caulker.

Today more than 40,000 acres of sugarcane are harvested by some 4,000 small farmers in northern Belize. Mennonites, who came to the Blue Creek, Shipyard, and Little Belize areas in the late 1950s, have contributed greatly to agriculture in the region, producing rice, corn, chickens, milk, cheese, and beans. And tourism, foreign retirement communities, and casino gaming are becoming important, especially in northern Corozal District.

one. Most buses on the busy Goldson Highway route will drop you in Orange Walk Town. Tropic Air provides air service most days between San Pedro and Caye Caulker and the Tower Hill airstrip just south of Orange Walk. One-way fares start at around BZ$70.

TIMING

The reason most visitors stop at Orange Walk Town is to take a day trip to Lamanai, up the New River. Several excellent local restaurants make a stopover in Orange Walk more pleasant.

What's in a Name?

The name *Belize* is a conundrum. According to *Encyclopaedia Britannica*, it derives from *belix*, an ancient Mayan word meaning "muddy water." Anyone who's seen the Belize River swollen by heavy rains can vouch for this description. Others trace the name's origin to the French word *balise* (beacon), but no one can explain why a French word would have caught on in a region once dominated by the English (Belize was known as British Honduras). Perhaps nothing more than a drinker's tale, another theory connects Belize to the Mayan word *belikin* (road to the east), which also happens to be the name of the national beer. A few even think the name may have come from Angola in West Africa, where some of the slaves who were brought to the West Indies and then to Belize originated, and where today there is a town called Belize. Some say Belize is a corruption of Wallace, the name of a Scottish buccaneer who founded a colony in 1620; still others say the pirate wasn't Wallace but Willis, that he wasn't Scottish but English, and that he founded a colony not in 1620, but in 1638.

There was indeed a pirate named Wallace, a onetime lieutenant of Sir Walter Raleigh's who later served as Tortuga's governor. Perhaps it was liquor or lucre that turned him into a pirate, but at some point in the early-to-mid-1600s he and 80 fellow renegades washed up near St. George's Caye. They settled in and lived for years off the illicit booty of cloak-and-dagger raids on passing ships. In 1798 a fleet of 31 Spanish ships came to exterminate what had now blossomed into an upstart little colony. Residents had a total of one sloop, some fishing boats, and seven rafts, but their maritime knowledge enabled them to defeat the invaders in two hours. That was the last Spanish attempt to forcibly dislodge the settlement, though bitter wrangles over British Honduras's right to exist continued for nearly a century.

We may never know whether Wallace and Willis were one and the same, but what's in a name, anyway? Grab a Belikin and come up with a few theories of your own.

SAFETY AND PRECAUTIONS
While generally safe, Orange Walk Town does have its share of drug problems, and the cheap bars can get rough on weekend nights.

Sights

Las Banquitas House of Culture
ARTS VENUE | FAMILY | This small museum—the name refers to the little benches in a nearby riverside park—presents changing exhibitions on Orange Walk District history and culture. Among the permanent displays are artifacts from Lamanai and Cuello. Las Banquitas is one of four House of Culture museums; the other three are in Belize City, Corozal Town, and Benque Viejo. These museums are operated by NICH, the National Institute of Culture and History. ✉ *Main and Bautista Sts.* ☎ *822/3302 NICH* ⊕ *www.nichbelize.org* 🎟 *Free, some exhibits have small fees* ⊙ *Closed weekends.*

Restaurants

★ Cocina Sabor
$$ | LATIN AMERICAN | FAMILY | Succulents populate the restaurant's patio, as do Orange Walk residents and a smattering

of tourists who know a good food joint when they find it. The reasonably priced menu is a mix of mestizo and other Belizean favorites and includes flavors such as coconut rum salsa and ginger-citrus glaze that give Belizean classics an energetic twist. **Known for:** authentic Belizean recipes; friendly service; generous portions. $ *Average main: BZ$20* ⊠ *South Belize-Corozal Rd., aka Philip Goldson Hwy.* ⊹ *South end of town on west side of street near L&R Liquor* ☏ *322/3482* ⊙ *Closed Tues.*

Maracas Bar and Grill

$$ | **LATIN AMERICAN** | **FAMILY** | A well-run option in Orange Walk Town, Maracas Bar and Grill has one of the town's most scenic settings overlooking the New River—you might even spot a crocodile. Sit in the covered riverside patio or in the air-conditioned dining room and start your meal with an appetizer of shrimp, conch, or lobster ceviche (lobster is available mid-June to mid-February and conch is usually October to late April). **Known for:** lovely open-air bar overlooking the river; succulent ceviche; exceptional service. $ *Average main: BZ$20* ⊠ *El Gran Mestizo hotel, Naranjal St.* ☏ *600/9143* ⊙ *Closed Mon. and Tues.*

★ Nahil Mayab

$$ | **LATIN AMERICAN** | Orange Walk Town may be the last place you'd expect to find an upscale restaurant like this, with its Maya-inspired decor, well-prepared food, and extra-friendly servers. Nonetheless, it opened here, on a corner behind the Shell station, to rave reviews. **Known for:** charming atmosphere; rice and beans with stew chicken (it sells out at lunch); friendly staff. $ *Average main: BZ$26* ⊠ *Guadeloupe and Santa Ana Sts.* ⊹ *Two blocks behind Shell station on Belize-Corozal Rd. (Goldson Hwy.)* ☏ *322/0831* ⊕ *www.nahilmayab.com* ⊙ *Closed Sun. and Mon.*

Hotels

★ El Gran Mestizo Riverside Cabins

$$ | **RESORT** | Operated by the same couple who own Hotel de la Fuente, the new El Gran Mestizo is now the top place to stay in the Orange Walk area. **Pros:** new cabin colony is top place to stay in Orange Walk Town; pleasant setting on the New River; range of rates and accommodations from hostel dorm to premium cabins. **Cons:** breakfast is not included; restaurant only open Thursday to Sunday; riverside location means mosquitos. $ *Rooms from: BZ$200* ⊠ *Naranjal St.* ☏ *322/2290* ⊕ *www.elgranmestizo.com* ⊷ *18 rooms* ⏌⊙⏌ *Free breakfast.*

★ Hotel de la Fuente

$ | **HOTEL** | Orlando and Cindy de la Fuente's place is a step up from other hotels in central Orange Walk Town, and the low rates for the standard rooms with air-conditioning, free Wi-Fi, cable TV, and continental breakfast put it among the best values in northern Belize. **Pros:** excellent value for attractive, modern rooms; central location; variety of tours offered. **Cons:** no pool; beds may be too firm for some; linens could be updated. $ *Rooms from: BZ$98* ⊠ *14 Main St.* ☏ *322/2290* ⊕ *www.hoteldelafuente.com* ⊷ *22 rooms* ⏌⊙⏌ *Free breakfast.*

Lamanai Landings Resort and Marina

$$$ | **RESORT** | **FAMILY** | With balconies perched above the New River, this Belizean-owned resort gives guests the feeling of being in the jungle—keep an eye out for the river crocs that often spend the night under the hotel—while conveniently located just south of Orange Walk Town. The private balconies make up for the lackluster decor. **Pros:** all-inclusive package with meals and tours available; each room has a balcony overlooking the river; easy river access to Lamanai ruins. **Cons:** room decor lacks flair; no swimming pool; so-so restaurant. $ *Rooms from: BZ$480* ⊠ *Tower Hill,*

Philip Goldson Hwy. ☎ *670/7846* 🌐 *www.lamanailandingsresortandmarina.com* 🛏 *24 rooms* 🍴 *Free breakfast.*

St. Christopher's Hotel
$ | **HOTEL** | **FAMILY** | On a quiet street near the Banquitos House of Culture and backing up on the New River, this family-run hotel has simple but clean rooms, with tile floors and brightly colored bedspreads, at very affordable rates. **Pros:** unpretentious, family-run hotel; central location near market and the river; a good value. **Cons:** not all rooms have a/c; no pool; furnishings a little tired. [$] *Rooms from: BZ$84* ✉ *10 Main St.* ☎ *302/1064* 🌐 *www.stchristophershotelbze.com* 🛏 *23 rooms* 🍴 *No meals.*

Lamanai

About 2½ hrs northwest of Belize City, or 24 miles (39 km) south of Orange Walk Town.

Overlooking a gorgeous lagoon, you'll find Lamanai ("submerged crocodile" in Yucatec Mayan), Belize's longest-occupied Mayan site, inhabited until well after Christopher Columbus "discovered" the New World in 1492. In fact archaeologists have found signs of continuous occupation from 1500 BC until AD 1700. The Jaguar Temple, Mask Temple, and High Temple are sights to behold.

GETTING HERE AND AROUND

There are several ways to get here. One option is to drive on the mostly unpaved road from Orange Walk Town. Turn west off the Goldson Highway (also known in Orange Walk Town as Queen Victoria Avenue or Belize-Corozal Road) at the Orange Walk fire station. From here go to Yo Creek, then southwest to San Felipe Village, a total of 24 miles (39 km). In San Felipe, go straight for another 12 miles (19 km) to reach the ruins. Another route by road is via Shipyard—the unpaved road to Shipyard is just south of Orange Walk. The best way to approach the ruins, however, is by boat, which takes about an hour and a half from Orange Walk. Boats leave around 9 am from the Tower Hill bridge over the New River on the Goldson Highway, about 6 miles (10 km) south of Orange Walk, and from a dock in town. If you are staying at Lamanai Outpost Lodge, the lodge has its own boats to take you up the river, departing from a dock just southwest of the dock where other Lamanai boats depart. Some hotels in Orange Walk Town arrange Lamanai tours, with pickup and drop-off at the hotel. You can also take a 15-minute charter plane trip from Belize City.

TIMING

Most people visit Lamanai as a day-trip, but to see the ruins and explore the New River Lagoon, you'll want to overnight at least and preferably stay two to three nights.

Sights

★ **Lamanai** (*"submerged crocodile"*)
ARCHAEOLOGICAL SITE | **FAMILY** | What makes Lamanai so special is its setting on the west bank of a beautiful 28-mile-long (45-km) lagoon, one of only two waterside Mayan sites in Belize (the other is Cerros, near Corozal Town). Nearly 400 species of birds have been spotted in the area and a troop of howler monkeys visits the archaeological site regularly.

For nearly 3,000 years Lamanai's residents carried on a lifestyle that passed from one generation to the next, until the Spanish missionaries arrived. You can still see the ruins of the missionaries' church near the village of Indian Church. The same village also has an abandoned 19th-century sugar mill. With its immense drive wheel and steam engine—on which you can still read the name of the manufacturer, Leeds Foundry of New Orleans—swathed in strangler vines and creepers, it's a haunting sight. In all, 50 to 60 Mayan structures are

The Mennonites in Belize

About 12,000 Mennonites live in a dozen different communities in Belize. Some communities, such as Blue Creek in northern Belize and Spanish Lookout in Cayo District, are "progressive." Modern vehicles and agricultural methods are used and the community even gets involved in the government. Others, such as Little Belize and Shipyard in northern Belize, are conservative—traditional, inward-looking, and shunning modern conveniences, opting for horses and buggies instead. Most Mennonites in Belize speak a Low German dialect among themselves. Although not unfriendly to visitors, they do not seek tourism, and there are few visitor facilities in Mennonite areas. However, Mennonites, known in Belize as hard-working and savvy about business, provide much of the food produced in Belize and dominate a good part of the construction business in the country.

spread over this 950-acre archaeological reserve. The most impressive is the largest pre-Classic structure in Belize—a massive, stepped temple built into the hillside overlooking the New River Lagoon. Many structures at Lamanai have been partially excavated. Trees and vines grow from the tops of some temples, and the sides of one pyramid are covered with vegetation. On the grounds you'll find a visitor center with educational displays on the site, and pottery, carvings, and small statues, some dating back 2,500 years. Local villagers from the Indian Church Village Artisans Center set up small stands on the grounds to sell handmade carvings, jewelry, and other crafts, along with T-shirts and snacks. Many visitors enjoy Lamanai not only for the stunning setting on the New River Lagoon, but also for the boat ride up the New River, where you are likely to see many birds, along with howler monkeys, crocodiles, and maybe even manatees. **■ TIP→ Lamanai is a popular destination for cruise ship excursions; some days there can be large numbers of day visitors from cruise ships.** ✉ *Near Indian Church Village* 🌐 *www.nichbelize.org* 🎫 *BZ$10.*

Hotels

★ Lamanai Outpost Lodge
$$$$ | RESORT | FAMILY | Perched on a low hillside on the New River Lagoon within walking distance of the Lamanai ruins, this eco-lodge's well-designed thatch cabanas sit amid lovely gardens and have porches with lagoon views. **Pros:** gorgeous setting on the New River Lagoon; easy access to Lamanai ruins; excellent tours. **Cons:** high rates; no a/c; no swimming pool. [$] *Rooms from: BZ$1,000* ✉ *Near Indian Church Village* ☎ *235/2441, 954/636–1107 in U.S.* 🌐 *www.lamanai.com* 🛏 *17 rooms* 🍴 *Some meals.*

Río Bravo Conservation and Management Area

2½ hrs west of Belize City.

Created with the help of distinguished British naturalist Gerald Durrell, the Río Bravo Conservation and Management Area spans 260,000 acres near where Belize, Guatemala, and Mexico meet. The four-hour drive from Belize City takes you through wildlands where you may encounter a troop of spider monkeys, wildcats, flocks of ocellated turkeys, a dense shower of butterflies—anything but another vehicle.

GETTING HERE AND AROUND

By car from Belize City or Corozal Town, drive to Orange Walk Town, going into town rather than taking the bypass. Turn west at the crossroads near the Orange Walk fire station toward Yo Creek. Continue on through Yo Creek, following the road that turns sharply south and goes through San Lazaro, Trinidad, and August Pine Ridge villages. At San Felipe, 24 miles (40 km) from Orange Walk Town, the road turns sharply to the west (right) at a soccer field. Follow this road for about 7 miles (12 km) to the Río Bravo bridge and into Programme for Belize lands. If you don't have your own car, contact Programme for Belize and ask if they can arrange transportation for you from Orange Walk Town, Belize City, or elsewhere.

CONTACTS Programme for Belize.
☎ 277/5616 Programme for Belize
⊕ www.pfbelize.org.

TIMING

If you decide to visit this remote part of Belize, you'll want to spend a minimum of two days, and preferably longer, so you can explore the jungle, La Milpa, and nearby mestizo villages.

SAFETY AND PRECAUTIONS

Once away from the field station grounds, you're in the bush. Keep a wary eye out for poisonous snakes, scorpions, stinging insects, and other denizens of the wild.

 Sights

Río Bravo Conservation and Management Area

NATURE PRESERVE | FAMILY | Managed by Belize City–based Programme for Belize, a not-for-profit organization whose mission is the wise use and conservation of Belize's natural resources, the Río Bravo Conservation Area contains nearly 400 species of birds, 70 species of mammals, and 200 types of trees. About one-half of Río Bravo is managed as a nature reserve, and the rest is managed to generate income, from forestry and other activities, including tourism. Programme for Belize is actively involved in research and conservation programs to protect endangered species including the yellow-headed parrot.

Within the reserve's borders are more than 60 Mayan sites; many have yet to be explored. The most important is **La Milpa**, Belize's largest site beside Caracol and Lamanai. At its height between AD 400 and 830, La Milpa was home to almost 50,000 people. The suburbs of this city spread out some 3 miles (5 km) from the city center, and the entire city encompassed some 30 square miles (78 square km) in area. So far, archaeologists have discovered 20 large courtyards and 19 stelae.

Visiting Río Bravo, like the other areas of northwestern Orange Walk, is best done in a four-wheel-drive vehicle. You must make arrangements to visit in advance with **Programme for Belize ,** as the entire Río Bravo Conservation Area is managed by this private, nonprofit organization, and the main road through its lands is gated. You also need advance reservations to stay at La Milpa Field Station. Staying overnight or longer at this field station is the best way to see Río Bravo, but you can visit it briefly on a day-trip. Another field station, at Hill Bank, primarily serves as a research base for sustainable forest management but visitors with an interest in forest research can be accommodated in two cabanas and a dorm that sleeps six. Contact Programme for Belize for information.

Guides and information are available at La Milpa Field Station. Chan Chich Lodge, Lamanai Outpost Lodge, and other hotels also can arrange visits with guides to La Milpa and the Río Bravo Conservation and Management Area. ✉ *Orange Walk Town* ☎ *227/5616 Programme for Belize* 🌐 *www.pfbelize.org.*

Hotels

La Milpa Field Station

$$$$ | B&B/INN | FAMILY | About 3 miles (5 km) from La Milpa Mayan site, this field station is a combination lodge and summer camp; stay in rustic thatched cabanas with a private bath or in a dorm that sleeps up to 30. **Pros:** you'll feel like an archaeologist or naturalist here; quiet and remote setting surrounded by nature; dining room serves filling Belizean dishes. **Cons:** accommodations are very basic; not easy to get to; can be buggy. [$] *Rooms from: BZ$610* ✉ *Programme for Belize, 1 Eyre St., Belize City* ☎ *227/5616* 🌐 *www.pfbelize.org* 🛏 *9 rooms* 🍴 *All meals.*

Gallon Jug

3½ hrs west of Belize City.

The 130,000 acres of Gallon Jug Estates, owned by the family of the late Sir Barry Bowen, is home to old-growth mahogany trees and many other tropical hardwoods along with more than 350 species of birds and many mammals and reptiles. The name Gallon Jug is said to come from the fact that an employee of Belize Estates Company, which formerly owned the property, discovered many discarded items from an old Spanish camp, including a number of ceramic gallon jugs.

GETTING HERE AND AROUND

The easiest and fastest way to get here is by charter airplane (about BZ$800 for two people to Gallon Jug Estates' own 3,000-foot airstrip). Javier Flying Service in Cayo District has three- and five-passenger Cessna airplanes, and charter flights are also available through Tropic Air. Chan Chich Lodge will arrange the flights for you. With advance permission, you can also drive to Chan Chich, about 3½ hours from Belize City. Follow the route to Río Bravo and continue on through Programme for Belize lands to the Cedar Crossing gatehouse and into Gallon Jug lands. It's a long but beautiful drive, and you're almost certain to see a considerable amount of wildlife along the dirt road. Chan Chich offers a transfer by road from Belize City.

> **Tip**
>
> Gallon Jug is best visited on an overnight or multinight stay. Both the Gallon Jug and Programme for Belize (Río Bravo) lands are private, with gated entrances, so you'll need advance permission to visit.

CONTACTS Javier Flying Service. ✉ *Central Farm, George Price Hwy., Central Farm Airstrip, San Ignacio* ☎ *824/0460* 🌐 *www.javiersflyingservice.com.*

TIMING

You'll want to spend at least two to three days at Chan Chich Lodge, longer if you have a keen interest in birding or wildlife spotting.

SAFETY AND PRECAUTIONS

Despite its remote location, Chan Chich is one of the safest places in Belize.

Sights

★ Gallon Jug Estates

ARCHAEOLOGICAL SITE | Once part of the venerable Belize Estates & Produce Company that owned one-fifth of all the land in Belize, Gallon Jug Estates is now 130,000 private acres that straddle the Orange Walk and Cayo Districts. There's a 3,000-acre working farm that produces coffee, grows cacao and corn, and raises cattle; it's the only truly commercial coffee operation in Belize. Gallon Jug also produces hot sauces and delicious mango and other jams, which sell in Belize and elsewhere. Tours of the coffee plantings and the production facility, along with other farm and jungle tours, can be arranged through Chan Chich Lodge. Jaguar sightings are fairly common around the Chan Chich Lodge, averaging around one a week. You're likely to see toucans, many different hummingbirds, flocks of parrots and ocellated turkeys, as well as deer. Chan Chich, one of the best jungle lodges in Central America, is the only place to stay in the area. It's possible to visit on a day-trip from La Milpa Field Station, Blue Creek Village, or even Lamanai or Orange Walk Town, but you need your own transportation and advance permission to come on the gated, private Gallon Jug lands. Gallon Jug has its own private landing strip. ✉ *Gallon Jug Estates* 🌐 *www.chanchich.com.*

Hotels

★ Chan Chich Lodge

$$$$ | **B&B/INN** | **FAMILY** | Arguably the most memorable lodge in Belize and one of the top lodges in all of Central America, Chan Chich is set in a remote, beautiful area literally on top of a Mayan ruin, with 12 rustic yet comfortable cabanas—the price of a vacation here is similar to a five-star hotel in New York, yet the high cost is worth it for a once-in-a-lifetime experience. **Pros:** some of the best birding and wildlife spotting in Belize; so safe you don't lock your cabana's door; magnificent setting within a Mayan site; understated but eminently comfortable accommodations. **Cons:** somewhat difficult and expensive to get to; pricey, but worth it; no air-conditioning except in two-bedroom villas. [$] *Rooms from: BZ$950* ✉ *Gallon Jug Estates* ☎ *223/4419 in Belize City, 877/279–5726 toll-free in U.S. and Canada* 🌐 *www.chanchich.com* 🛏 *13 rooms* 🍴 *All-inclusive.*

Corozal Town

95 miles (153 km) north of Belize City.

Settled by refugees from the Yucatán during the 19th-century Caste Wars, Corozal is now the haven of many North American expats. It's the last town before Río Hondo, the river separating Belize from Mexico. Though thoroughly ignored by tourists, this friendly town is great for a few days of easy living. It's hard not to fall into the laid-back lifestyle here—a sign at the entrance of a local grocery used to advertise "Strong rum, 55 Belize dollars a gallon."

English is the official language in Corozal, but Spanish is just as common here. The town was largely rebuilt after Hurricane Janet nearly destroyed it in 1955. Many houses are clapboard, built on wooden piles, and other houses are simple concrete-block structures, though the growing clan of expats is putting up new houses that wouldn't look out of place in Florida. One of the few remaining 19th-century colonial-era buildings is a portion of the old fort in the center of town, now the Corozal House of Culture.

GETTING HERE AND AROUND

Corozal Town is the last stop on the Goldson Highway before the Mexico border. There's frequent bus service from early morning to early evening on the Goldson Highway from Belize City. Maya Island Air and Tropic Air have about four or five daily flights between the Corozal airstrip and San Pedro Aiport. A daily water taxi, the *Thunderbolt,* runs between Corozal Town and San Pedro with a stop on demand at Sarteneja.

TIMING

Although from your base in Corozal Town you can make day trips to the ruins at Cerros and Lamanai, the main activity for visitors in Corozal is simply relaxing and hanging out.

SAFETY AND PRECAUTIONS

Corozal Town and the rural parts of the district are among the safer places in Belize, but crack cocaine has made its ugly appearance here (police seem oddly unable to find and close down the crack houses), which is one reason petty theft is an issue.

CONTACTS ADO Bus Line. ✉ *ADO Bus Terminal, Av. Insurgentes and Av. Belice, Chetumal* ☎ *800/369–4652, 998/887–9533 in Cancún* ⊕ *www.ado.com.mx.*

Sights

Commercial Free Zone

DUTY-FREE | FAMILY | About 600 wholesale and retail companies are located in the Corozal Commercial Free Zone/ Zona Libre Belice on the Belize side of the Belize-Mexico border. Visitors may find some bargains on clothing and household items imported from Asia, along with discounted gasoline and liquor, though the retail stores target Mexicans rather than Belizeans or U.S. or other international tourists. Three casinos also target the Mexican market, especially on weekends. Visitors going from Belize to the Free Zone must pay the Belize BZ$40 exit fee, which cuts into any savings on gas or merchandise, and pay duties on goods (especially liquor) brought back into Belize. ✉ *1 Freedom Ave., Belize-Mexico Border* ☎ *423/7010* ⊕ *www.belizecorozalfreezone.com.*

Corozal House of Culture

MUSEUM | The architecturally elegant old Corozal Cultural Center, for many years the main Corozal market, was completely renovated and is now the Corozal House of Culture. Located in one of the oldest buildings in northern Belize (other than ancient Mayan structures), the House of Culture was built in 1886. It's operated by the National Institute of History and Culture (NICH) as an art gallery and museum devoted to the history of Corozal Town

Hot Property

Corozal District has become a hot spot for U.S., Canadian, and European retirees and snowbirds. Several hundred expats live full-time in Corozal District, and the numbers are growing. They're attracted by the home prices—a two-bedroom, modern home in a nice area near the water can go for less than US$150,000. Two-bedroom rental apartments and small houses are available starting at US$250 to US$400 a month. An expat "friendship luncheon" is held monthly in Corozal Town. Newcomers and wannabes welcome.

and northern Belize. NICH operates other museums including ones in Belize City, Orange Walk Town, San Pedro, San Ignacio, and Benque Viejo, along with many Mayan archaeological sites. ✉ *1st Ave., near Corozal Bay* ☎ *422/0071* ⊕ *www.nichbelize.org* ☑ *Free* ☉ *Closed weekends.*

Corozal Museum

MUSEUM | FAMILY | This tiny one-room museum is the work of Lydia Ramcharam Pollard, a third-generation Indian Belizean, whose grandparents came to Belize as indentured servants in the mid-19th century and worked in the sugarcane and rice fields. Pollard has collected a variety of Corozal historical artifacts, including old domestic household items, sugarcane tools, tortilla-making equipment, and other mestizo pieces, along with some items that represent her family's history. ✉ *129 South End, aka Goldson Hwy.* ✛ *0.5 mile south of Corozal Town, in house on east side of highway* ☎ *402/3314* ☑ *By donation* ☉ *Closed Sun.*

Santa Rita

ARCHAEOLOGICAL SITE | Not far from Corozal are several Mayan sites. The closest, Santa Rita, is a short walk or drive from the town center. It's on a low hill across from the Coca-Cola plant near Corozal Hospital at the north end of town. Only one large temple building has been excavated. The government of Belize designated Santa Rita as an official "Wedding Garden of Belize," and a number of mostly Belizean weddings have been held there. Although there isn't a visitor center yet, a caretaker/guide will show you around and collect the admission fee. ✉ *Near Corozal Hospital and Coca-Cola plant* 🌐 *www.nichbelize.org* 🎟 *BZ$10.*

🍴 Restaurants

★ Corozo Blue's

$$ | **PIZZA** | **FAMILY** | This popular eatery in a stone building on the bay at the South End serves excellent wood-fired pizza, burgers, sandwiches, and ceviche, plus a few traditional Belizean dishes like rice and beans. By Corozal standards, prices are on the high side, but the atmosphere, bayside setting, and friendly staff make it well worth a visit. **Known for:** beautiful bay views; great wood-fired pizza; large menu. [$] *Average main: BZ$27* ✉ *South End* ☎ *422/0090.*

★ June's Kitchen

$ | **LATIN AMERICAN** | **FAMILY** | The best breakfast in Corozal is served by Miss June at her home, but there's only seating for about a dozen guests on the open-air patio. Everything is homemade, freshly prepared, and served by Miss June and her family. **Known for:** yummy home cooking; big breakfasts with great prices; friendliest service in town. [$] *Average main: BZ$12* ✉ *3rd St. S* ☎ *422/2559* 🕓 *Closed Sun. No dinner.*

★ Patty's Bistro

$$ | **LATIN AMERICAN** | **FAMILY** | Patty's Bistro (sometimes spelled Patti's) serves some of the best food in town, the service is sprightly and friendly, the atmosphere is no-frills, and prices are low. For a local treat, try the hearty conch soup (in season, usually October to late April). **Known for:** great Belizean and North American choices; conch soup; odd hours. [$] *Average main: BZ$19* ✉ *2nd St. N* ☎ *402/0174* 🕓 *Closed Sun.*

🛏 Hotels

★ Almond Tree Hotel Resort

$$ | **RESORT** | Directly on the bay just south of town, Almond Tree Hotel Resort raises the bar on Corozal Town lodging. **Pros:** attractively designed rooms; swimming pool; bayside setting with views. **Cons:** on the south end, a bit away from the main part of town; limited dining options at resort but good restaurants nearby; no TV. [$] *Rooms from: BZ$240* ✉ *425 Bayshore Dr., South End* ☎ *628/9224* 🌐 *www.almondtreeresort.com* 🔑 *10 rooms* 🍽 *No meals.*

George Hardie's Las Vegas Hotel & Casino

$$ | **HOTEL** | George Hardie's Las Vegas Hotel & Casino is northern Belize's largest and most upscale hotel, with a fitness center, swimming pool, bars, and a good restaurant on-site. **Pros:** swimming pool; large, full-service hotel with restaurant on-site; friendly staff. **Cons:** located in Free Zone, not in Corozal Town; visitors to Free Zone must pay BZ$40 Belize exit fee; caters mainly to gamblers. [$] *Rooms from: BZ$280* ✉ *Mile 91.5, Philip Goldson Hwy.* ✥ *In Corozal Commercial Zone aka Corozal Free Zone, on Belize territory but requiring official exit from Belize (Mexican visitors do not need to go through Belize customs and immigration)* ☎ *423/7000 in Belize* 🌐 *www.lvbelize.com* 🔑 *106 rooms* 🍽 *No meals.*

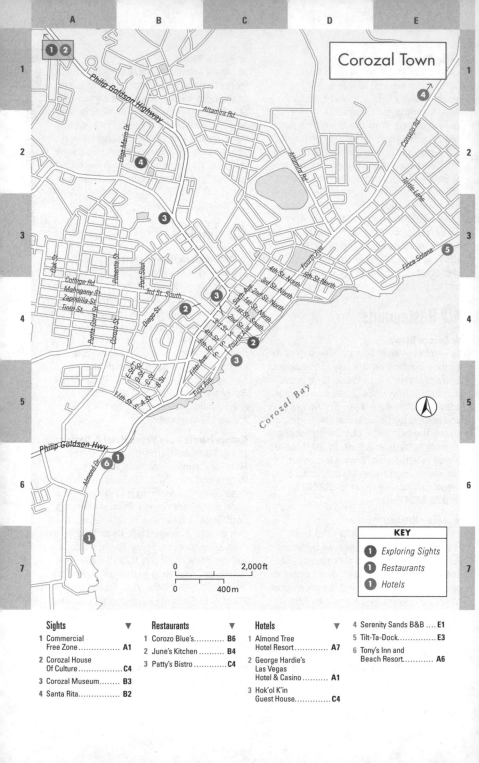

Corozal Town

KEY

1. Exploring Sights
1. Restaurants
1. Hotels

Sights ▼	**Restaurants** ▼	**Hotels** ▼	4 Serenity Sands B&B **E1**
1 Commercial Free Zone **A1**	1 Corozo Blue's **B6**	1 Almond Tree Hotel Resort **A7**	5 Tilt-Ta-Dock **E3**
2 Corozal House Of Culture **C4**	2 June's Kitchen **B4**	2 George Hardie's Las Vegas Hotel & Casino **A1**	6 Tony's Inn and Beach Resort **A6**
3 Corozal Museum **B3**	3 Patty's Bistro **C4**		
4 Santa Rita **B2**		3 Hok'ol K'in Guest House **C4**	

Hok'ol K'in Guest House

$ | **HOTEL** | **FAMILY** | Yucatec Mayan for "coming of the rising sun," Hok'ol K'in, founded by an American Peace Corps veteran and now operated by Belizeans, is a friendly small budget hotel on the Corozal bayfront. **Pros:** breezy bayfront location within walking distance of most shops and restaurants; friendly management; some handicap-accessible rooms. **Cons:** no-frills rooms; only half of the guest rooms have a/c; in-town location can get loud. $ *Rooms from: BZ$120* ✉ *89 4th Ave.* ☎ *422/3329* ⊕ *www.corozal.net* ⇱ *11 rooms* ❍| *No meals.*

★ **Serenity Sands B&B**

$ | **B&B/INN** | **FAMILY** | This upscale, eco-oriented bed-and-breakfast is hidden away off the Consejo Road north of Corozal Town, with four tastefully decorated rooms on the second floor with private balconies overlooking gardens, Belizean art, and locally made hardwood furniture. **Pros:** immaculately maintained grounds; family friendly; eco-oriented management. **Cons:** out-of-the-way location warrants a rental car; a short walk to bay; limited a/c. $ *Rooms from: BZ$190* ✉ *Mile 3, Consejo Rd.* ⊹ *From Corozal Town, take 4th Ave. N, which becomes unpaved Consejo Rd. Stay on Consejo Rd. 3 miles (5 km). Turn right at Serenity Sands sign. Follow Serenity Rd. 0.75 mile (1.2 km); turn at first right and follow this road turning left, then right until you reach Serenity Sands B&B* ☎ *669/2394* ⊕ *www.serenitysands.com* ⇱ *5 rooms* ❍| *Free breakfast.*

★ **Tilt-Ta-Dock**

$ | **RESORT** | These eight charming adults-only cabanas scattered along the bayshore are private and well appointed, and you'll wake each morning to gorgeous turquoise water views. **Pros:** great bay views and dock; pool, bikes, and kayaks; full kitchens. **Cons:** no restaurant on-site; some may prefer to stay in town; no real beach. $ *Rooms from: BZ$194* ✉ *George Price La.* ⊹ *Northern edge of town on the bay* ☎ *660/9692* ⊕ *www.tilttadockresortbelize.com* ⇱ *8 cabanas* ❍| *No meals.*

Tony's Inn and Beach Resort

$$ | **HOTEL** | **FAMILY** | One of the oldest hotels and restaurants in northern Belize, Tony's Inn is still going strong, with spacious, refurbished rooms and a popular bayside restaurant and bar, all on beautifully landscaped grounds. **Pros:** attractive rooms; breezy bayside setting with landscaped grounds; open-air restaurant; safe guarded parking. **Cons:** no swimming pool; can be buggy; no real beach. $ *Rooms from: BZ$207* ✉ *South End* ☎ *422/2055* ⊕ *www.tonysinn.com* ⇱ *24 rooms* ❍| *No meals.*

Copper Bank

12 miles (20 km) southeast of Corozal Town.

Copper Bank is a tidy and small (population around 500) mestizo fishing village on Corozal Bay. The village is something of a footnote to the nearby Mayan site, Cerros.

GETTING HERE AND AROUND

One way to get here is by boat from Corozal. You can also drive from Corozal Town, crossing the New River on the hand-pulled ferry. To get to the ferry from Corozal, take the Northern Highway south toward Orange Walk Town (watch for ferry sign). Turn left and follow this unpaved road for 2.5 miles (4 km) to the ferry landing. After crossing the river, drive on to a T intersection and turn left for Copper Bank. The trip from Corozal Town to Copper Bank takes about a half hour but longer after heavy rains, as the dirt road can become very bad. As you enter Copper Bank, watch for signs directing you to "Cerros Maya."

TIMING

Most visitors do only a day-trip to see the Cerros ruins, although if you want a quiet, off-the-main-path place to finish writing that novel, you won't find a better place than Cerros Beach Resort.

Sights

Cerros

ARCHAEOLOGICAL SITE | Like the Tulum site in Mexico, Cerros (also referred to as Cerro Maya, or Mayan Hill in Spanish) is unusual in that it's directly on the water. Unlike Tulum, however, there is little development around it, and at times you can have the place all to yourself. With a beautiful setting on a peninsula jutting into Corozal Bay, near the mouth of the New River, the late pre-Classic center dates to 2000 BC and includes a ball court, several tombs, and a large temple. Altogether, there are some 170 structures, many just mounds of stone and earth, on 52 acres. There's also a small visitor center. Bring plenty of bug spray—mosquitoes can be fierce here. **■TIP→ The easiest way to get to Cerros is to charter a boat in Corozal Town, for a 15-minute ride across the bay.** ✉ *2.5 miles (4 km) north of Copper Bank* ✣ *Follow signs from south end of Corozal Town and cross New River on Pueblo Nuevo hand-cranked ferry. At T intersection, go left to Copper Bank Village and follow signs west on unpaved roads to Cerros* ☎ *822/2106 NICH Institute of Archaeology* 🌐 *www.nichbelize.org* 🎫 *BZ$10.*

Restaurants

Tradewinds Restaurant

$$ | **AMERICAN** | **FAMILY** | The "house restaurant" for the Orchid Bay real estate development, Tradewinds is run by David and Demaris, an American-Belizean couple. The menu features adequate American pub food such as burgers and wings, along with ceviche and other seafood and some traditional Belizean dishes such as rice and beans with stew chicken. **Known for:** pub fare; beach vibes; ceviche. [$] *Average main: BZ$20* ✉ *Orchid Bay Club* ☎ *650/1925* 🌐 *www.orchidbay.bz.*

Hotels

Cerros Beach Resort

$ | **B&B/INN** | Cerros Beach Resort is an off-the-grid option for good food and simple lodging on Corozal Bay, near the Cerros ruins. **Pros:** low-key, crowd-free small resort on the bay; tasty food and home-brewed beer; good value. **Cons:** mosquitoes sometimes can be pesky; cabins are basic; hard to get to. [$] *Rooms from: BZ$131* ✉ *Cerros Beach Resort* ✣ *Near Cerros Mayan site on north side of Cerros peninsula; entering Copper Bank village, watch for signs to Cerros Beach Resort. The resort will arrange for pickup by boat from Consejo or Corozal Town for parties of five or more* ☎ *623/9530, 518/872–3052 in U.S.* 🌐 *www.cerrosbeachresort.com* 🕑 *Restaurant closed Mon.* 🛏 *4 rooms* 🍴 *No meals.*

Crimson Orchid B&B

$$ | **B&B/INN** | This stylish three-level, nine-room B&B is located in the middle of the somewhat off-the-beaten-path development just beyond the hand-pulled ferry across Laguna Seca, catering both to the handful of visitors who find themselves on the road to Sarteneja, and to prospective buyers at Orchid Bay. The air-conditioned rooms are attractively furnished, and there's a great view of Chetumal Bay from the rooftop terrace and bar. **Pros:** nicest accommodations in the Cerros-Sarteneja area; reasonable prices; full English breakfast included. **Cons:** out-of-the-way location in Orchid Bay development that gets few tourists; no pool; may be too quiet for some. [$] *Rooms from: BZ$218* ✉ *Pescadores Park, off Sarteneja Rd., at Orchid Bay development* ☎ *669/5076* 🛏 *9 rooms* 🍴 *Free breakfast.*

The laid-back fishing village of Sarteneja has low-key beaches.

Sarteneja

40 miles (67 km) from Corozal Town.

The bay setting of the mestizo and Creole community of Sarteneja makes it one of the most relaxed and appealing destinations in Belize. It's also the largest fishing village in Belize. You can swim in the bay here, though in many places the bottom is gunky.

Lobster fishing and pineapple farming are the town's two main industries, and Sarteneja is also a center for building wooden boats. Most residents speak Spanish as a first language, but many also speak English. Visitors and real-estate buyers are beginning to discover Sarteneja, and while tourism services are still minimalist, several small guesthouses are now open, and there are a few places to get a simple, inexpensive bite to eat.

GETTING HERE AND AROUND

Driving to Sarteneja from Corozal Town takes about 1½ hours via the New River ferry and a second, bayside ferry across Laguna Seca. The road is unpaved and can be very muddy after heavy rains. You also can drive to Sarteneja from Orange Walk Town, a trip of about 40 miles (67 km) and 1½ hours. There are several Sarteneja Bus Line buses a day, except Sunday, from Belize City via Orange Walk Town. The trip from Belize City takes 3½ to 4 hours.

The daily water taxi, *Thunderbolt,* which sails between Corozal Town and San Pedro, will drop you at Sarteneja on request. You also can hire a private boat in Corozal to take you and your party to Sarteneja.

Sarteneja has an airstrip, with flights on Tropic Air from San Pedro to Corozal Town stopping at Sarteneja on demand.

CONTACTS Tropic Air. ⊠ *San Pedro Airport, Coconut Dr., San Pedro Town*

☎ *226/2626 reservations in Belize* 🌐 *www.tropicair.com.*

TIMING

Once you visit Shipstern and take a splash in the sea, you've just about exhausted all there is to do in Sarteneja. So bring several good books and enjoy the slow-paced village life.

Sights

Shipstern Nature Reserve

NATURE PRESERVE | About 3½ miles (6 km) west of Sarteneja on the road to Orange Walk or Corozal is the Shipstern Nature Reserve; this is the driest place in Belize and best visited January through April. You pass the entrance and visitor center as you come into Sarteneja. The 31 square miles (81 square km) of tropical forest forming the reserve are, like the Crooked Tree Wildlife Sanctuary, a paradise for birders. Shipstern is managed by the Corozal Sustainable Future Initiative (CSFI), an NGO. More than 300 species of birds have been identified here. Look for egrets (there are 13 species), American coots, keel-billed toucans, flycatchers, warblers, and several species of parrots. Mammals are in healthy supply as well, including tapirs, pumas, and jaguars. The former butterfly farm next to the visitor center is now a small education area, and butterflies are being repopulated; don't apply bug spray if you are entering the butterfly enclosure. Nearby, a small museum at Mahogany Park focuses on the history and uses of this beautiful tropical hardwood. There is a botanical trail leading from the visitor center, with the names of many plants and trees identified on small signs. Admission, a visit to the butterfly center, and a guided tour of the botanical trail is BZ$10 per person. Other tours are available, including one to the lagoon at Xo-Pol (BZ$70 per person) to see birds and crocodiles; stop at the Shipstern visitor center for more information. Bring plenty of bug juice. ■ **TIP→ Although you can stay and eat in Sarteneja village, Shipstern offers basic cabin accommodations or a budget; meals are an added daily cost.** ✉ *Chunox-Sarteneja Rd., near Sarteneja village* ☎ *660/1807 Corozal Sustainable Future Initiative in Corozal Town* 🌐 *www.visitshipstern.com* 🎟 *BZ$10 per person, with minimum charge of BZ$20; birding tours BZ$50 per person, with a minimum charge of BZ$100.*

Restaurants

Liz's Fast Food

$ | **LATIN AMERICAN** | **FAMILY** | You can get a sack full of tacos, *sabutes* (corn tortillas topped with refried beans, shredded stewed chicken, lettuce, onions, tomatoes, and cilantro), empanadas, *garnaches* (fried corn tortillas with refried beans, grated cheese, onions, habanero pepper, and cilantro), and other mestizo dishes here for almost nothing. Most items, though small as a sand dollar, are extremely tasty and cost only a Belize dollar for two or three. **Known for:** tasty, inexpensive food; sabutes; fresh juice. [$] *Average main: BZ$2* ✉ *Av. Primitivo Aragon* ✥ *Near center of town* 💳 *No credit cards.*

Hotels

Fernando's Seaside Guesthouse

$ | **B&B/INN** | Lounge on the second-floor veranda of this small waterfront guesthouse and watch the fishing boats anchored just a few hundred feet away. **Pros:** across Front St. from the sea; water views from the second-floor porch; near the nature reserve. **Cons:** rooms at back lack a sea view; rooms are basic; no restaurant. [$] *Rooms from: BZ$109* ✉ *64 N. Front St.* ☎ *423/2085* 🛏 *4 rooms* 🍴 *No meals.*

Chapter 6

THE CAYO

Updated by
Rachel White

⊙ Sights	🍴 Restaurants	🏨 Hotels	🛍 Shopping	🍸 Nightlife
★★★★☆	★★☆☆☆	★★★☆☆	★★☆☆☆	★★☆☆☆

WELCOME TO THE CAYO

TOP REASONS TO GO

★ **National Parks and Reserves:** About 60% of the Cayo District is national parks and reserves. That's good news if you like hiking, birding, wildlife spotting, or canoeing.

★ **Caves:** Although there are caves in Toledo and elsewhere in Belize, Cayo has the biggest and most exciting ones. Actun Tunichil Muknal is the top caving experience in Belize.

★ **Mayan Sites:** The Cayo is home to the largest and most important Mayan site in Belize; Caracol has more than 35,000 buildings. Cayo also has the most easily accessible Mayan sites in the country.

★ **Jungle Lodges:** With more than 30 jungle lodges, the Cayo has far more than all the other districts of Belize combined. There's a lodge for every budget.

★ **Mountains:** The Mountain Pine Ridge's 2,000–3,600-foot mountains, with their waterfalls, caves, and rivers, provide a welcome respite from the heat and humidity of lowland Belize.

The Cayo's main connection to the coast is the George Price Highway (formerly the Western Highway), a paved two-lane road running 78 miles (128 km) between Belize City and the Guatemala border. Secondary roads, mostly unpaved and sometimes difficult to drive on, branch off the Price Highway, leading to small villages and to the Mountain Pine Ridge, the Spanish Lookout Mennonite area, and various jungle lodges.

At Belmopan the paved Hummingbird Highway is one of Belize's most scenic roads (its rival is the newer San Antonio Road toward the Guatemalan border in Toledo District), cutting 54 miles (90 km) southeast through the Maya Mountains to Dangriga, passing Blue Hole National Park. Mile markers on the Hummingbird start in Dangriga and increase as they go to Belmopan.

1 Belmopan City. Although hardly a tourism hot spot, Belmopan has a growing number of restaurants, hotels, and nearby jungle lodges.

2 San Ignacio. The hub of western Belize, San Ignacio is a bustling little town. Here you can arrange tours (often at lower prices than from jungle lodges), shop at the local market, and get a good meal, whether you're hungry for Indian, Italian, Chinese, Belizean, or even Sri Lankan.

3 Benque Viejo. The last town in Belize before you reach Guatamala, Benque Viejo has modest art and cultural attractions worth checking out, as well as a Mayan burial cave.

4 Mountain Pine Ridge. The largest forest reserve in Belize, the Mountain Pine Ridge covers almost 300 square miles (777 square km). Crisscrossed by old logging roads and small rivers, and dotted with waterfalls, the Mountain Pine Ridge—at elevations up to almost 3,400 feet, and noticeably cooler than other parts of the Cayo—is the gateway to the Chiquibul wilderness and to Caracol. It's also home to three top-notch jungle lodges.

5 Caracol. The largest and most important Mayan site in Belize, Caracol rivals Tikal in Guatemala in historical importance and archaeological interest.

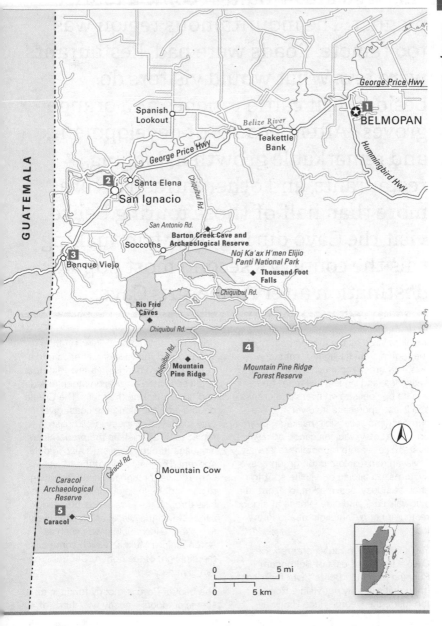

When the first jungle lodges opened in the early 1980s in the Cayo, few thought this wild area would become a tourist magnet. The mountainous region was too remote. Roads were bad. Restaurants were few. What would visitors do, besides visit cattle ranches and orange groves? After decades of development, and remarkable growth in lodging, restaurants, and other infrastructure, more than half of those touring Belize visit the Cayo during their trip, making this the country's second most popular destination after Ambergris Caye.

You'll be lured by the rugged beauty of the region, with its jagged limestone hills, low green mountains where tapirs, peccaries, and jaguars still roam free, and its boulder-strewn rivers and creeks. You'll also appreciate its diversity, in a compact and accessible package. Even on a short stay, you can canoe or kayak rivers, hike remote mountain trails, visit a Mayan ruin, explore underground cave systems, go birding or wildlife spotting, shop at a busy local market, chill out at a sidewalk café, and dine in style at a good restaurant or by lamplight at a jungle lodge.

You'll know when you've entered the Cayo a few miles east of Belmopan. Running along the Belize River for miles (though it's usually not visible from the road), the George Price Highway (formerly the Western Highway) then winds out of the valley and heads into a series of sharp bends. In a few minutes you'll see cattle grazing on steep hillsides and horses flicking their tails. The Creole people who live along the coast give way to Maya and mestizos; English is replaced by Spanish as the predominant language (though English is also widely spoken). The lost world of the Maya comes alive through majestic, haunting ruins. And the Indiana Jones in you can hike through the jungle, ride horseback, canoe down the Macal or Mopan River, and explore incredible caves such as Actun Tunichil Muknal, which some call the highlight of their entire Central American experience.

The best of Cayo is mostly found in its scenic outdoors—nearly two-thirds of the district is in national parks and forest reserves. But you should also take time to appreciate its towns and villages. Belmopan, once just a sleepy village, is in the middle of a boom, with new government and residential construction fueled by real-estate speculation. These days, it's officially known as Belmopan City, one of only two such official government city destinations, the other, of course, being Belize City. San Ignacio is a thriving little town, its downtown area usually busy with locals buying supplies and backpackers looking to book tours or grab a bite and a Belikin at one of San Ignacio's many inexpensive eateries. Santa Elena, just to the east of San Ignacio, merges seamlessly to turn the so-called Twin Towns into one. The village of San Antonio on the Cristo Rey Road is predominantly Mayan. Benque Viejo del Carmen, 2 miles (3 km) from the border, feels more Guatemalan than Belizean, and Spanish Lookout, the Mennonite center, with its well-kept farms and no-nonsense farm-supply and general stores, could as well be in the U.S. Midwest.

El Cayo is Spanish for "the caye" or key. Local residents still call San Ignacio Town "El Cayo," or just "Cayo," which can potentially create some confusion for outsiders. The name is thought to have originally referred to the small island formed where the Macal and Mopan Rivers meet at San Ignacio.

Planning

When to Go

The best time to visit the Cayo is late fall and winter, when temperatures generally are moderate. During the peak of the dry season, March to May or early June, at the lower elevations around San Ignacio and Belmopan daytime temperatures can reach 100°F, though it does cool off a bit

at night. Seasonal rains usually reach the Cayo in early June. In summer, after the rains begin, temperatures moderate a little, but humidity increases. Year-round the Mountain Pine Ridge is noticeably cooler and less humid than anywhere else in Belize, and at times in winter it can be downright chilly, but lodges in the Pine Ridge do have fireplaces.

Getting Here and Around

AIR TRAVEL
Most people bound for the Cayo fly into Belize City. Tropic Air has flights to Maya Flats airstrip on the Chial Road between San Ignacio and Benque Viejo. For charter flights, there also is an airstrip near San Ignacio at Central Farm. Blancaneaux Lodge and Hidden Valley Inn in the Mountain Pine Ridge have their own private airstrips and helipads.

★ **Maya Flats Airstrip**
The small Maya Flats Airstrip (MYF) is on the Chial Road off the Benque Viejo Road (aka George Price Highway) about midway between San Ignacio and Benque Viejo del Carmen. Currently it is served only by **Tropic Air** and a few private aircraft. Tropic has multiple 30-minute flights daily between San Ignacio and the international airport in Ladyville (near Belize City), plus flights daily from the municipal airport in Belize City. Some of the municipal airport flights stop at either the international airport or Belmopan. ✉ *Chial Rd., San Ignacio* ☎ *226/2626 in Belize, 800/422–3435 toll-free in U.S. and Canada* ⊕ *www.tropicair.com.*

BUS TRAVEL
A number of bus lines provide frequent service—about once every half hour during daylight and early evening hours—between Belize City and Cayo, with a stop in Belmopan. Among small bus companies authorized to operate on the George Price Highway are BBOC, D and E, Guerra's Bus Service, Middleton's, Shaw Bus, and Westline. James Line

runs from Belize City to Belmopan, and then down the Hummingbird and Southern Highways to Dangriga and Punta Gorda. Westbound buses depart from Belize City about every half hour beginning at around 5 am, with the last departures at 9 or 9:30 pm.

The cost between Belize City and San Ignacio is BZ$7 on a local and BZ$9 on an express if you can find one. From Belize City regular buses are about BZ$5 to Belmopan and BZ$8 to Benque Viejo. Buses are typically old U.S. school buses and are not air-conditioned. Most buses from Belize City leave from what is still called the Novelo's terminal on West Collet Canal Street, even though the Novelo's bus line is defunct. Look for any bus with "Cayo" or "Benque" on the front. There is a bus station in the center of Belmopan, while buses stop at a parking area next to the Cayo Welcome Center on Savannah Avenue in the center of San Ignacio. The Belize Bus Blog (⊕ *www. belizebus.wordpress.com*) has helpful information on bus travel.

Welcome Center Bus Area
From the bus terminal you have easy access to downtown San Ignacio. ⊠ *Savannah St., next to Cayo Welcome Center, San Ignacio.*

CAR TRAVEL
Other than the two-lane George Price Highway most roads in the Cayo are unpaved and dusty in the dry season, muddy in the rainy season. To get to the Cayo, simply follow the Price Highway west from Belize City. Watch out for "sleeping policemen" (speed bumps) near villages along the route. ■TIP→ Be **especially careful when driving the Price Highway. Most of the road lacks shoulders, and the surface can be extremely slick when wet. Horrific auto accidents occur frequently on this highway, which is long overdue for major upgrading.** If you didn't rent a car in Belize City, you can rent one in San Ignacio.

RENTAL INFORMATION Cayo Auto Rentals. ⊠ *89 Benque Viejo Rd., aka George Price Hwy., San Ignacio* ☎ *824/4779* ⊕ *www. cayoautorentals.com.* **Matus Car Rental.** ⊠ *18 Benque Viejo Rd., George Price Hwy., San Ignacio* ☎ *824/2005* ⊕ *www. matuscarrental.com.*

TAXI TRAVEL AND SHUTTLES
Taxis are plentiful in and around San Ignacio, but they're expensive if you're going to a remote lodge. For example, a taxi from San Ignacio to one of the Mountain Pine Ridge lodges is likely to be BZ$100–BZ$150, and to one of the lodges west of San Ignacio on the Macal River, about BZ$50–BZ$80 (rates are negotiable). Taxis within San Ignacio shouldn't be more than BZ$6 to most points and around BZ$15 to Bullet Tree. Collective taxis (they pick up as many passengers as possible) run to the Guatemala border from San Ignacio for BZ$5 (ask a local to show you where they pick up). *Colectivos* to Bullet Tree are BZ$2 to BZ$4. You can find taxis at Market Square in the middle of town, near Burns Avenue, or call **Cayo Taxi Association** (☎ *824/2196*) or **Savannah Taxi Association** (☎ *824/2155*), or, easiest of all, have your hotel call a taxi.

Many Cayo hotels and lodges provide van transportation from the international airport and other points in Belize City for about BZ$200–BZ$300 for up to four people one way. Several operators run shuttle vans between Belize City and San Ignacio for around BZ$70–BZ$100 per person. Among those currently offering shuttles are **William's Shuttle, Belize Shuttles and Transfers, and Discounted Belize Shuttles and Tours.** William's Shuttle is run by Dutch expat William Hofman, who is reliable, friendly, and knowledgeable; he charges around BZ$90 per person for two between Belize City and San Ignacio, or BZ$70 per person for three or more. Belize Shuttles and Transfers has both on-demand and fixed-time shuttle trips, the fixed-time shuttles to San Ignacio from either Belize City airport costing BZ$70 per person, plus 12.5% tax. Discounted Shuttles charges BZ$70 per person for two people from the international airport to Belmopan and BZ$90 per person to San Ignacio; these rates include tax. **Mayan World** and **PACZ Tours** also offer shuttles, including to Flores or Tikal in Guatemala (BZ$70 per person with a minimum of two people). Shuttles to Guatemala do not include the BZ$40 per person Belize exit fee. *For more information on these shuttles, please visit the Shuttle section in the Travel Smart chapter.*

A taxi from the international airport near Belize City to San Ignacio will cost around BZ$180–BZ$250 (for the cab, not per person), depending on your bargaining ability.

Safety

Although most visitors report feeling completely safe in the Cayo, in recent years occasional carjackings and robberies have occurred in border areas and in the Mountain Pine Ridge and Chiquibul areas. Belize Defence Forces soldiers usually accompany vehicles going to Caracol. Ask locally about any recent incidents before starting road trips to remote areas.

Being close to Guatemala's El Petén region, thousands of Cayo visitors take short trips across the border to view the fantastic ruins of Tikal. Its proximity to this tourist attraction is a boon for the Cayo but also a burden, as the poverty-stricken population of northern Guatemala spills over into relatively affluent Belize. On several occasions armed gangs from Guatemala have robbed tourists around San Ignacio, especially near the El Pilar Mayan site and in the Mountain Pine Ridge. Incidents also have occurred in Guatemala near Tikal and towns in the Petén. However, most visitors to the Cayo say they feel quite safe and as a visitor, you're unlikely to encounter any problems.

A silent killer in Cayo is the George Price Highway, formerly the Western Highway. The two-lane road is paved, but it's narrow and most sections have no shoulders on the side of the highway. Worse, the surfacing material on parts of the road is extremely slick when wet. More people die in traffic accidents on this highway than on any other road in Belize, so exercise extreme caution if you find yourself traveling this road.

Health

While the Cayo normally has relatively few mosquitoes, thanks to the porous limestone terrain that doesn't allow water to stand in puddles, there are occasional outbreaks of dengue fever. Dengue, which causes flulike symptoms, and, in more serious cases, death from internal bleeding, is transmitted by the bite of *Aedes aegypti* and *Aedes albopictus* mosquitoes. The Zika virus is also present in mosquitoes in Belize; Zika causes a rash and flulike symptoms as well as microcephaly in newborn babies when infected during pregnancy. These species of mosquitoes that carry Zika are most active in the early morning and late afternoon. Travelers, especially during the rainy season, should consider using insect repellent with DEET. There is as yet no preventative medicine for dengue or for Zika, although vaccines for both are currently under development. Pay close attention to travel warnings, and avoid travel to this region if you are pregnant or are thinking of becoming pregnant.

Health standards in the Cayo are high. The water in San Ignacio and Santa Elena comes from a treated municipal system, so it's safe to drink, though many people prefer the taste of bottled water. Resorts in the region have their own safe water systems.

Hotels

In the Cayo you have two very different choices in accommodations: jungle lodges and regular hotels. Jungle lodges, regardless of price or amenities, offer a close-to-nature experience, typically next to a river or in a remote mountain setting. Many lodges house their guests in thatch cabanas patterned after traditional Mayan houses. At the top end, lodges such as Blancaneaux Lodge and The Lodge at Chaa Creek deliver a truly deluxe experience, with designer toiletries, imported mattresses, and decor that wouldn't be out of place in *Architectural Digest*. At the other end, some budget lodges have outdoor bathrooms and thin foam mattresses. In between are a number of mid-level lodges providing an off-the-beaten-path experience at moderate prices.

Whereas the district's lodges are back-a-bush (a Belizean expression for "out in the jungle"), the Cayo's hotels are in towns or along the George Price Highway. The area's least expensive hotels are clustered in downtown San Ignacio, one of the backpacker centers of Belize. Hotels in and around Belmopan are a little more expensive because they cater to people in the capital on government business. Whether hotel or jungle lodge, most properties in the Cayo are small, typically run by the owners.

Generally, inexpensive hotels and lodges maintain the same rate year-round, though some may discount a little in the off-season (generally mid-April to early December). More expensive places usually have off-season rates 20% to 40% less than high season.

Restaurants

San Ignacio is the culinary center of the Cayo, with some two dozen restaurants. Most are small spots with only a few tables. Restaurants offer Indian, French, German, and even Sri Lankan fare as well as burritos and beans. Prices, designed to appeal to the budget and mid-level travelers who stay in town, rarely rise above the moderate level. At the jungle lodges outside San Ignacio prices are much higher. Some lodges charge BZ$70–BZ$80, or more, for dinner.

Restaurant and hotel reviews have been shortened. For full information, visit Fodors.com.

What it Costs in Belize Dollars

	$	$$	$$$	$$$$
RESTAURANTS				
	under BZ$15	BZ$15–BZ$30	BZ$31–BZ$50	over BZ$50
HOTELS				
	under BZ$200	BZ$200–BZ$300	BZ$301–BZ$500	over BZ$500

Tours

ADVENTURE

San Ignacio and, to a lesser extent, Belmopan are Belize's centers for outdoor adventure, including hiking, river canoeing, rafting, birding, caving, cave tubing, mountain biking, horseback riding, and other activities. Most lodges offer extensive tour options, either using their own guides or guides they know and trust. Jungle lodges and hotels often provide complimentary kayaks, canoes, and bikes or rent them for a modest charge.

Green Dragon Adventure Travel

ADVENTURE TOURS | FAMILY | Associated with the Belize Jungle Dome Lodge near Belmopan, Green Dragon Adventure Travel offers 3- to 14-day tours of Belize. Among them are four- and five-day adventure tours of the Cayo, incorporating visits to Mayan ruins and caves with activities including river kayaking, snorkeling in Shark-Ray Alley, and horseback riding. Rates for these Cayo tours are

BZ$2,500 to BZ$3,300 per person, not including airfare to Belize, alcohol, or gratuities. ✉ *Banana Bank, Mile 47, George Price Hwy., Belmopan* ☎ *822/2124* ⊕ *www.greendragonbelize.com.*

MOUNTAIN BIKING

Backroads

ADVENTURE TOURS | Pedal your way through Cayo and Tikal with a seven-day, six-night tour from Backroads. The tour takes you biking through the Mountain Pine Ridge and Tikal National Park, with a stay at the luxurious Blanceaneux Lodge. You also get to fly to southern Belize and snorkel on the Belize Barrier Reef. Packages start at around BZ$9,000 per person. ✉ *801 Cedar St., Berkeley* ☎ *800/462–2848 toll-free in U.S. and Canada, 510/527–1555* ⊕ *www.backroads.com.*

SEEING THE RUINS

San Ignacio makes a good jumping-off spot to see Tikal, either on a day-trip or overnight. It's also a good base for visiting Mayan sites in the Cayo, including **Caracol, Xunantunich, Cahal Pech,** and **El Pilar.** It's also a base for visiting Actun Tunichil Muknal, the amazing caves that introduce you to the Mayan underworld.

Belize Magnificent Mayan Tours

SPECIAL-INTEREST | Run by local tour guide Albert Williams, Belize Magnificent Mayan Tours (or BZM Tours for short) does tours to Caracol, Tikal, Xunantunich, and elsewhere. Day tours to Mayan sites range from around BZ$440 per person for Caracol to BZ$850 for an overnight trip to Tikal. BZM Tours also has tours to Xunantunich, Cahal Pech, and Chechem Ha Cave, with extras such as visiting the Belize Zoo and cave tubing. Book direct for a 10% discount. ✉ *3 Burns Ave., San Ignacio* ☎ *621/0312* ⊕ *www.bzmtours. com.*

★ PACZ Tours

SPECIAL-INTEREST | A long-established San Ignacio tour operator, PACZ specializes in tours to the spooky, wonderful Actun Tunichil Muknal near Belmopan (BZ$220 per person for a guided full-day tour). They also offer other Mayan tours, including ones to Tikal and Caracol. The day tour to Tikal is BZ$290 and includes transportation from downtown San Ignacio, lunch, and admission to Tikal. The full-day Caracol tour is BZ$220 and includes transportation from downtown San Ignacio, admission fees, lunch, and stops at some sites in the Mountain Pine Ridge including Rio On and Rio Frio Cave. ✉ *30 Burns Ave., San Ignacio* ☎ *824/0536, 604/6921* ⊕ *www.pacztours.net.*

Visitor Information

The Cayo Welcome Center has a visitor information center and displays of Mayan artifacts. The Belize Tourism Board website (⊕ *www.travelbelize.org*) has some information on visiting the Cayo. San Ignacio Town (⊕ *www.sanignaciotown. com*), though a commercial site, has considerable information on the Cayo. Belmopan City Online (⊕ *www.belmopancityonline.com*) has tourism information on the Belmopan area, along with local news of the capital city. For information on how Belize is governed, visit the National Assembly of Belize website (⊕ *www.nationalassembly.gov.bz*)—the site also explains how you can request a visit to the legislative assembly.

Belmopan City

50 miles (80 km) southwest of Belize City.

While it used to be said that the best way to see Belize's capital, which was moved here from Belize City in 1970, was through the rearview mirror as you head toward San Ignacio or south down the Hummingbird, a collection of lovely jungle lodges has made Belmopan a great base from which to do your jungle adventuring. With the relocation

Great Itineraries

If You Have 3 Days in the Cayo

Upon arrival at the international airport, immediately head to the Cayo by rental car, bus, or shuttle van. If you have time, stop en route at the Belize Zoo. Stay at one of the jungle lodges around San Ignacio if it's within your budget. On your first full day in the Cayo, explore the area around San Ignacio, visiting the Xunantunich and Cahal Pech Mayan ruins, the Belize Botanic Gardens, and Green Hills Butterfly Farm. Assuming you have the energy, walk the Rainforest Medicine Trail and spend a few minutes at the Natural History Center, both at The Lodge at Chaa Creek. On the second day, if you're not planning to move on to Tikal in Guatemala after your stay in the Cayo, at least take a day tour there. Guided tours from San Ignacio usually include van transportation to the Tikal park, a local guide at the site, and lunch. Alternatively, if you're heading to Tikal later, take a day trip to Caracol in the Mountain Pine Ridge. Bring a picnic lunch and make stops at Río On pools, the Río Frio cave, and a waterfall, such as Five Sisters on the grounds of Gaia Lodge,

or Big Rock Waterfall nearby. On your final day, take a full-day guided tour of Actun Tunichil Muknal. Have dinner at a restaurant in San Ignacio.

If You Have 5 Days in the Cayo

Rent a car at the international airport and drive to a jungle lodge near Belmopan. If you have time, stop en route at the Belize Zoo and do a quick driving tour of the capital. On your first full day, go cave tubing and take a zipline canopy tour at Nohoch Che'en Caves Branch Archeological Reserve, also called Jaguar Paw after a now-closed jungle lodge at the site. Alternatively, for a more strenuous day, take a trip with Caves Branch Adventure Camp, or do its cave-tubing trip. End your day with dinner at your lodge and a night wildlife-spotting tour. On your second day, drive down the Hummingbird Highway and take a dip in the inland Blue Hole. Also, visit St. Herman's Cave, or go horseback riding at Banana Bank Lodge near Belmopan. On the third day, move on to a jungle lodge near San Ignacio or in the Mountain Pine Ridge and follow the three-day itinerary above.

of several embassies (including the U.S. embassy) from Belize City to Belmopan, and new commercial activity around the capital, Belmopan—finally—has started showing signs of life. The population has grown to more than 18,000. Commercial and retail activities are booming, and there's a minor real-estate gold rush going on.

GETTING HERE AND AROUND

Belmopan is about 48 miles (79 km) on the George Price Highway from Belize City. By car, it takes about an hour. As

you approach the roundabout to Belmopan from the east, Guanacaste National Park is on your right. Turn south at Mile 47.4 on the Hummingbird Highway. In about 1¼ miles (2 km) you'll come to the main entrance road to Belmopan City. Turn left and soon you come to the Ring Road, a two-lane road that circles the city and provides access to the streets inside the ring. The jungle lodges near Belmopan are located either off the Price or Hummingbird Highway.

Butterfly Migrations

Belize is on the flyway for sulphur and other butterfly migrations from the United States and Canada to and through Central America. The summer migration usually starts in June and can last for several weeks. Among the species of butterflies migrating at this time are cloudless sulphur (*Phoebis sennae*), orange-barred sulphur (*Phoebis philea*), ruddy daggerwing (*Marpesia petreus*), great southern white (*Ascia monuste*), and giant swallowtail (*Heraclides cresphontes*),

among many others. Monarchs (*Danaus plexippus*) usually migrate south to and through Belize in the late fall, and northward in the early spring. (Monarchs are believed to be the only species that migrate both north and south.) Butterfly and moth expert Jan Meerman at **Green Hills Butterfly Farm** estimates that as many as 2 million butterflies and moths migrate through Belize in a single day during migration season.

TIMING

The highlights of Belmopan City itself can easily be seen in a couple of hours. If you're staying at a jungle lodge nearby, you can easily spend two to three days exploring the wider area, or longer, if you want to see the San Ignacio area while basing here.

Sights

At the edge of Belmopan City is **Guan-acaste,** Belize's smallest national park. **Actun Tunichil Muknal,** the cave that many view as one of the top sights and experiences in the region, is not far from Belmopan, off Mile 52.5 of the Price Highway. Neither is the **Nohoch Che'en Caves Branch** archaeological park far, accessible on a paved road off the Price Highway at Mile 37, with its exhilarating cave tubing. Belmopan is also the gateway to the **Hummingbird Highway,** one of Belize's most scenic roadways and home to the inland **Blue Hole** and what remains of **Five Blues Lake.** If you have an interest in Belizean history and politics, the **George Price Centre for Peace and Development** is a museum, library, and cultural center

focused on Belize's founding father and first prime minister.

Five Blues Lake National Park

NATIONAL/STATE PARK | At the 4,000-acre Five Blues Lake National Park, until 2006 you were able to hike 3 miles (5 km) of trails, explore several caves, and canoe and swim in a 10-acre lake with five shades of blue. The lake was a cenote, a collapsed cave in the limestone. In July 2006, despite heavy rains, the water level in the lake began to recede. On July 20, 2006, local residents heard a strange noise "as if the lake were moaning." A giant whirlpool formed, and most of the water in the lake was sucked into the ground. Many of the fish died, and the lake looked like a dry pit. Researchers believe that a sediment "plug" dissolved and the lake drained, like water from a bathtub, into underground sinkholes and caves. The lake has since refilled with water, but the park isn't what it was before 2006. The park entrance is about 3.5 miles (6 km) from the Hummingbird Highway, via a narrow and very rough dirt road. Bikes can be rented in St. Margaret's village, from which village volunteers manage the park, and homestays and overnight camping in the village also

Giving Back to Belize

Wonderful Belize is a developing nation. Its poverty rate hovers around one-third, concentrated higher in rural areas. School fees such as uniforms and books are prohibitively expensive for some families, and effects of colonialism link socioeconomic status to race. Women especially face obstacles to safety and secure income. What's more, Belize's ecosystems are fragile and depend on the work of conservation nonprofits. If you'd like to give back to Belize, here are some reliable organizations.

■ **American Crocodile Education Sanctuary:** This research and education facility advocates for wetlands and its inhabitants, and lets you "adopt a croc." ⊕ www.americancrocodilesanctuary.org

■ **Belize Bird Rescue:** Hard-working people have made prospects better for Belize's avian population. ⊕ www.belizebirdrescue.com

■ **The Belize Zoo:** This special nonprofit is famous for protecting native Belizean species, notably the jaguar. ⊕ www.belizezoo.org

■ **Cornerstone Foundation:** A branch of this international NGO is based in San Ignacio and provides excellent programs for children and women. ⊕ www.cornerstonefoundationbelize.org

■ **Oceana Belize:** Oceana advocates for the world's oceans. ⊕ www.belize.oceana.org

■ **Pack for a Purpose:** Many Belizean hotels have lists of items guests can bring for local schools or community projects. ⊕ www.packforapurpose.org

■ **UNIBAM:** The United Belize Advocacy Movement was founded by brave advocates of LGBTQ+ rights in Belize, who have faced tremendous opposition. ⊕ www.unibam.org

can be arranged. ✉ *At end of Lagoon Rd., off Mile 32, Hummingbird Hwy., St. Margaret's Village.*

George Price Centre for Peace and Development
LIBRARY | FAMILY | A permanent exhibit at this cultural center, library, and museum follows the life story of the Right Honorable George Price as he led the British colony to independence. Born in 1919 in Belize City, George Price was Belize's first and longest-serving prime minister. The "George Washington of Belize" is widely respected for his incorruptible dedication to the welfare of Belize and Belizeans. There's a sizeable library of books on human rights, peace, and national development, and the center hosts art shows, concerts, and film screenings. George Price passed away September 19, 2011, at age 92, just two days short of the 30th anniversary of Belize's independence. ✉ *Price Centre Rd., Belmopan* ☎ *822/1054* ⊕ *www.gpcbelize.com* ☯ *Closed Sat.*

Guanacaste National Park
NATIONAL/STATE PARK | FAMILY | Worth a quick visit on the way in or out of Belmopan is Belize's smallest national park, Guanacaste National Park, named for the huge guanacaste trees that grow here. Also called monkey's ear trees because of their oddly shaped seedpods, the trees tower more than 100 feet. (Unfortunately, the park's tallest guanacaste tree had to be cut down due to safety concerns that it might fall.) The 50-acre park, managed by the Belize Audubon Society, has a rich population of tropical birds,

Cornfields can be spotted along the scenic Hummingbird Highway.

including smoky brown woodpeckers, black-headed trogons, red-lored parrots, and white-breasted wood wrens. You can take one of the eight daily hourly tours, or you can wander around on your own. After, cool off with a refreshing plunge in the Belize River; there's also a small picnic area. ⊠ *Mile 47.7, George Price Hwy. (formerly Western Hwy.), Belmopan* ☎ *223/5004 Belize Audubon Society in Belize City* ⊕ *www.belizeaudubon.org* ✉ *BZ$5.*

★ **Hummingbird Highway**
SCENIC DRIVE | One of the most scenic roadways in Belize, the Hummingbird Highway, a paved two-lane road, runs 54.5 miles (91 km) from the junction of the George Price Highway (formerly Western Highway) at Belmopan to Dangriga. Technically, only the first 32 miles (53 km) is the Hummingbird—the rest is the Stann Creek District Highway, but most people ignore that distinction and call it all the Hummingbird. As measured from Belmopan at the junction of the George Price Highway, the Hummingbird

first winds through limestone hill country, passing St. Herman's Cave (Mile 12.2) and the inland Blue Hole (Mile 13.1). It then starts rising steeply, with the Maya Mountains on the west or right side, past St. Margaret's Village and Five Blues Lake (Mile 23). The views, of green mountains studded with cohune palms and tropical hardwoods, are incredible. At the Hummingbird Gap (Mile 26, elevation near 1,000 feet, with mountains nearby over 3,000 feet), you're at the crest of the highway and now begin to drop down toward the Caribbean Sea. At Middlesex Village (Mile 32), technically the road becomes the Stann Creek District Highway and you're in Stann Creek District. Now you're in citrus country, with groves of grapefruit and Valencia oranges. Near Steadfast Village (watch for signs around Mile 37) there's the 1,600-acre Billy Barquedier National Park, where you can hike to waterfalls. At Mile 48.7 you pass the turn-off to the Southern Highway, and at Mile 54.5 you enter Dangriga, with the sea just ahead. ■**TIP→ If driving, keep a watch for "sleeping policemen," speed**

Cayo History

The Maya began settling the Belize River Valley of the Cayo some 5,000 years ago. At the height of the Maya civilization, AD 300 to 900, Caracol, El Pilar, Xunantunich, Cahal Pech, and other cities and ceremonial centers in what is now the Cayo were likely home to several hundred thousand people, several times the population of the district today.

Spanish missionaries first arrived in the area in the early 17th century, but they had a difficult time converting the independent-minded Maya, some of whom were forcibly removed to the Petén in Guatemala. The first

significant Spanish and British settlements were logwood and mahogany logging camps. The town of San Ignacio and its adjoining sister town, Santa Elena, were established later in the 1860s. Though only about 70 miles (115 km) from Belize City, San Ignacio remained fairly isolated until recent times, because getting to the coast by horseback through the bush or by boat could take three days or longer. What was then the Western Highway was paved in the 1980s, making it easier to get here. The first jungle lodges began operation, and tourism now vies with agriculture as the main industry.

bumps to slow traffic near villages. Most are signed, but a few are not. Also, gas up in Belmopan, as there are few service stations until you approach Dangriga. ⊠ *Belmopan to Dangriga, Hummingbird Hwy., Belmopan.*

St. Herman's Blue Hole National Park

NATIONAL/STATE PARK | FAMILY | Less than a half hour south of Belmopan, the 575-acre St. Herman's Blue Hole National Park has a natural turquoise pool surrounded by mosses and lush vegetation, wonderful for a cool dip. The "inland Blue Hole" is actually part of an underground river system. On the other side of the hill is St. Herman's Cave, once inhabited by the Maya. There's a separate entrance to St. Herman's. A path leads up from the highway, but it's quite steep and difficult to climb unless the ground is dry. To explore St. Herman's cave beyond the first 300 yards or so, you must be accompanied by a guide (available at the park), and no more than five people can enter the cave at one time. With a guide, you also can explore part of another cave system here, the Crystal Cave (sometimes called the Crystalline Cave), which

stretches for miles; the additional cost is BZ$20 per person for a two-hour guided tour. The main park visitor center is 12.5 miles (20.5 km) from Belmopan. The park is managed by the Belize Audubon Society, which administers a network of seven protected areas around the country. ⊠ *Mile 42.5, Hummingbird Hwy., Belmopan* ☎ *223–5004 Belize Audubon Society in Belize City* ⊕ *www.belizeaudubon.org* 🅾 *BZ$8.*

🍴 Restaurants

In addition to the restaurants listed here, the food and produce stalls at the Belmopan market (**Market Square,** open Monday through Saturday, off Bliss Parade next to the bus terminal on Constitution Drive) are good places to buy tasty Belizean produce, snacks, and fruit at inexpensive prices—for example, you can get 8 or 10 bananas for BZ$1. If you can't wait to get to Belmopan to eat, near the Belize Zoo is a well-known roadside eatery where you can grab a good burger and a cold beer called **Cheers** (⊠ *Mile 31, Western Hwy.* ☎ *822–8014*).

Caladium

$$ | **LATIN AMERICAN** | In business since 1984, the Caladium is one of the oldest businesses in this young capital. Most Belizeans know it, since it's next to the bus station at Market Square. **Known for:** local specialties like conch fritters; large portions of authentic Belizean food; fast, friendly service. [$] *Average main: BZ$18* ✉ *Market Sq., Belmopan* ☎ *822/2754* ⏲ *Closed Sun.*

★ **Corkers Restaurant and Bar**

$$ | **ECLECTIC** | **FAMILY** | Next door to the Hibiscus Hotel, Corkers is run by the husband-and-wife team of Geoff Hatto-Hembling and Sam Buxton from the United Kingdom. To catch any breezes, sit in the covered, open-air patio, or you can dine inside in the cozy air-conditioned dining room. **Known for:** tasty burgers; half-price cocktails during happy hour 4–10 pm Thursday–Saturday; funky, casual decor. [$] *Average main: BZ$22* ✉ *Hibiscus Pl., Belmopan* ☎ *822/0400* 🌐 *www.corkers-belize.com* ⏲ *Closed Sun.*

Grove House Restaurant

$$ | **CARIBBEAN** | Inside the Sleeping Giant Lodge, you'll find a gastronomic delight. The Grove House serves up fresh-from-the-field, homemade meals that look amazing and taste even better. **Known for:** local, organic, field-to-table dining; stunning jungle and mountain views; beautiful presentation. [$] *Average main: BZ$30* ✉ *Sleeping Giant, Mile 36.5, Hummingbird Hwy., Belmopan* ☎ *822/3851* 🌐 *www.vivabelize.com/the-grove-house.*

Hotels

Banana Bank Lodge

$$ | **B&B/INN** | **FAMILY** | Set on the banks of the Belize River, this lodge is a good spot for families, especially those who like to ride horses, as equestrians of all skill levels have a choice of horses from their herd of about 100. **Pros:** swimming pool and bar; very friendly atmosphere; horseback riding. **Cons:** some object to the lodge's caged birds and animals; rooms are dated; loud birds at night may disturb light sleepers. [$] *Rooms from: BZ$283* ✉ *Banana Bank Ranch, Belmopan* ⊕ *By boat: Across Belize River, turn north at Mile 47 of George Price Hwy. Continue to split in road and keep right. At next sharp turn, keep right and continue 0.5 mile (1 km) to end of road, park, and bang gong to summon a boat from Banana Bank. By road: From Price Hwy., turn north at Mile 46.9 and cross bridge over Belize River. Follow gravel/dirt road 3 miles (5 km) to Banana Bank sign. Turn right and follow dirt road for 2 miles (3 km) to lodge* ☎ *832/2020* 🌐 *www.bananabank.com* 🛏 *18 rooms* 🍴 *Free breakfast.*

★ **Belize Jungle Dome**

$$ | **RESORT** | This well-appointed small inn near the Belize River has four attractively furnished small suites, with tile floors, lots of windows, and an uncluttered look. **Pros:** intimate and upscale accommodations with a/c in a lovely setting; large selection of tours with knowledgable guide; friendly and welcoming staff. **Cons:** stairs may be a problem for guests with mobility limitations; restaurant is a little pricey; some may not like eating with other guests at meals. [$] *Rooms from: BZ$207* ✉ *Banana Bank, off Mile 47, George Price Hwy., Belmopan* ⊕ *From George Price Hwy. turn north at Mile 46.9 and cross bridge over Belize River. Follow gravel/dirt road 3 miles (5 km) until you see Banana Bank sign. Turn right and follow dirt road 2 miles (3 km). Belize Jungle Lodge is on right just before Banana Bank Lodge* ☎ *822/2124* 🌐 *www.belizejungledome.com* 🛏 *5 rooms, 1 3-bedroom house* 🍴 *No meals.*

Dream Valley Jungle Lodge

$$ | **RESORT** | With somewhat eccentric decor and televisions in every room, Dream Valley is not quite luxurious and not quite rustic, but guests enjoy its intimacy and quiet location right at the jungle's edge. **Pros:** beautiful views

of Belize River; good value; tranquil, relaxed setiing. **Cons:** not as polished as some more established lodges; not that many dining options; need a rental car or taxi to go anywhere. [$] *Rooms from: BZ$286* ✉ *Young Gal Rd., Teakettle Village* ☎ *665/1000, 888/969–7829 toll-free in U.S. and Canada* 🌐 *www.dreamvalleybelize.com* 🛏 *15 rooms* 🍴 *No meals.*

Ian Anderson's Caves Branch Adventure Co. & Jungle Camp

$$$ | **RESORT** | **FAMILY** | This adventure lodge has gone upscale, adding hillside "treehouse suites" with jaw-dropping views, a multilevel swimming pool with whirlpool, and a botanical garden featuring orchids and bromeliads. **Pros:** some of the best adventure tours in Belize; lush jungle setting with beautiful orchid collection; nice swimming pool and botanical garden. **Cons:** long walks and steps to room may be problem for those with mobility issues; somewhat pricey; limited Wi-Fi. [$] *Rooms from: BZ$368* ✉ *Mile 42.5, Hummingbird Hwy., 12 miles (19.5 km) south of Belmopan, Belmopan* ☎ *610/3451* 🌐 *www.cavesbranch.com* 🛏 *29 rooms* 🍴 *No meals.*

★ Pook's Hill

$$$ | **B&B/INN** | **FAMILY** | When the lamps are lit each night on the polished rosewood veranda, this low-key, remote jungle lodge is one of the most pleasant places in the Cayo. **Pros:** well-managed jungle lodge in true jungle setting; on doorstep of Actun Tunichil Muknal; bar and dining room are conducive to guest interaction. **Cons:** insects can be a nuisance; with meals and tours lodge can get expensive; no a/c or Wi-Fi in rooms. [$] *Rooms from: BZ$476* ✉ *Pook's Hill, off Mile 52.5, George Price Hwy., Belmopan* ✥ *At Mile 52.5 of George Price Hwy., at Teakettle Village, head south on unpaved track for 5 miles (8 km)* ☎ *832/2017* 🌐 *pookshilllodge.com* 🛏 *11 cabanas* 🍴 *No meals.*

★ Rock Farm Guest House

$ | **B&B/INN** | **FAMILY** | Large, comfortable rooms nestled on a 52-acre farm greet you in this serene and eco-friendly guesthouse. **Pros:** large, comfortable rooms at modest prices; hotel guests have exclusive access to Belize Bird Rescue; proceeds go to bird sanctuary. **Cons:** no a/c; noise from birds not to everyone's liking; long bumpy road to get there. [$] *Rooms from: BZ$131* ✉ *Roar River Dr., Belmopan* ☎ *610/0400* 🌐 *www.belizebirdrescue.org* 🛏 *5 rooms* 🍴 *Some meals.*

★ Sleeping Giant Rainforest Lodge

$$$ | **RESORT** | This well-run lodge, just off the Hummingbird Highway near the Sibun River, offers luxury in a remote rain-forest setting. **Pros:** air-conditioned luxury accommodations in the foothills of the Maya Mountains; attractive grounds bordered by Sibun River; good food. **Cons:** caters to many groups; expensive; many steep stairs to get to some rooms. [$] *Rooms from: BZ$500* ✉ *Mile 36.5, Hummingbird Hwy., Belmopan* ☎ *786/472–9664 in U.S.* 🌐 *www.sleepinggiantbelize.com* 🛏 *20 rooms* 🍴 *No meals.*

Twin Palms B&B

$$ | **B&B/INN** | **FAMILY** | This unpretentious, pleasant B&B in Belmopan offers affordable, comfortable rooms with televisions, fans, and refrigerators, plus the bonus of two swimming pools. **Pros:** comfortable and friendly; reasonable rates; central location close to downtown. **Cons:** no a/c; homey decor may not be what some travelers are used to; not in the jungle. [$] *Rooms from: BZ$230* ✉ *8 Trio St., off Hummingbird Hwy., Belmopan* ✥ *From Hummingbird Hwy. at Belmopan look for Uno gas station. Entrance to Trio St. is across highway. Look for Twin Palms sign* ☎ *822/2831* 🌐 *www.belmopanbedandbreakfast.com* 🛏 *12 rooms* 🍴 *Free breakfast.*

🏃 Activities

Belmopan and San Ignacio offer a similar lineup of outdoor activities, and since they're only about 20 miles (33 km) apart, even if you are staying in San Ignacio you can enjoy the activities near Belmopan.

BIRDING

Although there's good birding in many areas around Belmopan, Pook's Hill Lodge, 5.5 miles (9 km) off the George Price Highway at Mile 52.5, is in a league of its own. The birding list from Pook's Hill includes the mealy parrot, spectacled owl, Aztec parakeet, and keel-billed toucan.

CANOEING AND KAYAKING

The Belize River, wide and mostly gentle (Class I–II), offers good canoeing and kayaking. It was once used by loggers to transport mahogany to Belize City and hosts the annual La Ruta Maya Mountains to the Sea Canoe Race. The multiday race is held in March during the Baron Bliss holiday. You can also canoe or kayak portions of the Caves Branch River (also Class I–II). Many hotels and lodges arrange canoe or kayak trips, including **Caves Branch Adventure Co. & Jungle Lodge** (☎ 822/2800), off the Hummingbird Highway. Full-day canoe or kayak trips start at around BZ$120 per person.

CANOPY TOURS

You may feel a little like Tarzan as you dangle 80 feet above the jungle floor, suspended by a harness, moving from one suspended platform to another.

CAVING

The area around Belmopan, with its karst limestone topography, is a paradise for cavers.

★ Actun Tunichil Muknal

HIKING/WALKING | A must-do adventure in Belize, the Actun Tunichil Muknal (ATM) cave system runs some 3 miles (5 km) through the limestone of Cayo, just a few miles from Belmopan. ATM is the resting place of the Crystal Maiden, a Maya girl

who was sacrificed here, along with at least 13 others, including seven children, centuries ago. If you visit Actun Tunichil Muknal ("Cave of the Stone Sepulcher" in the Mayan language), you will experience what many say are the most awesome sights in all of Central America. You'll see amazing limestone formations, thousand-year-old human calcified skulls and skeletons, and many Mayan artifacts including well-preserved pottery. As long as you are in adequate physical condition—you have to hike almost an hour, swim in neck-deep water, and clamber through dark, claustrophobic underground chambers—this is sure to be the most memorable tour you'll take in Belize. Cameras are banned from the cave, and the tour is not suitable for young children. ■TIP➜ **Although you can drive on your own to the staging area for ATM, you must have a licensed guide to visit it, as you'll be up close and personal with priceless Mayan artifacts.** It's easiest to do an all-day tour from San Ignacio or Belmopan. These tours run around BZ$200–BZ$280, including transportation, lunch, and the government admission fee. ✉ *Off Mile 52.5, George Price Hwy., road entrance at junction of Price Hwy. and Teakettle Village, Belmopan* ☎ *822/3302 National Institute of Culture & History (NICH)* 💲 *BZ$50, plus required guide fee.*

Caves Branch Adventure Co. & Jungle Camp
SPELUNKING | First on the scene was Ian Anderson of Caves Branch Adventure Co. & Jungle Camp. He and his friendly staff of highly trained guides run exhilarating adventure-themed caving, tubing, and hiking trips from an upscale jungle camp just south of Belmopan. They also run day and overnight kayaking trips in the Cayo District. ✉ *12 miles (19.5 km) south of Belmopan, Mile 42.5, Hummingbird Hwy., Belmopan* ☎ *866/357–2698 toll-free in U.S. and Canada, 610/3451 in Belize* ⊕ *www.cavesbranch.com.*

St. Herman's Blue Hole National Park

SPELUNKING | At St. Herman's Blue Hole National Park, at Mile 42 of the Hummingbird Highway, there are two large caves, St. Herman's and the Crystal Cave. Both require a guide to explore (guides are available at the national park visitor center), though you can go without a guide into the first 300 yards of St. Herman's. ✉ *Mile 42, Hummingbird Hwy., Belmopan* ⊕ *www.belizeaudubon.org* 🖃 *BZ$10.*

CAVE TUBING

An activity you'll find in few places outside Belize is cave tubing. You drift down a river, usually the Caves Branch River in the Cayo District, in a large rubber inner tube. At certain points the river goes underground, and you float through eerie underground cave systems, some with Mayan artifacts still in place. The only light is from headlamps.

In the last years since Jaguar Paw Lodge (now no longer operating as a lodge) and Caves Branch Adventure Co. & Jungle Lodge (☎ *673/3454, 866/357-2698* ⊕ *www.cavesbranch.com*) first introduced it, cave tubing has become one of the most popular soft-adventure activities in Belize. It's the number-one mainland shore excursion of cruise-ship passengers, and on days when several large ships are docked in Belize City you can expect inner-tube traffic jams.

Caves Branch River has two main entry points: near the former **Jaguar Paw Lodge** (✉ *off Mile 37 of George Price Hwy.*), at **Nohoch Che'en Caves Branch Archeological Reserve**, and near **Caves Branch Adventure Co. & Jungle Lodge** (✉ *off Hummingbird Hwy.* ☎ *822/2800*). The Jaguar Paw access attracts more people, and when several cruise ships are in port at Belize City the river here can be jammed. There's a parking area about 0.5 mile (1 km) from Jaguar Paw, and here you'll find a number of independent tour guides for cave-tubing tours, which vary in length. Cave-tubing trips from Caves Branch Lodge are longer, require more hiking, and cost more.

Cave tubing is subject to changes in the river levels. In the dry season (February through May or June), the river levels are often too low for cave tubing. Also, after heavy rains, the water level in the river may be too high to safely float through caves, so in the rainy season (June to November) cave-tubing trips may occasionally be canceled. Always call ahead to check if tours are operating.

Nohoch Che'en Caves Branch Archeological Reserve

PARK—SPORTS-OUTDOORS | Often still referred to as Jaguar Paw (the name of the jungle lodge formerly at this site), Nohoch Che'en Caves Branch is the most-visited archaeological site in Belize, mainly because of the number of cruise-ship day-trippers who come here. However, that doesn't diminish the grandeur—and just plain fun—you'll experience when you float on inner tubes in the Caves Branch River through caves that the ancient Maya held sacred. Many Belize City, Belmopan, and San Ignacio tour companies offer cave-tubing tours that include transportation, equipment, and a guide. If you have a rental car, you can drive to the park and do cave tubing on your own with a guide for lower cost. The site is at the end of a paved road off Mile 37 of the George Price Highway, and is now quite commercial with a large paved parking lot, changing rooms, concession stands, a bar, and shops. Tour operators at the site provide guides and equipment, and independent guides are also around to offer tours. Tours start with a 30-minute hike to the cave entrance, and then you float back to a point near the parking lot. Cave tubing is not recommended for young children— some operators have a 12-year-old age requirement. At times during the rainy season, and occasionally during other parts of the year, water may be too high for safe tubing. ✉ *Off Mile 37, George*

Price Hwy. ⊹ From Belize City, follow George Price Hwy. to Mile 37. Turn south (left) on paved road and follow about 6 miles (10 km) to Nohoch Che'en Caves Branch Archeological Reserve parking lot ☎ *226/2882* ⌦ *BZ$30.*

GOLF
Roaring River Golf Course
GOLF | The only public golf course on the mainland is Roaring River Golf Course. This 9-hole, 1,933-yard, par-32 jungle course (watch out for the crocs in the water traps) with double tees that let you play 3,892 yards at par 64, was the pet project of an expat South African, Paul Martin, who found himself with some extra time and a lot of heavy earth-moving equipment on his hands. Before long, he'd carved out the greens and bunkered fairways. It's not Pebble Beach, but it's fun, and affordable, too, as fees are only BZ$35 for 9 holes or BZ$50 for 18 holes. After a round of golf, you can sip a Belikin at the clubhouse. Roaring River Golf Course also has five air-conditioned cottages for rent, and a restaurant, The Meating Place, for guests and groups, with advance reservations only. ⌦ *Off Mile 50.25, George Price Hwy., Roaring River Dr., near Camalote Village, Belmopan* ⊹ *Turn south at Camalote Village at Mile 50.25 of Price Hwy. and follow signs* ☎ *820/2031* ⊕ *www.belizegolf.net.*

HORSEBACK RIDING
Banana Bank Lodge & Jungle Horseback Adventures
HORSEBACK RIDING | FAMILY | The largest equestrian operator in this part of Belize is Banana Bank Lodge, off the George Price Highway near Belmopan. Run by John Carr, a former Montana cowboy and rodeo rider, Banana Bank has more than 90 horses, mostly quarter horses, a large round-pen riding arena, stables, and miles of jungle trails on a 4,000-acre ranch. They offer occasional agricultural tours that introduce visiting farmers or others interested in agriculture to Mennonite and other farm operations in Belize. A two-hour ride costs BZ$120, and a four- to five-hour ride is BZ$180. A full-day jungle ride is BZ$200 per person and includes lunch. Night rides and horseback-riding packages are also available. ⌦ *Banana Bank, Belmopan* ☎ *832/2020* ⊕ *www.bananabank.com.*

⊘ Shopping

Art Box
ART GALLERIES—ARTS | FAMILY | With one of the largest selections of arts and crafts in Belize, Art Box is the place to go if you're looking for handcrafted gifts, books, jewelry, or souvenirs. Upstairs is a gallery featuring Belizean artists including Carolyn Carr. ⌦ *Mile 46, George Price Hwy., Belmopan* ☎ *623/6129* ⊕ *www.artboxbz.com.*

San Ignacio

23 miles (37 km) southwest of Belmopan.

When you see the Hawksworth Bridge, built in 1949 and the only public suspension bridge in Belize, you'll know you've arrived at San Ignacio, the hub of the Cayo district. San Ignacio, with its twin town Santa Elena just to the east, is an excellent base for exploring western Belize. Nearby are three Mayan ruins, as well as national parks and a cluster of butterfly farms.

With its well-preserved wooden structures, San Ignacio is a Belizean town where you might want to linger. Evenings are comfortable and usually mosquito-free, and the colonial-era streets are lined with funky bars and restaurants. It's worth coming at sunset to listen to the eerily beautiful sounds of the grackles, the iridescent black birds that seem to like the town.

GETTING HERE AND AROUND

San Ignacio is less than two hours by car on the George Price Highway from Belize City, an easy drive on a paved road. On the way you will pass the Mennonite settlement of Spanish Lookout, a thriving community. The Hawksworth Bridge to enter San Ignacio is one-way. You'll take another bridge when leaving town.

TIMING

San Ignacio and the jungle lodges around it are used by many visitors to explore western Belize, which easily takes a week or more if you want to see it all.

Sights

Most tours to **Actun Tunichil Muknal** leave from San Ignacio, although this amazing cave is actually near Belmopan.

★ Belize Botanic Gardens

GARDEN | FAMILY | The life's work of ornithologist Ken duPlooy, the personable Judy duPlooy, and their family is the 45-acre Belize Botanic Gardens. It's an extensive collection of hundreds of trees, plants, and flowers from all over Central America. Enlightening tours of the gardens, set on a bank of the Macal River at Sweet Songs Jungle Lodge, are given by local guides who can tell you the names of the plants in Mayan, Spanish, and English as well as explain their varied medicinal uses. An orchid house holds the duPlooys' collection of more than 100 orchid species, and there also is a palm exhibit. The Botanic Gardens also run gardening programs for Belize residents as well as great birding opportunities. ⊠ *Big Eddy, Chial Rd.* ⊹ *From San Ignacio, head 4.75 miles (7.5 km) west on Benque Rd., turn left on unpaved Chial Rd. and go about 5 miles (8 km) to Sweet Songs Jungle Lodge* ☎ *824/3201* ⊕ *www. belizebotanic.org* ⊠ *BZ$15 self-guided tour; BZ$30 guided tour.*

Belize Medicinal Plants Trail

TRAIL | FAMILY | Also called the Rainforest Medicine Trail, this trail was originally developed by natural medicine guru Rosita Arvigo and gives you a quick introduction to traditional Mayan medicine. The trail takes you on a short, self-guided walk through the rain forest on the grounds of Chaa Creek, giving you a chance to study the symbiotic nature of its plant life. Learn about the healing properties of such indigenous plants as red gumbo-limbo and see some endangered medicinal plants. The shop here sells Mayan medicinal products like Belly Be Good and Flu Away. ⊠ *The Lodge at Chaa Creek, Chial Rd.* ☎ *834/4010 in Belize, 877/709–8708 toll-free number in U.S. and Canada* ⊕ *www.chaacreek.com* ⊠ *BZ $10 self-guided tour, BZ$30 for a guided tour including Natural History Centre and Blue Morpho Breeding Center.*

Cahal Pech

ARCHAEOLOGICAL SITE | FAMILY | Just at the western edge of San Ignacio, on a tall hill, is a small, intriguing Mayan site, the unfortunately named Cahal Pech ("Place of the Ticks"). You probably won't be bothered by ticks now, however. It was occupied from around 1200 BC to around AD 900. At its peak, in AD 600, Cahal Pech was a medium-size settlement of perhaps 10,000 people with some three dozen structures huddled around seven plazas. It's thought that it functioned as a guard post, watching over the nearby confluence of the Mopan and Macal Rivers. It may be somewhat less compelling than the area's other ruins, but it's no less mysterious, given that these structures mark the presence of a civilization we know so little about. Look for answers at the small visitor center and museum. ⊠ *Cahal Pech Hill* ☎ *822/2016 NICH Belize Institute of Archeology* ⊕ *www.nichbelize.org* ⊠ *BZ$10.*

Cayo Welcome Center

INFO CENTER | FAMILY | The largest tourism information center in the country, the BZ$4 million Cayo Welcome Center was established in San Ignacio due to the

Cayo's archaeological sites and rain-forest jungle lodges getting an increasing number of visitors. Besides friendly staff who provide information about tours, lodging, restaurants, and sightseeing, the center has exhibits and photos of Mayan artifacts found in San Ignacio, along with contemporary art and cultural displays. Free Wi-Fi is available throughout. Food stalls and a burger restaurant are in or near the center complex, and there is easy access to the pedestrian-only section of Burns Avenue, with its tour guide offices, restaurants, bars, banks, shops, and budget hotels. The center also functions as a community center, with free movies and musical concerts by local bands some nights. ⊠ *Savannah St.* ☎ *623/3918, 800/624–0686 Belize Tourism Board in Belize City* ⊕ *www. travelbelize.org.*

Chaa Creek Natural History Centre & Blue Morpho Butterfly Farm

FARM | FAMILY | The Natural History Centre at The Lodge at Chaa Creek has a small library and lots of displays on everything from butterflies to snakes (pickled in jars). Outside is a screened-in blue morpho butterfly-breeding center. If you haven't encountered blue morphos in the wild, you can see them up close here and even peer at their slumbering pupae, which resemble jade earrings. Once you're inside the double doors, the electric blue beauties, which look boringly brown when their wings are closed, flit about or remain perfectly still, sometimes on your shoulder or head, and open and close their wings to a rhythm akin to inhaling and exhaling. Tours are led by a team of knowledgeable naturalists. You can combine a visit here with one to the Belize Medicinal Plants Trail. ⊠ *The Lodge at Chaa Creek, Chial Rd.* ☎ *834/4010 in Belize, 877/709–8708 Chaa Creek* ⊕ *www.chaacreek.com* ⊠ *BZ$10 self-guided tour; BZ$30 combined with guided Belize Medicinal Plant Trail tour.*

El Pilar

ARCHAEOLOGICAL SITE | Near the border of Belize and Guatemala, El Pilar is still being excavated under the direction of Anabel Ford, a professor at the University of California at Santa Barbara, and the MesoAmerican Research Center. El Pilar is three times larger than Xunantunich, but because it's at the end of a 7-mile (12 km) rough dirt road, you're likely to have the place to yourself; it gets only a few hundred visitors a year. Excavations of Mayan ruins have traditionally concentrated on public buildings, but at El Pilar the emphasis has been on reconstructing domestic architecture—everything from houses to gardens with crops used by the Maya. El Pilar, occupied from 800 BC to AD 1000, at its peak may have had a population of 20,000. Several well-marked trails take you around the site. Because the structures haven't been stripped of vegetation, you may feel as if you're walking through a series of shady orchards. ■**TIP➔ Don't forget binoculars: in the 5,000-acre nature reserve there's terrific bird-watching.** Behind the main plaza, a lookout grants a spectacular view across the jungle to El Pilar's sister city, Pilar Poniente, on the Guatemalan border. There is a visitor center, the Be Pukte Cultural Center of Amigos de El Pilar, in Bullet Tree Falls (usually open daily 9–5), where you can get information on the site and pay the admission fee. Note that several incidents of robbery have occurred at or near El Pilar. You may want to visit this site on a tour, available from several tour operators in San Ignacio including Crystal Paradise/Birding in Paradise. ⊠ *7 miles (12 km) northwest of Bullet Tree Falls, off Bullet Tree Rd., Bullet Tree Falls* ✛ *Take Bullet Tree Rd. in San Ignacio to Bullet Tree Falls. In Bullet Tree Falls, just before bridge over Mopan River on left you will see Be Pukte Cultural Center of Amigos de El Pilar. To go on to El Pilar, you will see signs to El Pilar Rd.* ☎ *822/2106 NICH Institute of Archeology* *in Belmopan* 🌐 *www.nichbelize.org* 🎟 *BZ$10.*

★ Spanish Lookout

TOWN | FAMILY | The hilltop community of Spanish Lookout, population 3,000, about 5 miles (8 km) north of the George Price Highway, is one of the centers of Belize's 11,000-strong Mennonite community, of which nearly 3,000 are in Cayo District. The easiest access to Spanish Lookout is via the paved Route 30 at Mile 57.5 of the Price Highway. The village's blond-haired, fair-skinned residents may seem out of place in this tropical country, but they're responsible for much of the construction, manufacturing, and agriculture in Belize. They built many of Belize's resorts, and most of the chickens, eggs, cheese, and milk you'll consume during your stay come from their farms. Many of the small wooden houses that you see all over Belize are Mennonite prefabs built in Spanish Lookout. In Belize's conservative Mennonite communities, women dress in cotton frocks and head scarves, and the men don straw hats, suspenders, and dark trousers. Some still travel in horse-drawn buggies. However, most Mennonites around Spanish Lookout have embraced pickup trucks and modern farming equipment. The cafés and small shopping centers in Spanish Lookout offer a unique opportunity to mingle with these sometimes world-wary people, but they don't appreciate being gawked at or photographed any more than you do. Stores in Spanish Lookout are modern and well-stocked, the farms wouldn't look out of place in the U.S. Midwest, and many of the roads are paved (the Mennonites do their own road paving). Oil in commercial quantities was discovered in Spanish Lookout in 2005, and several wells are still pumping, although the amount of oil pumped has diminished in recent years. ✉ *Spanish Lookout.*

Tropical Wings

NATURE PRESERVE | FAMILY | Besides thoughtful displays on the Cayo flora and fauna, Tropical Wings, a little nature center, raises about 20 species of butterfly including the blue morpho, owl, giant swallowtail, and monarch varieties. The facility, at The Trek Stop, also has a small restaurant and gift shop, along with cabins. ✉ *Mile 71.5, George Price Hwy., 6 miles (10 km) west of San Ignacio, San José Succotz* ☎ *823/2265* 🌐 *www.thetrekstop.com/tropwings.htm* 🎟 *BZ$10.*

🍴 Restaurants

Besides the restaurants listed here, most of the jungle lodges in the Cayo have their own restaurants. Those at Table Rock Lodge, Mystic River Lodge, The Lodge at Chaa Creek, and Sweet Songs Lodge are especially good. Nearer town, the restaurants at Ka'ana Boutique Resort and San Ignacio Resort Hotel also are noteworthy. On the other end of the price scale, street vendors set up barbecue grills and food stalls on the Price Highway just east of the Hawksworth Bridge in Santa Elena, and you can get big plates of food for little money.

The Crave

$$$ | ECLECTIC | At what might be the smallest restaurant in the Cayo, there's room for just one table inside and one outside, but you'll be rewarded with San Ignacio's take on gourmet dining. Choose from a small number of menu options that change daily (steak, pasta, lamb ribs, and pork chops are usually served in some way), selected by the chef/owner and cooked in an open kitchen beside the inside table. **Known for:** charming atmosphere; open kitchen; delectable desserts like chocolate roulade. [$] *Average main: BZ$35* ✉ *24 West St.* ☎ *602/0737* 💳 *No credit cards.*

Erva's

$$ | LATIN AMERICAN | FAMILY | Nothing fancy here, just down-home Belizean dishes at moderate prices, and that's exactly why it's popular. Go for the traditional beans-and-rice dishes or a fish platter; the ceviche is good, too. **Known for:** eclectic menu with something for everyone; spicy Creole flavors; filling burritos. [$] *Average main: BZ$20* ✉ *4 Far West St.* ☎ *824/2821* ⏲ *Closed Sun.*

★ Guava Limb Café

$$ | ECLECTIC | FAMILY | Located in a remodeled colonial framehouse on the far end of Burns Avenue, Guava Limb Café serves an eclectic mix of delicious soups, seafood, salads, and local and American dishes that have given it a reputation as the best restaurant in San Ignacio. Run by the owners of The Lodge at Chaa Creek, there's open-air seating and a bar on the first level, while a second-level veranda overlooks Macal River Park. **Known for:** farm-to-table ingredients; Caribbean food and Asian dishes like gado gado; vegetarian friendly. [$] *Average main: BZ$26* ✉ *79 Burns Ave.* ☎ *824/4837.*

Hode's Place Bar & Grill

$ | LATIN AMERICAN | FAMILY | Hodes is often the busiest place in town, with its large shaded patio next to a citrus grove, swings, slides, and ice-cream bar (it's much bigger than it looks from the outside). The fried chicken with french fries is some of the best in the Cayo. **Known for:** cold beer; karaoke; fried chicken. [$] *Average main: BZ$14* ✉ *Savannah St., across from sports stadium* ☎ *804/2522.*

★ Ko-Ox Han-Nah

$$ | ECLECTIC | FAMILY | From the Mayan language, Ko-Ox Han-Nah roughly translates to "let's go eat." It's far from fancy—you eat on simple tables in what is essentially a large open-front building on busy Burns Avenue—but service is cheerful, and the food is inexpensive and well prepared. Much of the food is raised on the farm of the Zimbabwe-born owner. **Known for:** farm-to-table food; Belizean rice and beans; international options including Indian lamb curries and Korean chicken. [$] *Average main: BZ$19* ✉ *5 Burns Ave.* ☎ *824/3014.*

Pop's Restaurant

$ | LATIN AMERICAN | FAMILY | The most popular place for breakfast in San Ignacio is here at Pop's, where it's served all day from 6:30 am to 3 pm. You can get an American full breakfast here, but you can also try a Belizean breakfast such as a cheese and chaya omelet, Belizean bacon, refried beans, and fry jacks. **Known for:** fry jacks; early breakfast to fuel your tour; tasty fare at affordable prices. [$] *Average main: BZ$14* ✉ *West St. near Waight St.* ☎ *824/3366* 💳 *No credit cards.*

Sanny's Grill

$$ | LATIN AMERICAN | FAMILY | With sizzling spices, this restaurant transforms basics like chicken or pork chops beyond standard fare. Try the pork in brandy-mustard sauce, the coconut chicken, or the piña colada fish. **Known for:** quaint atmosphere; grilled fish; friendly service. [$] *Average main: BZ$26* ✉ *E. 23rd St.* ☎ *824/2988* ⏲ *No lunch.*

Hotels

SAN IGNACIO

Hotels in downtown San Ignacio are all budget-to-moderate spots. On the western edge of town, with hotels such as the San Ignacio Resort Hotel and Ka'ana, lodgings become more upscale. The lodges along the Mopan River, a river that winds into Belize from Guatemala, tend to be in the budget-to-moderate range. Most lodges on the Macal River, such as The Lodge at Chaa Creek and Sweet Songs Lodge, are upmarket, though there are some exceptions. A number of lodges, including Mystic River, Inn the Bush, Table Rock, and Mariposa, have opened on the Cristo Rey Road en route to the Mountain Pine Ridge, most also with access to the Macal River.

Aguada Hotel & Restaurant

$ | HOTEL | FAMILY | Frugal travelers jump at the opportunity to stay in this tidy, attractive, and inexpensive hotel with air-conditioned rooms and a saltwater swimming pool in Santa Elena, the low-key town adjoining San Ignacio. **Pros:** clean, inexpensive rooms with a/c; one of the few budget hotels with a pool; nice on-site restaurant. **Cons:** a bus or short taxi ride away from downtown San Ignacio; spotty Wi-Fi; some traffic noise. $ Rooms from: BZ$150 ⊠ La Loma Luz area, off George Price Hwy. across from La Loma Luz hospital, Santa Elena ☎ 804/3609 ⊕ www.aguadabelize.com ⤢ 25 rooms ♦ No meals.

Amber Sunset Jungle Resort

$$ | B&B/INN | Owned by a family originally from Belize City, this jungle resort makes a real effort to show the diversity of Belize; the five cabanas, built into the jungle canopy, are each decorated to reflect one of Belize's major population groups (Creoles, mestizos, Maya, Garifuna, and the Mennonites). **Pros:** unique theme focusing on diversity; nice swimming pool; great restaurant. **Cons:** no a/c; steep climbs required to reach cabanas and restaurant; out-of-town location on a bumpy road. $ Rooms from: BZ$300 ⊠ Mile 59, George Price Hwy. ☎ 824/3141 ⊕ www.ambersunsetbelize.com ⤢ 5 cabanas ♦ No meals.

Cahal Pech Village Resort

$ | RESORT | Once you make it up the steep hill, you'll enjoy the best views in the Cayo at this hotel at the western edge of San Ignacio, near the Cahal Pech Mayan site. **Pros:** great views; enticing pool; good value. **Cons:** some rooms and cabanas need upgrading; limestone dirt road up to hotel is very steep, especially if you're walking; a/c doesn't entirely cool some cabanas. $ Rooms from: BZ$190 ⊠ 1 mile (2 km) west of town, off George Price Hwy., Cahal Pech Rd., Cahal Pech Hill ☎ 824/3740, 239/494–3281 in U.S.

⊕ www.cahalpech.com ⤢ 78 rooms ♦ No meals.

Martha's Guesthouse and Restaurant

$ | B&B/INN | FAMILY | With clean rooms, a good restaurant, and convenient tours, the four-story Martha's Guesthouse provides just about everything you need right in the heart of downtown San Ignacio. **Pros:** handy downtown location; tasty food on-site. **Cons:** can be noisy; rates are higher than most other downtown hotels. $ Rooms from: BZ$142 ⊠ 10 West St. ☎ 804/3647 ⊕ www.marthasbelize.com ⤢ 16 rooms ♦ No meals.

Rumors Resort

$ | HOTEL | This roadside hotel just west of San Ignacio provides a pool, an affordable restaurant and bar, and a convenient location, all at moderate prices. **Pros:** easy access to San Ignacio without the parking and traffic; pleasant rooms with a/c and Wi-Fi; affordable. **Cons:** some standard rooms could use upgrades; pool may be open to public at times; not an actual "resort." $ Rooms from: BZ$140 ⊠ Mile 68, George Price Hwy., about 3 miles (5 km) west of downtown San Ignacio ☎ 824/2795 ⊕ www.rumorsresort.com ⤢ 11 rooms ♦ No meals.

★ San Ignacio Resort Hotel

$$$$ | RESORT | Queen Elizabeth II once stayed at this resort with well-appointed rooms that have verandas facing a nature reserve, making you feel like you're outside the city environs. **Pros:** in-town location that feels like it's in the jungle; great restaurant and bar; attention to detail makes you feel welcome. **Cons:** a little pricey for what you get; some rooms may need updating; on-property tours not worth the money. $ Rooms from: BZ$571 ⊠ 18 Buena Vista Rd. ☎ 824/2034, 855/488–2624 toll-free in U.S. and Canada ⊕ www.sanignaciobelize.com ⤢ 26 rooms ♦ No meals.

ALONG THE MOPAN RIVER
Clarissa Falls Resort
$ | RESORT | FAMILY | The low gurgle of nearby Mopan River rapids is the first and last sound of the day at Clarissa Falls Resort. **Pros:** quiet, pastoral riverside setting; good food; very friendly and welcoming owners. **Cons:** resort is on a ranch and not in a true jungle setting; may be too rustic for some. $ Rooms from: BZ$164 ⌧ Mile 70, George Price Hwy., 5.5 miles (9 km) west of San Ignacio ☎ 833/3116 ⊕ www.clarissafallsresort.com ⌁ 11 cabanas, 1 bunkhouse ⏇ Some meals.

Ka'ana Boutique Resort
$$$$ | RESORT | Ka'ana brings a level of luxury to San Ignacio with tranquil gardens, a wine cellar, and spacious rooms outfitted with 500-count cotton sheets, high-end toiletries, and flat-screen TVs. **Pros:** convivial staff; luxury amenities; good bar and restaurant; family friendly. **Cons:** not a true jungle lodge; pricey; some may prefer no children. $ Rooms from: BZ$630 ⌧ Mile 69.25, George Price Hwy. ☎ 824/3350 in Belize, 866/494–2807 toll-free in U.S. ⊕ www.kaanabelize.com ⌁ 15 rooms ⏇ No meals.

Mahogany Hall Boutique Resort
$$$ | HOTEL | An upmarket alternative to fancy jungle lodges is this resort in Bullet Tree Falls, on the banks of the Mopan River. **Pros:** gorgeous suites; lovely views of the Mopan River. **Cons:** somewhat unusual location—neither a jungle lodge nor in-town hotel; steep stairs with no handrails and no elevator. $ Rooms from: BZ$490 ⌧ Paslow Falls Rd., Bullet Tree Falls ⊹ From east, turn left off Bullet Tree Rd. just before bridge over Mopan River ☎ 622/4325, 800/610–9821 ⊕ www.mahoganyhallbelize.com ⌁ 8 rooms ⏇ No meals.

Parrot Nest
$ | HOTEL | If ever since you were a kid you've wanted to sleep in a tree house by a river, this is your chance. **Pros:** rustic but cute cabanas and tree houses; good value; helpful and friendly owners. **Cons:** not truly in the jungle; cabanas are small; some traffic and noise from nearby properties. $ Rooms from: BZ$109 ⌧ Off Bullet Tree Rd., on Mopan River, Bullet Tree Falls ☎ 669/6068 ⊕ www.parrot-nest.com ⌁ 7 cabanas, 2 tree houses ⏇ No meals.

ALONG THE MACAL RIVER
★ Black Rock River Lodge
$$$ | RESORT | FAMILY | Some 800 feet above limestone cliffs and the Macal River gorge, across from Elijio Panti National Park, Black Rock Lodge has one of the most beautiful settings of any lodge in the country. **Pros:** remote, gorgeous setting; eco-conscious management; excellent birding on property. **Cons:** isolated setting means you're stuck here for somewhat pricey meals and tours; lack of Wi-Fi may bother some; no a/c. $ Rooms from: BZ$400 ⌧ On Macal River, 13 miles (22 km) upriver from San Ignacio ☎ 834/4038 ⊕ www.blackrocklodge.com ⌁ 20 rooms ⏇ No meals.

★ The Lodge at Chaa Creek
$$$$ | RESORT | FAMILY | This was the first true jungle lodge in the Cayo, and owners Mick and Lucy Fleming (he's from England, she's from the United States) have spent more than three decades polishing The Lodge at Chaa Creek to a fine, rich patina, while adding features like a gorgeous bi-level swimming pool. **Pros:** stunningly landscaped grounds; all tours are included in your stay; green and socially conscious owners. **Cons:** lodging, meal, and tour prices may strain your budget; spacious grounds mean long walks to get from room to restaurant and pool; most rooms lack air conditioning. $ Rooms from: BZ$798 ⌧ Chaa Creek Rd., off Chial Rd. ⊹ From San Ignacio go 4.75 miles (7.5 km) west on Benque Rd., aka George Price Hwy., turn left on Chial Rd. and go about 4.5 miles (7 km). Follow signs to Chaa Creek ☎ 824/2037 local reservations, 877/709–8708 toll-free in

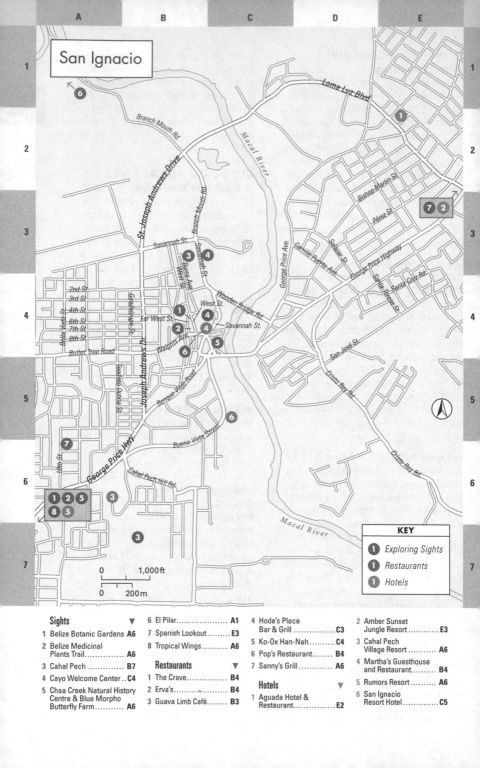

San Ignacio

KEY

- ① Exploring Sights
- ① Restaurants
- ① Hotels

Sights ▼

1 Belize Botanic Gardens **A6**
2 Belize Medicinal
   Plants Trail............... **A6**
3 Cahal Pech **B7**
4 Cayo Welcome Center .. **C4**
5 Chaa Creek Natural History
   Centre & Blue Morpho
   Butterfly Farm........... **A6**

6 El Pilar.................... **A1**
7 Spanish Lookout......... **E3**
8 Tropical Wings.......... **A6**

Restaurants ▼

1 The Crave................. **B4**
2 Erva's.................... **B4**
3 Guava Limb Café........ **B3**

4 Hode's Place
   Bar & Grill **C3**
5 Ko-Ox Han-Nah.......... **C4**
6 Pop's Restaurant........ **B4**
7 Sanny's Grill **A6**

Hotels ▼

1 Aguada Hotel &
   Restaurant................ **E2**

2 Amber Sunset
   Jungle Resort **E3**
3 Cahal Pech
   Village Resort **A6**
4 Martha's Guesthouse
   and Restaurant.......... **B4**
5 Rumors Resort **A6**
6 San Ignacio
   Resort Hotel **C5**

U.S. and Canada 🌐 *www.chaacreek.com* 🛏 *37 rooms* 🍴 *Free breakfast.*

Sweet Songs

$$$$ | **RESORT** | **FAMILY** | High above a bend in the Macal River is this remarkable, relaxing lodge whose grounds include the 45-acre Belize Botanic Gardens. **Pros:** botanic gardens on-site; first-rate birding; eco-conscious management. **Cons:** costs for meals, transfers, and tours all add up; road to lodge is long and bumpy; some may miss a/c. [$] *Rooms from: BZ$640* ✉ *Chial Rd.* ✥ *From San Ignacio head 4.75 miles (7.5 km) west on George Price Hwy., turn left on Chial Rd., and go about 5 miles (8 km)* ☎ *824/3101 in Belize, 512/243–5285 in U.S.* 🌐 *sweetsongslodge.com* 🛏 *14 rooms* 🍴 *Free breakfast.*

Table Rock Jungle Lodge

$$$ | **HOTEL** | Kick back in a hammock and listen to the river trickle by and the birds chirp on your private veranda in these eco-friendly jungle cabanas. **Pros:** luxe saltwater infinity pool; easy access to swimming, canoeing, and tubing on the river; cabanas offer secluded privacy but open-air views of the jungle and river. **Cons:** long walks to cabanas may be difficult for those with limited mobility; no a/c but rooms cool off at night; limited Wi-Fi. [$] *Rooms from: BZ$350* ✉ *Mile 5, Cristo Rey Rd., Cristo Rey Village* ☎ *672/4040* 🌐 *tablerockbelize.com* 🛏 *11 rooms* 🍴 *No meals.*

Activities

San Ignacio is the center for touring in western Belize. Just walk along busy Burns Avenue and you'll see signs for all kinds of tours and find the offices of several tour operators. Individual tour guides, who by law must be Belizean citizens and be licensed by the government, may work for tour operators, work for a lodge or hotel, or freelance on their own. Some hang out at restaurants in town, especially those on Burns Avenue, and post notices at bulletin boards in downtown hotels and restaurants. PACZ Tours, Mayan Heart World, and others have offices downtown. You can compare prices and sign up for the next day's tours. Obviously, the more layers of costs involved, the higher the price for you, but on the other hand larger operators and hotel tour companies have more resources, and they have their long-term reputations to protect, so they may be more reliable. Tours from lodges usually are more costly than if booked with an independent tour operator. Also, some lodges try to sell packages of tours rather than individual ones.

Most jungle lodges offer a full range of day-trips, either using their own guides or working with independent guides and tour companies. The largest lodge-affiliated tour operation is Chaa Creek Expeditions, but Black Rock Lodge, Crystal Paradise, Sweet Songs, Cahal Pech Village, San Ignacio Resort Hotel, and other hotels and lodges also do many tours and trips.

If you have a rental car, you can visit all of the Mayan sites in the Cayo on your own, along with other attractions such as the butterfly farms, the Belize Botanic Gardens, Medicinal Plants Trail, and many of the attractions in the Mountain Pine Ridge. We do recommend having a guide, since you'll get more out of any tour and learn more than you would on your own. Also, for most caving tours, notably Actun Tunichil Muknal, a guide is mandated by law. Local guides also are critical for nature hikes and birding trips, as many of these guides have remarkable local knowledge and ability to spot things you probably wouldn't see otherwise.

BIRDING

The area around San Ignacio is good for birding because it contains such a variety of habitats—river valleys, foothills, lagoons, agricultural areas, and broadleaf jungle—each of which attracts different types of birds. For example, Aguacate

Lagoon near Spanish Lookout attracts water birds such as night herons, neotropic cormorants, and whistling ducks. Open land and pastures are good for spotting laughing falcons, vermillion flycatchers, eastern meadowlarks, and white-tailed kites.

There's good birding on the grounds of most of the lodges along the Mopan and Macal Rivers, including **Chaa Creek, Sweet Songs, Crystal Paradise,** and **Clarissa Falls.** In addition, local guides and tour companies run birding trips.

Paradise Expeditions

BIRD WATCHING | FAMILY | Based in Cayo and connected with Crystal Paradise Lodge, Paradise Expeditions is a family operation with decades of experience in the Cayo. You can do day-trips for BZ$150–BZ$200, or the Tut family group has 5- to 11-night birding trips to various parts of Belize, starting at BZ$2,500 per person for a five-night, six-day birding trip in central Belize, and ranging up to around BZ$3,000 per person for a 12-day, 11-night expedition that covers much of the country. ⊠ *Cristo Rey Rd.* ☎ *610/5593* ⊕ *www.birdinginbelize.com.*

CANOEING AND KAYAKING

The Cayo's rivers, especially the Mopan and Macal, make it an excellent place for canoeing and kayaking. Most of the larger resorts, like **Chaa Creek, Table Rock,** and **Sweet Songs,** have canoes or inflatable kayaks that you can use for free, paddling upriver, then leisurely floating back down. If you're not staying at a resort that has canoes for use, you can put in at the Macal and paddle and float down to the Hawksworth Bridge at San Ignacio, a trip that takes two or three hours depending on your starting point. If you're not one for tubing, canoeing can be a great alternative as some companies offer canoe trips to caves where you'll learn about archaeology and Mayan history.

Do exercise caution. You won't believe how fast the rivers, especially the Macal, can rise after a heavy rain. Following rains in the Mountain Pine Ridge, it can reach a dangerous flood stage in just a few minutes. Also, in the past there have been a few rare incidents of visitors in canoes being stopped and robbed on the Macal. Watch weather forecasts, and ask locally about safety on the rivers.

Mayawalk Tours

CANOEING/ROWING/SKULLING | Mayawalk guides will take you to Barton Creek, where you first get to the Mennonite community, then board your canoes and go to Barton Creek Caves, where you'll switch on your headlights and canoe through darkness, observing crystal formations and learning about Mayan history. ⊠ *19 Burns Ave.* ☎ *824/3070* ⊕ *mayawalk.com* ✆ *BZ$170.*

CAVING

Over the millennia, as dozens of swift-flowing rivers bored through the soft limestone, the Maya Mountains became pitted with miles of caves. The Maya used them as burial sites and, according to one theory, as subterranean waterways that linked the Cayo with communities as far north as the Yucatán. Previously, the caves fell into a 1,000-year slumber, disturbed only by the nightly flutter of bats. In recent years, the caves have been rediscovered by spelunkers.

Belize Magnificent Mayan Tours

ADVENTURE TOURS | Operated by Albert Williams and his family, Belize Magnificent Mayan Tours (usually known as BZM) has a large variety of caving tours in the Cayo, including day-trips to ATM, Barton Creek Cave, Crystal Cave, and Chechem Ha. It also does trips to the Chiquibul, Mountain Pine Ridge, and other destinations. ⊠ *16B San José Succotz, San José Succotz* ☎ *621/0312* ⊕ *www. bzmtours.com.*

★ PACZ Tours

HIKING/WALKING | Arguably the top Actun Tunichil Muknal tour operator, PACZ has been operated by Emilo Awe since 1998, with a sizeable group of tour guides. The ATM tour costs around BZ$190 from downtown San Ignacio, including lunch and admission. PACZ also does a Barton Cave trip, for BZ$160. You can meet the PACZ tour guides at the office on Burns Avenue, or they will pick you up at hotels around San Ignacio. ⊠ *30 Burns Ave.* ☎ *824/0536* ⊕ *www.pacztours.net.*

COOKING

Marie Sharp's Tourist Center & Culinary Class

CULTURAL TOURS | If you're enamored with the Belizean cuisine and especially the ubiquitous Marie Sharp's hot sauce, learn how to prepare some dishes using Marie's own recipes. After a visit to the market with your instructor, you'll learn about Belizean culture and how food plays an important role, while cooking up traditional favorites like stew chicken, coconut rice and beans, and ceviche, all while sampling traditional rum punch. ⊠ *Rainforest Haven Inn, 2 Victoria St.* ☎ *674/1984* ⊕ *rainforesthavens.com* ☜ *BZ$100.*

HIKING

Most of the lodges have hiking trails. **Black Rock River Lodge, Chaa Creek, Table Rock,** and **Sweet Songs** all have especially good areas for hiking. If you want even more wide-open spaces, head to the Mountain Pine Ridge, which offers hundreds of miles of hiking trails, mostly old logging roads. For more adventurous hikes and overnight treks, you'll want to go with a guide.

Maya Guide Adventures

HIKING/WALKING | Marcos Cucul and son Francis, who run Maya Guide Adventures, are Ket'chi Mayans who are trained in cave and wilderness rescue. They can take you on day adventures or overnight caving, canoeing, and kayaking trips, or guide you in Elijio Panti National Park or other national parks and reserves. A day-trip into the crystal cave will cost around BZ$170 per person; overnight trips start at around BZ$300 per person, depending on length and number of people. ⊠ *Yaxche Jungle Camp, Belmopan* ☎ *600/3116* ⊕ *www.mayaguide.bz.*

HORSEBACK RIDING

The Lodge at Chaa Creek

HORSEBACK RIDING | With its stable of well-cared-for riding horses, the Lodge at Chaa Creek offers two- to three-hour guided horseback trips, with morning or afternoon options. The trips cost BZ$90 per person, and rides cover about 5 miles (8 km). ⊠ *Chaa Creek Stables, Chaa Creek Rd., off Chial Rd.* ☎ *834/4010 in Belize, 877/709–8708 toll-free in U.S. and Canada* ⊕ *www.chaacreek.com.*

Mountain Equestrian Trails

HORSEBACK RIDING | When it comes to horseback-riding adventures, whether on the old logging roads of the Mountain Pine Ridge or on trails in the Slate Creek Preserve, the local experts are found at Mountain Equestrian Trails. Five-night riding packages including accommodations, meals, and daily rides are around BZ$5,500 for two people in season. Day rides also are offered for around BZ$140 per person. ⊠ *Mile 8, Mountain Pine Ridge Rd.* ☎ *669/1124 in Belize, 800/838–3918 toll-free in U.S.* ⊕ *www.metbelize.com.*

🛍 Shopping

Creek Art Walter Castillo Home Art Gallery

ART GALLERIES | Noted artist Walter Castillo, a San Pedro native, has moved his gallery workshop from Bullet Tree Falls. His highly collectible paintings are among the best-known contemporary works on Belizean life. Call ahead for directions to the gallery and to arrange a time to visit. ⊠ *Walter St., Bullet Tree Falls* ☎ *622/4936* ⊕ *www.waltercastilloart.com.*

★ Orange Gallery

CRAFTS | This has one of the best selections of Belizean and Guatemalan crafts in Belize. It has an especially good selection of wood items from tropical hardwoods, including bowls, small pieces of furniture, and carvings. There's also a small restaurant and guesthouse here. ⊠ *Mile 60, George Price Hwy., east of San Ignacio* ☎ *824/3296* ⊕ *www.orangegifts.com.*

★ San Ignacio Market

MARKET | **FAMILY** | On Saturday morning, San Ignacio Market comes alive with farmers selling local fruits and vegetables. Vendors also hawk crafts, clothing, and household goods. Some vendors show up on other days as well, but Saturday has by far the largest market. A smaller vegetable and fruit market is open weekdays near Burns Avenue, closer to town. ⊠ *Savannah St., across from soccer stadium.*

Benque Viejo

7 miles (11 km) southwest of San Ignacio.

Old Bank, or Benque Viejo in Spanish, is the last town in Belize before you reach Guatemala. Modest in size and population (about 9,000), Benque is low-key in other ways, too, but the little House of Culture is worth a short stop, and neighboring San José Succotz village is home to the Xunantunich Mayan site. The Poustinia Land Art Park is perhaps the most unusual element of Belize's art scene.

◉ Sights

Actun Chechem Ha (Chechem Ha Cave)

ARCHAEOLOGICAL SITE | On private land, Actun Chechem Ha, which means "Cave of the Poisonwood Water," is a Mayan burial cave with artifacts that date back three millennia. There are many pots and a stela used for ceremonial purposes. This cave may have the largest collection of Mayan pottery in one place anywhere in Belize, possibly the world. To examine the pottery, you'll have to climb ladders, and getting to the cave requires a 35- to 45-minute walk, mostly uphill. The cave is on private property, and the landowner's family sometimes gives tours. Tour companies, with registered guides, also visit here from San Ignacio and Belmopan, charging from BZ$150 per person. ■TIP→ **Belize Magnificent Tours in San Ignacio, which charges BZ$190 per person, is one recommended tour company for this trip.** Due to the hike to the cave entrance and climbing in the cave, you need to be reasonably physically fit to visit Chechem Ha. ⊠ *10 miles (17 km) south of Benque Viejo, Mile 7, Hydro Rd., near Vaca Falls, Benque Viejo del Carmen* ☎ *653/0799* ⌨ *Tours to Chechem Ha including transportation from San Ignacio or your lodge, lunch, admission fee, and sometimes swimming at Vaca Falls are around BZ$150–BZ$200 per person.*

Benque House of Culture

MUSEUM | The mission of Benque House of Culture, one of the government-sponsored houses of culture in Belize (others are in Belize City, Orange Walk Town, Corozal Town, San Pedro, and San Ignacio/Santa Elena), is "promoting beauty and goodness." Housed in the former Benque police station, this little museum (and we do mean *little*) has displays on the history of Benque Viejo and also offers classes for local schoolchildren and their teachers. There is also a large rosewood and mahogany marimba (a xylophone-like musical instrument) on display. ⊠ *64 Joseph St., 7 miles (11.5 km) west of San Ignacio, Benque Viejo del Carmen* ☎ *823/2697* ⊕ *www.nichbelize.org* ⌨ *By donation.*

Poustinia Land Art Park

ARTS VENUE | One of the most unusual and least-known attractions in Belize, Poustinia Land Art Park is a collection of about 30 original works by artists from a dozen countries, including Belize, Norway, Guyana, Brazil, Guatemala, and England, scattered about some 60 acres of a former cattle ranch. It's owned by an architect, who calls Poustinia an "environmental project." Among the works of outdoor art, which some would call funky and others fascinating, are *Downtown,* by Venezuelan artist Manuel Piney, and *Returned Parquet,* a reference to Belize's colonial history in mahogany parquet flooring by Tim Davies, a British artist. Nature is taking over the artworks, which apparently is part of the plan. Getting around the park, which is open by appointment only, requires sometimes strenuous hiking; bring insect repellent. Make arrangements to visit the park and for a tour guide at the Benque House of Culture in Benque Viejo. ✉ *Mile 2.5, Hydro Rd., Benque Viejo del Carmen* ✣ *2.5 miles (5 km) south of Benque Viejo, 8 miles (13 km) southwest of San Ignacio* ☎ *823/269 Benque House of Culture* 🎟 *BZ$20.*

Xunantunich

ARCHAEOLOGICAL SITE | FAMILY | One of the most accessible Mayan sites in Belize, Xunantunich (pronounced shoo-nan-too-nitch) is located on a hilltop site above the Mopan River west of San Ignacio. You take a hand-pulled ferry across the river (it carries pedestrians and up to four vehicles) near the village of San José Succotz. The ferry is free, but tip the operator a Belizean dollar or two if you wish. Tour guides offer their services as you board the ferry, but you do not need a guide to see the ruins. After crossing the Mopan on the ferry, drive or hike about a mile to the visitor center and the ruins. Although settlement of Xunantunich occurred much earlier, the excavated structures here, in six plazas with about two dozen buildings, date from AD 200 to 900. El Castillo, the massive 120-foot-high main pyramid and still the second-tallest structure in Belize after Caana at Caracol, was built on a leveled hilltop. The pyramid, which you can climb if you have the energy, has a spectacular 360-degree panorama of the Mopan River valley into Guatemala. On the eastern wall is a reproduction of one of the finest Mayan sculptures in Belize, a frieze decorated with jaguar heads, human faces, and abstract geometric patterns telling the story of the Moon's affair with Morning Light. ✉ *Near San José Succotz Village, 6.5 miles (11 km) southwest of San Ignacio, George Price Hwy. (Benque Rd.), San José Succotz* ☎ *822/2106* 🌐 *www.nichbelize.org* 🎟 *BZ$10.*

🍴 Restaurants

★ Benny's Kitchen

$ | LATIN AMERICAN | This little open-air restaurant near Xunantunich has won many fans who come for hearty Mayan, mestizo, and Creole dishes at rock-bottom prices. You'll find mostly locals here, many from San Ignacio, Benque Viejo, and other parts of Cayo District. **Known for:** cheap, good food; pibil (pork cooked in an underground oven); chilimole (chicken with mole sauce). [$] *Average main: BZ$10* ✉ *Across Benque Rd. (George Price Hwy.) from ferry to Xunantunich, San José Succotz* ✣ *Turn south just west of Xunantunich ferry and follow signs about 3 blocks* ☎ *823/2541.*

Mountain Pine Ridge

17 miles (27 km) south of San Ignacio.

The best way to describe Mountain Pine Ridge is to paraphrase Winston Churchill: it's a puzzle wrapped in an enigma. Instead of the tropical vegetation you'd expect to find, two-thirds of this large reserve is pine forest, mainly Honduras pines. Most pines are young, due to losses from wildfires and beetle infestations. Old logging roads cut through red clay, giving the region an uncanny resemblance to northern Georgia in the United States. Sinkholes, caves, and waterfalls are common in limestone areas. With elevations up to 3,335 feet, winter temperatures can drop into decidedly untropical low 40s, yet exotic wildlife abounds, including orange-breasted falcons, toucans, tapirs, jaguars, and crocodiles. It's widely considered the best place in Belize to see waterfalls and to go mountain biking.

GETTING HERE AND AROUND

From the George Price Highway, there are two routes into the Mountain Pine Ridge, both just east of San Ignacio: the Mountain Pine Ridge Road (also sometimes called the Chiquibul Road or the Georgeville Road), at Georgeville at Mile 61.6 of the George Price Highway; and the Cristo Rey Road, with the turnoff at Mile 66.5 of the George Price Highway. From the George Price Highway, the entrance to the Mountain Pine Ridge is 10.2 miles (17 km) via the Mountain Pine Ridge Road and 14.8 miles (25 km) via the Cristo Rey Road. Note that Cristo Rey Road is now partly paved, and even the nonpaved portions are well maintained, while the Georgeville Road is often filled with ruts and limestone shards that can easily cause a flat tire.

Heading southeast from San Ignacio on the Cristo Rey Road, a little beyond San Antonio, the Cristo Rey Road meets the Mountain Pine Ridge Road coming from Georgeville. Turn right to go into the Mountain Pine Ridge. After 2.5 miles (4 km) a guard at a gatehouse will record your name, destination, and license-plate number. The main road through the Mountain Pine Ridge is a mostly dirt road that can become almost impassable after heavy rains, but is otherwise a decent road without the bumps that plague many other backroads in the Cayo.

There is no public bus transportation into the Mountain Pine Ridge. Charter flights by Javier's Flying Service and Tropic Air can fly into private airstrips at Blancaneaux Lodge and Hidden Valley Inn. Tour operators in San Ignacio offer day-trips to the Pine Ridge and also to Caracol in the Chiqibul.

Entrance into the Mountain Pine Ridge is free, though there is a nominal charge collected if you go to the viewing area for Thousand Foot Falls.

CONTACTS Javier's Flying Service. ⊠ *Central Farm Airstrip, Central Farm, San Ignacio* ☎ *824/0460* ⊕ *www.javiersflyingservice.com.* **Tropic Air.** ☎ *226/2626 reservations in Belize, 800/422–3435 toll-free in U.S. and Canada* ⊕ *www.tropicair.com.*

TIMING

You could spend a week or longer exploring the streams, waterfalls, and distant trails of the Mountain Pine Ridge.

SAFETY AND PRECAUTIONS

The Mountain Pine Ridge is a remote and lightly populated area. Occasionally, bandits have taken advantage of this to stop and rob visitors, and some Guatemalan squatters have tried to move across the border in search of free land, prompting run-ins with Belize authorities. Guatemalan *xateros*, hunters for the prized *xate* palm, also are a problem in parts of the area. Currently, Belize Defence Forces soldiers accompany vehicles to Caracol. If you drive on your own to Caracol, it is at your own risk. However, the main danger to most visitors is not bandits but getting sunburned on a hiking trail or old logging road.

Sights

Barton Creek Cave and Archeological Reserve

ARCHAEOLOGICAL SITE | FAMILY | This wet cave, now a part of the Barton Creek Archeological Reserve in a remote area off the Mountain Pine Ridge Road, offers a canoeing adventure in Xibalba (the Mayan underworld). You'll float through about a mile of a long underground chamber—the cave is nearly 5 miles (8 km) long and parts have never been completely explored. You'll see Mayan ceramics along with ancient calcified skeletal remains and skulls. You can go on a tour from San Ignacio or from your lodge. PACZ Tours, for example, offers a six-hour tour, including lunch and admission to the cave, for BZ$170 plus tax per person, and Chaa Creek offers a half-day tour for one to four persons for BZ$310 plus BZ$50 per person for park admission and equipment plus tax. You can also drive to the cave yourself, rent a boat and gear, and hire a guide near the cave. Getting to the cave is an adventure in itself, requiring a long drive on rough roads. Parts of the road and the cave itself may be inaccessible after hard rains. Be careful in the cave; it's best to tour with a reputable tour company with an experienced tour guide and reliable, well-maintained equipment such as float vests. ⊠ *Barton Creek Cave* ⊹ *Turn at Mile 62 of George Price Hwy. (formerly Western Hwy.) onto Mountain Pine Ridge Rd. aka Georgeville Rd. or Chiquibul Rd. Go about 3 miles (5 km) and, at Cool Shade, turn left. Go 4 miles (6 km) on a rough, unpaved road through Lower Barton Creek Mennonite community to Upper Barton Creek and cave. Watch for signs for Barton Creek Outpost, Mike's Place, and cave* ☎ *822/2106 Institute of Archaeology* ⊕ *www.nichbelize.org* ☞ *BZ$10.*

Elijio Panti National Park

NATIONAL/STATE PARK | Named after the famed Guatemala-born herbal healer who died in 1996 at the age of 106, Elijio Panti National Park (Noj K'a'ax Meen Elijio Panti National Park) is part of Belize's extensive national parks system. It spans about 13,000 to 16,000 acres (the exact area is undetermined) around the villages of San Antonio, Cristo Rey, and El Progreso and along the Macal River. In the park are Sakt'aj waterfalls and two dry caves known as Offering and Cormorant. The hope is that with no hunting in this park, more birds and wildlife will return to western Belize. Development of the park has been slowed by differing

perspectives among those in San Antonio Village, including Maria Garcia (a relative of Elijio Panti) of the Itzamna Society, various departments of the government of Belize, and other parties. Even today, there is no one official website for the park. Currently you must be accompanied by a licensed tour guide to enter the park. For information on the park and how to visit it, check with tour guides in San Ignacio or San Antonio. ⊠ *Off Cristo Rey Rd., San Antonio Village* ⊕ *www. epnp.org* ☞ *BZ$10.*

Green Hills Butterfly Ranch and Botanical Collections

FARM/RANCH | FAMILY | The largest and the best of Belize's butterfly farms open to the public, Green Hills has about 30 native species in a huge flight area on display at any given time. Jan Meerman, who has published a book on Belize's butterflies and moths, runs the place with Dutch partner Tineke Boomsma and other staff, who speak a variety of English, Spanish, Dutch, Yucatec Mayan, and Creole. On the 100-acre grounds there are also many flowers, including passion flowers, bromeliads, heliconias, and orchids. Birding is good here as well, with more than 300 species sighted in the area. Bring lunch and eat it in the Green Hills picnic area. ⊠ *Mile 8, Mountain Pine Ridge Rd. (aka Chiquibul Rd., aka Georgeville Rd.), El Progreso/7 Mile* ☎ *834/4017* ⊕ *www.green-hills.net* ☞ *Guided tour BZ$25.*

Mountain Pine Ridge Forest Reserve

NATURE PRESERVE | This reserve is a highlight of any journey to Belize and an adventure to explore, although the scenery may remind you more of the piney woods of the far southern Appalachians than of tropical jungle. The Mountain Pine Ridge Forest Reserve is in the high country of Belize—low mountains and rolling hills are covered in part by vast pine forests and crisscrossed with old logging roads. Waterfalls and streams abound, and there are accessible caves, such as Rio Frio. The higher elevations, up to near 3,400 feet, provide cooler temperatures and outstanding views. The best way to see this area, which covers more than 106,000 acres, is on a mountain bike, a horse, or your own feet. It's also not a bad ride in an SUV, which you'll need to get you through the Pine Ridge to the Chiquibul wilderness and the magnificent ruins of Caracol. Aside from the Honduras pines, 80% of which were damaged in recent years by the southern pine beetle but are now recovering, you'll see lilac-color mimosa, Saint-John's-wort, and occasionally a garish red flower appropriately known as hotlips. Look for the craboo, a wild tree whose berries are used in a brandy-like liqueur believed to have aphrodisiac properties (the fruit ripens June through August). Birds love this fruit, so any craboo is a good place to spot orioles and woodpeckers. You may not see them, but the Pine Ridge is home to many of Belize's large mammals, including tapirs, cougars, jaguars, and ocelots, and in the streams are a few Morelet's crocodiles. ✉ *Mountain Pine Ridge, San Antonio Village.*

Rio Frio Caves
CAVE | FAMILY | These caves are only a few miles by car down a steep track, but ecologically speaking, they are in a different world. In the course of a few hundred yards, you drop from pine savanna to tropical forest. Few other places in Belize illustrate its extraordinary geological diversity as clearly as this startling transition. A river runs right through the center of the main cave—actually it's more of a tunnel, open at both ends—and, over the centuries, has carved the rock into fantastic shapes. Swallows fill the place, and at night ocelots and margays pad silently across the cold floor in search of slumbering prey. Seen from the dark interior, the light-filled world outside seems more intense and beautiful than ever. About a mile (2 km) away are the Cuevas Gemelas (Twin Caves), best seen with a guide. Due to occasional bandit activity in the area, at times a Belize Defence Forces escort is required to visit the Rio Frio Caves—if driving on your own, ask at your hotel or at the Douglas Da Silva forestry station, where private vehicles meet up with a Defence Force escort. ✉ *Mountain Pine Ridge* ✣ *From entrance gate of Mountain Pine Ridge, go 14 miles (23 km). Turn right at Douglas de Silva forestry station at Rio Frio sign and drive 5 miles (8 km) to caves* 🎟 *Free.*

Thousand Foot Falls (*Hidden Valley Falls*)
BODY OF WATER/WATERFALL | Inside the Mountain Pine Ridge Forest Reserve, Thousand Foot Falls actually drops nearly 1,600 feet, making it the highest waterfall in Central America. A thin plume of spray plummets over the edge of a rock face into a seemingly bottomless gorge below. The catch is that the viewing area, where there is a shelter with some benches and a public restroom, is some distance from the falls. Many visitors find the narrow falls unimpressive from this vantage point. To climb closer requires a major commitment: a steep climb down and up the side of the mountain is several hours. ✉ *Mountain Pine Ridge* ✣ *From the Mountain Pine Ridge gate, go 2 miles (3 km) and turn left toward Hidden Valley Inn. Go 4 miles (6 km) to the falls observation area. It's well signed* 🎟 *BZ$4.*

Hotels

NEAR MOUNTAIN PINE RIDGE

Crystal Paradise Resort
$$ | B&B/INN | This family-run jungle lodge has a range of accommodations, from two simple rooms to a collection of traditional thatched cabanas with views of the Macal River Valley. **Pros:** Belizean owned; good guided tours; lots of birds. **Cons:** no-frills rooms and cabanas; can be buggy; no a/c. [$] *Rooms from: BZ$290* ✉ *Cristo Rey Rd., Cristo Rey Village* ☎ *615/9361* 🌐 *www.crystalparadise.com* 🛏 *12 rooms* 🍴 *No meals.*

Gumbo Limbo Jungle Resort
$$ | **HOTEL** | Well priced, with a lovely hilltop setting, and amenities such as a pool, this small lodge is an attractive option just 2 miles (3 km) from the George Price Highway at Georgeville. **Pros:** attractive cottage accommodations; lovely views; nice swimming pool. **Cons:** steep hill on dirt access road is a doozy. [$] *Rooms from: BZ$290* ✉ *Mile 2, Mountain Pine Ridge Rd. (aka Chiquibul Rd. or Georgeville Rd.), Georgeville* ☎ *650/3112* 🌐 *www.gumbolimboresort.com* 🛏 *4 cottages* 🍴 *No meals.*

Inn the Bush Eco-Jungle Lodge
$$ | **B&B/INN** | With only three cabanas, every guest gets personal attention at this small ecolodge where you can lounge in a four-poster king bed and then jump in the pool for a refreshing swim. **Pros:** personal service; reasonable rates; peace and quiet. **Cons:** access road is rough. [$] *Rooms from: BZ$250* ✉ *Mile 6, Cristo Rey Rd., Macaw Bank, off Cristo Rey Rd., Cristo Rey Village* ☎ *670/6364* 🌐 *www.innthebushbelize.com* 🛏 *3 cabanas* 🍴 *No meals.*

Macaw Bank Jungle Lodge
$$ | **B&B/INN** | This small, laid-back ecolodge on 50 acres adjoining the Macal River is for travelers seeking a no-frills spot where you can hear the jungle hum outside your doorstep and where the air bristles with the promise of bird and animal sightings. **Pros:** laid-back ecolodge with moderate rates; great food. **Cons:** not a luxury lodge; need a rental car. [$] *Rooms from: BZ$283* ✉ *Cristo Rey Rd., Cristo Rey Village* ☎ *665/7241* 🌐 *www.macawbankjunglelodge.com* 🛏 *5 cottages* 🍴 *No meals.*

Mariposa Jungle Lodge
$$$ | **RESORT** | This small, intimate lodge has six well-designed cabanas set in the shade on a low hill, with pimento walls, thatched roofs, and furniture handmade at the lodge and elsewhere in Belize. **Pros:** personalized service; attractive cabanas, with a/c; swimming pool. **Cons:** 20-minute drive from San Ignacio; with lodging, meals, tours, and transfers, rates are a little spendy; vegan cuisine may disappoint carnivores. [$] *Rooms from: BZ$464* ✉ *Cristo Rey Rd., near junction with Mountain Pine Ridge Rd., San Antonio Village* ☎ *670/2113 in Belize, 304/244–2136 in U.S.* 🌐 *www.mariposajunglelodge.com* 🛏 *9 rooms* 🍴 *No meals.*

Mountain Equestrian Trails
$$ | **HOTEL** | MET, as most people call it, is one of Belize's top equestrian spots, offering five-night room and horseback-riding packages that come with full days of riding, lodging, and meals. **Pros:** equestrian charm abounds; reasonable prices for cabanas; eco-friendly. **Cons:** facilities a bit too rustic for some; limited options at restaurant; no electricity in cabins may be off-putting. [$] *Rooms from: BZ$288* ✉ *Mile 8, Mountain Pine Ridge Rd. (aka Chiquibul Rd. or Georgeville Rd.), El Progresso/7 Mile* ☎ *669/1124 in Belize, 800/838–3918 toll-free U.S. reservations* 🌐 *www.metbelize.com* 🛏 *10 cabanas* 🍴 *Some meals.*

★ **Mystic River Resort**
$$$ | **RESORT** | Operated by a French-American couple, this jungle resort on the Macal River is a step up in luxury, service, and dining from other run-of-the-mill lodges in the area. **Pros:** stylishly decorated cottages all with views and fireplaces; excellent food; friendly management. **Cons:** a little pricey; no a/c; isolated location. [$] *Rooms from: BZ$400* ✉ *Mile 6, Cristo Rey Rd., San Antonio Village* ☎ *672/4100* 🌐 *www.mysticriverresort.com* 🛏 *6 cottages* 🍴 *No meals.*

MOUNTAIN PINE RIDGE

★ **Blancaneaux Lodge**
$$$$ | **RESORT** | As you sweep down Blancaneaux's hibiscus- and palm-lined drive, past the big main swimming pool, you may get a whiff of Beverly Hills, and indeed the lodge is owned by film director Francis Ford Coppola. **Pros:** fabulous

grounds; deluxe cabanas and villas; wonderful food and service. **Cons:** many steep steps may pose problems for some; very expensive. $ *Rooms from: BZ$680* ✉ *Mountain Pine Ridge ⚓ Turn right at Blancaneaux sign 4.5 miles (7.5 km) from Mountain Pine Ridge entrance gate* ☎ *866/356–5881 toll-free reservations in U.S. and Canada* ⊕ *www.thefamilycoppolaresorts.com/en/blancaneaux-lodge* ⛺ *20 villas* ⦿ *Free breakfast.*

Gaia Riverlodge

$$$ | **RESORT** | Drive deep into the Mountain Pine Ridge and you'll find, perched on a steep hill above the Five Sisters waterfalls, this elegant lodge and staging ground for exploration. **Pros:** appealing small lodge; a little less expensive than other lodges in the Mountain Pine Ridge; eco-friendly. **Cons:** some standard cabanas don't have much of a view; no pool or TV. $ *Rooms from: BZ$450* ✉ *Mountain Pine Ridge ⚓ From main Mountain Pine Ridge Rd., turn right at Blancaneaux and Five Sisters signs 4.5 mile (7 km) from Pine Ridge entrance gate. Continue past Blancaneaux airstrip about 1 mile (2 km)* ☎ *834/4024* ⊕ *www.gaiariverlodge.com* ⛺ *16 cabanas* ⦿ *Some meals.*

★ Hidden Valley Inn & Reserve

$$$$ | **B&B/INN** | Sitting on 7,200 acres, Hidden Valley has more than a dozen waterfalls, at least two private caves, and 90 miles (150 km) of hiking and mountain biking trails. **Pros:** charming lodge atmosphere; wonderful waterfalls; excellent birding and stunning pool. **Cons:** meals are pricey; loss of many mature pines due to the pine beetle means it can be hot and dry on the trails. $ *Rooms from: BZ$670* ✉ *4 Cooma Cairn Rd. ⚓ From main Mountain Pine Ridge Rd., turn left at Hidden Valley Inn sign 3.75 miles (6.25 km) from Pine Ridge entrance gate* ☎ *822/3320, 844/ 859–2227 toll-free reservations number in U.S. and Canada* ⊕ *www.hiddenvalleyinn.com* ⛺ *12 cottages* ⦿ *Some meals.*

Activities

BIRDING

Birding is great in the Mountain Pine Ridge, and, surprisingly, it's even better now that many of the pines were felled by the southern pine beetle. Without the tall pines, it's much easier to spot orange-breasted falcons, blue crown motmots, white king vultures, stygian owls, and other rare birds.

CAVING

Easily accessible in the Cayo is the Rio Frio Cave. You can also do trips to Barton Creek Cave, about 8 miles (13 km) northwest of the Mountain Pine Ridge entrance gate, off Mountain Pine Ridge Road, and to Actun Tunichil Muknal from Mountain Pine Ridge. Hidden Valley Inn has two caves open only to guests of the inn.

HIKING

With its karst limestone terrain, extensive network of old logging trails and roads, and cooler temperatures, the Mountain Pine Ridge is ideal for hiking. All the lodges here have miles of marked trails. You can also hike along the roads (mostly gravel or dirt), as there are very few cars in the Pine Ridge. Most people find this more pleasant than trying to fight their way through the bush. The mountain area around Baldy Beacon, the highest point in the Pine Ridge at around 3,335 feet, is especially beautiful; it may remind you of part of the Highlands of Scotland.

All of the Mountain Pine Ridge and Chichibul Wilderness is lightly populated, and some of the residents, such as unemployed squatters who have moved into this remote area, may not always have your best interests at heart. Cell phones don't usually work here, although there has been talk of installing some cell-phone towers as a security measure. Lodges such as Hidden Valley Inn provide radio phones to guests who are hiking. Always leave word with a responsible party about your hiking plans and time of

A Crime of Flowers

A rather plain-looking palm leaf has become a big-money target for poachers in Belize—and a huge problem for the Forest Department. The leaves in question, xate (pronounced sha-tay), are widely used in the floral industry because they stay fresh-looking for 45 to 60 days after harvest. They come from three *Chamaedorea* palm species: *C. elegans*, known as parlor palm; *C. oblongata*, called xate macho; and *C. ernesti-augustii*, or fishtail. The latter is the most sought-after, fetching up to US$1 at its final destination, though poachers get only a fraction of that.

Xate grows wild in Belize, and also in parts of Guatemala and Mexico. Guatemalan xate collectors, called xateros, have stripped much of their own El Petén jungles and have now moved on to Belize, crossing the border into the Chiquibul and other remote areas. Xateros earn more collecting xate than working at regular jobs, if they can even find work in the economically depressed rural areas of El Petén. Not surprisingly, Belizeans are increasingly joining the ranks of xate poachers. The harvesters sweep through the jungle, removing the palm leaves with a pocketknife or machete. Each palm plant produces two to five usable leaves.

Unfortunately, the poachers do more than just collect xate. They sometimes stumble across Mayan sites and loot them for priceless artifacts. Some trap toucans, rare parrots, and endangered scarlet macaws for sale on the black market, and they hunt wild animals, including protected tapirs, for food. The Belize Forest Department has reported significant depletion of native wildlife in areas with large numbers of xate collectors. In a few cases, xateros have been implicated in robberies or in attacks on researchers and on Belize Defence Forces soldiers. With little chance of getting caught and only modest fines if they are, xate poachers are working at minimal risk.

What can you do to reduce the damage done by illegal xate collectors? First, avoid buying flower arrangements that contain xate, unless you're sure that the xate was harvested legally. You can also support an effort by the Natural History Museum in London, in cooperation with the Belize Ministry of Natural Resources and the Belize Botanic Gardens at Sweet Songs Lodge near San Ignacio, to encourage sustainable, organic growing of xate by Belizean farmers.

expected return. Carry plenty of water, food, a compass, and basic medical supplies, especially on long hikes to remote areas. You may want to hire a guide.

HORSEBACK RIDING

In this remote area with virtually no vehicular traffic and many old logging roads, horseback riding is excellent. **Blancaneaux Lodge** and **Hidden Valley Inn** offer horseback riding, and **Mountain Equestrian Trails** runs horseback tours into the Pine Ridge.

MOUNTAIN BIKING

Mountain Pine Ridge has the best mountain biking in Belize on hundreds of miles of remote logging roads. Mountain biking is especially good on the 90 miles (150 km) of private hiking and mountain biking trails at Hidden Valley Inn. Blancaneaux and Hidden Valley Inn provide complimentary mountain bikes to guests.

San Ignacio is home to several Mayan sites, including Cahal Pech and El Pilar.

The Lodge at Chaa Creek also offers mountain biking.

ZIPLINING
Calico Jack's Jungle Canopy & Zip Line
ZIP LINING | FAMILY | Calico Jack's zipline is more than a half mile (1 km) long. The "Ultimo Explorer" zipline tour has nine runs on 15 platforms at more than 2,700 feet. Ziplining starts at BZ$80 plus tax. There are five caves on the grounds, two open for exploring with a guide. Calico Jack's Village also has cabanas for rent and a restaurant. ⊠ *Off Mile 7, Mountain Pine Ridge Rd., El Progreso/7 Mile* ☎ *832/2478.*

Caracol

55 miles (89 km) south of San Ignacio.

Caracol (Spanish for "snail") is the most spectacular Mayan site in Belize, as well as one of the most impressive in Central America. It was once home to as many as 200,000 people (almost two-thirds the population of modern-day Belize).

GETTING HERE AND AROUND
Caracol is about 55 miles (89 km) from San Ignacio, and about 35–40 miles (57–66 km) from the major lodges in the Mountain Pine Ridge. Because roads are mostly unpaved and often in poor condition, cars or tour vans take about two hours from the Pine Ridge lodges and about three hours from San Ignacio, sometimes longer after heavy rains.

Advance permission to visit Caracol is no longer required. Although only about a 10-mile (17-km) section of the road to Caracol from San Ignacio is paved, once in the Mountain Pine Ridge the road is generally in good shape, except after heavy rains. The Belize government has plans to eventually pave the entire road to Caracol.

SAFETY AND PRECAUTIONS
Occasional holdups of tourists by armed gangs believed to be from Guatemala occurred here over the past several years. For caution's sake, trips to Caracol are now in a group convoy, protected by Belize Defence Forces troops. The

meet-up point is Augustine De Silva village, a few miles into the Pine Ridge. As off-putting as that may seem, Caracol is well worth seeing. The robbery incidents have occurred very rarely, and the tour operators to Caracol know the ropes and will work to make sure your trip to Caracol is rewarding and safe.

TIMING

You generally can't overnight at Caracol, so you have to visit on a day-trip. You can see the excavated area of Caracol in a few hours.

TOURS

Most visitors to Caracol come as part of a tour group from San Ignacio or from one of the lodges in the Mountain Pine Ridge. Full-day tours from San Ignacio, which often include a picnic lunch and stops at Rio Frio Cave, Rio On, and other sights in the Mountain Pine Ridge, cost from about BZ$160 to BZ$220 per person, including the BZ$20 admission fee to Caracol, depending on what is included and the number of people going. Tours from independent operators generally cost less than those from lodges. Lodges in the Mountain Pine Ridge charge around BZ$200–BZ$250 per person for tours to Caracol, including tax.

Because of its remote location, Caracol gets only about 12,000 visitors a year. That's about one-tenth the number who visit Altun Ha, one-fifth the number who visit Xunantunich, and a smaller fraction of the number who see Tikal. Thus, you're in exclusive company, and on some slow days you may be one of only a handful of people at the site. Excavations by a team from the University of Central Florida usually are carried out in the winter, typically January through March.

 Sights

★ **Caracol**

ARCHAEOLOGICAL SITE | FAMILY | Once a metropolis with five plazas and 32 large structures covering almost a square mile, Caracol once covered an area larger than present-day Belize City. Altogether it is believed there are some 35,000 buildings at the site, though only a handful of them have been excavated. Excavations at Caracol are being carried on by Diane and Arlen Chase of the University of Central Florida. The latest excavations are in an area approximately 500 yards southeast of Caracol's central plaza. Once Caracol has been fully excavated it may dwarf even the great city of Tikal, which is a few dozen miles away (as the toucan flies) in Guatemala. The evidence suggests that Caracol won a crushing victory over Tikal in the mid-6th century, a theory that Guatemalan scholars haven't quite accepted. Until a group of *chicleros* (collectors of gum base) stumbled on the site in 1936, Caracol was buried under the jungle of the remote Vaca Plateau. It's hard to believe it could have been lost for centuries, as the great pyramid of Caana, at nearly 140 feet, is still Belize's tallest structure.

The main excavated sections are in four groups, denoted on archaeological maps as A, B, C, and D groups. The most impressive structures are the B Group at the northeast end of the excavated plaza. This includes Caana (sometimes spelled Ca'ana or Ka'ana), or "Sky Palace," listed as Structure B19-2nd, along with a ball court, water reservoir, and several large courtyards. Caana remains the tallest structure in Belize. The A Group, on the west side of the plaza, contains a temple, ball court, and a residential area for the elite. The Temple of the Wooden Lintel (Structure A6) is one of the oldest and longest-used buildings at Caracol, dating back to 300 BC. It was still in use in AD 1100. To the northwest of the A Group is the Northwest Acropolis, primarily a residential area. The third major plaza forming the core of the site is at the point where a causeway enters the "downtown" part of Caracol. The D Group is a group of structures at the South Acropolis.

Near the entrance to Caracol is a small but interesting visitor center. If you have driven here on your own (with a Belize Defence Forces escort) instead of with a tour, a guide usually can be hired at the site, but you can also walk around on your own. Seeing all of the excavated area involves several hours of hiking around the site. Wear sturdy shoes and bring insect repellent. Also, watch for anthill mounds and, rarely, snakes. This part of the Chiquibul Forest Reserve is a good place for birding and wildlife spotting. Around the ruins are troops of howler monkeys and flocks of ocellated turkeys, and you may also see deer, coatimundis, foxes, and other wildlife at the site or on the way. ✚ *From Mountain Pine Forest Ridge reserve entrance, head south 14 miles (23 km) to village of Douglas Da Silva (where you can meet up with a Belize Defence Forces escort), turn left and go 36 miles (58 km)* ⊕ *www.caracol.org* ✉ *BZ$20.*

Chapter 7

THE SOUTHERN COAST

Updated by
Jeffrey Van Fleet

👁 Sights	🍽 Restaurants	🛏 Hotels	🛍 Shopping	🍸 Nightlife
★★★★☆	★★★★★	★★★★★	★★★☆☆	★★★☆☆

WELCOME TO THE SOUTHERN COAST

TOP REASONS TO GO

★ **Beaches:** The mainland's best beaches are on the Placencia Peninsula and around Hopkins. Although they're narrow ribbons of khaki rather than wide swaths of talcum-powder sand, they're ideal for lazing in a hammock under a coco palm. And you don't have to fight the crowds for a spot—at least not yet.

★ **Jaguars:** The world's first jaguar preserve is the Cockscomb Basin Wildlife Sanctuary. Chances are you won't actually see one of these big, beautiful cats in the wild, as they roam the high bush mainly at night, but you may see tracks or hear a low growl in the darkness.

★ **Water Sports:** Anglers won't be disappointed by the bonefish, tarpon, and other sport fishing. The Barrier Reef here is generally 15 miles (25 km) or more off the coast, so it's a long trip out, even with the fast boats the dive shops use. However, there are patch reefs around closer islands, with excellent snorkeling. Serious divers will find two of Belize's three atolls, Turneffe and Glover's, within reach.

From the north, the Hummingbird Highway leads from Belmopan south to Dangriga. The road is paved and it is the most scenic drive in the country. The Coastal Road looks like a shortcut on a map, but it's a loose gravel roadway and it does not hug the coast, despite the name. Stick with the Hummingbird.

Off the spine of the Southern Highway, various shorter roads lead to villages on the coast and inland: from the highway it's about 4 miles (7 km) to Hopkins; 25 miles (42 km) to Placencia Village, nicely paved all the way, although the speed bumps are irritating; and 5 miles (8 km) to Big Creek/Independence on a paved road.

1 Dangriga. Dangriga is the largest Garifuna settlement in Belize and a jumping-off spot for several offshore cayes. From here you can reach Gales Point, a small Creole village with a beautiful waterside setting, known for the manatees in nearby lagoons.

2 Hopkins. The most accessible and friendly Garifuna village in Belize, Hopkins has good beaches and a growing tourism industry.

3 Cockscomb Basin Wildlife Sanctuary. One of Belize's best nature reserves is the place to spot jaguars and is easily reached no matter where you stay in this region.

4 Maya Beach. The first community you encounter as you approach the Placencia Peninsula from the north is seeing an expanding number of resorts.

5 Seine Bight. Quiet (for now) Seine Bight maintains its Garifuna heritage in the light of growing tourism development.

6 Placencia Village. This fun, cluttered village is the "metropolis" of its namesake peninsula.

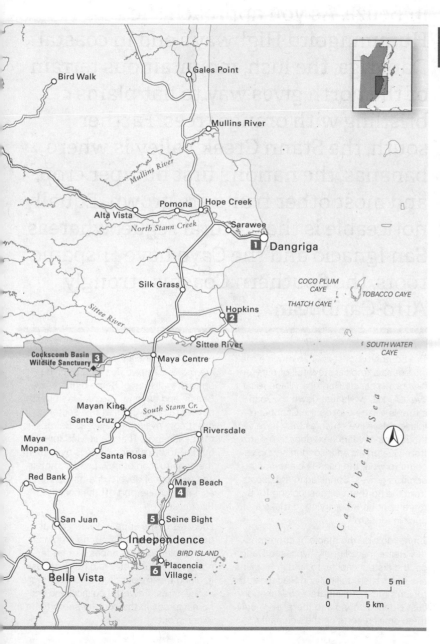

The transition from one landscape to another is often swift and startling in Belize. As you approach the Hummingbird Highway's end in coastal Dangriga, the lush, mountainous terrain of the north gives way to flat plains bristling with orange trees. Farther south, the Stann Creek Valley is where bananas, the nation's first bumper crop, and most other fruits are grown. Equally noticeable is the cultural segue: whereas San Ignacio and the Cayo have Hispanic roots, the Southern Coast is strongly Afro-Caribbean.

The Southern Coast isn't so much a melting pot as a tropical stew full of different flavors. A seaside Garifuna village recalls West Africa, while just down the road a Creole village evokes the Caribbean. Inland, Maya live much as they have for thousands of years next door to mestizos from Guatemala and Honduras who've come to work the banana plantations or citrus groves. Sprinkled in are expats from the northern climes looking for a retirement home or trying to make a buck in tourism.

Tourist dollars, the staple of contemporary Belize, have largely bypassed Dangriga, the district capital, to land in Hopkins and, even more tellingly, in Placencia, the region's most striking travel destination. Just a decade or so ago there were only three small resorts on the peninsula north of Placencia Village. Now there are more than two dozen, stretching up to the villages of Seine Bight, Maya Beach, and beyond. The region's boosters never tire of saying that this sector of coast now rivals the cayes as Belize's top destination. That's a stretch for now, but the tourism boom here is evident in the construction of new condos, hotels, and residential developments, as well as a new cruise port off the coast of Placencia.

Local residents appear divided about the dramatic changes. Some embrace the development in hopes of a better economic future; others bitterly oppose it, citing the impact on the coast's fragile ecosystems. Powerful political and economic forces in the country seem to be winning out.

The surfacing of the Southern Highway from Dangriga all the way to Punta Gorda and the Guatemalan border has made this region more accessible than ever. Off the main highway, however, most roads consist of red dirt and potholes. The road that once was the worst in the region, the dirt track from the Southern Highway to Placencia Village, has been transformed, thanks to a loan from the Caribbean Development Bank, into a smooth, paved, two-lane thoroughfare. The repaving of the Hopkins Road has also been completed, although the main road through Hopkins Village is still like a bed of nails.

Real-estate sales are a driving force in Placencia, Hopkins, and elsewhere along the coast. The lure is the beaches. The Southern Coast has the best beaches on the mainland, although as elsewhere inside the protecting Barrier Reef, the low wave action means the beaches are narrow and there's usually sea grass in the water close to shore. (Sea grass—not seaweed, which is an algae—may be a nuisance for swimmers, but it's a vital part of the coastal ecosystem, acting as a nursery for sea life.) Much of the seafront land is being divided into lots awaiting development. If things continue at this pace, the boast about this region one day rivaling Ambergris Caye as Belize's top beach destination will come true.

MAJOR REGIONS

Thanks to its good beaches, **the Southern Coast**—the area from Gales Point to Placencia—is the up-and-coming part of Belize, with a growing number of resorts and restaurants, especially in Hopkins and Placencia.

The **Placencia Peninsula** is fast becoming one of the major visitor destinations in Belize, one that may eventually rival Ambergris Caye as the most popular resort area in the country. It's one 16-mile-long (26-km-long) peninsula, with three different but complementary communities: Northern Peninsula/Maya Beach, Seine Bight, and Placencia Village.

Planning

When to Go

The weather on the Southern Coast is similar to that in central and northern Belize, only a little wetter. Expect some rain about half the days of the year—usually thanks to late fall and winter cool fronts or summer tropical fronts passing through. These showers are generally followed by sunshine. Summer daytime temperatures along the coast reach the high 80s, occasionally the 90s. Humidity is high most of the year, typically 80% or more.

Getting Here and Around

AIR TRAVEL

You'll arrive fresher if you fly. From Belize City (both international and municipal airports) there are frequent flights to Dangriga (DGA) and Placencia (PLJ) on Maya Island Air and Tropic Air. There are more than 20 flights daily between Belize City and Placencia and more than a dozen to Dangriga. You'll generally fly in small aircraft, such as the 14-passenger Cessna Caravan C208. Fares tend to be slightly lower on Maya Island Air.

CONTACTS Maya Island Air. ⊠ *Placencia airstrip, Placencia Rd., Placencia Village* ☎ *523/3443 at Placencia airstrip, 223/1403 in Belize City for reservations countrywide, 522/522–0617 at Dangriga airstrip* ⊕ *www.mayaislandair.com.* **Tropic Air.** ⊠ *Placencia airstrip, Placencia Rd., Placencia Village* ☎ *523/3410 at Placencia airstrip, 226/2626 in Belize for reservations, 800/422–3435 in U.S. for reservations, 522/2129 at Dangriga airstrip* ⊕ *www.tropicair.com.*

BOAT, CRUISE, AND FERRY TRAVEL

A small boat named the *Hokey Pokey* provides water-taxi service between Placencia Village and Independence, a village on the west side of Placencia Lagoon. Currently there are eight round trips each way daily, except on Sunday, when there are six or seven. Schedules for the boat are set to coincide with James Bus Line stops in Independence, so you can make connections to Punta Gorda to the south or Dangriga, Belmopan, and Belize City to the north.

From Placencia, a weekly boat, the *Pride of Belize,* runs to Puerto Cortes, Honduras, on Friday, with a stop in Big Creek across the lagoon to clear immigration and customs. It departs from the Placencia Municipal Pier at the south end of Placencia Village. In Puerto Cortes, the boat arrives at Laguna and returns from Puerto Cortes on Monday morning. You can buy tickets at Barefoot Beach Bar, which is on the beachfront next to Tipsy Tuna in Placencia.

From Dangriga, boats go out daily to Tobacco Caye. There are no fixed schedules, but the boats generally leave around 9 to 9:30 am. Ask at the Riverside Café or at the boats docked in the Stann Creek River near the café.

Happy Go Luckie Tours in Hopkins has a water-taxi service from Hopkins to Dangriga, Tobacco Caye, Placencia, and a few other destinations. There is no fixed schedule; passengers must book trips in advance and prices are based on a minimum of two persons. The company also provides sea and river tours, fishing and snorkeling tours, and custom charter tours to cayes and atolls off the Southern Coast.

You can arrive directly to this region by cruise ship too. Norwegian Cruise Line (NCL) operates its own port facility at Harvest Caye, an island three miles (5 km) off the coast of Placencia. NCL has designed its Harvest Caye port call to be a day at a self-contained private island, but the cruise line offers shore excursions to the mainland as well.

CONTACTS Pride of Belize. ✉ *Placencia Municipal Pier, at south end of Main St., Placencia Village* ☎ *626/8835.* **Happy Go Luckie Tours.** ☎ *635/0967* ⊕ *www.hgltours.com.* **Hokey Pokey.** ✉ *MNM Gas Station Dock, Placencia Rd., Placencia Village* ✥ *Follow signs for MNM Gas Station Dock, just north of heart of village* ☎ *622/3213.*

BUS TRAVEL

In the south, James Bus Line runs from Belize City via Belmopan to Dangriga and Independence and then Punta Gorda. Schedules are subject to change, but James Bus Line has about 10 buses daily. The buses don't stop in Placencia, they stop across the lagoon in Independence, where you can connect with the *Hokey Pokey* boat to Placencia Village. Ritchie's Bus Service has four buses daily each way between Dangriga and Placencia, with reduced service on Sunday. BEBB Bus Line has twice-daily service between Placencia and Dangriga, with a stop in Hopkins. Fares on all buses between Placencia and Dangriga are BZ$10. With connections, the trip from Belize City to Dangriga and Hopkins is three to five hours; Placencia is around five to six hours, depending on the number of stops and connections. Buses are usually old U.S. school buses or ancient Greyhound buses, are often crowded, and don't have air-conditioning or restrooms. The James Bus Line buses generally are in the best condition. In Placencia, buses are not supposed to go into the main part of Placencia Village due to traffic congestion and the narrow street, but some do. A temporary bus station is in a vacant parking lot on the east side of the main road at the north end of Placencia Village. ⚠ **Several charter buses bring workers from nearby villages to Placencia, but they do not pick up other passengers.**

CONTACTS BEBB Bus Line. ✉ *Placencia Rd., Placencia Village.* **James Bus Line.** ✉ *7 King St., Punta Gorda* ☎ *722/0117 in Punta Gorda.* **Ritchie's Bus Service.** ✉ *Main Rd., Placencia Village* ☎ *523/3806* ⊕ *www.ritchiesbusservice.com.*

CAR TRAVEL

To get to this region, head southeast from Belmopan on the Hummingbird Highway, one of Belize's better roads, as well as one of its most scenic. On your right rise the jungle-covered Maya Mountains, largely free of signs of human habitation except for the occasional field of corn or beans. As you approach Dangriga you'll see large citrus groves. South of Dangriga on the Southern Highway you'll pass a number of large banana plantations—the blue plastic bags protect the bananas from insect damage.

Barefoot Services, Budget, and Placencia Car Rental rent cars in Placencia. Many companies and larger hotels rent scooters and golf carts, which can be driven on the roads. Budget, based in Belize City, has a branch in Placencia. The car rental companies in Placencia will deliver cars to Dangriga, Hopkins, and other areas nearby, but you'll have to pay a delivery fee.

CONTACTS Barefoot Services. ✉ *Caribbean Travel and Tours Office, Main St., Placencia Village* ✛ *On east side of main road, near Rumfish y Vino* ☎ *523/3066* ⊕ *www.barefootservicesbelize.com.* **Budget.** ✉ *Live Oak Pl., south of airstrip, Placencia Village* ☎ *223/2435 in Belize City, 523/3068 in Placencia* ⊕ *www. budget-belize.com.* **Placencia Car Rental.** ✉ *Placencia Rd., Seine Bight Village* ✛ *On main road just north of Robert's Grove* ☎ *523/3284* ⊕ *www.placenciacarrental. com.*

TAXI TRAVEL

If you need a ride to the airport in Dangriga, have your hotel call a taxi. Taxis usually meet arriving flights at the Dangriga and Placencia airstrips, but many hotels in Placencia provide free pickup services at the airstrip and also provide scheduled van service from the hotel to and from Placencia Village. Taxis are expensive on the Placencia Peninsula.

Hotels

There are two kinds of lodging to choose from on the Southern Coast: small, basic hotels, often Belizean owned, and upscale beach resorts, usually owned and operated by Americans or Canadians. The small hotels are clustered in Placencia Village, Hopkins Village, and Dangriga Town. The beach resorts lie mostly on the Placencia Peninsula north of Placencia Village and also just south of Hopkins Village. Several of these resorts are among the best hotels in Belize. Vacation rental houses are becoming as prominent as hotels near Hopkins and on the Placencia Peninsula.

Restaurants

Broiled, grilled, fried, sautéed, cooked in lime juice as ceviche, or barbecued on the beach: any way you eat it seafood is the life-stuff on the Southern Coast. Restaurants serve fish, lobster, conch, and shrimp, often fresh from the boat, or, in the case of shrimp, straight from the shrimp farms near Placencia.

Expect mostly small, locally owned restaurants: some breezy beachside joints with sand floors, others wood shacks. Placencia has by far the largest number of eateries, with Hopkins a distant second. Chef Rob's is Hopkins's best restaurant. Some of the upscale restaurants are in resorts such as Turtle Inn. The Bistro at Maya Beach Hotel is one of the country's best dining spots. And it's worth making a trip to Placencia just to sample the incredible gelato at Tutti-Frutti.

Off-season, especially in late summer and early fall, restaurants in Placencia and Hopkins may close for a few weeks, and on any day the owners may decide to close early if there are no customers, so call ahead. It's also a good idea to make reservations so the cooks will have enough food on hand.

HOTEL AND RESTAURANT PRICES
Restaurant and hotel reviews have been shortened. For full infromation, visit Fodors.com.

What It Costs in Belize Dollars

	$	$$	$$$	$$$$
RESTAURANTS				
	under BZ$15	BZ$15– BZ$30	BZ$31– BZ$50	over BZ$50
HOTELS				
	under BZ$200	BZ$200– BZ$300	BZ$301– BZ$500	over BZ$500

Tours

Altogether, Placencia has about 150 licensed tour guides and around two dozen licensed tour operators; Hopkins and Dangriga also have licensed tour guides and operators. Most of the guides, except some fishing guides, work on a contract basis for resorts or tour operators. These tour guides and operators offer dive and snorkel trips to Laughing Bird, the Belize Barrier Reef, and Turneffe and Glover's Atolls; wildlife tours to Monkey River; birding tours to Red Bank and elsewhere; hiking trips to Cockscomb Basin Wildlife Sanctuary and Mayflower Bocawina National Park; and excursions to Mayan ruins near Punta Gorda.

The larger resorts on the Placencia Peninsula, including Chabil Mar, Turtle Inn, and Robert's Grove, offer a variety of tours and trips, using tour guides they have come to trust. Likewise, in Hopkins the larger resorts such as Hamanasi offer both land and sea tours.

To book tours and trips, check with your hotel; in Placencia Village, several of the tour operators have small offices along Main Street. Also check with the Belize Tourism Industry Association's (BTIA) visitor information office; the staff in Placencia can advise you on tours. You'll probably pay a little less by booking in the village instead of at your hotel, but the savings may not be worth the effort.

ADVENTURE TOURS
Toadal Adventure Belize
Toadal Adventure provides top-notch multiday sea and river expedition kayak trips in southern Belize. Trips can be customized to your specific schedule and interests. ⊠ *Near Sidewalk, Placencia Village* ☎ *523/3207* ⊕ *www.toadaladventure.com.*

BOATING, SAILING, AND WATER SPORTS
Snorkeling trips inside the reef, to Laughing Bird Caye and other snorkel spots, are popular tour options, as are half-day boat trips to Monkey River and boat excursions on the Placencia Lagoon to look for manatees. Most full-day trips include a picnic lunch. If you're going to an area with an admission or marine reserve fee often the fee is additional. Also available from Placencia are bareboat and crewed sailboat charters by charter operators such as the Moorings.

★ **Destinations Belize**
Destinations Belize is especially strong in arranging guided fishing trips, but it also offers land and sea tours of all kinds, as well as help with overall Belize trip planning, including booking hotels and transportation. ⊠ *Placencia Village* ☎ *561/315–6161 in U.S.* ⊕ *www.destinationsbelize.com.*

The Moorings
An international yacht charter company, the Moorings offers 7- to 14-night sailing charters from Placencia aboard a catamaran or monohull sailboat. Stops include a number of small cayes including Hatchett

Caye. Prices in season for a weekly bareboat charter for two ranges start at BZ$7,800, not including provisions. An all-inclusive skippered charter with a cook for a week in high season begins at BZ$30,000. ⊠ *Placencia Rd., Laru Beya Marina, Seine Bight Village* ☎ *800/416-0820 in U.S., 523/3351 in Placencia* ⊕ *www.moorings.com.*

SCUBA DIVING AND SNORKELING

This far south, the reef is as much as 20 miles (33 km) offshore, necessitating boat rides of 45 minutes to nearly two hours to reach dive sites. Because this part of the reef has fewer cuts and channels, it's also more difficult to get out to the seaward side, where you'll find the best diving. As a result, most of the diving in this region is done from offshore cayes, which are surrounded by small reefs, usually with gently sloping drop-offs of about 80–100 feet. This isn't the place for spectacular wall dives—you're better off staying in the north or heading out to the atolls. Near Moho Caye, southeast of Placencia, you'll find brilliant red-and-yellow corals and sponges that rarely appear elsewhere in Belize.

Two marine reserves off Placencia are popular snorkeling and diving spots. Laughing Bird Caye, Belize's smallest marine reserve, about 13 miles (22 km) off Placencia, is a popular spot for snorkeling. Whale sharks, *Rhincodon typus,* gentle giants of the sea, appear off Placencia in the Gladden Spit area, part of the Gladden Spit and Silk Caves Marine Reserves 26 miles (43 km) east of Placencia, in late spring and early summer. You can snorkel or dive with them on day-trips from Placencia. The best time to see whale sharks is three or four days before and after a full moon, March through June. Admission fee to each of these marine reserves is BZ$20; the admission typically is included in the dive or snorkel shop fee.

Diving costs a little more in Placencia than most other places in Belize, in part due to the distance to the reef and the atolls. Most of the larger resorts, like the Inn at Robert's Grove and Turtle Inn, have dive shops and also offer snorkel trips. Avadon Divers and the Splash Dive Center are considered two of the best dive shops in the region.

Ranguana Caye

BEACHES | FAMILY | For an idyllic island getaway with good snorkeling from the shore, consider a day-trip to Ranguana Caye. The trip, run by the people who manage the caye, includes kayaking, paddleboarding, and snorkeling, as well as a beach barbecue. ■ TIP→ If you have time, grab a few cold ones at Billy's Beach Bar on the island (drinks are extra). The fee is BZ$250 per person. You'll also find overnight accommodation here in the form of three cabanas. ⊠ *Placencia Municipal Pier, Placencia Village* ☎ *674/7264* ⊕ *www.ranguanacaye.com.*

★ Splash Dive Center

SCUBA DIVING | One of the best dive shops in southern Belize, Splash Dive Center offers many dive and snorkel trips that include visits to the inner and outer reefs and Glover's atoll. Opportunities to dive with whale sharks at Gladden Spit are also available in late spring and early summer. ⊠ *Splash Dive Center, Placencia Village* ☎ *523/3080* ⊕ *www.splashbelize. com.*

Visitor Information

The Placencia location of the Belize Tourism Industry Association (BTIA) is located behind Re/Max Real Estate on Main Street across from ScotiaBank. The BTIA publishes the *Placencia Breeze,* an informative monthly newspaper; it has a helpful website that lists accommodations, restaurants, and bars.

INFORMATION Belize Tourism Industry Association. (*BTIA*) ⊠ *Main St., behind Re/Max Property Center, Placencia Village* ☎ *523/4045* ⊕ *www.placencia.com.*

Great Itineraries

If You Have 3 Days on the Southern Coast

Base yourself in Placencia. On your first full day, walk the Sidewalk in Placencia Village, hear the latest gossip, and get to know a little of village life. Hang out on the beach at your hotel and get on Belize time, then have drinks and dinner in the village, perhaps at Rumfish y Vino, Secret Garden, or La Dolce Vita. If you still have energy, tip down a Belikin at the Barefoot Bar or Tipsy Tuna, both directly on the beach. On your second day, take a snorkel trip to Laughing Bird Caye or another snorkel area, or, if you dive, do a full-day dive trip to Turneffe or Glover's atoll. On your final day, drive or take a guided tour to Cockscomb Basin Wildlife Sanctuary. Be sure to stop at the Maya Center craft cooperative for gift shopping. If there's time, also visit the Mayflower Bocawina National Park, with its Mayan sites and waterfalls. End the day with dinner at The Bistro at Maya Beach Hotel, one of the best restaurants in Belize.

If You Have 5 Days on the Southern Coast

Drive or fly to Dangriga (the closest airport to Hopkins). Proceed by taxi or rental car to Hopkins to stay at one of its beach resorts such as Hamanasi, one of the top beach resorts in Belize, or in a luxurious beachfront suite at Villa Margarita. On your first full day, take a walk on the beach in the morning, then tour Cockscomb Basin

Wildlife Sanctuary and hike the jungle trails. Be sure to stop at the Maya Center craft cooperative. Have dinner at one of the local restaurants in Hopkins Village such as Innies or Chef Rob's. On your second full day, get an early start and visit the Mayflower Bocawina National Park with its small Mayan sites and big waterfalls, perhaps doing the zipline at Bocawina Rainforest Resort. Return to Hopkins and spend the late afternoon napping and recovering on the beach. On your third day, rise early and drive (or go by taxi) to Placencia. If the weather's good, take a snorkel trip. Have dinner in Placencia Village (don't miss gelato at Tutti-Frutti) or at The Bistro at Maya Beach Hotel. End the evening with a drink on the beach at Tipsy Tuna. On your fourth day, if you dive, do a day dive trip to Turneffe or Glover's atoll. If you're there April to June around a full moon, consider doing a snorkel or dive tour to see the huge but gentle whale sharks at Gladden Spit. Alternatively, you could go fishing for tarpon or permit, and if you catch a snapper or something else edible, have one of the local restaurants prepare it for you for dinner. Or simply spend a lazy day in a hammock at the beach and around the pool. Spend your final day in Dangriga, Belize's center of Garifuna culture, little known to the outside world. Take in the Garifuna Museum and stop by a couple of Garifuna-themed shops, the Pen Cayetano Gallery and Mercy Sabal.

Locals bike through the streets of Dangriga.

Dangriga

99 miles (160 km) southeast of Belmopan.

With a population of around 9,500, Dangriga is the largest town in the south and the administrative capital of the Stann Creek District. Dangriga also anchors the heartland of Belize's Garifuna people. (Strictly speaking the collective form is "Garinagu," although no one uses that term in English.) Avoid the sometimes-heard term "Black Caribs," considered pejorative and a remnant of colonialism. There's not much to keep you in Dangriga. Though the town is on the coast, there are no good beaches, no truly first-class hotels, few restaurants, and, except for a small museum on Garifuna culture in the outskirts of town, not much to see. Rickety clapboard houses on stilts and small shops line the downtown streets, and the town has a kind of end-of-the-road feel. Dangriga isn't really dangerous, and in fact it's friendlier than

it first seems, though it has a rough vibe, a little like Belize City, that's off-putting for many visitors.

Each year, on November 19 and the days around it, the town cuts loose with a week of carnival-style celebrations. Garifuna drumming, costumed Jonkunu dancers, *punta* music, and a good bit of drinking make up the festivities of Garifuna Settlement Day, when these proud people celebrate their arrival in Belize and remember their roots.

GETTING HERE AND AROUND

You can arrive in Dangriga by car, bus, or airplane. The Hummingbird Highway, one of Belize's most scenic roads, runs 54 miles (89 km) from Belmopan to Dangriga. James Line and other bus lines have frequent service during the day from Belize City via Belmopan to Dangriga. The bus station in Dangriga is seven blocks south of town on the main road. By air, Maya Island and Tropic together have more than a dozen flights daily to Dangriga's airstrip from the international

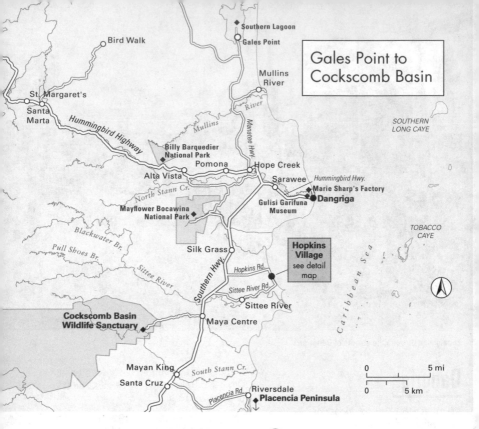

SOUTHERN
LONG CAYE

Southern Lagoon
Gales Point

Bird Walk

Mullins
River

St. Margaret's
Santa
Marta

Hummingbird Highway

Mullins

Manatee Hwy.

Billy Barquedier
National Park
Pomona

Hope Creek

Alta Vista

Sarawee   Hummingbird Hwy.

North Stann Cr.   Marie Sharp's Factory
Dangriga

Mayflower Bocawina
National Park

Gulisi Garifuna
Museum

Blackwater Br.

Pull Shoes Br.

TOBACCO
CAYE

Silk Grass

Hopkins Rd.

Caribbean Sea

Hopkins
Village
see detail
map

Sittee River Rd.

Sittee River

Cockscomb Basin
Wildlife Sanctuary

Maya Centre

Mayan King   South Stann Cr.
Santa Cruz

Placencia Rd.   Riversdale
Placencia Peninsula

0   5 mi
0   5 km

and municipal airports in Belize City. The airstrip is at the north edge of town.

TIMING

Candidly, Dangriga isn't exactly a tourist mecca. (Some hotels have Dangriga mailing addresses, even though they're physically located in Hopkins or on an offshore caye or elsewhere.) Unless you have a special interest in Garifuna culture, need to overnight there on your way to Tobacco Caye, Southwater Caye, or another offshore caye, or simply have a yen to visit quirky, Graham Greene–ish spots, you'll probably spend only a few hours in Dangriga, if that.

SAFETY AND PRECAUTIONS

Visitors may get hassled a little on the streets of Dangriga, and care should be exercised if walking around town after dark.

◉ Sights

Billy Barquedier National Park

NATIONAL/STATE PARK | FAMILY | This 1,600-acre park lies along the Hummingbird Highway between Miles 16.5 and 19 in Stann Creek District. Established in 2001, the park is still relatively young, and although it offers no spectacular sights, it does have rustic hiking trails. The Barquedier Waterfall (locally sometimes called Bak-a-Der Waterfall) is about a 20-minute hike from the entrance. The park is part of a community co-management program for nature reserves. It's best to enter the park via the northern entrance at Mile 16.5 of the Hummingbird Highway. Camping is available in the park for BZ$20 per person, plus the park entrance fee. ✉ Main entrance, Mile 16.5, Hummingbird Hwy., Steadfast

Southern Coast History

As elsewhere in Belize, the Maya were here first. They had settlements in what is now Stann Creek District at least from the early Classic period (around AD 300) until the post-Classic period (about AD 1200). However, this part of Belize did not have the large Mayan cities that existed elsewhere. Few of the known Mayan sites in the area have been extensively excavated; all appear to have been small ceremonial centers.

In the 1600s, small numbers of English, some of whom were pirates, settled on the Placencia Peninsula, though most eventually left the area. Creoles, slaves from Jamaica, came to Stann Creek in the 1700s, mainly to work in logging, and, later, in fishing. In the next century English traders and farmers arrived in what is now Dangriga. They called their coastal trading posts "stands," which was corrupted to "stann." Hence the administrative district's name, Stann Creek. On November 19, 1823, a group of Garinagu from the Bay Islands of Honduras, Africans who had intermarried with indigenous Carib peoples in the southern Caribbean, arrived at the mouth of the Stann Creek River, at what was then called Stann Creek Town. This date is still celebrated in Belize as Garifuna Settlement Day.

In the late 1800s several families, originally from Scotland, Portugal, Honduras, and elsewhere, arrived in Placencia. The names of these families—Garbutt, Leslie, Westby, and Cabral—are still common on the peninsula. In the 19th and early 20th centuries the fertile soils of the coastal plain were found to be ideal for growing bananas and citrus, and soon agriculture became the most important industry in the region. The first railroad in Belize, the Stann Creek Railway, built by the United Fruit Company to transport bananas, started operation around World War I. The railroad closed in the 1950s.

The first small tourist resorts were developed on the Placencia Peninsula in the 1960s and '70s, but the lack of infrastructure meant that few visitors made it this far south. The first fishing cooperative was established in Placencia in 1962. Although fishing is still a way of life for a few people on the coast, the big money now is real-estate development and tourism. Shrimp farming, once an up-and-coming industry around Placencia, has run into problems due to competition from Asia, and several Belize shrimp farms have closed.

Village ☎ 668/0183 ⊕ www.billybarquedier.org ☞ BZ$8.

Gales Point

TOWN | The small Creole village of Gales Point, population about 500, has an idyllic setting on the Southern Lagoon. The lagoon and nearby waters are home to many manatees. You can drive to Gales Point via the unpaved Coastal Highway, and tours are available from Dangriga and Hopkins. ✉ Gales Point ✛ From Dangriga, go northwest on Hummingbird Hwy. 8.5 miles (14 km) to village of Melinda; turn right on Manatee Hwy. (Coastal Rd.) and follow 13 miles (21 km) to turnoff, a sharp right turn. This dirt road to Gales Point Village runs about 2.5 miles (4 km) until it ends at lagoon and Manatee Lodge.

★ Gulisi Garifuna Museum

MUSEUM | FAMILY | Named after a Garifuna heroine who came to Belize with her 13 children and founded the village of Punta Negra in Toledo District, this museum has a number of displays on Garifuna history and life. Exhibits cover the Garifuna migration from Africa to St. Vincent, then to Roatan and Belize. Another exhibit is on Thomas Vincent Ramos, a visionary Garifuna leader who, in 1941, established the first Garifuna Settlement Day. Other displays are on Garifuna food, clothing, medicinal plants, and music and dance. The museum also has rotating displays of paintings by Garifuna artists including Pen Cayetano. ⊠ *Chuluhadiwa Park, Stann Creek Valley Rd.* ⊹ *About 2 miles (3 km) west of Dangriga* ☎ *699/0639* ⊕ *www.ngcbelize.org* ⊠ *BZ$10* ☾ *Closed Sun.*

★ Marie Sharp's Factory

FACTORY | You can visit the source of one of Belize's few well-known exports, Marie Sharp's Hot Sauce, made in about a dozen different heat levels from Mild to Beware. (Hillary Clinton is a big fan. She described her yen for the spicy condiment in her 2017 post-campaign book *What Happened.*) The small factory, with about 25 workers and still a Sharp family business, is open to interested visitors weekdays, but for a tour it's best to call in advance. Besides the factory tour, you can also see the entire selection of products manufactured by Marie Sharp, and most are offered for sale along with Marie Sharp T-shirts and tote bags. Her products are sold in nearly every grocery in Belize and sit on tables in most restaurants in Belize. ■**TIP**➜ **Marie Sharp's main office is on 3 Pier Road in Dangriga, where there also is a small shop.** ⊠ *1 Melinda Rd., 8 miles (13 km) west of Dangriga, Stann Creek Valley* ⊹ *Watch for sign on east side of Hummingbird Hwy. as you near junction of Hummingbird and Southern Hwys.* ☎ *520/2087* ⊕ *www.mariesharps.bz* ⊠ *Free.*

★ Mayflower Bocawina National Park

ARCHAEOLOGICAL SITE | Mayflower Bocawina has small Mayan ruins, lovely waterfalls, and good hiking on more than 7,000 acres. A private lodge, Bocawina Rainforest Resort, is in the park and has upscale lodging, food and drink, and the longest zipline in Belize. The park has three minor Mayan ceremonial sites: Mayflower, T'au Witz, and Maintzunum, near Silk Grass Creek. Nearby are the three waterfalls: Bocawina Falls, Three Sisters Falls, and Antelope Falls. Access to Mayflower is easiest from Hopkins, about 20 minutes by car. However, tours are offered from Placencia and Dangriga as well as from Hopkins. The entrance to the park is about 4.5 miles (7.5 km) on a dirt road off the Southern Highway. From the visitor center, to get to Bocawina and Three Sisters Falls, which are close together, it's an easy hike of about 1.25 miles (2 km) on the marked Bocawina Falls trail. The trail to Antelope Falls, about 1.75 miles (3 km), is somewhat more difficult due to some steep sections that can be slick after rains. Maps of the trails are available at the small visitor center. So far, little excavation has been conducted at the Mayan sites, but the parklike setting at the base of the Maya Mountains is beautiful. ⊠ *Southern Hwy.* ⊹ *From Mile 6 on Southern Hwy., go west 4.5 miles (7.5 km) on dirt road to park visitor center* ☎ *523/7223* ⊕ *www.mayflowerbocawina.org* ⊠ *BZ$10.*

Southern Lagoon

BODY OF WATER | FAMILY | One of the most beautiful lagoons in Belize, Southern Lagoon is about 25 miles (41 km) north of Dangriga—a 45-minute car ride. This lagoon is home to many West Indian manatees, and on beaches nearby, hawksbill turtles nest May to October. The Northern and Western Lagoons also are in this area. ⊠ *Gales Point* ⊹ *From Dangriga, drive west on Stann Creek Hwy./Hummingbird Hwy. to Melinda; turn right on unpaved Coastal Hwy. and go about 12 miles (20 km) to turnoff for*

Gales Point and follow 2.5 miles (4 km) to lagoon and Gales Point Village.

🍴 Restaurants

King Burger

$ | LATIN AMERICAN | No, it has nothing to do with the U.S. chain Burger King, but it is one of the best places in Dangriga to get an honest plate of chicken and rice and beans. Prepared by the Cuban owner, the fresh fish is good, and, yes, so are the hamburgers. **Known for:** great fish dishes; friendly, local atmosphere; BYOB. [$] *Average main: BZ$14* ✉ *135 Commerce St.* ✣ *On Dangriga's main street just north of the bridge of North Stann Creek River* ☎ *522/2476* 💳 *No credit cards* ⏲ *Closed Sun.*

Riverside Café

$ | LATIN AMERICAN | The Creole and Garifuna dishes here are hearty, tasty, and prepared fresh. The restaurant is often busy with fishermen and the guys who run boats out to Tobacco Caye and other offshore cayes, but it's basic and clean. **Known for:** filling breakfasts; hearty rice and beans; local fisherman's vibe. [$] *Average main: BZ$12* ✉ *Riverside and Oak Sts., on west side of North Stann Creek River* ☎ *661/6390* 💳 *No credit cards.*

🛏 Hotels

Bocawina Rainforest Resort

$$ | RESORT | Located within the beautiful Mayflower Bocawina National Park, the Bocawina Rainforest Resort has comfortable accommodations that include four spacious deluxe suites (with two queen beds, a table and chairs in a sitting area with jungle views through large windows), two thatched casitas (one has two bedrooms that can be rented together or as individual units), and six standard rooms that share a single veranda. **Pros:** hard-to-beat location in national park; lots of wildlife and birds; on-site zipline. **Cons:** you may need lots of bug spray; no a/c; remote location. [$] *Rooms from: BZ$238* ✉ *Mayflower Bocawina National Park* ✣ *Near Mayflower archaeological site, 5 miles (8 km) off Mile 6, Southern Hwy.* ☎ *670–8019, 844/894–2311 in U.S.* 🌐 *www.bocawina.com* 🛏 *12 rooms* 🍴 *Free breakfast.*

Chaleanor Hotel

$ | HOTEL | A friendly family operates this good-value lodging in the tallest building in town—you can't miss it. **Pros:** central location; family-run hotel; helpful staff. **Cons:** economy rooms have no a/c; a few rooms have shared bath; you contend with flights of stairs if staying on upper floors. [$] *Rooms from: BZ$155* ✉ *35 Magoon St.* ☎ *522/2587* 🌐 *www.chaleanorhotel.bz* 🛏 *18 rooms* 🍴 *No meals.*

Pelican Beach Resort

$$$ | HOTEL | This waterfront hotel on the north end of Dangriga, near the airstrip, is the best the town has to offer. **Pros:** charming colonial-era main building; breezy seaside location; the best in-town lodging in Dangriga. **Cons:** not the beach of your dreams; not all rooms have a/c; about 30-minute walk to center of town. [$] *Rooms from: BZ$346* ✉ *Scotchman Town, North End* ☎ *522/2044* 🌐 *www.pelicanbeachbelize.com* 🛏 *20 rooms* 🍴 *Free breakfast.*

👜 Shopping

Dangriga has some interesting, offbeat shopping, notably for Garifuna arts and crafts. Collectors may want to spend a day looking for items that are rarely available outside Belize and in some cases may not be available elsewhere in Belize. Noted Garifuna artist Pen Cayetano has a studio and gallery.

Garinagu Crafts Gallery

ART GALLERIES | This small gallery sells Garifuna drums, masks, wood carvings and other locally made items. In the gallery is a small museum on Garifuna life. ✉ *46 Oak St., at Tubroose St.* ☎ *522/2596* ⏲ *Closed weekends.*

The Garifuna Struggle

Perhaps the most extraordinary of the ethnic groups calling Belize home, the Garifuna have a story that is both unusual and moving, an odyssey of exile and dispossession in the wake of the imposition of the Old World on the New. The Garifuna descended from a group of Nigerians who were shipwrecked on the island of St. Vincent in 1635. (Although the Nigerians were taken as slaves, their descendents vociferously deny they were ever slaves.) The Caribs, St. Vincent's indigenous population, fiercely resisted the outsiders at first, but they eventually overcame their distrust.

In the eyes of the British colonial authorities, the new ethnic group that developed after years of intermarriage was an illegitimate and troublesome presence. Worse still, the Garifuna sided with, and were succored by, the French. After nearly two centuries of guerrilla warfare, the British decided that the best way to solve the problem was to deport them en masse.

After a circuitous and tragic journey across the Caribbean, during which thousands perished of disease and hunger, some of the exiles arrived in Belize, while others ended up on the coasts of Honduras, Guatemala, and Nicaragua. With widespread emigration from Central America in recent decades, the world's largest Garifuna community today lives in New York City.

That the Garifuna have preserved their cultural identity testifies to Belize's extraordinary ability to encourage diversity. They have their own religion, a potent mix of ancestor worship and Catholicism; their own language, which, like Carib, has separate male and female dialects; their own music, a percussion-oriented sound known as punta rock; and their own social structure, which dissuades young people from marrying outside their community. In 2002 the United Nations designated the Garifuna as a World Heritage culture.

Mercy Sabal

CRAFTS | Dangriga craftswoman Mercy Sabal hand-stitches Garifuna dolls in traditional dress. Prices range from BZ$50 to BZ$100. ☒ 22 Magoon St. ۞ Closed weekends.

Pen Cayetano Studio Gallery

ART GALLERIES | Punta rocker and internationally known Garifuna artist Pen Cayetano displays his bold, colorful paintings at his studio and gallery at his home in Dangriga. Works by his wife, Ingrid, and daughter, Mali, are also displayed. The house, built around 1900 and totally redone by Cayetano, including painted murals on the exterior walls, alone is worth a visit, as it is one of the

most interesting old buildings in Dangriga. ☒ 3 Aranda Crescent, at Gallery St. ☎ 628/6807 ⊕ www.cayetano.de ☒ BZ$5 ۞ Closed weekends.

Hopkins Village

10 miles (17 km) south of Dangriga on the Southern Hwy., then 2 miles (3.3 km) east on a partially paved road.

Hopkins is an intriguing Garifuna coastal village of about 1,800 people, halfway between Dangriga and Placencia. Garifuna culture is more accessible here than in Dangriga. Hopkins has the same toast-color beaches as Placencia, and

A Garifuna troupe plays the drums in Hopkins Village.

a number of new resorts have opened to take advantage of them, including resorts, restaurants, and shops just to the south of Hopkins Village. Americans, Canadians, and Europeans are snapping up beachfront land here at prices only slightly lower than in Placencia or on Ambergris Caye. If there's a downside to the area, it's the sand flies, which can be biting at times.

GETTING HERE AND AROUND

The turnoff to Hopkins from the Southern Highway is 10 miles (16 km) south of the junction of the Hummingbird and Southern Highways. The Hopkins Road is nicely paved. James Bus Line will drop you at the entrance road to Hopkins along Southern Highway, but a few come into Hopkins itself. (Always check.) Shuttles also transfer visitors from the international airport in Belize City to Hopkins. Dangriga (DGA) is the closest airstrip. Take a taxi to Hopkins if your hotel doesn't provide a shuttle.

TIMING

The highlights of Hopkins can be seen in half a day, but if this is your beach destination, you can profitably spend several relaxing days here enjoying activities on the water.

Sights

Lebeha Drumming Center

ARTS VENUE | You can watch young Garifuna boys hone their drumming skills at the Lebeha Drumming Center. *Lebeha* means "the end" in the Garifuna language, a reference to the school's location at the north end of the village. The drums are of mahogany or mayflower wood, with deerskin on the drumhead. Other instruments include *shakas,* or shakers, calabash gourds filled with fruit seeds and turtle shells. The drumming goes on nightly, though most activity is on weekends. Donations are accepted. You can take drumming lessons and purchase a CD of Lebeha drumming. ⊠ *Main Rd., near north end of village, Hopkins* ☎ *665/9305* ⊕ *www.lebeha.com.*

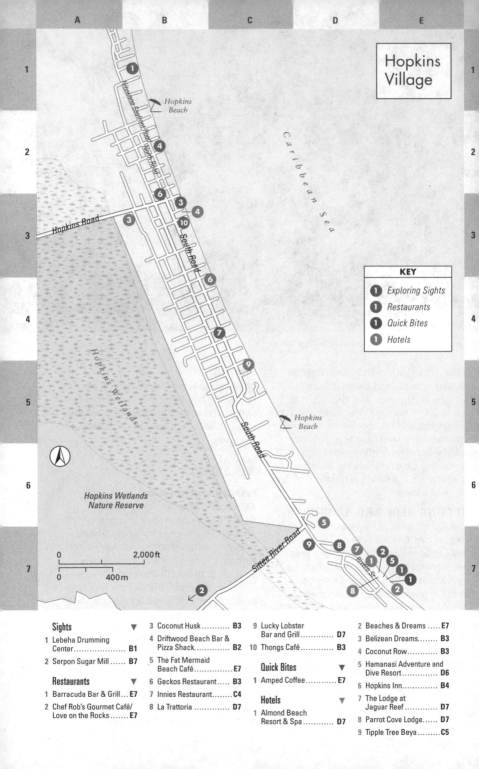

Hopkins Village

Caribbean Sea

Hopkins Beach

Hopkins Beach

Hopkins Wetlands Nature Reserve

Hopkins Wetlands

Hopkins Road

0   2,000ft
0   400m

KEY

- ① Exploring Sights
- ① Restaurants
- ① Quick Bites
- ① Hotels

Sights ▼

1 Lebeha Drumming Center.................... **B1**

2 Serpon Sugar Mill **B7**

Restaurants ▼

1 Barracuda Bar & Grill... **E7**

2 Chef Rob's Gourmet Café/ Love on the Rocks **E7**

3 Coconut Husk **B3**

4 Driftwood Beach Bar & Pizza Shack.............. **B2**

5 The Fat Mermaid Beach Café................ **E7**

6 Geckos Restaurant..... **B3**

7 Innies Restaurant........ **C4**

8 La Trattoria **D7**

9 Lucky Lobster Bar and Grill.............. **D7**

10 Thongs Café............. **B3**

Quick Bites ▼

1 Amped Coffee............ **E7**

Hotels ▼

1 Almond Beach Resort & Spa **D7**

2 Beaches & Dreams **E7**

3 Belizean Dreams........ **B3**

4 Coconut Row............. **B3**

5 Hamanasi Adventure and Dive Resort **D6**

6 Hopkins Inn.............. **B4**

7 The Lodge at Jaguar Reef **D7**

8 Parrot Cove Lodge...... **D7**

9 Tipple Tree Beya **C5**

Serpon Sugar Mill

FACTORY | Arguably Belize's most offbeat sight are these ruins of a 19th-century sugar mill, now eerily engulfed by the jungle over a century after its abandonment. Sugar once fueled the economy of this region, and American Southerners fleeing the defeated Confederacy established the Serpon Plantation after the Civil War. At its peak, the steam-powered mill produced 1,700 pounds of sugar a month. By the early 20th century, mills in northern Belize were able to harvest and generate sugar more efficiently, and Serpon ceased operation. You'd think the heat and humidity would take their toll, but the cast-iron equipment remains remarkably well preserved with little rust. You can visit the site on your own—it's a tad hard to find—and hire a guide at the small information center at the entrance. Hopkins and Placencia tour operators can also arrange visits. ⊠ *Hopkins* ⊹ *Watch for signs for Sittee River Village on Southern Highway. Entrance to mill is 1 mile (2 km) off highway on the right.* 🎟 *BZ$10.*

 Beaches

★ **Hopkins Beach**

BEACH—SIGHT | Five miles of golden sand stretch north and south of Hopkins. The water has less sea grass than other mainland beaches, making Hopkins Beach better and cleaner for swimming. The barrier reef lies only 8 to 10 miles (13–16 km) out, meaning you don't have to boat out so far to find good snorkeling. **Amenities:** food and drink; parking (no fee); toilets; water sports. **Best for:** partiers; snorkeling; solitude; sunrise; swimming; walking. ⊠ *North and south of village, Hopkins.*

 Restaurants

Barracuda Bar & Grill

$$$ | SEAFOOD | This beachside bistro, part of Beaches and Dreams Seafront Inn, is one of the best eateries on the Southern Coast, with delicious dishes like fresh grilled snapper and smoked chicken or ribs. Catch the sea breezes on the covered, open-air deck while you munch a handmade pizza or enjoy a burger. **Known for:** fresh grilled snapper; smoked chicken; great sea breezes on beachside deck. $ *Average main: BZ$40* ⊠ *Sittee Point, Hopkins* 🕾 *523/7259* ⊕ *www. beachesanddreams.com.*

★ **Chef Rob's Gourmet Café/Love on the Rocks**

$$$ | CARIBBEAN | You'll recognize this restaurant by the big sign out front made from one side of a red 1964 Peugeot 404, and inside the restaurant at Parrot Cove Lodge, the eclectic Caribbean-style, locally sourced food is nothing but contemporary and delicious. The place is really a two-for-one, with the adjoining Love on the Rocks restaurant, where guests cook their own food on lava rock. **Known for:** eclectic, rotating menu; one of Belize's top restaurants; option to cook your own food. $ *Average main: BZ$50* ⊠ *Parrot Cove Lodge, Sittee River Rd., Hopkins* 🕾 *663/1529* ⊕ *www.chefrobbelize.com.*

Coconut Husk

$$ | LATIN AMERICAN | A fun dining experience on an open-air porch adjoining the Coconut Row Hotel awaits you at one of Hopkins's newer eateries, which features a menu using local and organic ingredients. Coconut Husk truly shines at breakfast with filling pancakes or fry jacks with toast and natural fruit juices. **Known for:** filling breakfasts; great evening appetizers; cool local atmosphere. $ *Average main: BZ$18* ⊠ *Front St., Hopkins* 🕾 *675/3000* ⊕ *www.coconutrowbelize. com* ⊗ *No dinner Tues. and Wed.* ⊟ *No credit cards.*

Driftwood Beach Bar & Pizza Shack

$$ | PIZZA | Driftwood arguably has the best pizza in southern Belize, served up in a friendly, casual atmosphere in a beachfront thatch palapa. Try the Driftwood combo pizza, with red sauce, pepperoni, Italian sausage, peppers,

onion, mushrooms, and black olives (in three sizes). **Known for:** best pizza on the Southern Coast; good selection of pasta and seafood; Sunday afternoon beach barbecue. $ *Average main: BZ$25* ✉ *North end, Hopkins* ☎ *664/6611* ☾ *Closed Wed.*

The Fat Mermaid Beach Café

$$ | **MIDDLE EASTERN** | You'll find the full spectrum, from meaty to vegan, at this eatery south of the village, but if you follow a vegetarian, vegan, or gluten-free diet, make this place your Hopkins address. The focus is on Asian and Middle Eastern cuisine, with a good selection of falafels and curries. **Known for:** great options for all diets; terrific views; terrific burgers. $ *Average main: BZ$18* ✉ *Sittee River Rd., Hopkins* ☎ *662/5550* ☾ *Closed Tues. No dinner Mon.*

Geckos Restaurant

$$ | **CARIBBEAN** | One of the best-loved eateries in Hopkins, Geckos is a place where everybody knows your name; James cooks and Tina tends bar. Within minutes, you'll be friends with everybody, and you'll be enjoying a rum and tonic, jerk chicken, Gecko Balls (don't ask, just try 'em), and world-class, fresh-cut fries. **Known for:** an everybody-knows-everybody atmosphere; amazing fries; yummy jerk chicken. $ *Average main: BZ$24* ✉ *Main St. at Hopkins Rd., Hopkins* ✛ *Just north of T intersection at entrance to Hopkins* ☎ *629/5411* ⊕ *geckos-restaurant.business.site* ☾ *Closed Sun. and Tues.* ▭ *No credit cards.*

Innies Restaurant

$ | **LATIN AMERICAN** | At Innies, as at most local restaurants in Hopkins, you're eating in a spot that was once somebody's house or back porch. Here, you can dine inside or outside and get the full flavor of village life. **Known for:** traditional Garifuna cooking; tamer dishes such as rice and beans for the less adventurous; homestyle service. $ *Average main: BZ$14* ✉ *191 South, south end of village, Hopkins* ☎ *503/7333* ☾ *No dinner Sun.*

La Trattoria

$$$ | **ITALIAN** | The aromas waft out to the street and entice you in to this upscale—upscale for Hopkins, that is—Italian spot just south of town. Kick off a meal with a wide variety of bruschetta, followed by a Caprese salad, mushroom ravioli, and tiramisu for dessert. **Known for:** ample Italian wine list; bruschetta; friendly service. $ *Average main: BZ$34* ✉ *Sittee River Rd., Hopkins* ☎ *630/3606* ☾ *Closed Wed.*

Lucky Lobster Bar and Grill

$$ | **AMERICAN** | You might feel like you've stumbled into a bar in the States, but this open-air bar just has all those trappings—several TVs tuned to sports channels, nice restrooms, and efficient service. If you're craving fried-not-greasy food, get the Chicklets (chicken tenders skillfully battered in buttermilk and cornmeal), or the Lucky Clucker Lollipops (chicken skewers). **Known for:** sports-bar vibe; great bar food; souvenirs. $ *Average main: BZ$18* ✉ *Sittee River Rd., Lot 6, Hopkins* ☎ *676/7777* ☾ *Closed Mon. and Tues.*

Thongs Café

$ | **CAFÉ** | This European-run coffee shop and bistro is small but stylish, with Belizean wood carvings and paintings on the walls and free Wi-Fi. Expect good coffee, well-prepared breakfast omelets, and satisfying smoothies. **Known for:** filling breakfasts; great selection of salads at lunch; prime seating on front patio. $ *Average main: BZ$12* ✉ *Main St., south of main T-intersection, Hopkins* ☎ *622/0110* ☾ *No dinner. Closed Mon.*

☕ Coffee and Quick Bites

Amped Coffee

$ | **CAFÉ** | The line forms early for Amped's savory meat pies, baked fresh each day. They'll fortify you for a morning of sightseeing. **Known for:** good coffee to get you going; great place to hang out; area tours offered too. $ *Average main: BZ$8*

Development, Belize-Style

The building of $500,000 houses on $5,000 roads has been the story of development in Belize, as huge condos and luxury houses sprout up along narrow, muddy golf-cart trails. In some areas huge 4,000- to 6,000-square-foot homes are being built where there is no municipal water or sewage system and in more remote parts of the country no electricity or telephone.

Belize's lack of infrastructure is nothing new. As late as the 1980s open sewers were common all over Belize City. Even today, in some rural villages, telephone service is a rare commodity, and drinking water comes from a community well. With the unemployment rate in Belize in the low double digits, and with good, high-paying jobs scarce, many hope that the new housing boom will provide a needed economic boost and sustainable job growth. But environmentalists take a darker view.

In the Hopkins area, near Sittee Point, environmentalists worry that some of the tallest mangroves in the Western Hemisphere will fall prey to developers. It is illegal to remove endangered mangroves in Belize without a government permit, but this rule, like many other environmental protections, is often ignored. It isn't unusual for homeowners and developers with waterfront property to simply tear out these precious trees and deal with possible fines later.

Belize effectively has no zoning or comprehensive land-use planning, though there is now a country-wide building code that applies to individual buildings and houses. Environmental regulations, while strict in theory—every development is required to have a formal Environmental Impact Plan approved by the national government—often fail in practice. Protective regulations and permit procedures are circumvented, flouted, or just plain ignored. Government officials, whose resources are stretched thin, often can't provide oversight on development projects. According to environmentalists, some government officials are corrupt; they believe that developers can do what they like, if the price is right.

Economic growth, the environment, and the housing boom in Belize are complex, with parties facing off on a multitude of issues. Who knows if everyone will ever see eye to eye?

✉ *Sittee River Rd., Hopkins* ☏ *523/7259* ⊘ *No dinner.*

Hotels

In addition to the resorts and hotels, Hopkins has several small guesthouses, mostly run by local villagers but also by some expats who have found that the easygoing Hopkins life suits them. Most don't look like much from the outside but have the necessities including electricity and, usually, private baths. At these guesthouses it's usually not necessary to make reservations. When you arrive in the village, just walk around until you find one that suits you.

Almond Beach Resort & Spa

$$$$ | **RESORT** | **FAMILY** | Variety is the spice of beach life here, with an assortment of rooms, suites, and villas, some of which can be combined into über-suites for families. **Pros:** variety of accommodations; full-service spa; complimentary bikes

and kayaks. **Cons:** not inexpensive; a few reports of lackadaisical service; lots of families, so not a place to go if you want adults-only quiet. [$] *Rooms from: BZ$698* ✉ *Sittee Rd., Hopkins* ☎ *888/822–2448 in U.S., 533/7040 Belize for Almond Beach* 🌐 *www.vivabelize.com/almond-beach* 🛏 *25 rooms* 🍴 *No meals.*

Beaches & Dreams
$$$ | **RESORT** | **FAMILY** | A three-story boutique hotel, two octagonal cottages, and various "tree houses" (really just cabins among trees at the back of the property that accommodate up to five people) make up this popular laid-back beach spot. **Pros:** kick-off-your-shoes atmosphere; steps from the sea; good restaurant. **Cons:** comfort, not luxury; restaurant prices not cheap; some rooms on the basic side. [$] *Rooms from: BZ$450* ✉ *Sittee Point Rd., Hopkins* ☎ *523/7259, 888/266–9193 in U.S.* 🌐 *www.beachesanddreams.com* 🛏 *11 rooms* 🍴 *No meals.*

Belizean Dreams
$$$$ | **RESORT** | This collection of seaside villas is among the most upmarket accommodation choices on the Southern Coast. **Pros:** deluxe condo-style apartments; units can be combined and configured to meet your needs; friendly service. **Cons:** pool is small; some units have a minimum stay during high season; not all units have sea views. [$] *Rooms from: BZ$788* ✉ *Sittee River Rd., Hopkins* ☎ *670/2251, 800/456–7150 in U.S.* 🌐 *www.belizeandreams.com* 🛏 *9 villas* 🍴 *No meals.*

Coconut Row
$$ | **RENTAL** | This property is made up of three different accommodation types—Coconut Row, Palm Cove Cabins, and Buttonwood Guesthouse—which provides guests with a range of options to choose from including standard rooms, apartments, and cabins. **Pros:** beachfront units with Wi-Fi and fridges; a step up from other in-village accommodations; reasonable prices. **Cons:** a/c only at night unless you pay extra; a few units don't have sea views. [$] *Rooms from: BZ$220* ✉ *Front St., Hopkins* ☎ *675/3000, 518/658–6377 in U.S.* 🌐 *www.coconutrowbelize.com* 🛏 *12 rooms* 🍴 *No meals.*

★ Hamanasi Adventure and Dive Resort
$$$$ | **RESORT** | With beautifully landscaped grounds, top-notch accommodations, and an excellent scuba program, Hamanasi (Garifuna for "almond") is among Belize's very best beach and dive resorts. **Pros:** well-run resort; deluxe lodging in beautiful beachside setting; high-quality dive trips and inland tours. **Cons:** expensive restaurant; pricey accommodations (but worth it); diving requires a long boat trip to the reef or atolls. [$] *Rooms from: BZ$836* ✉ *Sittee River Rd., Hopkins* ☎ *533/533–7073, 844/235–4930 in U.S.* 🌐 *www.hamanasi.com* 🛏 *12 rooms, 13 tree houses* 🍴 *Free breakfast.*

★ Hopkins Inn
$ | **B&B/INN** | **FAMILY** | This cozy beachfront cottage keeps the guests returning. **Pros:** on the beach; helpful, enthusiastic young owners; good value. **Cons:** you may be awakened by the sound of roosters; simple rooms. [$] *Rooms from: BZ$190* ✉ *Hopkins* ☎ *623/1848* 🌐 *www.hopkinsinn.bz* 🛏 *4 cottages* 🍴 *Free breakfast.*

The Lodge at Jaguar Reef
$$$$ | **RESORT** | **FAMILY** | At the original upscale resort in Hopkins, Jaguar Reef's original whitewashed duplex garden and beachfront thatch cabanas is supplemented with newer colonial suites with local artwork, salt-tile floors, and custom-made hardwood furnishings. **Pros:** attractive and well-kept grounds; lovely beachside location; friendly staff. **Cons:** beautiful restaurant but meals are pricey; parking for guest vehicles is limited; poolside rooms are not as quiet. [$] *Rooms from: BZ$598* ✉ *Sittee River Rd., Hopkins* ☎ *888/822–2448 in U.S., 533/7040 in Belize* 🌐 *www.thebelizecollection.com/jaguar-reef* 🛏 *20 units* 🍴 *No meals.*

Parrot Cove Lodge

$$$ | RESORT | FAMILY | This small beach-front resort with rooms in earth tones arranged around a courtyard with a pool is an attractive option if you don't need all the amenities of the larger resorts but want an excellent restaurant. **Pros:** beachfront location; excellent restaurant on-site; friendly service. **Cons:** bit of a hike to activities in Hopkins Village; beach gets shade in the afternoon; smallish rooms. $ *Rooms from: BZ$398* ✉ *False Sittee Point, Sittee River Rd., Hopkins* ☎ *523/7225* ⊕ *www.parrotcovelodge. com* ➪ *12 units* ❍ *Free breakfast.*

Tipple Tree Beya

$ | B&B/INN | This small beachfront guesthouse in the heart of Hopkins Village provides a comfortable, no-frills alternative to the coast's upmarket resorts. **Pros:** steps from the water; hammocks on the porch; much more comfort and space in adjoining apartments. **Cons:** basic, not overly large rooms; no a/c in inn; apartments double the price of inn rooms. $ *Rooms from: BZ$90* ✉ *Hopkins* ⊕ *On beach in heart of village* ☎ *615/7006* ⊕ *tippletree-belize.com* ➪ *7 units* ❍ *No meals.*

🏃 Activities

BIRD-WATCHING

Cockscomb Basin Wildlife Sanctuary has excellent birding, with some 300 species identified in the reserve. You can also sometimes see the jabiru stork, the largest flying bird in the Western Hemisphere, in the marsh areas just to the west of Hopkins Village. Keep an eye out as you drive into the village from the Southern Highway. North of Hopkins is Fresh Water Creek Lagoon, and south of the village is Anderson Lagoon. These lagoons and mangrove swamps are home to many waterbirds, including herons and egrets. A kayak trip on the Sittee River should reward you with kingfishers, toucans, and various flycatchers. About 30 minutes by boat off Hopkins is Man-o-War Caye, a bird sanctuary that has one of the largest

---

Distances

Hopkins is less than 10 minutes by road (rough and potholed) from the paved Southern Highway and is ideally situated for a variety of outdoor adventures, both land and sea. Here's the distance from Hopkins to selected points of interest:

- Belize Barrier Reef: 10 miles (17 km)

- Cockscomb Basin Wildlife Sanctuary: 10 miles (17 km)

- Glover's and Turneffe Atolls: 25 miles (42 km)

- Mayflower Bocawina National Park: 15 miles (25 km)

---

colonies of frigate birds in the Caribbean, more than 300 nesting birds. Hamanasi, Jaguar Reef, and other hotels arrange bird-watching trips.

CANOEING AND KAYAKING

When kayaking or canoeing on the Sittee River, you can see many birds and, possibly, manatees and crocodiles. Manatees and porpoises are often spotted in the sea just off the Hopkins shore. Several hotels in Hopkins, including Tipple Tree Beya Hotel, Hopkins Inn, and Jungle Jeanie's, rent kayaks, canoes, and other water equipment by the hour or day. Although it's possible to do sea kayaking from Hopkins, often the water is choppy. Long sea-kayaking trips should be tried only by experienced kayakers, preferably with a guide.

CAVING

Caving tours from Hopkins typically go to St. Herman's Cave and the Crystal Cave at Blue Hole National Park on the Hummingbird Highway.

HIKING

Most hiking trips go to Cockscomb Basin Wildlife Sanctuary, where there are a dozen short hiking trails near the visitor center. If you're a glutton for punishment, you can go on a guided hike to Victoria Peak, the second-highest mountain peak in Belize. The 40-mile (67-km) hike from the visitor center at Cockscomb Basin Wildlife Sanctuary to the top entails inclines of 45 to 60 degrees. Most of these trips require at least three days up and back. One guide who will take you on jungle tours is Marcos Cucul, a jungle survival guide who is a member of the Belize National Cave and Wilderness Rescue Team.

Maya Guide Adventures
Marcos Cucul leads a team of jungle survival guides who belong to the Belize National Cave and Wilderness Rescue Team. All can help you explore the region. ⌂ *Hopkins* ⊕ *www.mayaguide.bz.*

HORSEBACK RIDING

Local lodges arrange horseback-riding trips, working with ranches near Belmopan and Dangriga. A full-day horseback trip usually includes transportation to the ranch and lunch.

MANATEE-WATCHING TOURS

Local lodges offer trips to Gales Point and the Southern Lagoon to try to spot Antillean manatees, a subspecies of West Indian manatees. These large aquatic mammals—adults weigh 800 to 1,200 pounds—are related to elephants. They're found in shallow waters in lagoons, rivers, estuaries, and coastal areas in much of Belize and are especially common in the lagoons around Gales Point. These gentle herbivores can live 60 years or longer. Under Belize government guidelines, you're not permitted to feed manatees, to swim with them, or to approach a manatee with a calf.

SCUBA DIVING AND SNORKELING

Diving and snorkeling off Hopkins is very good to terrific, though expensive compared with the northern cayes. The Barrier Reef is closer here—about 10 miles (17 km) from shore—than it is farther south. Dive shops with fast boats can also take you all the way to the atolls—Turneffe, Glover's, and even Lighthouse. These atoll trips generally start early in the morning, at 6 or 7, and last all day. In late spring, when whale sharks typically show up, local dive shops offer dives to see the Belizean behemoths at Gladden Spit Marine Reserve. Keep in mind that there are marine park fees (sometimes included in dive trip charges) for South Water Caye, Glover's, and Gladden Spit marine reserves, as well as additional rental fees for regulators, BCD, wet suits, and other equipment.

★ **Hamanasi**
DIVING/SNORKELING | One of the best diving operations in southern Belize is at Hamanasi. They have three large, well-equipped dive boats, including a 45-foot boat with three 200-horsepower outboard engines. ⌂ *Hopkins* ☎ *533/7073, 844/235–4930 in U.S.* ⊕ *www.hamanasi. com.*

WINDSURFING

Windsurfing is a growing sport in Hopkins, as the wind is a fairly consistent 10 to 15 knots, except in August and September, when it sometimes goes calm. The best winds are in April and May.

Windschief
WINDSURFING | Windschief rents well-maintained windsurfing equipment for BZ$20 for the first hour, then BZ$10 for additional hours, or BZ$60 a day. Private lessons are BZ$60 an hour. Windschief also has beach cabanas and a bar. ⌂ *Hopkins* ☎ *668/2117* ⊕ *www. windsurfing-belize.com.*

Shopping

Shopping is limited in Hopkins, where the local "shopping center" is a small clapboard house. Locals traditionally make much of what they use in daily life, from cassava graters to fishing canoes and paddles, and drums and shakas. Around the village, you'll see individuals selling carvings and other local handicrafts made from shells and coconuts. Also, several small shops and stands are scattered around the main part of the village. You can bargain for the best price, but remember that there are few jobs around Hopkins and that these craftspeople are trying to earn money to help feed their families.

GariMaya

CRAFTS | The biggest gift shop on the Southern Coast, GariMaya has a large selection of Garifuna and Mayan crafts, including masks, clothing, jewelry, and wood carvings, although some items appear to be imported from Guatemala and Mexico. You'll also find a good selection of souvenir T-shirts too. ⊠ *Sittee River Rd., Hopkins* ☎ *666/7970.*

Cockscomb Basin Wildlife Sanctuary

10 miles (17 km) southwest of Hopkins Village.

The mighty jaguar, once the undisputed king of the Central and South American jungles, is now endangered. But it has a haven in the Cockscomb Basin Wildlife Sanctuary, which covers 128,000 acres of lush rain forest in the Cockscomb Range of the Maya Mountains. With the Bladen Nature Reserve to the south, the jaguars have a continuous corridor of about 250,000 acres. Thanks to these reserves, as well as other protected areas around the country, Belize has the highest concentration of jaguars in the world.

GETTING HERE AND AROUND

Maya Center, at the entrance of the road to Cockscomb, is at Mile 15 of the Southern Highway. You can drive here, or any local bus on the Southern Highway will drop you. From Maya Center it's 6 miles (10 km) to the park. You can drive, hike (about two hours), or take a local taxi. There is a co-op crafts shop at Maya Center, which is a good place to buy locally made Mayan crafts; however, prices here generally are no lower than elsewhere in Belize.

TIMING

Most visitors come to Cockscomb only on a day visit with a guided tour. Quite frankly, that is the easier option. However, for the best chance to see wildlife and even the elusive jaguar, an overnight stay is best.

Sights

★ Cockscomb Basin Wildlife Sanctuary

NATURE PRESERVE | FAMILY | Some visitors to Cockscomb are disappointed that they don't see jaguars and that wildlife doesn't jump out from behind trees to astound them as they hike the trails. The experience at Cockscomb is indeed a low-key one, and seeing wildlife requires patience and luck. You'll have the best chance of seeing wild animals, perhaps even a jaguar or one of the other large cats, if you stay overnight, preferably for several nights, in the sanctuary. You may also have better luck if you go for an extended hike with a guide. Several nearby lodges, such as Hamanasi, offer night hikes to Cockscomb, departing around dusk and returning around 9 pm.

Cockscomb Basin has native wildlife aside from the jaguars. You might see other cats—pumas, margays, and ocelots—plus coatis, kinkajous, deer, peccaries, and, last but not least, tapirs. Also known as the mountain cow, this shy, curious creature appears to be half horse, half hippo, with a bit of cow and elephant thrown in. Nearly 300 species of birds have been identified in the Cockscomb Basin, including the keel-billed toucan, the king vulture, several hawk species, and the scarlet macaw, a species of parrot.

Within the reserve is Belize's best-maintained system of jungle and mountain trails, most of which lead to at least one outstanding swimming hole. The sanctuary also has spectacular views of Victoria Peak and the Cockscomb Range. Bring serious bug spray with you—the reserve swarms with mosquitoes and tiny biting flies called no-see-ums—and, if you can tolerate the heat, wear long-sleeve shirts and long pants. The best times to hike anywhere in Belize are early morning, late afternoon, and early evening, when temperatures are lower and more animals are on the prowl.

The road from Maya Center to the Cockscomb ranger station and visitor center winds 6 miles (10 km) through dense vegetation—splendid cahune palms, purple mimosas, orchids, and big-leaf plantains—and as you go higher the marvelous sound of tropical birds, often resembling strange windup toys, grows stronger and stronger. This is definitely four-wheel-drive terrain. You may have to ford several small creeks as well as negotiate deep, muddy ruts. At the end, in a clearing with hibiscus and bougainvillea bushes, you'll find a little office, where you can buy maps of the nature trails, along with restrooms, several picnic tables, cabins, and a campground. The Belize Audubon Society manages the Cockscomb and can assist in making reservations for the simple accommodations in the sanctuary.

Altogether there are some 20 miles (33 km) of marked trails. Walking along these 12 nature trails is a good way to get to know the region. Most are loops of 0.5–1.5 miles (1–2 km), so you can do several in a day. The most strenuous trail takes you up a steep hill; from the top is a magnificent view of the entire Cockscomb Basin. Longer hikes, such as to Victoria Peak, require a guide and several days of strenuous walking.

Hotels and tour operators and guides in Hopkins, Placencia, and Dangriga offer tours to Cockscomb; Hopkins is closest to the sanctuary but easily accessible from any of these coastal areas. ✉ *Maya Center, Mile 15, Southern Hwy.* ☎ *227/7369 Maya Center, 223/5004 Belize Audubon Society in Belize City* 🌐 *www.belizeaudubon.org* 🎟 *BZ$10.*

Hotels

Cockscomb Campgrounds and Cabins
$ | **RENTAL** | Inside the Cockscomb Wildlife Reserve, a small house and three cabins, each with private bath, can accommodate up to four or six people (BZ$120–BZ$170 per house/cabin) and make for a rustic yet comfortable way to experience nature here. **Pros:** true jungle setting; inexpensive; staying overnight offers different way to experience the reserve. **Cons:** don't expect upscale amenities; remote location; need to bring food and water. [$] *Rooms from: BZ$120* ✉ *Cockscomb Basin Wildlife Sanctuary* ✣ *Near visitor center* ☎ *223/5004 Belize Audubon Society in Belize City* 🌐 *www.belizeaudubon.org* 🛏 *4 rooms* 🍴 *No meals.*

Tutzil Nah Cottages
$ | **B&B/INN** | Gregorio Chun and his family, Mopan Maya who've lived in this area for many generations, provide affordable accommodations in simple thatch cabanas. **Pros:** close to Cockscomb; owners highly knowledgeable about the region; interesting tours available. **Cons:** very basic accommodation; furnishings need upgrading; two rooms share bath. [$] *Rooms from: BZ$50* ✉ *Mile 13.5, Southern Hwy., Cockscomb Wildlife Sanctuary* ✣ *Near Maya Center* ☎ *636/4750* 🌐 *www.mayacenter.com* 🛏 *4 rooms* 🍴 *No meals* 💳 *No credit cards.*

Placencia Peninsula

28 miles (47 km) south of Dangriga by road.

The Placencia Peninsula is fast becoming one of the major visitor destinations in Belize, one that may eventually rival Ambergris Caye as the most popular resort area in the country. It's one 16-mile-long (26-km-long) peninsula, with three different but complementary areas: Northern Peninsula/Maya Beach, Seine Bight, and Placencia Village.

The road—25 miles (41 km) from the Southern Highway to the tiny community of Riversdale and then down the peninsula to Placencia Village—is paved and in excellent condition. (You'll mutter under your breath at the frequent speed bumps, however.) Beginning at Riversdale, at the elbow where the actual peninsula joins the mainland, you'll get a quick glimpse through mangroves of the startlingly blue Caribbean. As you go south, the Placencia Lagoon is on your right, and behind it in the distance rise the low Maya Mountains, the Cockscomb Range ruffling the tropical sky with its jagged peaks. On your left, a few hundred feet away, beyond the remaining mangroves and a narrow band of beach, is the Caribbean Sea. A broken line of uninhabited cayes grazes the horizon.

Condo construction is fast filling in the once-vacant area between Riversdale and the village of Maya Beach. The beaches toward the upper end of the peninsula are some of the best on mainland Belize, and more restaurants and shops are starting to open here. Roughly midway down the peninsula is the Garifuna village of Seine Bight, struggling to adapt to change. At both the north and south ends of the village upscale resorts and condo developments have sprung up to take advantage of the appealing beaches.

On a sheltered half-moon bay at the southern tip of the peninsula is Placencia Village. Founded by pirates, and long a Creole village, the community is now inhabited by an extraordinary mélange of people, local and expatriate. Most of the hotels in the village are modest, and most shops have tiny selections. Two new lodgings—one upscale and the second very upscale—have joined the in-village offerings. Once you arrive, you'll probably just want to lie in a hammock with a good book, perhaps getting up long enough to cool off in the gentle waves or to sip a Belikin at one of the village saloons.

GETTING HERE AND AROUND

Both Tropic Air and Maya Island Air fly from Belize City to Placencia (PLJ), usually with a quick stop in Dangriga, and also north from Punta Gorda. The airstrip is about 2 miles (3 km) north of the center of Placencia Village.

By road, from the Southern Highway at Mile 22.2, it's about 8 miles (14 km) to Riversdale (the "bend" in the peninsula road), 15 miles (26 km) to Maya Beach, 19 miles (31 km) to Seine Bight, and 25 miles (41 km) to Placencia Village. The road is completely paved. Ritchie's Bus Line and BEBB have buses between Dangriga and Placencia several times a day. James Bus Lines, the dominant bus service in the south, has 9 or 10 buses a day each way between Belize City and Punta Gorda, but these buses stop across the lagoon in Independence rather than on the Placencia Peninsula itself.

Since there's no point-to-point bus service on the peninsula, and taxis are expensive, a rental car can be handy. If you haven't rented one in Belize City, you can rent one locally. Currently there are a couple of car-rental agencies on the peninsula, plus a branch of Belize City's Budget agency.

Just off Placencia Village, Ranguana Caye is a popular day-trip for snorkelers.

TIMING

It takes a couple of days to explore the entire Placencia Peninsula. How long you spend here depends on how much beach and water-sports time you want. Many visitors stay a week or longer, and some end up buying a lot or a house with the intention of living here permanently. (You might encounter real estate agents who plant that notion in your mind. Make no rash decisions, of course. If you lean in that direction, the experts suggest doing a trial rental of a few months to see if expat life is for you. Keep in mind that living in Belize is quite different than being on vacation here.)

SAFETY AND PRECAUTIONS

Overall the Placencia Peninsula is safe, but take the standard travel precautions of watching your things and avoiding flashing money and expensive items.

Northern Peninsula and Maya Beach

36 miles (61 km) south of Dangriga by road.

Some of the best beaches on the Placencia Peninsula—and therefore on mainland Belize—are at the northern end of the peninsula and the Maya Beach areas. The light khaki-color sand is soft, the surf is gentle, and, while the Barrier Reef is miles off the coast here as it is elsewhere in this part of Belize, there is good snorkeling a short kayak ride away, around False Caye just east of Maya Beach.

GETTING HERE AND AROUND

From the Southern Highway you go about 8 miles (14 km) east to Riversdale, where the Placencia Peninsula formally meets the mainland. From there, head south through the northern end of the peninsula 7 miles (12 km) to Maya Beach.

🍴 Restaurants

★ Maya Beach Hotel Bistro

$$$ | **SEAFOOD** | **FAMILY** | This bistro by the beach is, hands down, one of the best restaurants in the entire country. The setting, in a covered patio by the swimming pool with breezes from the sea, which is just a few yards away, is everything you come to the Caribbean to enjoy. **Known for:** creative, always-changing seafood menu; its popularity, which makes online reservations a must for dinner; scrumptious appetizer selection. [$] *Average main: BZ$38* ✉ *Placencia Rd., Maya Beach* ☎ *533/8040* 🌐 *www.mayabeachhotel.com.*

🛏 Hotels

Barnacle Bill's Beach Bungalows

$$ | **RENTAL** | **FAMILY** | A pair of wooden Mennonite-style bungalows are set among palm trees here on a lovely beach, with each on stilts. **Pros:** friendly spot; helpful owners; nice place just to relax. **Cons:** don't expect luxury; no kids under 12; five-night minimum stay. [$] *Rooms from: BZ$230* ✉ *23 Maya Beach Way, Maya Beach* ☎ *533/8110* 🌐 *www.barnaclebills-belize.com* 🛏 *2 cottages* 🍴 *No meals.*

Green Parrot Beach Houses

$$$ | **B&B/INN** | **FAMILY** | This resort has Mennonite-built cottages along a nice stretch of beach, each with a kitchenette and dining area. **Pros:** good option for families; pleasant beach area; good value. **Cons:** two-level units not to everyone's taste; you may not like outdoor showers in some units; not a good option if you crave action. [$] *Rooms from: BZ$340* ✉ *1 Maya Beach, Maya Beach* ✣ *4 miles (6.5 km) north of Seine Bight* ☎ *533/8188, 734/667–2537 in U.S.* 🌐 *www.greenparrot-belize.com* 🛏 *8 rooms* 🍴 *Free breakfast.*

Maya Beach Hotel

$$ | **B&B/INN** | **FAMILY** | This is the kind of small, unpretentious beachfront hotel that many come to Belize to enjoy, but few actually find. **Pros:** like a small Caribbean beach hotel should be; good value; one of Belize's best restaurants. **Cons:** rooms on the basic side; Wi-Fi is a little spotty; a couple of rooms get noise from the restaurant. [$] *Rooms from: BZ$260* ✉ *Placencia Rd., Maya Beach* ☎ *533/8040* 🌐 *www.mayabeachhotel.com* 🛏 *10 rooms* 🍴 *No meals.*

★ Naïa Resort and Spa

$$$$ | **RESORT** | **FAMILY** | This resort aspires to be the country's ultimate spa-centric seaside luxury destination, and we'd agree it succeeds. **Pros:** luxury villas and houses, some with private pools; large spa complex with the latest treatments and technologies; beautiful beach and lake setting. **Cons:** not inexpensive; vast 19-acre grounds; a bit of a jaunt to the village. [$] *Rooms from: BZ$750* ✉ *Cocoplum, Placencia Rd., Maya Beach* ☎ *523/4600, 888/439–5866* 🌐 *www.naiaresortandspa.com* 🛏 *35 villas* 🍴 *No meals.*

Singing Sands Inn

$$ | **B&B/INN** | The six free-standing thatched-roof cabanas here face the beach and are nicely decorated with polished hardwood floors. **Pros:** pleasant cottages set among tropical gardens; reasonable prices; good Asian restaurant. **Cons:** smallish cabana rooms; no a/c in some rooms; simple accommodation. [$] *Rooms from: BZ$280* ✉ *714 Maya Beach Rd., Maya Beach* ✣ *6 miles (10 km) north of airstrip* ☎ *533/3022, 440/579–3386 in U.S.* 🌐 *www.singingsands.com* 🛏 *10 rooms* 🍴 *No meals.*

🍸 Nightlife

Casino at The Placencia

CASINOS | A small casino holds court next to The Placencia Hotel with some 150 gaming machines and several live tables for blackjack and roulette. ✉ *The Placencia Hotel, Placencia Rd., Mile 13, Maya Beach* ☎ *807/6868* 🌐 *www.theplacencia.com.*

Activities

Jaguar Lanes
BOWLING | FAMILY | About the last place you'd expect to find a bowling alley is Maya Beach, but Jaguar Lanes is here, and it's fun! This little four-lane alley—air-conditioned, with jaguar murals on the walls and pine ceilings—has everything your lanes back home have, except you have to keep score on paper. ✉ *Maya Beach* ☎ *629/3145* 🕒 *Closed Thurs.*

Seine Bight

47 miles (77 km) south of Dangriga.

Like Placencia, its Creole neighbor to the south, Seine Bight is a small village. It may not be for long, though, as Placencia's resorts are stretching north to and through this Garifuna community, one of six predominantly Garifuna centers in Belize. The beach, especially south of Seine Bight, is excellent, though the village garbage sometimes mars the view. Hotels do rake and clean their beachfronts, and several community cleanups have been organized in an effort to solve this problem. All the businesses catering to tourists are along the paved main road (actually, it's the only road) that leads south to Placencia Village. The name Seine Bight derives from a type of net, called a seine, used by local fishermen. *Bight* means an indentation or inward bend in the coastline.

GETTING HERE AND AROUND

By road, Seine Bight is around 19 miles (31 km) from the junction at Southern Highway. By air, you'll fly into the Placencia airstrip, about a 10-minute drive.

TIMING

Seine Bight has no sights, per se, although it does contain one worthwhile shopping stop. How long you stay depends on how much beach and water time you want. Many visitors stay a week.

Hotels

Laru Beya Resort
$$$ | RENTAL | A condo colony whose name means "on the beach" in the Garifuna language, Laru Beya sits on seven beachfront acres, with well-priced rooms and suites that are bright and sunny. **Pros:** well-designed rooms and suites; a good value; friendly staff. **Cons:** minigolf course needs maintenance; a lot of steps to the third floor; a bit of a jaunt to the village. [$] *Rooms from: BZ$406* ✉ *Off Placencia Rd., Seine Bight Village* ✣ *0.5 miles (1 km) south of Seine Bight, south of Robert's Grove* ☎ *522/0384, 800/890–8010 in U.S.* 🌐 *www.larubeya.com* 🛏 *30 units* 🍴 *Free breakfast.*

Robert's Grove Beach Resort
$$$ | RESORT | Robert's Grove is one of the largest (44 units including standard rooms, suites, and one-, two- and three-bedroom apartments, and lagoon-side villas) and most complete resorts in southern Belize, with kayaks, windsurfers, small sailboats, and boats for diving. **Pros:** complete resort facilities; lovely seaside rooms and suites; lots of tours and on-site activities. **Cons:** nothing particularly exotic here; expensive; not what it used to be. [$] *Rooms from: BZ$410* ✉ *Placencia Rd., Placencia Village* ✣ *0.5 mile (1 km) south of Seine Bight* ☎ *523/3565, 800/565–9757 in U.S.* 🌐 *www.robertsgrove.com* 🛏 *44 rooms* 🍴 *Free breakfast.*

🛍 Shopping

Lola's Art

ART GALLERIES | Painter and writer Lola Delgado's workshop displays her bold, cheerful acrylic paintings of local women and scenes (BZ$100 and up). She also sells hand-painted cards, painted gourd masks, and some of her husband's wood carvings. Espresso and pastries are available. The workshop is up a flight of steps in a tiny wooden house off the main street, behind the football field. ⊠ *Seine Bight Village* ☎ *601/1913, 523/3342.*

Placencia Village

5 miles (8 km) south of Seine Bight, 52 miles (85 km) south of Dangriga.

Placencia Village is a mini, downscale version of Key West, laid-back, hip, and full of atmospheric watering holes. At the end of the road, the village is the main residential center on the peninsula, with a population of close to 1,000, predominantly Creoles. It is also the peninsula's commercial hub—if you can call a small village a hub—with a half-dozen grocery stores, a couple of hardware stores, and the majority of the region's restaurants and bars. Traffic on the Main Road (also called Main Street, and farther north Placencia Road) through the village is surprisingly heavy, and parking can be problematic. The village proper contains two snazzy places to stay; budget digs make up the rest of its accommodation options. Just north of the village, between it and the airport, are upscale beach resorts and condo developments.

Sometimes billed as the world's narrowest street or longest sidewalk, the Sidewalk is a single concrete path that winds through the village. Setting off purposefully from the town's southern end near the harbor, the path meanders through everyone's backyard. It passes wooden cottages on stilts overrun with bougainvillea and festooned with laundry, along with a few shops and tour offices, and then, as if it had forgotten where it was headed in the first place, peters out abruptly in a little clearing. Paved sidewalks and dirt paths run between the Sidewalk and the Main Road through Placencia Village. Stroll along the Sidewalk, and you've seen the entire community. If you don't mind it being a little rough around the edges, you'll be utterly enchanted by this rustic village, where the palm trees rustle, the waves lap the shore, and no one is in a hurry.

GETTING HERE AND AROUND

By road, Placencia Village is around 25 miles (41 km) from the Southern Highway. By air, you'll fly into the Placencia airstrip. Plan on about 10 minutes from the airstrip to the village, a BZ$12 taxi ride for up to two people, BZ$6 each for three or more. You can also get here by boat, the *Hokey Pokey,* from Independence/Mango Creek across the Placencia Lagoon (BZ$10). There are several Ritchie and BEBB buses a day between Placencia Village and Dangriga, and the BEBB buses stop in Hopkins. James Bus Line buses don't go to Placencia but stop in Independence, connecting with the *Hokey Pokey* to Placencia Village.

TIMING

Placencia Village is small and can be seen in a day or less. Popping into all the shops and cafés along the Sidewalk makes for a pleasant day. How long you choose to stay depends on how much relaxing and beach and water time you desire. Many visitors stay a week or longer, and a few never leave.

SAFETY

Most visitors say they feel safe in the village. However, petty theft has become a problem. Some budget travelers have reported thefts from their hotel rooms. A few Placencia hotels, and most of the more upscale resorts up the peninsula, have security guards. Note that at night the village and its beachfront are not well lighted.

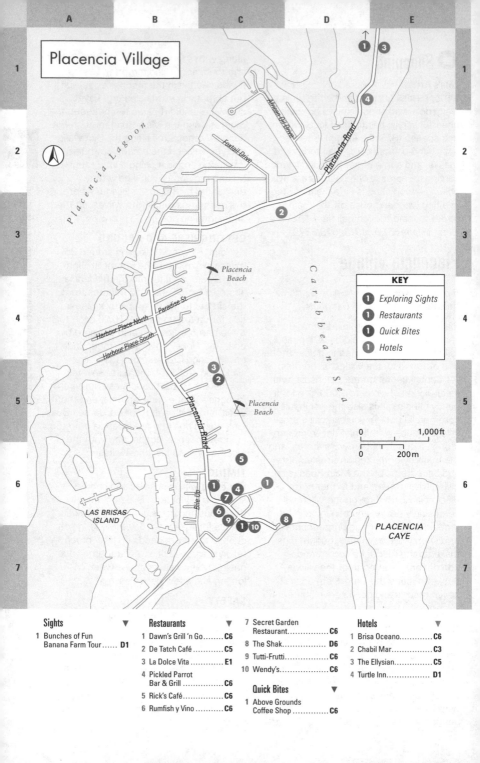

Placencia Village

KEY

- ① Exploring Sights
- ① Restaurants
- ① Quick Bites
- ① Hotels

Placencia Lagoon

Caribbean Sea

African Oil Drive

Foxtail Drive

Placencia Road

Placencia Beach

Paradise St.

Harbour Place North

Harbour Place South

Placencia Road

Bite Up

LAS BRISAS ISLAND

PLACENCIA CAYE

0   1,000 ft
0   200 m

Sights

Bunches of Fun Banana Farm Tour

FARM/RANCH | Nearby Honduras was history's original "Banana Republic." Belize, the former British Honduras, remains one of Britain's and the European Union's prime sources of bananas today. A two-hour tour at a plantation north of Maya Beach takes you through the cultivation and processing of the country's third most important agricultural crop. (Sugarcane and citrus fruits surpass bananas in their contribution to Belize's economy.) Tours take place Monday through Saturday at 8 and 10 am and 1 pm and are by reservation only. ✉ *Maya Beach* ✥ *Riverdale, 30 km (18 miles) north of Placencia Village* ☎ *624/4297* 🌐 *www.bunchesoffuntours.com* 🎫 *BZ$40* ⏲ *Closed Aug.–Nov.*

Beaches

Placencia Beach

BEACH—SIGHT | Whether the peninsula's 16 miles (26 km) of sand (the longest in Belize) is one beach or multiple is open to debate. All residents do agree that their golden strand stretching from Maya Beach to Seine Bight to Placencia Village is the mainland's best—most outsiders do, too. Some sections hum with activity, especially those in the village itself; others, you'll have all to yourself. The Barrier Reef lies a distant 20 miles (32 km) away, making snorkeling immediately offshore not ideal. **Amenities:** food and drink; parking (no fee); toilets; water sports. **Best for:** partiers; sunrise; solitude; swimming; walking. ✉ *Placencia Village north to Maya Beach.*

Restaurants

Dawn's Grill 'n Go

$$ | **LATIN AMERICAN** | **FAMILY** | Friendly service, local atmosphere, good food simply prepared, modest prices, ice-cold beer—what more could you want? Dawn's Grill 'n Go is in a small no-frills building with screened windows (no a/c) on the main street in Placencia Village. **Known for:** sausage omelets; fish tacos; fun local vibe. [$] *Average main: BZ$20* ✉ *Main St., next to BTL office* ☎ *602/9302* 💳 *No credit cards* ⏲ *Often closed several weeks July and Aug.*

De Tatch Café

$$ | **SEAFOOD** | This open-air bar and restaurant near the sea with a "tatch" (thatch) roof has long been a popular hangout in the village. Try the huge shrimp burrito and wash it down with a few cold Belikins. **Known for:** filling breakfasts; cool sea breezes; shrimp burritos. [$] *Average main: BZ$20* ✉ *Placencia Village* ✥ *In village near Seaspray Hotel* ☎ *503/3385* ⏲ *Closed Tues.*

★ **La Dolce Vita**

$$$ | **ITALIAN** | **FAMILY** | In a slightly Fellini-esque setting, upstairs over Wallen's Store, the often-underrated La Dolce Vita brings authentic antipasti, bruschetta, and pasta dishes to Placencia. With opera music playing softly in the background, it's like being in a small, family-run restaurant in Italy. **Known for:** spaghetti carbonara; penne dolce vita; good wine selection. [$] *Average main: BZ$32* ✉ *Main St., above Wallen's Store* ☎ *523/3115* ⏲ *Closed Mon. No lunch.*

Pickled Parrot Bar & Grill

$$ | **AMERICAN** | **FAMILY** | This popular thatch-roof restaurant and bar sits smack-dab in the heart of Placencia Village between the main road and the Sidewalk. Try the Philly cheesesteak or the burgers and fries. **Known for:** yummy cheesburgers; mouthwatering fries; owners' dogs. [$] *Average main: BZ$22* ✉ *Off main road, behind Wallen's Market* ☎ *636/7068* 💳 *No credit cards* ⏲ *Closed Tues. Closed several wks in late summer.*

Rick's Café

$$ | **CARIBBEAN** | **FAMILY** | This little place on the Sidewalk is a nice stop for fresh ceviche and cold beer at lunch; just sit on the

open-air veranda and watch the village life pass by. If you're craving greens, it also has some of Placencia's best salads. **Known for:** pineapple shrimp quesadillas; great salad selection; attentive owner and staff. [$] *Average main: BZ$20* ✉ *Sidewalk* ✣ *Near center of village, on west side of Sidewalk* ☎ *666/8466* 🕘 *Closed Wed.* 💳 *No credit cards.*

Rumfish y Vino

$$$ | **SEAFOOD** | This hip spot run by transplanted New Yorkers, in a breezy second-floor location near Tutti-Frutti, is a good place to have drinks, tapas, interesting seafood creations, and Italian pasta. Try the small plates of Thai shrimp cakes or *pescado relleno* (red snapper stuffed with shrimp). **Known for:** good seafood selection; yummy Thai appetizers; great wine selection. [$] *Average main: BZ$38* ✉ *Placencia Village Square, off Main St., near Tutti-Frutti* ☎ *523/3293* 🌐 *www.rumfishyvino.com.*

★ Secret Garden Restaurant

$$$ | **ECLECTIC** | This upmarket place serves sophisticated international meals at dinner in an open-air, palm-lined, romantically lighted garden. Enjoy the friendly service and an eclectic mix of dishes including ceviche, jerk chicken, black bean soup, and bacon-wrapped steak. **Known for:** upscale place for Placencia; vegan and gluten-free options available; key lime pie. [$] *Average main: BZ$35* ✉ *Sunset Pointe, in village* ☎ *523/3420* 🌐 *www.secretgardenplacencia.com* 🕘 *Closed Sun. No lunch.*

The Shak

$$ | **CAFÉ** | In a shack at the beginning of the Sidewalk, overlooking the harbor, The Shak is the spot for fruit smoothies. For lunch and dinner, there are several curries, wraps, sandwiches, and stir-fries. **Known for:** best smoothies in town; curries and stir-fries; local vibe. [$] *Average main: BZ$20* ✉ *Placencia Harbor, at beginning of Sidewalk* ☎ *622/1686* 💳 *No credit cards* 🕘 *No dinner Sun. and Tues.*

★ Tutti-Frutti

$ | **CAFÉ** | Authentic, Italian-style gelato is the thing here, and it's absolutely delicious, the equal of any you'll find in Rome. Try the tropical fruit flavors, such as banana, lime, coconut, papaya, and mango, or an unusual flavor such as sugar corn, all created from natural ingredients. **Known for:** gelato that rivals anything in Italy; rotating daily selection of flavors; knowledgable staff who'll explain the exotic flavors to you. [$] *Average main: BZ$8* ✉ *Main Square, Main Rd.* 💳 *No credit cards* 🕘 *Closed Wed. and up to two months in July and Aug.*

Wendy's

$$ | **LATIN AMERICAN** | **FAMILY** | Long-established Wendy's—no, not that Wendy's—always delivers good, no-frills food at reasonable prices. The Belizean breakfast of fry jack (the local version of beignets without the sugar), bacon, eggs, and refried beans is nearly perfect. **Known for:** filling breakfasts; great prices; solid Belizean dishes like gibnut, fry jack, and cow-foot soup. [$] *Average main: BZ$24* ✉ *Main St.* ☎ *523/3335.*

☕ Coffee and Quick Bites

★ Above Grounds Coffee Shop

$ | **CAFÉ** | Above Grounds sells shade-grown, organic Guatemalan coffee straight up, in lattes, iced, or however you like it. Fresh-roasted coffee by the pound is also for sale. **Known for:** great bagels; fresh donuts; good selection of coffee drinks. [$] *Average main: BZ$6* ✉ *Main St.* ✣ *South end of village across from south end of football field* ☎ *634/3212* 🕘 *No dinner. No lunch Sun.* 💳 *No credit cards.*

🛏 Hotels

Brisa Oceano

$$ | **HOTEL** | A step above the mostly budget options in Placencia Village—but nowhere near as pricey as The Ellysian—is this all-blue-on-the-outside collection

of condo-like units. **Pros:** convenient to everything in the village; good value; suites make for good base for staying in the area. **Cons:** not all rooms have ocean view; must contend with stairs if staying on upper floors; a few rooms get noise from the sidewalk. $ *Rooms from: BZ$286 ⊠ Placencia Village ☎ 523/3259, 877/418–2561 in U.S. ⊕ www.brisaoceano.com ↪ 50 rooms |⊙| Free breakfast.*

★ Chabil Mar
$$$$ | RESORT | FAMILY | Chabil Mar means "beautiful sea" in Kek'chi Mayan, and the sea and almost 400 feet of beach are indeed gorgeous at this gated luxury condo-style resort. **Pros:** beautiful grounds; lovely stretch of beach; every comfort and convenience at hand. **Cons:** walls hide the beauty of the grounds and beach; expensive, but you get your money's worth; a bit of a hike to the village. $ *Rooms from: BZ$980 ⊠ 2284 Placencia Rd. ✛ Between airstrip and Placencia Village ☎ 523/3606, 866/417–2377 in U.S. ⊕ www.chabilmarvillas.com ↪ 20 villas |⊙| No meals.*

★ The Ellysian
$$$$ | HOTEL | An exception to the general rule that "there are only budget lodging options in the village" is this snazzy, new beachfront retreat, smack-dab in the center of Placencia, set off enough to maintain an air of luxurious privacy. **Pros:** top option in Placencia Village; impeccable service; convenient to everything in the village. **Cons:** pricey; must climb stairs if staying on upper floors; not a place to stay if you seek a secluded resort. $ *Rooms from: BZ$750 ⊠ 1 Williams Dr. ☎ 523/4898, 501/232–0018 in U.S. ⊕ www.theellysian.com ↪ 12 rooms, 1 penthouse |⊙| Free breakfast.*

★ Turtle Inn
$$$$ | RESORT | FAMILY | Francis Ford Coppola's second hotel in Belize is nothing if not exotic, with the furnishings, art, and most of the construction materials bought in Bali by the film director and his wife. **Pros:** exotic Balinese furnishings;

delightful outdoor showers; beautiful seaside setting. **Cons:** no a/c; lodging, food, and drink are surprisingly pricey; two-night minimum stay during high season. $ *Rooms from: BZ$1,500 ⊠ Placencia Rd., 2 miles (3 km) north of Placencia Village ☎ 824/4912, 866/356–5881 in U.S. ⊕ www.thefamilycoppolahideaways.com ↪ 25 villas |⊙| Free breakfast.*

▣ Nightlife

Barefoot Beach Bar
BARS/PUBS | After dark, Barefoot gets its share of seaside sippers. For a bar, the food is good, and it has one of the best selections of rums on the peninsula, as well as occasional live music. ⊠ *Beachfront ✛ Next to Tipsy Tuna ☎ 523/3515.*

The Flying Pig
BARS/PUBS | This busy roadside sports bar serves ribs, burgers, pizza, and other bar food, along with quantities of Belikin beer, with local musicians on open-mic nights. ⊠ *Placencia Rd., 0.5 mile (1 km) north of airstrip on east side of road ☎ 602/6391.*

Hobbs Brewing Company
BREWPUBS/BEER GARDENS | A local microbrewery is giving Belize's ubiquitous Belikin beer some competition in this part of the country. Hobbs's line includes Wildcat India Pale Ale, Hummingbird Golden Ale, and Blue Marlin Coffee Stout. Stop by for a weekday brewery tour and sample the goods day or evening in the brewpub north of the village near the airstrip. ⊠ *Placencia Rd., Mile 21 ✛ Just north of airstrip ☎ 674/6227 ⊕ www. hobbsbrewingcompany.com.*

Pickled Parrot Bar & Grill
BARS/PUBS | The Thursday-night trivia contests here are a village institution. Weekend evenings give way to live music. ⊠ *Off main road ✛ Behind Wallen's Market ☎ 636/7068.*

Pyramid House

WINE BARS—NIGHTLIFE | This Mayan pyramid–shaped wine store/wine bar offers, arguably, the best selection of the fruit of the vine in the country. Stop by for wine and appetizers in an artsy, sophisticated setting. Call ahead if coming in the evening. The place keeps irregular evening hours, especially during the summer off-season. ✉ *Placencia Rd.* ✛ *At north entrance to Placencia Village* ☎ *636/5745.*

Tipsy Tuna

BARS/PUBS | Known for friendly service, Tipsy Tuna is Placencia's largest open-air beach bar. There's live music some weekend nights, and you can always shoot pool or watch sports on a big-screen TV. Fill up on bar snacks like burgers, fajitas, tacos, and shrimp baskets. There's karaoke some nights and Garifuna drumming occasionally. ✉ *Beachfront* ☎ *523/3089* ⊕ *www.tipsytunabelize.com.*

Shopping

Art 'n Soul Gallery

ART GALLERIES | This little gallery on the south end of the Sidewalk has paintings by owner Greta Leslie, along with work by other Belizean artists and some locally made jewelry from seashells, too. ✉ *South end of the Sidewalk* ☎ *503/3088.*

Activities

The fly-fishing on the flats off the cayes east of the Placencia Peninsula is some of Belize's best. This is one of the top areas in the world for permit. The area from Dangriga south to Gladden Caye is called "Permit Alley," and the mangrove lagoons off Punta Ycacos and other points south of Placencia are also terrific permit fisheries. You'll encounter plentiful tarpon—they flurry 10 deep in the water at times—as well as snook. You can also catch king mackerel, barracuda, wahoo, and cubera snapper. However, a lingering impact of Hurricane Iris in 2001 is that there are no longer as many good bonefish flats close to shore at Placencia. Bonefish are still around, but they're now several miles away, off the cayes.

Most of the better hotels also hook you up with a guide, many of whom pair with specific hotels. Fishing guides in Placencia are down-to-earth, self-taught guys who have fished these waters for years. They use small skiffs called *pangas.* For more information and help matching a local guide to your specific needs, get in touch with Mary Toy at Destinations Belize. ■TIP➔ **If you're on a budget, you can rent a canoe and try fishing the Placencia Lagoon on your own, where you may catch snook, barracuda, and possibly other fish.**

Guides usually provide trolling gear for free, but they'll charge you to rent light spin-casting tackle gear. If you're serious about fly-fishing, of course you'll want to bring your own gear. Don't forget to bring polarized sunglasses, a good fishing hat, insect repellent, lots of sunscreen and lip salve, and, if you're wading, thick-soled flats boots.

Destinations Belize

FISHING | Destinations Belize can connect you with local fishing guides and arrange fishing trips of all kinds. ☎ *523/4018 in Belize, 561/315–6161 in U.S.* ⊕ *www. destinationsbelize.com.*

Seahorse Dive Shop

DIVING/SNORKELING | The long-established Seahorse Dive Shop offers local reef dives for BZ$250 including tax, lunch, reserve admission, and gear. Glover's Atoll diving is BZ$340 including tax, gear, park fees, and lunch. If you don't dive, you can snorkel Glover's Atoll for BZ$170. Whale shark diving is BZ$370, and snorkeling is BZ$200 including all fees, gear, and lunch. ✉ *On dock at end of main road* ☎ *523/3166, 800/991–1969 in U.S.* ⊕ *www.belizescuba.com.*

Chapter 8

THE DEEP SOUTH

8

Updated by
Jeffrey Van Fleet

⊙ Sights	⊛ Restaurants	⊟ Hotels	⊜ Shopping	⊛ Nightlife
★★★★☆	★★★☆☆	★★★☆☆	★★★☆☆	★★☆☆☆

WELCOME TO THE DEEP SOUTH

TOP REASONS TO GO

★ **Rain Forests:** The greenest, lushest jungles in Belize are in Toledo, fed by heavy rains and temperatures that stay mostly above 70°F. Red ginger, bright yellow-and-orange lobster claw, masses of pink on mayflower trees, and orchids of all colors splash the emerald-green landscape. Scarlet-rumped tanagers, black-headed trogans, green kingfishers, several species of parrots, and roseate spoonbills join hundreds of other birds in the rain-forest cacophony.

★ **Outpost Atmosphere:** Punta Gorda gives you that last-place-on-Earth vibe. It is no longer the literal end of the road—the Southern Highway now continues beyond the town—but you get the feeling that you could hide out here and not be found.

★ **Fishing:** Among serious anglers, Southern Belize has a reputation for having one of the world's great permit fisheries, and for its large populations of tarpon and bonefish. The flats off Punta Ycacos are prime permit and bonefish grounds, and freshwater lagoons near Punta Negra hold tarpon.

The main road to the Deep South is the paved Southern Highway, which runs 100 miles (164 km) from the intersection of the Hummingbird Highway/Stann Creek District Highway to Punta Gorda and beyond.

As you travel south on the Southern Highway, the Great Southern Pine Ridge looms on your right, starting at about Mile 55. Farther in the distance are the Maya Mountains. On your left (though not visible from the highway) is the Caribbean Sea, and farther south, beyond Punta Negra, the Gulf of Honduras.

Branching off the Southern Highway are mostly unpaved roads, some barely more than muddy trails that lead to small villages. The San Antonio Road, from the Southern Highway about 14 miles (23 km) north of Punta Gorda, is paved all the way to the Guatemala border, where no official border crossing exists at this writing. Local residents cross back and forth freely, but you cannot.

1 Punta Gorda. This sleepy, friendly, overgrown village with a beautiful setting on the bay is the capital and "metropolis" of the Toledo district.

2 The Mayan Heartland. Nothing else in Belize is quite like the Mayan Heartland, where contemporary Mayan villages sit next to ancient ruins. Here also you'll see verdant rain forests, rice plantations, and cacao farms.

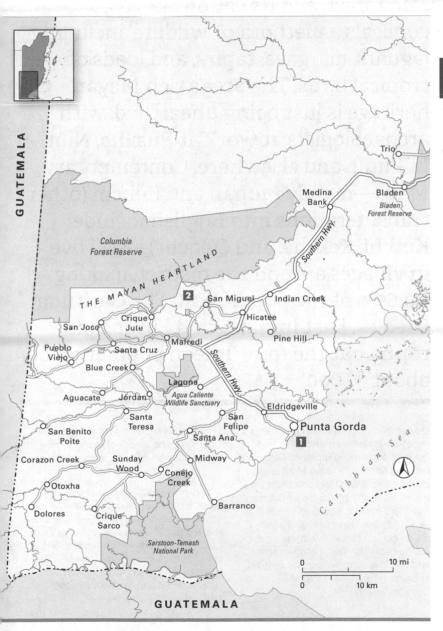

GUATEMALA

Trio

Medina
Bank

Bladen

Bladen
Forest Reserve

Columbia
Forest Reserve

Southern Hwy.

THE MAYAN HEARTLAND

2 San Miguel Indian Creek

Hicatee

San José Crique
Jule

Pine Hill

Pueblo
Viejo Santa Cruz Mafredi

Blue Creek

Laguna Southern Hwy.

Agua Caliente
Wildlife Sanctuary

Aguacate Jordan

Eldridgeville

Santa
Teresa San
Felipe

San Benito
Poite Santa Ana

1 Punta Gorda

Corazon Creek Sunday
Wood Midway

Caribbean Sea

Otoxha Conejo
Creek

Dolores Crique
Sarco Barranco

Sarstoon-Temash
National Park

0 10 mi

0 10 km

GUATEMALA

Toledo District in the Deep South has Belize's only extensive, genuine rain forest, and its canopy of trees conceals a plethora of wildlife, including jaguars, margays, tapirs, and loads of tropical birds. The area's rich Mayan heritage is just being unearthed, with archaeologists at work at Pusilha, Nim Li Punit, and elsewhere. Contemporary Maya—mainly Mopan and Kek'chi (other transliterations into English include Ket'chi, Kekche, and Q'eqchi')—still live in villages around the district, making up 60% of the population. The Garifuna, Creoles, East Indians, and Europeans round out the total Toledo population of about 36,000.

Lush, green, tropical Toledo also calls to chocolate lovers, as it's home to hundreds of small cacao growers. Cadbury's Green & Black gets some of its organic chocolate for Maya Gold chocolate bars from Toledo, and several small Belizean chocolate makers, including Cotton Tree, Goss, Ixcacao, Copal Tree, and others, create gourmet chocolate from organic Toledo cacao beans. An annual cacao festival billed as the Chocolate Festival of Belize takes place in late May, around Commonwealth Day.

Toledo also has rice plantations, citrus orchards, and stands of mangos, pineapples, bananas, and coconuts, so you'll never go hungry here.

For many years, ill-maintained roads, spotty communications, and the country's highest annual rainfall—as much as 180 to 200 inches—kept Belize's southernmost region off-limits to all but the most adventurous of travelers. The precipitation hasn't changed, but with improvements to the Southern Highway—beautifully paved the entire way from Dangriga to Punta Gorda—and the opening of new lodges and hotels, the riches of Toledo District are finally becoming accessible. The San Antonio Road, from the area called "The Dump" on the Southern Highway to the Guatemala border, has been paved, opening up easy access to a number of Mayan villages. Eventually, when a border crossing is completed and approved by the Guatemalan and Belizean governments, new development, trade, and immigration will be introduced to Toledo.

Other areas of Belize (not to mention Guatemala, Honduras, and Mexico) may have more spectacular ruins than Toledo, but where the Deep South shines is in its contemporary Mayan culture. Dozens of Mopan and Kek'chi villages exist much as they have for centuries, as do the Garifuna villages of Punta Negra and Barranco and the town of Punta Gorda. You can visit some of the villages and even stay awhile in guesthouses or homestay programs. If don't have time to do an overnight, you can participate in a one-day Mayan learning experience tour in local homes in Big Falls Village or take a tour of an organic cacao farm.

Don't expect to come to Toledo and lounge on the sand. The area doesn't have good beaches except for a few accessible only by boat. The coastal waters of the Gulf of Honduras are often muddy from silt deposited by numerous rivers flowing from the Maya Mountains. What *can* you expect? Exceptional fishing (Toledo has one of the world's best permit fisheries) and cayes off the coast that are well worth exploring. The closest are the Snake Cayes; farther out are the Sapodilla Cayes, the largest of which is Hunting Caye, with a horseshoe-shaped bay at the caye's eastern end with beaches of white coral where turtles nest in late summer. The downside is that visits to the cayes and to inland sites usually require expensive tours, as distances are considerable, and public transportation is limited.

Planning

When to Go

The Deep South never completely dries out, but this is the lushest, greenest part of the country all year long. June through September is the peak of the rainy season in Toledo, and when we say rainy we mean it—sometimes a few inches of precipitation a day. October through January are *drier*, but still with good chances of getting wet. Ideally, you should come between February and May, when most of Toledo gets only about an inch of rain a week.

Getting Here and Around

AIR TRAVEL
Maya Island Air and Tropic Air fly south to Punta Gorda (PND) from both the municipal and international airports in Belize City, sometimes with brief stops at Dangriga and Placencia. Depending on stops, flights take from 1 to 1½ hours. There are four or five flights daily to Punta Gorda on each airline. The airstrip is on the town's west side; from the town's main square, walk four blocks west on Prince Street.

CONTACTS **Maya Island Air.** ✉ *Punta Gorda Airstrip, Punta Gorda* ☎ *722/2072 in Punta Gorda, 233/1403 in Belize* ⊕ *www.mayaislandair.com.* **Tropic Air.** ✉ *Punta Gorda Airstrip, Prince St., Punta Gorda* ☎ *722/2008 in Punta Gorda, 226/2626 in Belize, 800/422–3435 in U.S.* ⊕ *www.tropicair.com.*

BOAT TRAVEL
Requena's, a long-established and reliable operator, offers daily boat service to Puerto Barrios, Guatemala; departure is at 9:30 am from the docks on Front Street, Punta Gorda. The trip takes about an hour and can be rough. The Pichilingo boat, as of this writing, departs Punta Gorda at 2 pm. From Puerto Barrios,

Pichilingo departs at 10 am and Requena's at 2:30 pm. On Tuesday and Friday only, most boats have service at 10 am from Punta Gorda to the charming tourist town of Livingston, Guatemala. Memo runs a daily boat from Punta Gorda to Livingston at 1 pm and returns daily at 3 pm (fare varies depending on the number of passengers). ■TIP➜ **Times and fares are subject to change, especially during the off-season and bad weather.**

These boats are small open boats for pedestrians only; there is no auto ferry between Guatemala and Punta Gorda. You must pay an exit fee when departing from Punta Gorda to Guatemala and when departing from Guatemala for Belize.

CONTACT Memo's Boat Service. ✉ *Punta Gorda Docks, Front St., Punta Gorda* ☎ *651/4780.* **Pichilingo.** ✉ *Punta Gorda Docks, Front St., Punta Gorda.* **Requena's Charter Service.** ✉ *12 Front St., Punta Gorda* ☎ *722/2070.*

BUS TRAVEL

James Bus Lines dominates the route between Punta Gorda and points north. Currently there are nine daily local bus departures from Punta Gorda to Belize City, and one express. The first bus is at 3:50 am and the last one at 3:50 pm. Eight local and two express James Line buses come from what is still called the Novelo's bus station in Belize City (Novelo's bus company no longer exists) to Punta Gorda daily, beginning at 5:15 am, with the last bus at 3:45 pm. It's a six- to seven-hour trip to or from Belize City via Belmopan, Dangriga, and Independence, depending on whether it's an express or local bus. Most buses are old U.S. Bluebird school buses—they're usually crowded, cramped, and have no air-conditioning. If you have the budget, fly. Any nonexpress bus will pick up and drop you anywhere along the route.

Off the Southern Highway in Toledo public transportation is limited. On market days (generally Monday, Wednesday, Friday, and Saturday) buses leave the main plaza near the clock tower in Punta Gorda around noon. Buses, mostly old American school buses operated by local entrepreneurs, go to different villages, returning on market days very early in the morning. There's no published schedule—you have to ask locally. As of this writing, buses from Punta Gorda serve the villages of Aguacate, Barranco, Big Falls, Crique Sarco, Dolores, Golden Stream, Indian Creek, Jalacte, Laguna, Medina, San Antonio, San Benito Poite, San Jose, San Miquel, San Pedro Columbia, Santa Ana, San Vicente, Pueblo Viejo, and Silver Creek. Bus service to villages along the San Antonio Road, including Manfredi, San Antonio, Santa Cruz, and Jalacte, has increased in frequency and speed because of the new road.

CONTACT James Bus Line. ✉ *7 King St., Punta Gorda* ☎ *702/2049 in Punta Gorda.*

CAR TRAVEL

The paving of the Hummingbird and Southern Highways has made the journey to Punta Gorda much shorter and more pleasant than ever. The drive from Belize City to Punta Gorda can be done in around four hours. Off the Southern Highway most Toledo roads, excepting the San Antonio Road, are unpaved. In dry weather they're bumpy yet passable, but after heavy rains the dirt roads can turn into quagmires even for four-wheel-drive vehicles. Most tertiary roads are not well marked, so you may have to stop frequently for directions. Despite this, expensive taxis and infrequent bus service to and from the Mayan villages and elsewhere in Toledo are arguments for renting a car. There are no major car-rental companies in Punta Gorda. Your best option is to rent at the international airport in Belize City, where there are about 10 rental car companies, or in Placencia, especially if you're stopping there on your way south. Bruno Kuppinger at SunCreek Lodge about 14 miles (22.5

km) northwest of Punta Gorda has a few cars available to rent. Belize City–based Budget has a satellite office in Placencia and can deliver a rental car from its Placencia fleet in Punta Gorda for an extra fee. Barefoot Services in Placencia also will bring a vehicle to Punta Gorda for a similar drop fee.

Barefoot Services
Barefoot Services in Placencia will deliver rental cars to Punta Gorda and elsewhere in Toledo. A one-time drop fee of BZ$250 applies. ⊠ *Main St., Placencia Village* ☎ *523/3066* ⊕ *www.barefootservicesbelize.com.*

★ **Budget Belize**
The Placencia office of Budget will deliver a vehicle to Punta Gorda for a one-time drop fee of BZ$250. High-season rates are around BZ$450 to $650 a week, plus 12.5% tax. ⊠ *Live Oaks Pl., South of Placencia airstrip, Placencia Village* ☎ *523/3068, 800/284–4387 in U.S.* ⊕ *www.budget-belize.com.*

TAXI TRAVEL
Taxis in the Deep South are available mostly in Punta Gorda. Your hotel can call one for you. You can also hire a taxi to take you to nearby villages, but negotiate the rate in advance.

Safety

Punta Gorda is generally a safe, friendly town. Indeed, Toledo District has some of the lowest crime rates in the country. With normal precautions you should have no problem walking around, even after dark. The nearby Mayan villages are also relatively free of crime.

Hotels

The entire Toledo District has only about 30 hotels, nearly all of them in and around Punta Gorda. Most are small and owner-run. You can usually show up

without reservations and look for a place that suits you.

Restaurants

With relatively few tourists coming to the region, and most local residents unable to afford to eat out regularly, restaurants in Toledo are fewer in number than elsewhere in Belize. Most are basic spots serving local fish and staples like stew chicken with beans and rice. Prices are low—you'll rarely pay more than BZ$30 for dinner, unless you're eating at an expensive lodge such as Copal Tree. Nearly all Toledo restaurants are in Punta Gorda.

HOTEL AND RESTAURANT PRICES
Restaurant and hotel reviews have been shortened. For full information, visit Fodors.com.

What it Costs in Belize Dollars			
$	$$	$$$	$$$$
RESTAURANTS			
under BZ$15	BZ$15–BZ$30	BZ$31–BZ$50	over BZ$50
HOTELS			
under BZ$200	BZ$200–BZ$300	BZ$301–BZ$500	over BZ$500

Homestays

A few programs offer the chance to live with the modern-day Maya or Garifuna at a homestay or village guesthouse. They are very inexpensive, but keep in mind that accommodations and meals are extremely basic; lodging may lack electricity and running water. You can also spend several days learning how to process cacao or learning to cook Belizean—including Mayan—recipes.

Aguacate Homestay Program
ECOTOURISM | FAMILY | The Aguacate Homestay Program gives you the

opportunity to have an authentic Mayan cultural experience in a Kek'chi Mayan village of fewer than 400 people. Guests live in a Mayan home, eat with the family, and participate in household and farm chores. Keep in mind that the living conditions are spartan at best. The homes are traditional thatch huts with dirt floors and no electricity, running water, or indoor plumbing. You pay BZ$20 per person including tax for lodging, BZ$7 per person per meal, and a BZ$10 per person registration fee. Part of the money goes to the host family and part to the village for improvements. Transportation by bus between Aguacate Village and Punta Gorda is available four or five days a week at nominal cost. ⊠ *Aguacate Village* ☎ *633/9954* ⊕ *www.aguacatebelize.com.*

The Living Maya Experience

MUSEUM VILLAGE | Learn about Kek'chi crafts, culture, and cuisine in a hands-on private experience in Mayan homes of participating villages in Big Falls. You could be involved in anything from building a traditional thatch house to making corn tortillas. Call in advance for what's available, times, and charges, or ask at your hotel or the BTIA Visitor Information Center in Punta Gorda to help arrange the Living Maya trip. If you're traveling solo, any nonexpress James Line bus will drop you off and pick you up at Big Falls Village (watch for Las Faldes restaurant on the Southern Highway) near the Living Maya Experience homes where the hosts live. Costs vary depending on which learning experiences you choose and the length of them, but most are under BZ$50 (not including transportation and additional tour company fees). ⊠ *Southern Hwy., Big Falls* ☎ *627/7408, 632/4585.*

★ Toledo Ecotourism Association (T.E.A.) Maya Village Guesthouse Program

ADVENTURE TOURS | **FAMILY** | The T.E.A. program allows visitors to participate in the village life of the Maya while maintaining some personal privacy. You stay overnight in small guesthouses in one of five Mopan and Kek'chi Mayan villages in Toledo District, currently including Santa Elena, San Antonio, San Jose, San Miguel, and Laguna; village guesthouse locations change from time to time. The guesthouses are very simple, with traditional thatch roofs and outdoor latrines. There is no running water or electricity in the guesthouses. You take meals in the homes of villagers and participate in the routines of village life. The program, endorsed by the Belize Tourism Board, is a collective owned by more than 200 members and is designed to promote cultural exchange. The cost is around BZ$100 a day per person, including meals and village activities. Other packages go from BZ$40 per person for a day-trip to BZ$190 per person for a two-night stay. ⊠ *BTIA Office, 46 Front St., Punta Gorda* ☎ *702/2119* ⊕ *www. belizemayatourism.org* ✈ *From BZ$40 per person.*

Tours

ADVENTURE TOURS

Big Falls Extreme Adventures

AMUSEMENT PARK/WATER PARK | Big Falls Extreme Adventures offers ziplining, river tubing, and hiking over, on, and around Rio Grande. Ziplining and river tubing are BZ$80 each, and if you do both there's a combination rate. Food is available at Las Faldas restaurant; lunch is around BZ$20. ⊠ *Southern Hwy., Big Falls* ☎ *634/5185* ⊕ *www.bigfallsextremeadventures.com* ✈ *BZ$80 and up.*

Romero's Charters and Tours

Romero's Charters and Tours has a driver service with vans and other vehicles that can take you to any of the inland destinations. ⊠ *Cattle Landing, Punta Gorda* ☎ *662/5791* ✎ *rcharters@btl.net.*

Toledo Cave & Adventure Tours

Toledo Cave & Adventure's excursions are not for couch potatoes. This outfitter offers such high-energy tours as multiday trips to the Maya Divide and to Doyle's Delight, Belize's highest peak. ⊠ *San Antonio Rd., Punta Gorda* ☎ *604/2124* ⊕ *www.tcatours.com.*

CULTURAL TOURS

Eladio's Chocolate Adventure

ECOTOURISM | FAMILY | Eladio Pop provides a tour of his Agouti Cacao Farm in San Pedro Columbia Village, followed by a chocolate tasting and a traditional Mayan lunch. Cost for this combination is BZ$50 per person, with à la carte tour options starting at BZ$25. Mr. Pop also offers a homestay with meals for BZ$30 per person. ⊠ *Agouti Cacao Farm, San Pedro Columbia Village, San Pedro Columbia* ☎ *624/0166* ⊕ *www.agouticacaofarm. wordpress.com.*

PG Tours

ADVENTURE TOURS | From a storefront office on Front Street, PG Tours arranges land and sea trips around Punta Gorda, including visits to area Mayan sites, cacao farm tours, cooking lessons, and drumming lessons. ⊠ *42 Front St., Punta Gorda* ☎ *636/6162* ⊕ *www.pgtoursbelize.com.*

Toledo Cacao Growers Association

During the Chocolate Festival in May, and by advance arrangement at other times, the Toledo Cacao Growers Association (TCGA), which represents more than 1,100 small organic cacao growers in southern Belize, offers tours of working cacao farms. ⊠ *Main Middle St., Punta Gorda* ☎ *722/2992.*

Warasa Garifuna Drum School

ARTS VENUE | Master Garifuna drummer and teacher Ronald Raymond McDonald is a self-taught drummer who has been performing since age five with his family, and the experience here acquaints you with local culture through drumming, drum making, and dance. McDonald gives private lessons in the Garifuna community of Punta Gorda, with private lessons starting at BZ$25. Call or email to arrange lessons or demonstrations, or you can do so through your hotel or the

BTIA Visitor Information Center on Front Street. ⊠ *New Rd., St. Vincent Garifuna Reserve, Punta Gorda* ☎ *632/7701* ⊕ *www.warasadrumschool.com* ✉ *one-on-one lessons start at BZ$25.*

Visitor Information

The office of the Belize Tourism Industry Association (BTIA), at 46 Front Street near the water-taxi dock, is open weekdays 8–4 and Saturday 8–11:30.

INFORMATION **Belize Tourism Industry Association.** ⊠ *Toledo Tourism Information Center, 46 Front St., Punta Gorda* ☎ *722/2531* ⊕ *www.btia.org.* **Toledo Tour Guides Association.** ⊠ *Visitor Information Center at BTIA, 46 Front St., Punta Gorda* ☎ *722/2531.*

Punta Gorda

102 miles (164 km) south of Placencia.

Most journeys south begin in the region's administrative center, Punta Gorda. "PG" (as it's affectionately known) isn't your typical tourist destination. Though it has a wonderful setting on the Gulf of Honduras, it has no real beaches. There are few shops of interest to visitors, a few simple restaurants, little nightlife, and but one in-town "sight," its landmark clock tower, which you can use to get your bearings.

So why, you ask, come to Punta Gorda? First, simply because it isn't on the main tourist track. The accoutrements of mass tourism are still, refreshingly, missing here. Schoolchildren may wave at you, and residents will strike up a conversation. Toledo has stunning natural attractions, too, such as clean rivers for swimming and cave systems with Mayan artifacts that rival those in the Cayo District. Also, with several new or upgraded hotels to choose from, it's a comfortable base from which to visit surrounding

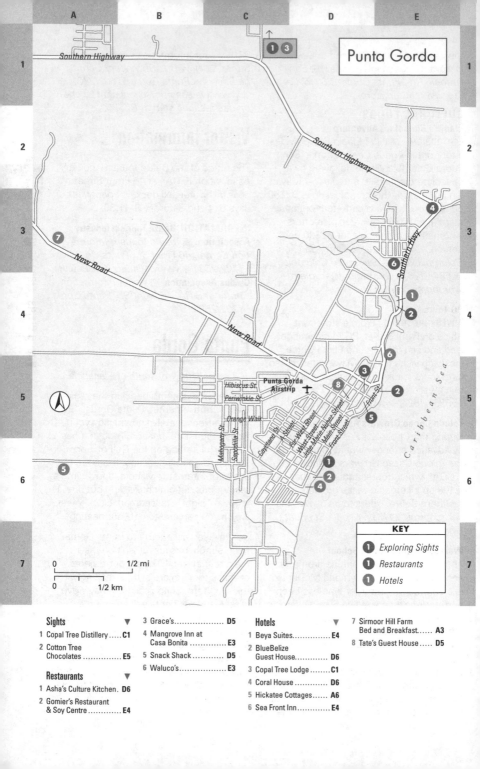

Punta Gorda

KEY

- ① Exploring Sights
- ① Restaurants
- ① Hotels

Sights ▼
1 Copal Tree Distillery **C1**
2 Cotton Tree
  Chocolates **E5**

Restaurants ▼
1 Asha's Culture Kitchen. **D6**
2 Gomier's Restaurant
  & Soy Centre **E4**

3 Grace's **D5**
4 Mangrove Inn at
  Casa Bonita **E3**
5 Snack Shack **D5**
6 Waluco's **E3**

Hotels ▼
1 Beya Suites **E4**
2 BlueBelize
  Guest House **D6**
3 Copal Tree Lodge **C1**
4 Coral House **D6**
5 Hickatee Cottages **A6**
6 Sea Front Inn **E4**

7 Sirmoor Hill Farm
  Bed and Breakfast **A3**
8 Tate's Guest House **D5**

Mayan villages, offshore cayes, and the high bush of the Deep South.

Settled in 1867 by ex-Confederate immigrants from the United States and later a magnet for religious missionaries, Punta Gorda once had 12 sugar estates, each with its own mill, but the sugar industry in Toledo has been replaced by rice farming, citrus groves, and small cacao plantations. After World War II, Great Britain built an important military base here, but when that closed in 1994 the linchpin of the local economy was yanked out. With some increase in tourist dollars and foreigners' growing interest in real estate here, Punta Gorda is starting to pick up again but hasn't lost its frontier atmosphere.

GETTING HERE AND AROUND
To best see the sights of Toledo, a rental car is ideal; otherwise you'll be stuck paying high tour rates or waiting for infrequent bus service. Many people drive down from Belize City, Hopkins, or Placencia. If you've flown or bused in to Punta Gorda, have a vehicle delivered to you from Budget in Placencia. If you'd like a knowledgeable local guide to ride with you in your rental car, that's also possible.

From the intersection of the Hummingbird and Southern Highways it's a straight shot 100 miles (164 km) down the Southern, with only a well-marked right turn near Independence to slow you down. On the Southern Highway about 20 miles (33 km) north of Punta Gorda, at about Mile 83, you'll come to an intersection. If you turn left you'll stay on the Southern Highway to Punta Gorda; if you bear right onto the San Antonio Road, you'll go comfortably to Lubaantun, San Antonio Village, and other Mayan villages, as well as the Guatemala border. Assuming that you continue on the Southern Highway, at about Mile 95 you have two options for reaching downtown Punta Gorda. You can turn right on the mostly unpaved Saddleback Road and go 5 miles (8 km). To enter from the prettier Bay of Honduras

side, as most visitors do, stay straight on the paved Southern Highway and go the same distance.

◉ Sights

Copal Tree Distillery
WINERY/DISTILLERY | Copalli, a smooth new Belizean rum, comes from the grounds of the Copal Tree Lodge, a few miles outside Punta Gorda, and is quickly gaining prestige in international circles. Copalli's organic process bypasses the molasses stage, distilling the rum directly from sugarcane, rain-forest water, and organic yeast. The end results are a white rum and a barrel-aged rum, equally smooth. A two-hour mixology class gives you ideas for mixing farm-fresh ingredients with your rum cocktails. A half-day distillery tour guides you through the rum-making process and includes a tasting and lunch. Both tours require advance reservations and are open to nonguests of the lodge. ✉ Machaca Hill, Wilson Rd. ☎ 722/0051, 877/417–9478 in U.S. ⊕ www.copallirum.com ⤳ Mixology class $45, distillery tour $75.

Cotton Tree Chocolates
FACTORY | **FAMILY** | From cacao beans to final candy bars, you can see how chocolate is made at Cotton Tree Chocolates, a small chocolate factory on Front Street in Punta Gorda. It's associated with Cotton Tree Lodge. You'll get a short guided tour of the chocolate-making process and you can buy bars of delicious milk or dark chocolate. Cotton Tree Lodge also offers guests a program on sustainable cacao growing, producing, and harvesting. ✉ 2 Front St. ☎ 621/8776 ⊕ www.cottontree-chocolate.com ⤳ Free ⊙ Closed Sun.

⑪ Restaurants

★ Asha's Culture Kitchen
$$ | **LATIN AMERICAN** | **FAMILY** | In a rustic wood shack built right over the water, Asha's has the best views of any restaurant in Punta Gorda. Asha's specializes in fresh seafood served Creole style, such

as fried conch with mashed potatoes or grilled snapper with plantains and beans and rice. **Known for:** solid Creole cooking; rotating menu each day; great views of the bay. [$] *Average main: BZ$22* ✉ *74 Front St.* ☎ *651/8366* 💳 *No credit cards* 🕒 *Closed Mon.*

Gomier's Restaurant & Soy Centre
$$ | **VEGETARIAN** | **FAMILY** | Count your lucky stars if you find Gomier's open—the owner doesn't always follow his posted hours—and enjoy an excellent vegetarian meal from organic ingredients grown locally, along with some seafood. Go with the vegetarian dish of the day, which could be stir-fried tofu or vegan spaghetti. **Known for:** fresh seafood dishes; tofu-making and cooking classes; Friday Garifuna-style lunches. [$] *Average main: BZ$20* ✉ *Alejandro Vernon St., behind "Welcome to Punta Gorda" sign on Front St.* ☎ *722/2929* 💳 *No credit cards* 🕒 *No dinner Fri. No lunch weekends.*

Grace's
$ | **LATIN AMERICAN** | An established spot, Grace's has genuine value, a down-home feel, and hearty plates of beans and rice and other Belizean staples on the menu. Get a seat near the entrance and eye the town's street life. **Known for:** hearty Belizean breakfasts; nice variety of non-Belizean food; place to watch the goings-on in Punta Gorda. [$] *Average main: BZ$14* ✉ *21 Main St.* ☎ *702/2414.*

Mangrove Inn at Casa Bonita
$$ | **LATIN AMERICAN** | **FAMILY** | No pretense here—instead, you're seated on the second-floor veranda of the chef-owner's house across the street from the water in the Cattle Landing area of Punta Gorda. You'll find different dishes every evening but usually with a choice of seafood (snapper, snook, or shrimp) or a hearty dish like a thick pork chop or lasagna. **Known for:** terrific prices; BYOB; friendly local vibe. [$] *Average main: BZ$16* ✉ *Southern Hwy., Cattle Landing area* ☎ *623/0497* 💳 *No credit cards* 🕒 *Closed Sun. No dinner.*

To Market, To Market

On market days—Monday, Wednesday, Friday, and Saturday, with Wednesday and Saturday usually being the largest—Punta Gorda comes to life with vendors from nearby Mayan villages and even from Guatemala. They pack the downtown market area at the central plaza (look for the large clock tower) with colorful fruit and vegetable stands. Fresh fish also is sold in a building at the market, daily except Sunday. On Front Street are stalls selling clothing, crafts, and other items.

Snack Shack
$ | **LATIN AMERICAN** | Burritos are the thing here, and in fact usually just about the only thing, except for smoothies, shakes, coffee, and the occasional daily special. You get a selection of fillings and type of flour tortilla. **Known for:** huge breakfast burritos; brisk take-out business; terrific smoothies. [$] *Average main: BZ$10* ✉ *Main St., in BTL parking lot* ☎ *620/3499* 💳 *No credit cards* 🕒 *Closed Sun. No dinner.*

★ Waluco's
$$ | **LATIN AMERICAN** | Hands down Punta Gorda's best and most pleasant restaurant, Waluco's is a project of TIDE, a local conservation organization, and profits go to support its work. Go for the fresh-grilled fish of the day, which might be snook, snapper, or another local catch. **Known for:** grilled catch of the day; great prices; Thursday karaoke night. [$] *Average main: BZ$16* ✉ *Hopeville, Mile 1, Southern Hwy.* ✥ *Across the street from the water, midway between downtown Punta Gorda and Cattle Landing* ☎ *702/2129* 🕒 *Closed Mon. and Tues.*

Hotels

Beya Suites

$ | **HOTEL** | **FAMILY** | From the verandas on the second- or third-floor rooftop terrace of this bright pink, waterfront hotel (*beya* means beachfront in the Garifuna language) within walking distance of downtown Punta Gorda, you have expansive views of the sea. **Pros:** views of the water; Belizean owned; friendly staff. **Cons:** most units are not really suites; breakfast is very basic; back rooms lack views. $ *Rooms from: BZ$180* ⊠ *6 Front St.* ☎ *722/2188* ⊕ *www.beyasuites.com* ⇨ *10 rooms* ⍟ *No meals.*

BlueBelize Guest House

$ | **B&B/INN** | **FAMILY** | At this pleasant small spot overlooking the water, you can settle in and do your own thing in one of the six attractive self-catering flats, with kitchens or kitchenettes, spacious bedrooms, TVs, and verandas with hammocks. **Pros:** spacious self-catering apartments; reasonable rates; breezy waterfront location. **Cons:** no a/c but sea breeze generally keeps rooms cool; no on-site restaurant. $ *Rooms from: BZ$170* ⊠ *139 Front St.* ☎ *722/2678* ⊕ *www.bluebelize.com* ⇨ *6 rooms* ⍟ *Free breakfast.*

★ Copal Tree Lodge

$$$ | **RESORT** | The luxury suites, impeccable service, and gorgeous spa here offer a level of indulgence not seen in this part of the country, and the lodge is committed to conservation and sustainability to boot. **Pros:** great views of forest and ocean from hilltop location; incredible spa; the top lodge option near Punta Gorda. **Cons:** higher-end rooms here are pricey; the hillside cable car is occasionally out of order. $ *Rooms from: BZ$400* ⊠ *Machaca Hill, Wilson Rd.* ☎ *722/0051, 877/417–9478 in U.S.* ⇨ *16 suites, 1 villa* ⍟ *No meals.*

★ Coral House

$$ | **B&B/INN** | A 1938 British colonial–era home serves as one of the most pleasant small guesthouses in the country, with breezy views of the Bay of Honduras and warm hospitality from owners and staff. **Pros:** one of the best small inns in Belize; a/c and Wi-Fi included; reasonable prices. **Cons:** no restaurant; back rooms get a little more street noise; about a 10-minute walk to town center. $ *Rooms from: BZ$220* ⊠ *151 Main St.* ⊹ *Across from Punta Gorda hospital* ☎ *722/2878* ⊕ *www.coralhouseinn.com* ⇨ *6 rooms* ⍟ *Free Breakfast.*

★ Hickatee Cottages

$ | **B&B/INN** | Just a mile (1.5 km) from downtown Punta Gorda, this delightful small lodge has lovely Caribbean-style cottages with zinc roofs and private verandas; it's nestled in lush jungle foliage where you'll hear howler monkeys and see a wide variety of birds. **Pros:** lovely cottages; lush jungle setting but near town; excellent value. **Cons:** no a/c; battery power for basics but not for appliances; occasionally muddy final road to get here. $ *Rooms from: BZ$190* ⊠ *Ex-Servicemen Rd., about 1 mile (1.5 km) from Punta Gorda* ⊹ *Coming into Punta Gorda on the bay side, follow Front St. into town, past Uno gas station, through market area, and then turn right immediately past St. Peter Claver church. Take next left onto Main St. and continue past hospital; bear right where road becomes Cemetery La. Follow Cemetery La. for three blocks and, when you reach small children's playground, turn "half left" onto Ex-Servicemen Rd. (also known as Boom Creek Rd.). Go 1 mile (1.5 km) farther to Hickatee Cottages, on left* ☎ *662/4475* ⊕ *www.hickatee.com* ⇨ *6 rooms* ⍟ *Free breakfast.*

Sea Front Inn

$ | **B&B/INN** | **FAMILY** | With its pitched roofs and stone-and-wood facade, this four-story hotel overlooking the Gulf of Honduras may remind you of a Swiss ski lodge in a tropical setting. **Pros:** appealing waterfront location; one-of-a-kind rooms; majestic architecture. **Cons:** upper-story rooms require climbing a lot of steps;

Belize's calm Rio Grande is perfect for river tubing and fishing.

prices are a little higher than similar accommodations in Punta Gorda; larger than most Punta Gorda lodgings so not a place if you crave solitude. $ *Rooms from: BZ$170* ✉ *4 Front St.* ☎ *722/2300* ⊕ *seafrontinn.com* ⌁ *20 units* ⦿ *No meals.*

★ Sirmoor Hill Farm Bed and Breakfast

$$ | **B&B/INN** | **FAMILY** | In a restored century-old colonial home on a 775-acre farm near Punta Gorda, this bed-and-breakfast is among the most appealing small lodgings in Belize, but it's more like visiting a friend's home in the country than a hotel. **Pros:** gorgeous rural setting; beautifully restored colonial home; swimming pool. **Cons:** not much privacy; more like visiting friend's home; shared bath. $ *Rooms from: BZ$220* ✉ *New Rd. MLS3, near Belize Defence Force camp* ☎ *722/0052* ⊕ *www.sirmoorhillfarm.com* ⌁ *2 rooms* ⦿ *Free breakfast.*

Tate's Guest House

$ | **B&B/INN** | **FAMILY** | If you don't demand luxury, you couldn't find a nicer budget spot in Punta Gorda than this guesthouse on a quiet residential street. **Pros:** clean accommodations with a/c, Wi-Fi, and cable TV at affordable rates; central location in downtown Punta Gorda; friendly, helpful owner. **Cons:** no-frill rooms; no breakfast. $ *Rooms from: BZ$100* ✉ *34 Jose Maria Nunez* ☎ *722/0147* ⊟ *No credit cards* ⌁ *5 rooms* ⦿ *No meals.*

Activities

Punta Gorda and Toledo offer great opportunities for outdoor activities—fishing, diving, snorkeling, sea and river kayaking, and caving. Due to so few visitors to the Deep South and the limited number of tour operators, visitors often arrive to find that only certain tours are actually available on a given day, or if they are running, tended to cost much more than in other parts of Belize. Still, with tourism slowly increasing, more tours are being offered, and prices are becoming more reasonable, given the high cost for gasoline and supplies. Try to go with a group of four to six, as many tours have a price

History

The Maya, mostly a group called the Manche Chol Maya, established sizable ceremonial centers and midsize cities in Toledo beginning almost 2,000 years ago. In the Classic period, Lubaantun, which flourished in the 8th and 9th centuries, is thought to have been the administrative center of the region, but for reasons still unclear it was abandoned not long after this. In southern Belize as elsewhere in Mesoamerica, the Mayan civilization began a long, slow decline a little more than 1,000 years ago.

Spanish conquistadors, including Hemán Cortés himself in 1525, came through southern Belize in the early 16th century, but the Maya resisted Spain's and, later, Britain's attempts to control and tax them. The British, who arrived as loggers, tried to put the Maya in "reservations" and eventually, in the 18th and 19th centuries, moved nearly the entire Manche Chol population to the highlands of Guatemala.

In the late 19th century, groups of Mopan and Ket'chi Maya began moving into southern Belize from Guatemala, establishing more than 50 villages around Toledo. Around the same time, Garifuna from Honduras settled in Punta Gorda, Barranco, and Punta Negra.

Southern Belize, with its rain and remoteness from Belize City, has languished economically for most of the 20th century. The paved Southern Highway and new road from Guatemala should help boost tourism and development in the region in coming years.

8

The Deep South PUNTA GORDA

based on a group of up to six people, not per person.

Among the most popular tours are those to the Snake Cayes with a full day of snorkeling, fishing, and beach bumming. Another popular tour combines Blue Creek caves or Agua Caliente Wildlife Sanctuary with a tour to Lubaantun, or possibly a visit to Rio Blanco National Park and its waterfall.

FISHING

For bonefish and tarpon, head to the estuary flats in the Port Honduras marine reserve at the end of the Rio Grande, or go northward to Punta Ycacos. Anglers must pay a park fee in the Marine Reserve, but there is no fee for the Punta Ycacos, unless you fish in the Port Honduras reserve. To arrange for a guide with a boat, contact TIDE Tours or Garbutt's Marine.

★ **TIDE Tours**

FISHING | TIDE Tours has trained more than 60 tour guides in Toledo, and can arrange fly-fishing guides for bonefish or permit in Payne's Creek National Park and Port Honduras Marine Reserve, from around BZ$900 per day for two persons, not including tax or reserve fees. TIDE Fish Fest Weekend is an annual event held in October that raises awareness for environmental issues and also celebrates the region's natural resources. ■**TIP→ TIDE can also arrange a variety of other tours throughout Toledo.** ⊠ Front St., Hopeville area ☎ 722/2274 TIDE office ⊕ www.tidetours.org.

SCUBA DIVING AND SNORKELING

This far south the reef has pretty much broken up, but individual cayes have their own small reef systems. The best of the bunch is at the Sapodilla Cayes with great wall dives. Lime Caye has camping, and Hunting Caye has a lighthouse. The only drawback is that because they're 40 miles (64 km) off the coast, a day's dive trip can be pricey, depending on how many people go. The Snake Cayes, with several notable dive sites, are closer in, about 18 miles (30 km) northeast of Punta Gorda. The four Snakes—East, West, South, and Middle—are so named because of boa constrictors that once lived there.

The turquoise waters lapping up the shores of the usually deserted white-sand beach on Snake Caye are good for snorkeling, as are the Sapodilla Cayes at the southern end of the Belize Barrier Reef.

Garbutt's Marine

DIVING/SNORKELING | All-day diving and snorkeling trips are available to the Snake and Sapodilla Cayes as well as to Port Honduras Marine Reserve; overnight stays at Lime Caye is also an option. The three Garbutt brothers, Scully, Oliver, and Eworth, also do guided fishing trips and have cabins for rent. ⊠ *Joe Taylor Creek, Southern Hwy.* ☎ *604/3548* ⊕ *www. garbuttsfishinglodge.com.*

Reef Conservation International

SCUBA DIVING | Reef Conservation International operates marine conservation trips in the Sapodilla Cayes Marine Reserve from Punta Gorda. You can stay at the Reef CI camp based on Tom Owens Caye, in basic accommodations—there's Internet but no hot water. You'll get plenty of snorkeling and diving, but you can also assist marine biologists and other Reef CI staff in monitoring and preserving the reef. One-week dive packages including diving, dive equipment, lodging, and meals start at BZ$2,660 per person, not including air fare to Belize or transfers to southern Belize. ⊠ *Mile 18, Placencia Rd., Stann Creek District* ☎ *626/1429 in Placencia, 513/334–9393 in U.S.* ⊕ *www. reefci.com.*

Shopping

Maya Bags

GIFTS/SOUVENIRS | Some 100 Mayan women from eight local villages sew handbags, purses, fitness bags, travel bags, and other items, which are sold in a fair-trade shop in Punta Gorda near the airstrip and, on a larger scale, to stores in the United States and via mail order elsewhere. ⊠ *Airport St., near Punta Gorda airstrip* ☎ *917/697–2203 in U.S.* ⊕ *www. mayabags.org* ⊗ *Closed weekends.*

Punta Gorda Market at Central Plaza

CRAFTS | Fresh fruits and vegetables, local coffee and cacao beans, and some craft items are sold at indoor and outdoor stalls at the central plaza near the clock tower. The busiest market days usually are Tuesday, Wednesday, Friday, and Saturday, but not as much activity takes place here as it does on Front Street. ⊠ *Punta Gorda Central Park, Main Middle St., at clock tower* ⊗ *Closed Sun.*

Punta Gorda Market on Front Street

CLOTHING | Wednesday and Saturday are the big market days in the area along Front Street near the Civic Center, with Monday and Friday seeing a bit less activity. You'll find food stalls, and vendors sell fruit and vegetables, chocolate, and copal incense, reputed to be useful for energy cleansing. Some crafts and miscellaneous household items are for sale here. (Many of the crafts here come from neighboring Guatemala.) ⊠ *Front Street Market, Front St.* ⊗ *Closed Tues., Thurs., and Sun.*

The Mayan Heartland

Drive a few miles outside of Punta Gorda, and you find yourself in the heartland of the Mayan people. Half the population of Toledo is Maya, a far higher proportion than in any other region in Belize. The Toledo Maya Cultural Council has created an ambitious network of Mayan-run

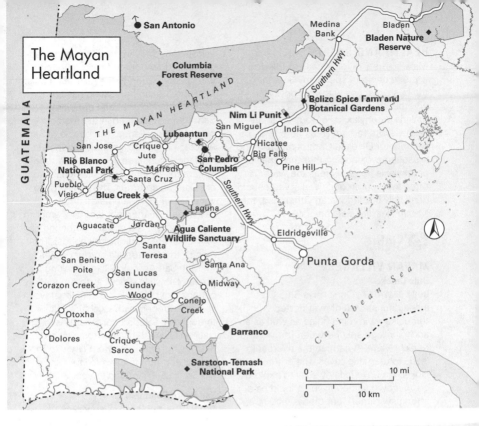

The Mayan Heartland

guesthouses, and it also manages the Mayan Mapping Project. By collating oral history and evidence of ancient Mayan settlements, the project hopes to secure rights to land that the Maya have occupied for centuries but that the Belizean government has ceded to multinational logging companies. There's also a separate Mayan homestay program, where you stay in local homes rather than in guesthouses.

The Maya in Belize divide into two groups: Mopan Maya and Kek'chi-speaking (also spelled Q'eqchi') peoples from the Guatemalan highlands. Some of the latter are relatively recent arrivals, refugees from active repression by the Guatemalan government during the 1970s and 1980s. Each group tends to keep to itself, living in separate villages and preserving unique traditions. Among the Kek'chi villages in Toledo are Crique Sarco, San Vincente, San Miguel, Laguna, San Pedro Columbia, Santa Teresa, Sunday Wood, Mabelha, and Corazon. Mopan Maya villages include San Antonio, Pueblo Viejo, and San José.

GETTING HERE AND AROUND

Because bus service to rural villages is limited at best, a car is a necessity unless you want to take guided tours. Happily, the paved San Antonio Road from the Southern Highway to Jalacte Village at the Guatemalan border has opened up much of the Mayan Heartland, making it much faster and easier to see this region.

TIMING

You can see the highlights in a day or two, but to explore the region thoroughly takes longer. Distances are not great, but most tertiary roads are poor to terrible, and it takes time just to get around the district.

HEALTH AND SAFETY

Malaria exists in rural areas of Toledo. If you're going to spend any time in the bush, discuss with your physician whether to use chloroquine or other malaria prophylaxis. For routine, short-term visitors to rural areas here, the U.S. Centers for Disease Control recommend mosquito avoidance rather than malaria prophylaxis. In rural areas the water is often from community wells; you should drink only bottled water. Otherwise, the Mayan Heartland is very safe.

Sights

MAYAN VILLAGES

Blue Creek

BODY OF WATER | Don't miss Blue Creek, a beautiful stretch of river dotted with turquoise swimming holes as well as an anchor village split between Mopan and Kek'chi Maya. A path up the riverbank leads to dramatic caves. The entrance to Hokeb Ha Cave is fairly easy to explore on your own (although you should be a strong swimmer), but others require a guide or a tour. To be on the safe side, we recommend going with a tour operator in any case. TIDE Tours and other operators offer trips to Blue Creek, providing lights and other necessary equipment. ⚠ **Don't swim in the river at night—the fer-de-lance, a highly poisonous snake, likes to take nocturnal dips.** ☒ *Hokab Ha Cave, Blue Creek Village* ⊕ *Drive north on Southern Hwy. to area called The Dump and turn west on San Antonio Rd. Drive to village of Mafredi and turn left toward Blue Creek. Go about 9 miles (15 km) to entrance to Blue Creek research station.*

★ San Antonio

TOWN | The Mopan Mayan village of San Antonio, 35 miles (56 km) west of Punta Gorda, is Toledo's second-largest town, with a population of about 1,000. It was settled by people from the Guatemalan village of San Luis, who revere their former patron saint. The impressive village church, built of stones carted from surrounding Mayan ruins, has a stained-glass window donated by another city with a connection to the saint: St. Louis, Missouri. Cacao harvesting has brought a bit of development and prosperity to San Antonio not seen in the region's other Mayan villages. The people of San Antonio haven't forgotten their ancient heritage: each June 13, they take to the streets for a festival that dates back to pre-Columbian times. The San Antonio waterfall sits a mile outside of town. It cascades a scant eight feet over smooth limestone and is a popular gathering spot for picnickers (and hummingbirds). The road to the Guatemala border passes through San Antonio Village, making access easy. No official accommodation options exist here, but overnight stays can be arranged with local families through the Toledo Ecotourism Association (T.E.A.). ☒ *San Antonio Village* ⊕ *Drive north on Southern Hwy. to The Dump, and turn left and follow San Antonio Rd. to San Antonio Village.*

San Pedro Columbia

TOWN | The Kek'chi Mayan village of San Pedro Columbia (population 700) is a cheerful cluster of brightly painted buildings and thatch houses off the San Antonio Road. Several local women sell hand-woven embroidery. ■**TIP**➔ **The Mayan site of Lubaatun is nearby.** ☒ *San Pedro Columbia* ⊕ *From Punta Gorda, drive north on Southern Hwy. to The Dump, and turn west on San Antonio Rd. Just before village of San Antonio, turn right on dirt track (watch for sign) to San Pedro Columbia.*

GARIFUNA VILLAGES

Barranco

TOWN | **FAMILY** | Although the Maya are by far the largest population in rural Toledo, this also forms part of Belize's Garifuna homeland. Barranco, a small village of fewer than 200 people about an hour by road from Punta Gorda, is the largest Garifuna center in Toledo. This southernmost coastal village in Belize has electricity, a couple of shops, a bar, a police station, a health clinic, and a school. It was the birthplace of Andy Palacio, the famed *punta* rock musician. A guided village tour includes, in addition to a visit to Palacio's gravesite, stops at the Dabuyaba (Garifuna temple), the House of Culture, and a cassava factory. Lunch in a local home is also possible. TIDE Tours, PG Tours, and other tour operators offer trips to Barranco, or you can drive yourself. ⊠ *Barranco* ⊕ *From Punta Gorda, drive north to Jacinto Village (watch for water tower) and turn west on dirt road to San Felipe, Santa Ana, and Barranco Villages. It's about 9 miles (15 km) on dirt road to Barranco, but it may take you as long as 45 mins after you leave Southern Hwy.* ☎ *709/2010 Barranco community phone.*

MAYAN RUINS
★ Lubaantun

ARCHAEOLOGICAL SITE | FAMILY | Lubaantun, which lies beyond the village of San Pedro Columbia, is a Late Classic site discovered in 1924 by German archaeologist Thomas Gann, who gave it a name meaning "place of fallen stones." Lubaantun must have been an awe-inspiring sight: on top of a conical hill, with views to the sea in one direction and the Maya Mountains in the other, its stepped layers of white-plaster stone would have towered above the jungle like a wedding cake. No one knows exactly what function the structures served, but the wealth of miniature masks and whistles found suggests it was a center of ceramic production. (The altars so common to other Mayan sites are nowhere to be found here.) The trio of ball courts and the central plaza with tiered seating for 10,000 spectators seems like a Mayan Madison Square Garden, and you'll occasionally see kids kicking around a soccer ball here. There's a small visitor center at the site. Although this is southern Belize's largest Mayan site, visitors are few during the week, and you might find you have the whole place to yourself.

Most tour operators in Punta Gorda can arrange trips to Lubaantun, or you can visit by rental car, an easy trip down the San Antonio Road. ⊠ *San Pedro Columbia* ⊕ *20 miles (33 km) northwest of Punta Gorda, about 1 mile (1.5 km) from village of San Pedro Columbia* ☎ *822/2016 NICH Institute of Archaeology in Belmopan* ⊕ *www.nichbelize.org* ⊠ *BZ$10.*

★ Nim Li Punit

ARCHAEOLOGICAL SITE | FAMILY | Nim Li Punit, a Late Classic site discovered in 1976, has 26 unearthed stelae, including one, Stela 14, that is 30 feet tall—the largest ever found in Belize and the second largest found anywhere in the Mayan world. Nim Li Punit, which means "Big Hat" in the Kek'chi Mayan language, is named for the elaborate headgear of a ruler pictured on Stela 14. Shady trees cool you off as you walk around the fairly small site (you can see it all in an hour or so). Stop by the informative visitor center on the premises to learn more about the site. Nim Li Punit is near the Kek'chi village of Indian Creek, and children (and some adults) from the village usually come over and offer jewelry and crafts for sale. It is easily accessible via a short dirt road off the Southern Highway. ⊠ *Mile 72.5, Southern Hwy., Indian Creek Village* ⊕ *From Punta Gorda, drive north on Southern Hwy. about 27 miles (44 km) to Indian Creek Village. Turn west at Nim Li Punit sign and go about 0.5 mile (1 km) on dirt road to site. James Line buses (locals, not express) will drop you at entrance road* ☎ *822/2106 NICH Institute of Archaeology in Belmopan* ⊕ *www.nichbelize.org* ⊠ *BZ$10.*

NATURE RESERVES
Agua Caliente Wildlife Sanctuary

NATURE PRESERVE | FAMILY | Hot springs, freshwater lagoons, caves, and hiking trails dot the 6,000-acre Agua Caliente Wildlife Sanctuary. The sanctuary is known for its water birds, including ibises, herons, egrets, woodstorks, and kingfishers. A half-mile boardwalk gives

Lubaantun and the Crystal Skull

In the last century Lubaantun became the scene of what is allegedly the biggest hoax in modern archaeology. After it was excavated in the 1920s, a British adventurer named F. A. Mitchell-Hedges claimed to have stumbled on what became known as the Crystal Skull. Mitchell-Hedges described the incident in a potboiler, *Danger, My Ally*, in 1951. According to the book, the Crystal Skull was found under an altar at Lubaantun by his daughter Anna. Mitchell-Hedges portrayed himself as a serious archaeologist and explorer: in truth, he was a magazine hack who was later exposed in England as an adventurer. The Crystal Skull made good copy; also known as the Skull of Doom, it was supposedly used by Mayan high priests to zap anyone they didn't like. Mitchell-Hedges claimed it was 3,600 years old and had taken 150 years to fashion by rubbing a block of pure rock crystal with sand. A similar skull, in the possession of the British Museum, shows signs of having been manufactured in modern times with a dentist's drill. However, some archaeologists believe the Crystal Skull may be authentic, possibly of Aztec origin. Anna Mitchell-Hedges, who died in 2007, adamantly refused to allow the Crystal Skull to be tested and denied all requests by the Belizean government to return it. It is now owned by her caregiver, Bill Homann.

access to the visitor center. A local guide is recommended. During the dry season you can hike under the forest canopy and through wetlands to the warm springs at the base of the Agua Caliente hills. During the rainy season, canoes are available for hire. ⊠ *About 13 miles (21 km) west of Punta Gorda, Toledo* ✢ *From Punta Gorda, take Southern Hwy. 10 miles (16 km) north. Turn left on Laguna Rd. and go 3 miles (5 km). The trail to wildlife sanctuary begins in Laguna Village.*

Belize Spice Farm and Botanical Gardens

FARM/RANCH | FAMILY | See exotic spices such as cardamom, vanilla, nutmeg, clove, cinnamon, and sandalwood growing at this spice farm just off the Southern Highway at Golden Stream. Currently, only black pepper is grown in enough quantity (about 10,000 pounds of peppercorns per year) for commercial sales in Belize, but plans are to expand other spice production for domestic and, eventually, international sales. The spice farm is part of a 500-acre tract now producing mostly citrus fruits. Visitors are given a guided tour of the farm on a cart with seats pulled by a tracked tractor; walking tours are also available. Usually the last stop on the tour is the drying room, full of wonderful spice aromas. Tours generally start every hour on the hour from 8 to 4, but it's advisable to call ahead. The restaurant accommodates tour groups and other visitors. ⊠ *Southern Hwy., Golden Stream* ☎ *670/1338* ⊕ *www.belizespicefarm.com* 🖃 *BZ$40.*

Bladen Nature Reserve

NATURE PRESERVE | FAMILY | Ever been freshwater snorkeling? Check out the Bladen River in the Bladen Nature Reserve. The river snakes through the reserve, allowing for excellent kayaking, canoeing, swimming, and, yes, some freshwater snorkeling. The 100,000-acre Bladen Reserve is comanaged by the Belize Forestry Department and the Ya'axche Conservation Trust, an environmental NGO based in Punta Gorda. Bladen is the center piece of the Maya Mountain Corridor, creating a crucial link in the last remaining large, intact block of forest in the region. Additional parts of this corridor are protected by the Cockscomb

Basin Wildlife Sanctuary, the Columbia River Forest Reserve, and the Chiquibul National Park and Forest Reserve, all bordering Bladen. Tours of the Bladen Reserve also are given by interns from a private reserve managed by the Belize Foundation for Research and Environmental Education (BFREE). Camping and simple bunkhouse accommodations are available for around BZ$80–BZ$120 per person per day, meals included. Additional charges may apply for transportation, canoe rental, laundry, and other services. ⊠ *Bladen Nature Reserve* ☎ *352/231–2772 in U.S., 722/0108 in Punta Gorda* ⊕ *www.yaaxche.org.*

Columbia Forest Reserve

FOREST | One of the largest undisturbed tropical rain forest areas in Central America is the Columbia Forest Reserve in a remote area north of San José Village. The karst terrain—an area of irregular limestone in which erosion has produced sinkholes, fissures, and underground streams and caves—is difficult to navigate, so the only way to see this area is with a guide and with advance permission from the Belize Forestry Department. It has extremely diverse ecosystems because the elevation ranges from about 1,000 to more than 3,000 feet, with sinkholes as deep as 800 feet. You'll find areas of true "high bush" here: old-growth tropical forest with parts that have never been logged at all. Much of the rich flora and fauna of this area has yet to be documented. For example, one brief 12-day expedition turned up 15 species of ferns never found before in Belize, along with several new species of palms, vines, and orchids. Check with the Toledo Tour Guide Association at the BTIA visitor information office in Punta Gorda to try to find a guide to take you to this remote reserve. ⊠ *North of San José Village, San José* ☎ *637/2000 Toledo Tour Guide Association.*

Rio Blanco National Park

NATIONAL/STATE PARK | **FAMILY** | This tiny national park (500 acres) has a big waterfall—the Rio Blanco, which splashes over rough limestone boulders into a deep pool; you can jump into it for a refreshing swim. The waterfall can be reached via a well-marked hiking trail. Upstream a short distance from the falls is a nice area for a picnic, shaded by trees and flowering bushes. The park is managed by residents of nearby Mayan villages including Santa Elena, Santa Cruz, Golden Stream, and Pueblo Viejo. You can visit on your own, though Punta Gorda tour operators include Rio Blanco in their offerings. ⊠ *Santa Cruz* ⊕ *30 miles (49 km) northwest of Punta Gorda between Santa Cruz and Santa Elena Villages, off San Antonio Rd. to Jalacte—watch for signs.*

Sarstoon-Temash National Park

NATIONAL/STATE PARK | **FAMILY** | One of the wildest and most remote areas of Belize is the Sarstoon-Temash National Park, between the Temash and Sarstoon Rivers in the far south of Toledo District on the border of Guatemala. Red mangroves grow along the river banks; animals and birds rarely seen in other parts of Belize, including white-faced capuchin monkeys, can be spotted here, along with jaguars (if you're lucky), ocelots, and tapirs, along with more than 200 species of birds. The only way to see this 42,000-acre area is with a guide by boat. Contact the Sarstoon-Temash Institute for Indigenous Management (SATIIM), which manages the park in conjunction with the Belize Forestry Department, for a guide, or check with the BTIA office on Front Street in Punta Gorda, home to the Toledo Tour Guide Association. SATIIM, among other things, is involved in efforts to oppose oil and gas exploration in the Sarstoon-Temash. ⚠ **The park has been a flashpoint in Guatemala's long-standing claims to Belizean territory, most recently in spring 2019. Check with the institute for**

developments. ✉ *Punta Gorda* ✥ *About 13 miles (21 km) south of Punta Gorda by boat* ☎ *722/0103* 🌐 *www.satiim.org.bz* 🎟 *BZ$20.*

🍴 Restaurants

Coleman's Café

$ | **LATIN AMERICAN** | This longtime local favorite serves simple but tasty Belizean dishes such as stew chicken or pork with beans and rice. Sit at tables with oilcloth tablecloths under a covered patio, open to the breezes, and enjoy genuine Belizean hospitality at lunch and dinner. **Known for:** tasty stew pork; periodic lunch buffets on no fixed schedule; nothing fancy, but friendly local vibe. [$] *Average main: BZ$14* ✉ *Main St., Big Falls Village, Big Falls* ✥ *Near rice mill* ☎ *720/2017* 💳 *No credit cards* ⏲ *No dinner.*

🛏 Hotels

Cotton Tree Lodge

$$$ | **RESORT** | **FAMILY** | This jungle lodge is named after the silk cotton tree (also called the kapok or ceiba), and, fittingly, the lodge strives to provide a silky-smooth experience for guests. **Pros:** stunning riverside setting; lots of activities; rope swing over the river. **Cons:** sometimes buggy; no a/c. [$] *Rooms from: BZ$400* ✉ *Moho River, near San Felipe Village, San Felipe* ☎ *212/529–8622 in U.S., 670/0557* 🌐 *www.cottontreelodge.com* 🛏 *15 rooms* 🍽 *All-inclusive.*

The Farm Inn

$$ | **B&B/INN** | **FAMILY** | On a 52-acre farm near San Antonio Village, off the San Antonio Road, this South African–run lodge has six nicely designed rooms and suites. **Pros:** quiet, natural setting near traditional Mayan villages; friendly international management; reasonable prices. **Cons:** no a/c; you'll need a car to stay here. [$] *Rooms from: BZ$220* ✉ *San Antonio Rd., San Antonio Village* ✥ *From Punta Gorda, drive north on Southern Hwy. to The Dump, turn left on San Antonio Rd. Drive to San Antonio Village, and continue about 2 miles (3.3 km). Watch for Farm Inn sign on right. Turn right and follow drive a few hundred yards to lodge* ☎ *614/4911* 🌐 *www.thefarminnbelize.com* 🛏 *6 rooms* 🍽 *Free breakfast.*

The Lodge at Big Falls

$$$ | **HOTEL** | **FAMILY** | Relax beside a meandering jungle river, listen to otters splash, and admire colorful tropical birds and butterflies at this small lodge on 30 placid acres beside the Rio Grande. **Pros:** fun to tube or swim in the river; excellent birding; good food. **Cons:** meals are pricey; you'll need a car to stay here. [$] *Rooms from: BZ$482* ✉ *Off Mile 79, Southern Hwy., Rio Grande, Big Falls* ☎ *732/4444* 🌐 *www.thelodgeatbigfalls.com* 🛏 *9 rooms* 🍽 *No meals.*

SIDE TRIP TO GUATEMALA

Updated by
Rachel White

👁 **Sights**
★★★★★

🍽 **Restaurants**
★★★☆☆

🛏 **Hotels**
★★★★☆

💼 **Shopping**
★★☆☆☆

🍸 **Nightlife**
★☆☆☆☆

WELCOME TO SIDE TRIP TO GUATEMALA

TOP REASONS TO GO

★ **Tikal:** Tikal is usually ranked as the most impressive of all Mayan sites. You can climb many of the structures and, looking across the jungle canopy, feel humbled by the history's gravitas.

★ **Other Mayan Ruins:** Tikal is the best known, but hardly the only important, Mayan site in El Petén. El Mirador was a giant city-state, perhaps larger than Tikal, and in the Mirador Basin are the remains of at least four other centers, including Nakbé, El Tintal, Xulnal, and Wakná.

★ **Wildlife:** The ancient world amazes, but when you see a spider monkey munching allspice berries just feet away, you may think the best part of the Mayan world is what still inhabits it.

★ **Flores and Lago Petén Itzá:** The island town of Flores has a muted, old-world ambience in the middle of an oceanic lake.

★ **Shopping for Handicrafts:** The indigenous population is known for a variety of handicrafts. There's an open-air market in Santa Elena, and Flores has a number of little shops.

The Petén is rugged country, where major roads are few and far between and traffic is thin. Because there are only two airports—one in Guatemala City, the other in Flores—you'll do most of your travel by land. Most roads you'll traverse are paved, such as the road from Santa Elena–Flores to Tikal, the road from Río Dulce in the south to Santa Elena–Flores, and a few others.

Proximity to Las Verapaces and the Atlantic lowlands—it's four to five hours from either region—make the Petén a reasonable overland combination with either, and air links to Guatemala City simplify travel here from almost any other region of the country.

1 Tikal. Arguably the most impressive of all Mayan sites, and rivaling even Machu Picchu in Peru and Angkor Wat in Cambodia in its ancient splendor, Tikal is a must-see.

2 Flores. Set at the end of the causeway in Lake Petén, the town of Flores is an enchanting and walkable small town, tourist oriented, with almost a charmed Mediterranean air.

3 Santa Elena. This bustling commercial center is far less frequented by tourists than Flores (so it's the perfect place to get an authentic sense of how people live in El Petén).

4 El Remate. Close to Tikal and on the lake, the village of El Remate is another pleasant (though perhaps less enchanting) base for exploring the region.

5 North Shore, Lake Petén Itzá, and Quexil Lagoon. These small villages are known for their beautiful lake vistas.

6 El Mirador. This is a must-see (but lesser-seen) Mayan ruin you can reach by hiking.

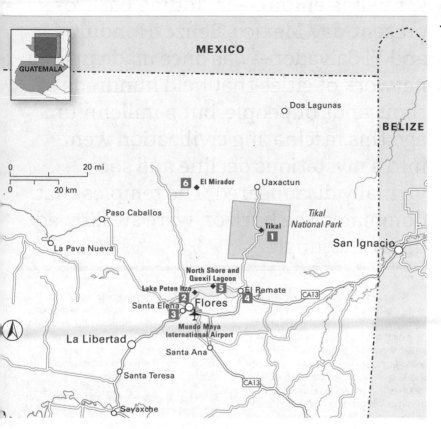

The jungles of El Petén were once the heartland of the Mayan civilization. The sprawling empire—including parts of present-day Mexico, Belize, Honduras, and El Salvador—was once made up of a network of cities that held hundreds of thousands of people, but a millennium ago this fascinating civilization went into a mysterious decline and soon virtually disappeared. The temples that dominated the horizon were swallowed up by the jungle.

Today ancient ruins seem to emerge as if nourished by El Petén's soil. In comparison with the rest of Guatemala, which has 15 million people in an area the size of Tennessee, El Petén is relatively sparsely populated, although this is changing. Fifty years ago El Petén had fewer than 20,000 residents. Due to massive immigration from other areas of Guatemala, El Petén now has more than half a million people (almost twice the population of the entire country of Belize). Still, nature reigns supreme, with vines and other plants reclaiming everything that stands still a little too long. Whatever your primary interest—archaeology, history, birding, biking—you'll find plenty to do and see in this remote region.

Four-wheel-drive vehicles are required to get to many of the archaeological sites (but not to Tikal), while others, such as those in the Mirador Basin, are reachable only by boat or on foot. The difficulty doesn't just enhance the adventure, it gives you time to take in the exotic scenery and rare tropical flora and fauna that are with you all the way. Most major roads in the Petén are now beautifully paved, and the towns of Flores and Santa Elena bustle with activity.

The Petén may be vast and remote, but the traveler's focus takes in a far more limited area. Ruins dot the entire region, but excavation has begun on only a few of them. In the center of the region on Lago Petén Itzá sits Flores, its administrative center, and its twin town of Santa Elena, the site of the regional airport. Northeast lie the famed ruins of Tikal.

HISTORY
At its peak, the Mayan civilization developed one of the earliest forms of writing, the very first mathematical system to use zero, complex astronomical calculations, advanced agricultural systems, and an inscrutable belief system. It was

during this zenith that spectacular cities such as Tikal were built. By the time the Europeans arrived, the Mayan civilization had already mysteriously collapsed.

Until the 1960s the Petén region was a desolate place. This all changed when the Guatemalan government began offering small tracts of land in El Petén for US$25 to anyone willing to settle it. The landless moved in droves, and today the population is more than 500,000—a 25-fold increase in around 50 years.

Unemployment in El Petén is high, and tourism—mostly associated with Tikal and other Mayan sites—is the main industry. Many make ends meet through subsistence farming, logging, hunting for *xate* (palm leaves used in the floral industry) in the wild, and marijuana cultivation. Exploration for oil is under way in a few areas as well.

MAJOR REGIONS

Tikal. Arguably the most impressive of all Mayan sites, and rivaling even Machu Picchu in Peru and Angkor Wat in Cambodia in its ancient splendor, Tikal is a must-see.

Tikal Environs. Set at the end of the causeway in Lake Petén, the town of Flores is an enchanting and walkable small town, tourist oriented, with almost a charmed Mediterranean air. The village of El Remate, closer to Tikal and on the lake, is another pleasant (though perhaps less enchanting) base for exploring the region.

Other Mayan Sites in El Petén. The complexes of El Mirador, Nakúm, Uaxactún, and El Zotz, among others, are scattered around Tikal. They're all close, but poor roads limit the number of visitors, especially during the rainy season.

Planning

When to Go

It's very warm here year-round. The rainy season is May to November, and the rain takes itself seriously. Occasional showers are a possibility the rest of the year, but shouldn't interfere with your plans. March and April are the hottest months, with December and January a few degrees cooler than the rest of the year. July and August see an influx of visitors during prime North American and European vacation time.

Getting Here and Around

AIR TRAVEL

Aeropuerto Internacional Santa Elena (FRS), or the Mundo Maya International Airport, often just referred to as the Flores airport, is less than 0.5 mile (1 km) outside town. Taxis and shuttles meet every plane and charge about 20 quetzales per person to take you into Flores. The airport has service to and from Belize City, Guatemala City, and Cancún.

Avianca, Tropic Air, and TAG operate flights between Guatemala City and Santa Elena-Flores that take less than an hour. Tropic Air and TAG run flights between Belize City and Flores.

CONTACTS Avianca Airlines. ☎ *800/284– 2622 in U.S.* ⊕ *www.avianca.com.* **TAG.** ☎ *502/2380–9400 in Guatemala* ⊕ *www.tag.com.gt.* **Tropic Air.** ✉ *Philip Goldson International Airport, Belize City* ☎ *501/226–2626 in Belize, 800/422–3435 in U.S.* ⊕ *www.tropicair.com.*

BUS TRAVEL

Linea Dorada and Autobuses Fuente del Norte offer daily direct bus service between the Marine terminal in Belize City and Santa Elena–Flores. The five-hour trip on air-conditioned buses with comfortable reclining seats, TVs, and bathrooms costs around US$25 one way. Call at least one day ahead for reservations. Inexpensive local service is available, but those buses stop in every village along the way, which adds hours to the trip. The same lines also offer service between Guatemala City and Santa Elena–Flores.

In Santa Elena, the main local bus terminal is a bustling center where your questions can be easily answered. (To and from the bus station, a tuk-tuk should be a mere Q5.) Here you can catch a scheduled minibus shuttle, operated by San Juan Travel and other companies, that makes the 42-mile (70-km) trip on a good paved road to Tikal several times in the morning and return trips in the evening. Service is usually reduced during slow periods. They cost around US$6.50 one way per person and take 1 ½ hours or more, depending on stops.

From the town bordering Belize, Melchor de Mencos, there are frequent chicken buses, often packed, which cost about Q30 (around US$4). They'll take you to Santa Elena–Flores but not to Tikal. To get to Tikal from the Belize border, you have to get off at El Cruce (the Crossroads) and wait for another bus en route to Tikal. The frequency of buses depends on the time of year and is not wholly reliable, but roughly every two hours until the early afternoon.

CONTACTS Linea Dorada. ⊠ *Mercado Nuevo Interior, Zona 2, Santa Elena* ☎ *502/7924–8434, 502/7924–8535* ⊕ *www.lineadorada.com.gt.* **Zippy Zappy Mayan Travels.** ⊠ *111 N. Front St., Belize City* ☎ *502/7947–7070 Grupo del Fuente, 501/223–1200 Mundo Maya Travel in Belize* ⊕ *www.travelmundomaya.com.*

CAR TRAVEL
Main roads in El Petén, such as between Flores/Santa Elena and Tikal, are paved and in very good shape. Secondary roads, however, often are in poor repair and not very well marked. Some roads are impassable during the rainy season, so check with the tourist office before heading out on seldom traveled roads, such as those to the more remote ruins surrounding Tikal.

If you're not booked on a tour, one way to get around El Petén is to rent a four-wheel-drive vehicle. If you rent a vehicle in Belize and plan to travel to Guatemala, Crystal Auto Rentals is the only company that allows you to take their cars across the border. Let them know your plans and they will give you all of the appropriate paperwork you will need when crossing the border. Many rental agencies, including Hertz, have offices at Mundo Maya International Airport in Flores. You need a valid driver's license from your own country to drive in Guatemala.

It is ill-advised to drive after dark in Guatemala; use extreme caution when driving. ⚠ **Armed attacks on cars have occurred between Guatemala City and Petén, and between the Belize border and Tikal. Check official crime and safety reports before traveling.**

LOCAL AGENCIES Hertz. ⊠ *Mundo Maya Airport, Santa Elena* ☎ *502/3274–4424 Hertz in Santa Elena, 800/654–3001 Hertz international rentals* ⊕ *rentautos.com.gt.* **Tabarini.** ⊠ *Mundo Maya International Airport, Santa Elena* ☎ *502/ 7926–0253* ⊕ *www.tabarini.com.*

TAXI TRAVEL
Taxis from the Santa Elena–Flores airport to Tikal are around US$50. A taxi from the Santa Elena airport into Flores is Q20 (about US$2.50) per person.

Emergencies

El Petén's only hospital is in San Benito, a suburb of Santa Elena. Medical facilities in El Petén are not as modern as in the rest of the country. If you're really sick, consider getting on the next plane to Guatemala City. Centro Médico Maya in Santa Elena has physicians on staff, though little or no English is spoken.

CONTACT EMERGENCY SERVICES Centro Médico Maya. ⊠ *2 Av. y 4 Calle, Zona 1, Santa Elena* ☎ *502/7926–0180.* **Hospital Nacional.** ⊠ *Calle Principal, San Benito* ☎ *502/7932–1111.* **Police.** ☎ *110 for police emergency, 120 for ambulance.* **Tourist Emergency Assistance.** ☎ *502/2421–2810, 1500.*

Safety

Most crimes directed at tourists in El Petén are pickpocketings, muggings, and thefts from cars. However, there have been a number of incidents over the years involving armed groups stopping buses, vans, and private cars at Tikal park.

In town, don't wear flashy jewelry and watches, keep your camera in a secure bag, and don't handle money in public. Hire taxis only from official stands at the airport, outside hotels, and at major intersections. If you can avoid it, don't drive after sunset. One common ploy used by highway robbers is to construct a roadblock, such as logs strewn across the road, and then hide nearby. When unsuspecting motorists get out of their cars to remove the obstruction, they are waylaid. ■TIP→ **If you come upon a deserted roadblock while driving, don't stop; turn around.**

INGUAT, the national institute for tourism, has voluntary security caravans to escort cars from Santa Elena–Flores to Tikal. To inquire about an escort, it is recommended to contact INGUAT directly by email at least three days in advance (info@inguat.gob.gt).

The increase in adoption of Guatemalan children has caused some people—particularly rural villagers—to fear that children will be abducted by foreigners. Limit your interaction with children you do not know, and be discreet when taking photographs.

Hotels

El Petén has a wide range of lodging options, from suites at luxurious lakeside resorts to stark rooms in budget hotels. Flores has many lodging choices, though most are merely adequate, and the number of hotels there keeps prices competitive. The hotels in much larger Santa Elena, the gateway to the island town of Flores, are generally larger and more upscale than the places in Flores, but with less atmosphere. El Remate, about 22 miles (35 km) from Flores on the road to Tikal, is a pleasant alternative, with several excellent small, mostly inexpensive hotels. At Tikal itself are three lodges that have the great advantage of being right at the park. On the north side of Lago de Petén Itzá are several hotels, including a couple of the most upscale in the region: Francis Ford Coppola's La Lancha and the largest resort hotel in the area, Hotel Camino Real Tikal.

Many hotels in El Petén have high and low seasons. They charge higher rates during the dry season, December through April, especially at the peak times of Christmas and Easter, and sometimes also during the July-to-August vacation season. Advance reservations are a good idea during these periods, especially at Tikal park lodges.

Restaurants

In El Petén you have a couple of choices for dining: *comedores,* which are small eateries along the lines of a U.S. café or diner, with simple and inexpensive local food; and restaurants, that, in general, are a little nicer and serve a wider selection of food, often with an international or American flavor. Restaurants are mostly in Flores and other towns. In more remote lodgings, you'll probably eat in the hotel dining room.

Some restaurants serve wild game, or *comida silvestre*. Although often delicious, the game has usually been taken illegally. You might see *venado* (venison), *coche del monte* (mountain cow or peccary), and *tepezcuintle* (paca, a large rodent) on the menu.

RESTAURANT AND HOTEL PRICES

Restaurant and hotel reviews have been shortened. For full information, visit Fodors.com

What It Costs in Guatemalan Quetzales

	$	$$	$$$	$$$$
RESTAURANTS				
	under Q70 ($9)	Q70–Q100 ($9–$13)	Q101–Q130 ($14–$18)	over Q130 ($18)
HOTELS				
	under Q360 ($50)	Q360–Q560 ($50–$75)	Q561–Q760 ($75–$100)	over Q760 ($100)

Extended Tours

Aside from hotel-run overnight or multi-day tours, ARCAS runs special ecotours. Martsam Travel offers many different types of tours in the area. Tip tour guides about 10% of the tour price.

CONTACTS ARCAS EcoTours. ⊠ *Mayan Biosphere Reserve, Flores* ✛ *Near Zoológico Petencito* ☎ *502/5208–0968.* **Martsam Travel.** ⊠ *Calle 30 de Junio, lobby of Capitán Tortuga, Flores* ☎ *502/7926–0346 in Flores, 305/395–3935 in U.S. and Canada* ⊕ *www.martsam.com.*

FROM BELIZE

Many tour operators in the San Ignacio, Belize, area operate day and overnight or multinight Tikal tours. You'll pay more in Belize than in Guatemala, but you reduce the hassle factor significantly—you'll probably be picked up at your Cayo hotel, whisked across the border, provided

with a guide to Tikal, and fed lunch (hotel accommodations are arranged if you're staying overnight). You'll typically pay US$150 for a day tour to Tikal from San Ignacio. Overnight tours can be as much as US$450 but include a sunrise tour. When comparing tour costs, check to see if border fees and Tikal admission are included.

Visitor Information

CONTACTS ARCAS. ⊠ *Mayan Biosphere Reserve, Flores* ✛ *Near Zoológico Petencito* ☎ *502/5208–0968 Dr. Fernando Martinez (Rescue Center Director)* ⊕ *www.arcasguatemala.org.* **INGUAT.** ⊠ *Mundo Maya International Airport, Santa Elena* ☎ *502/2421–2800* ⊕ *www. visitguatemala.com.*

Tikal

22 miles (35 km) north of El Remate, 42 miles (68 km) northeast of Flores.

GETTING HERE AND AROUND

There are several ways to get to Tikal. If you're in Belize City, you can take a bus on the Fuente del Norte or Linea Dorada lines to Santa Elena–Flores. At higher cost, you can fly Tropic Air from the Philip S. W. Goldson International Airport, which has flights every day. If in San Ignacio, Belize, take a taxi or cheaper collective taxi to the Guatemalan border. From there you'll walk across the border and either take a taxi straight to Tikal, or a bus to El Cruces (the crossroads between Santa Elena–Flores and Tikal) where you'll wave down another bus. From the border (referred to as Melchor de Mencos), a taxi is by far the easier option, cheaper in a group if you can find friendly passengers at the border with whom to split the cost. *See Petén Getting Here and Around for more information.*

If you choose to rent a car, a paved, well-patrolled 42-mile (70-km) highway

Several temples and acropolises make Tikal one of the most impressive Mayan sites of all.

connects Santa Elena–Flores and Tikal, passing through the town of El Remate at about its halfway point. The most expensive but least stressful option is an escorted tour from San Ignacio.

TIMING

You can visit Tikal on a day-trip and get a good sense of its grandeur. Depending on your schedule, you may choose to spend the night either at Tikal National Park so you can see the ruins in the morning (a must for birders), or in Flores, El Remate, or elsewhere along the shores of Lake Petén Itzá. You can easily spend two days, or longer, exploring the ruins. You may want to hire a guide for your first day, then wander about on your own on the second. If you have additional time, consider an extension in El Petén. The town of Flores, with its lakeside bistros and cobblestone streets, merits at least a half-day stroll.

SAFETY AND PRECAUTIONS

Taxis and tourist buses seem to be magnets for bandits in El Petén. The bandits take passengers' valuables; occasionally passengers have been assaulted. Keep in mind that some 300,000 international visitors come to Tikal every year, and the vast majority of them have no problems with crime.

Sights

TIKAL WITH A GUIDE

Most people find a guide worth it. Guides can be booked at the concrete information kiosk near the parking lot; some can be booked ahead. They make the visit more interesting, though don't believe everything they tell you, as some guides have their own pet theories on the decline of the Maya or other subjects that they love to expound to tourists. Rates are highly negotiable, but expect to pay about US$60 for a tour for up to four or five people. In a large group you may pay as little as US$10 per person. If you're staying more than one day, hire a guide for the first day, and then wander on your own after that.

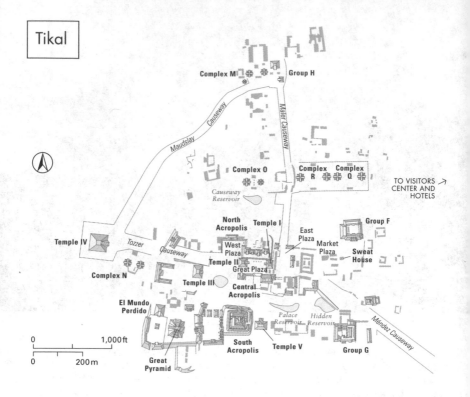

Tikal

Complex M · Group H

Maudslay Causeway

Mater Causeway

Complex O

Causeway Reservoir

Complex R · Complex Q

TO VISITORS CENTER AND HOTELS

North Acropolis · Temple I

East Plaza

Group F

Temple IV

Tozzer Causeway

West Plaza

Market Plaza

Sweat House

Complex N

Temple II

Great Plaza

Temple III

Central Acropolis

El Mundo Perdido

Palace Reservoir · Hidden Reservoir

Méndez Causeway

0 ——— 1,000 ft

0 ——— 200 m

South Acropolis · Temple V · Group G

Great Pyramid

ON YOUR OWN

Pack well: Wear hiking or walking shoes and bring plenty of water (a liter a person per hour is advised)—you'll be walking about 6 miles (10 km) and up a lot of stairs if you intend to see the whole site. Take along your bug spray, as you'll likely sweat off the first layer. Snacks and sunscreen are smart to have. There are bathrooms inside the park but not potable water.

The ticket-taker and gate to Tikal is at the left of the roundabout where the information kiosk sits. (Signs are not plentiful.) When you pass the gate, keep to the middle trail. You'll soon arrive at the ancient city's center, filled with awe-inspiring temples and acropolises. The pyramid that you approach from behind is **Temple I**, known as the Temple of the Great Jaguar because of the

feline represented on one of its carved lintels. It's in what is referred to as the **Great Plaza**, one of the most beautiful and dramatic in Tikal. The Great Plaza was built around AD 700 by Ah-Cacao, one of the wealthiest rulers of his time. His tomb, comparable in magnitude to that of Pa Cal at the ruins of Palenque in southern Mexico, was discovered beneath the Temple of the Great Jaguar in the 1960s. The theory is that his queen is buried beneath **Temple II**, called the Temple of the Masks for the decorations on its facade. It's a twin of the Temple of the Great Jaguar. In fact, construction of matching pyramids distinguishes Tikal from other Mayan sites.

The **North Acropolis**, to the west of Ah-Cacao's temple, is a mind-boggling conglomeration of temples built over layers and layers of previous construction.

Exploring Tips

Visitors are not allowed inside the ruins after opening hours, which are 6 am to 6 pm.

There are tales of tourists sneaking in or slipping guards bribes to pass, but we advise against that. The trails are not lit and climbing the pyramids is risky in the dark. There's also a slight menace of robbery.

If you stay at one of the three lodgings on the grounds, you get a jump-start on the day-tour visitors and have the advantage of being here late in the afternoon, after everyone else has left.

In order to take a famous sunrise tour, you must stay in the park the night before. Tours begin at 4 am, and you'll pay the day's Q150 ticket fee to the park, plus an extra Q100 for entrance

before the park opens, plus the cost of the tour. They don't guarantee the sun, and there's often a cloud canopy, but seeing the park awaken is a marvel.

Signs indicate whether a structure cannot be climbed ("No Subrir"), which is not always obvious. Look for these signs and respect the rules.

In the past, if you purchased an entrance ticket after 3 pm, you could use the same ticket for your next day's entry, but at the time of writing that's unfortunately no longer the case. It doesn't hurt to ask upon purchase.

⚠ There are no ATMs inside Tikal National Park. Hotels usually exchange dollars for quetzales or will direct you to a business that will. Be sure to have plenty of cash before heading to Tikal.

Excavations have revealed that the base of this structure is more than 2,000 years old. Be sure to see the stone mask of the rain god at Temple 33. The **Central Acropolis,** south of the Great Plaza, is an immense series of structures assumed to have served as administrative centers.

If you climb to the top of one of the pyramids, you'll see the gray roof combs of others rising above the rain forest's canopy but still trapped within it. **Temple V,** to the south, underwent a $3 million restoration project and is now open to the public. **Temple IV,** to the west, is the tallest-known structure built by the Maya. Although the climb to the top is steep, the view is unforgettable.

To the southwest of the plaza lie the **South Acropolis,** which hasn't been reconstructed, and a 105-foot-high pyramid, similar in construction to those at Teotihuacán. A few jungle trails, including the marked Interpretative Benil-ha Trail, offer

a chance to see howler monkeys and other wildlife. You also may see packs of the hook-tailed coatimundi (*pizote* in Spanish), adorable relatives of the racoon. Outside the park, a somewhat overgrown trail halfway down the old airplane runway on the left leads to the remnants of old rubber-tappers' camps, and is a good spot for bird-watching.

TIKAL MUSEUMS

At park headquarters are two small archaeological museums that display Mayan artifacts, plus a new exhibit on current restoration and conservation projects. These are good resources for information on the enigmatic rise and fall of the Maya, though little information is in English. You will need to purchase tickets for the museum separately at the same time as you buy tickets to enter Tikal itself.

El Centro de Conservación e Investigación de Tikal

ARCHAEOLOGICAL SITE | The Center of Conservation and Research is a collaboration with the government of Japan. There's a small exhibition and info center about its restoration and conservation work. ✉ *Tikal* ⊕ *www.mcd.gob.gt/el-centro-de-conservacion-e-investigacion-de-tikal.*

El Museo Lítico (*Stelae Museum*)

ARCHAEOLOGICAL SITE | El Museo Lítico or Stelae Museum has stelae (commemorative stone slabs) found at Tikal and interesting photos from early archaeological excavations. ✉ *Near visitor center* 🖾 *Q30 admission to both museums.*

El Museo Tikal (*Tikal Sylvannus G. Morley Museum*)

ARCHAEOLOGICAL SITE | El Museo Tikal has a replica of Ha Sawa Chaan K'awil's burial chamber and some ceramics and bones from the actual tomb (the jade, however, is a replica). ✉ *Near visitor center* 🖾 *Q30 admission to both museums.*

Hotels

There are three hotels on the park grounds: Tikal Inn, Jungle Lodge, and Jaguar Inn. At all of these you pay for the park location rather than good amenities and great service. Electric power is from generators, which usually run for part of the morning and evening, although batteries may provide limited lighting throughout the night. None of the hotels at the park have air-conditioning. Since the hotels here have a captive audience, service is not always as friendly or helpful as it could be, and reservations are sometimes "lost," even if you have a confirmation email. However, when contrasted with the massive concessionaire-owned lodges inside national parks around the rest of the world, these hotels are intimate and atmospheric. If you want to be even closer to the cry of howler monkeys, good camping is available at the park campsite (Q50, or

about US$6.50, per person and around the same for tent or hammock), where you'll sleep under a small thatch gazebo. Or you can camp at the Jaguar Inn, which will provide an inflatable mattress and linens in a modern pop-up tent and access to public bathrooms and showers (approximately Q100, or about US$13, per person). Two comedores are at the entrance to the park; Comedor Tikal on the right of the entrance is the better and cheaper. The tiny Caffé Ital near the souvenir stands serves coffee and candy bars. All three hotels have restaurants open to the public, with inflated pricing. The hotels have room-only rates, but if you are booking through a travel agent you may be required to take a package that includes meals and a Tikal tour.

Jaguar Inn

$$$ | **HOTEL** | **FAMILY** | This hotel has the feel of a backpacker's lodge, only not at backpacker prices, but it's in the park, and despite the less-than-luxe mattress, you'll awaken to birdsong. **Pros:** conveniently in the park; 24-hour electricity; camping available. **Cons:** basic rooms somewhat jammed together; hot water limited to three hours in the morning and three hours in the evening; very pricey for what you get. $ *Rooms from: Q677* ⊠ *Parque Nacional Tikal* ☎ *502/7926 2411, 315/359-4926* ⊕ *www.jaguartikal.com* ⟳ *30 rooms and camping* ⍰ *No meals.*

★ Jungle Lodge

$$$$ | B&B/INN | FAMILY | Easily the best accommodations in Tikal, this lodge's cobblestone footpaths will lead you through a tamed jungle (but not so tame as to deny you a hello from a spider monkey or an iguana) to remodeled bungalows, painted with elegant interpretations of Mayan motifs. **Pros:** dynamic interiors and exteriors; Edenic jungle gardens; swimming pool; suites for a range of budgets. **Cons:** due to renovations, rooms are more expensive; dining options underwhelming and overpriced; electricity and water are turned off at set times of the day. $ *Rooms from: Q1,175* ⊠ *Parque Nacional Tikal* ☎ *502/2477 0570* ⊕ *www.junglelodgetikal.com* ⟳ *49 rooms* ⍰ *No meals.*

Tikal Inn

$$ | B&B/INN | FAMILY | The cluster of bungalows, set farthest from the park entrance, wraps around a well-manicured garden and a pool, which you will be very happy to see after trekking through the ruins. **Pros:** good location in the park; swimming pool; decent service; packages can be a bargain. **Cons:** rooms can be hot since there is no power for fans at night; limited hot water and electricity; dated accommodations. $ *Rooms from: Q384* ⊠ *Parque Nacional Tikal* ☎ *502/7861-2444* ⊕ *www.tikalinn.com* ⟳ *25 rooms* ⍰ *Some meals.*

🏃 Activities

Many folks make a lifelong career out of guiding tours at Tikal, and can be found around the information kiosk centered in the roundabout inside the park. Inquire whether they are INGUAT certified, about

their guidance experience, tour costs, and whether there's a chance a tour would be cancelled if not enough tourists sign on. If you prefer to book ahead of time, there are multiple options.

Canopy Tours Tikal

TOUR—SIGHT | FAMILY | The fun folks at Canopy Tours Tikal have expeditions that take you to the true heart of the rain forest—not on ground level, but more than 100 feet up in the air, where you can " *vuele como Superman.*"Even more exhilarating, you may see monkeys in their homes and/or other wildlife. Each zipline costs US$30 (approx. Q188) per person (plus park entrance fee). Inquire and they'll provide transport from inside the park, Remate, or Flores for a small extra fee. Canopy Tours Tikal also offers hiking, bird-watching, and horseback riding. ⊠ *Near entrance gate to Tikal park, El Remate* ⊹ *About 40 mins by car from Flores* ☎ *502/5615 4988* ⊕ *www.tikalcanopy.com* ⌑ *Q230.*

Ecotourism & Adventure Specialists

TOUR—SIGHT | FAMILY | This company's professionally run tours like canopy, birding, and archaeological, include an option for hotel pickup in Flores in the morning, and then hotel drop-off in the late afternoon after a day of guided exploration. Tours can be reserved through their website. ⊠ *Guatemala City* ☎ *502/2367-2837* ⊕ *www.tikalpark.com.*

Flores

133 miles (206 km) north of Río Dulce, 38 miles (61 km) northeast of Sayaxché.

Flores is the blue-ribbon rose in the bouquet of green that is El Petén. If you're traveling in the region, it would be a shame to miss this historic little island, where you can stay in a cozy inn, eat well, and explore the hilly cobblestone streets on foot.

The red-roof town, on an island in the waters of Lago Petén Itzá connected to the mainland by a main road, is on the site of the ancient city of Tatyasal. This was the region's last unconquered outpost of Mayan civilization, until it finally fell to the Spanish in 1697. The conquerors destroyed the city's huge pyramids.

Today, from afar the provincial capital looks like a toy village neatly assembled; up close it has narrow streets lined with buildings in buttermint pastels, and flowers spilling over balconies, making every corner photogenic. There's a central square presided over by a colonial church, and the pint-sized motorized tuk-tuks give you a real sense of being *elsewhere*. Touristy, yes, but still charming.

To stay in some of Flores's hotels is to experience a different era; you almost expect to see it through a yellow-tinted filter. Some hotels are quaint and unfussy; some are simply pedestrian, even mediocre. Frame your expectations well, and their eccentricities can enhance the experience.

Connected to the mainland by a bridge and causeway—don't be put off by the Burger King at the entrance to the causeway—Flores serves as a base for many travelers to El Petén. It's also the center of many nongovernmental organizations working for the preservation of the Mayan Biosphere, an endangered area covering nearly all of northern Petén. Flores is also one of the last remaining vestiges of the Itzá, the people who built Mexico's monumental Chichén Itzá.

GETTING HERE AND AROUND

Once in Flores, all will be a hop-skip-jump (or just a stroll) away. Wave down a zooming tuk-tuk if the hills are looking unfriendly.

TIMING

Even if you fall in love with Flores, which is possible and almost inevitable, a night or two is enough for most to steep in the charm of the *islita*.

🍴 Restaurants

★ Achiote

$$ | INTERNATIONAL | FAMILY | A broad menu features *comida típica* as well as familiar plates, so you can order a tasty hamburger (with optional whiskey sauce) or *pollo al achiote*, chicken spiced with the red, red pre-Colombian herb. The atmosphere is tasteful and relaxing, so you won't even miss the lake, which is a couple of blocks away. **Known for:** lovely ambience; delectable dishes; good cocktails and wine list. [$] *Average main: Q70* ✉ *Av. Reformes, at Hotel Isla de Flores* ☎ *502/7867–5176* 🌐 *www.hotelisladeflores.com* 💳 *No credit cards.*

Café Arqueológico Yaxhá

$ | LATIN AMERICAN | Combining a cultural and educational experience with good food, this restaurant is the creation of German architect Dieter Richter, who has worked on projects at Yaxhá and Naranjo. You can browse a collection of books, photos, maps, and other information about the Mayan world while you enjoy a *hamburguesa* or a Mayan dish such as *Pollo Xni Pec* (chicken in a chili sauce served with rice and yucca). **Known for:** unique Mayan dishes; laid-back boho atmosphere; friendly, helpful staff. [$] *Average main: Q60* ✉ *Av. 15 de Septiembre* ☎ *502/5830–2060* 🌐 *www.cafeyaxha.com.*

Capitán Tortuga

$$ | PIZZA | FAMILY | The large, cartoonlike Capitán Turtle sign may fool you into thinking this restaurant is just for kids, but the grilled meats, pizza, tacos and burritos, and other options make this one of Flores's better choices for a meal with a view. The *pinchos* (grilled kebabs) are cooked on an open barbecue, sending enticing aromas throughout the restaurant. **Known for:** stunning lake views; fresh whitefish; friendly service. [$] *Average main: Q100* ✉ *Calle 30 de Junio and Callejón San Pedrito* ☎ *502/7867–5089.*

Cool Beans (*El Café Chilero*)
$ | CAFÉ | You'll feel appropriately cool chilling in a hammock or shooting the breeze with another wanderer in this leafy garden café, sipping lemonade or an ice latte. If you're bored by the national beers, Gallo in Guatemala or Belikin in Belize, this café serves real IPAs and a selection of imported craft beers. **Known for:** craft beer; tasty coffee; great prices. Ⓢ *Average main: Q55* ✉ *Calle 15 de Septiembre* ☎ *502/5571–9240* ☾ *Closed Sun.*

★ Il Terrazzo
$$ | ITALIAN | FAMILY | This terrace is so lovely and the Italian food so rich that the lake will seem swapped for the Mediterranean in a delicious sleight of hand. The best plates are the bowls of house-made pasta slick with olive oil and dense with shrimp, bacon, tomatoes, squash, basil, or whatever tops your dish of choice. **Known for:** must-try avocado salad; killer sunset views; homemade pasta. Ⓢ *Average main: Q100* ✉ *Calle la Union* ☎ *502 /7867–5479* ☾ *Closed Sun.* ▭ *No credit cards.*

Legumbres Mayas
$ | VEGETARIAN | "Legumes" might not be the sexiest feature of a restaurant name, but this little cinder-block, rickety-tabled joint has plates and plates of those fresh veggies you've been missing—and not the boring kind, either. Heaping helpings of beans and rice can be had for about Q20. **Known for:** vegan and vegetarian nirvana; friendly family service; great value. Ⓢ *Average main: Q25* ✉ *Calle 15 de Septiembre* ☎ *502 /4324–7259* ▭ *No credit cards.*

★ Raíces Bar and Grill
$ | LATIN AMERICAN | Grilled meats come piping hot off the *parrilla* (grill) and give this palapa restaurant swagger. Tacos with practically an artist's palette of sauces are also popular, and the steamed fish is excellent. **Known for:** great location overlooking the lake; tacos; happy hour. Ⓢ *Average main: Q50* ✉ *Flores* ☎ *502/7867–5743* ▭ *No credit cards.*

Hotels

Hotel Casona de La Isla
$$ | HOTEL | FAMILY | Rooms here are just functional; but Lake Petén Itzá is a few skips across the street and verandas in tones of blue and orange make for lovely places to sit. **Pros:** beautiful lake views; swimming pool; helpful staff. **Cons:** outdated decor; unless you get a special, rooms are not a bargain; small rooms. Ⓢ *Rooms from: Q522* ✉ *Calle 30 de Junio, at Calle 10 de Noviembre* ☎ *502/7867–5200* ⊕ *www.hotelesdepeten.com* ☞ *26 rooms* ⦿ *Free breakfast.*

Hotel Petén
$$ | HOTEL | FAMILY | The common areas, with lake views and cheery colors are lovelier places to be than the simple rooms, but the oldest hotel in Flores remains a reliable one. **Pros:** classic hotel with great views of the lake from some balcony rooms; clean and quaint; decent value. **Cons:** four flights of stairs to get to top-floor rooms; modest rooms; some complaints of bugs. Ⓢ *Rooms from: Q448* ✉ *Calle 30 de Junio, off Calle Centroamérica* ☎ *502/2366–2841* ⊕ *www. hotelesdepeten.com* ☞ *21 rooms* ⦿ *No meals.*

★ La Isla de Flores Hotel
$$$$ | B&B/INN | FAMILY | A fresh sensibility, which includes distressed wood and acid-washed concrete tastefully layered over historic architecture and original beams, makes this Flores's most stylish hotel and very easy to recommend. **Pros:** airy rooms with inspired design; lovely rooftop bar; lake views on upper floors. **Cons:** not on the water; higher rates than older hotels; service may not be on par with other similarly priced hotels. Ⓢ *Rooms from: Q860* ✉ *Av. la Reforma* ☎ *7867–5176* ⊕ *www.hotelisladeflores. com* ☞ *30 rooms* ⦿ *No meals.*

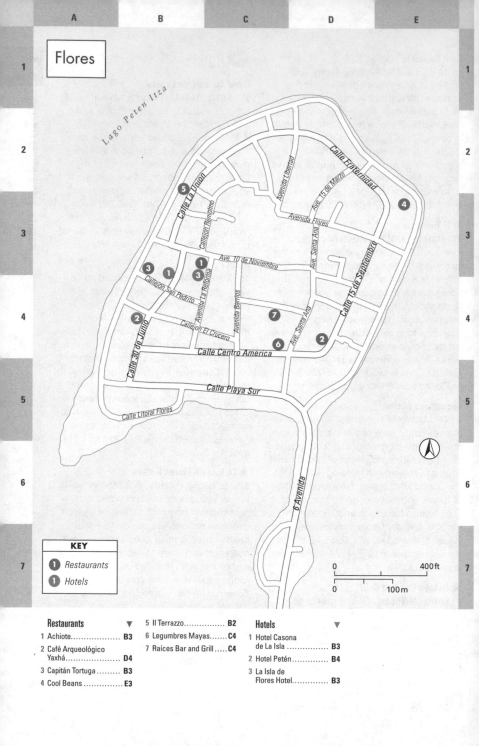

Flores

Lago Peten Itza

Calle La Union
Callejón Benidimo
Avenida Libertad
Calle Fraternidad
Ave. 15 de Marzo
Avenida Flores
Ave. Santa Ana
Ave. 10 de Noviembre
Callejón San Pedrito
Avenida La Reforma
Avenida Barrios
Calle 15 de Septiembre
Callejón El Crucero
Ave. Santa Ana
Calle 30 de Junio
Calle Centro America
Calle Playa Sur
Calle Litoral Flores
6 Avenida

KEY

🛈 Restaurants

🛈 Hotels

| 0 | 400 ft |
| 0 | 100 m |

Nightlife

The best of Flores nightlife involves having a mojito while watching the moon and the lake do their nightly dance. Not a bad way to close the day. In truth, there's not much partying; but Il Terrazzo, Raíces Bar and Grill, and Cool Beans are all lovely places for a drink. Most have generous happy hours; many close before midnight.

Activities

BOATING

Boat trips on Lake Petén Itzá can be arranged through most hotels in Flores or by haggling with boat owners who congregate behind the Hotel Santana. Tours often include a stop at Paraíso Escondido, a small mainland park northwest of Flores.

Kinkajou Kingdom and ARCAS

ZOO | FAMILY | Take a 10-minute boat ride across the lake to the wonderful exhibit Kinkajou Kingdom, featuring the big-eyed honey-bear cuties, as well as spider monkeys, margays, and other nonreleasable animals. This education service of the conservation NGO ARCAS is seldom taken advantage of by visitors but you should try to make time for it. Though you can drop in, reservations are recommended. ⊠ *Mayan Biosphere Reserve* ⊹ *Near Zoológico Petencito* ☎ *502/5208–0968* ⊕ *www.arcasguatemala.org* ⊠ *Q15.*

Santa Elena

0.25 mile (0.5 km) south of Flores.

Although it lacks the charms of neighboring Flores, gritty Santa Elena is pretty much unavoidable. Most services that you'll need for your trip to El Petén are usually offered here. There are also more upscale hotels here than in Flores.

GETTING HERE AND AROUND

Tuk-tuks—the motorized three-wheeled taxi rickshaws manufactured in Asia—ply the streets of Flores and Santa Elena. Five minutes and Q5 will get you between the two towns.

TIMING

Santa Elena is a place to sleep in a decent hotel, get money from an ATM, and buy picnic supplies. There's little to see in Santa Elena itself. At most, you'll use it as a base for exploring other parts of El Petén, so how long you stay here depends on your exploration plans.

SAFETY AND PRECAUTIONS

Some gas stations in Santa Elena have armed guards 24 hours a day, so that should tell you something. The better hotels are quite safe, however, and most visitors never experience any crime.

Hotels

Hotel La Casona del Lago

$$$$ | HOTEL | FAMILY | Santa Elena's spiffiest hotel puts you in mind of an old-time lighthouse, dignified in blue and white and sitting lakeside, with splendid views of Flores across the water. **Pros:** short walk or tuk-tuk ride across causeway to Flores; views of Flores and the lake; pool. **Cons:** rooms on street side can be noisy; gets a good deal of group business; expensive (for this part of Guatemala). Ⓢ *Rooms from: Q798* ⊠ *Calle Litoral on Lago* ☎ *502/7952–8700* ⊕ *www.hotelesdepeten.com* ⊅ *48 rooms* ⦿ *No meals.*

Villa Maya

$$$ | HOTEL | FAMILY | You could lie in bed and count the birds flying by your window at these villas on Lake Petenchel, east of Santa Elena, where pyramidal angles invoke the temples at Tikal. **Pros:** beautiful lake views; retreat-like setting; pleasant pool. **Cons:** not convenient to a selection of restaurants and shopping; bugs can be bothersome; some rooms far from restaurant and reception. Ⓢ *Rooms from: Q691* ⊠ *Laguna Petenchel* ⊹ *5 miles (8*

Private hideaways and wildlife reserves surround El Remate, Guatemala.

km) east of Santa Elena ☎ 502/7931–8350
hotel, 502/2223–5000 in Guatemala City
⊕ www.villasdeguatemala.com ↩ 56
rooms ⏏⃝ No meals.

Activities

Ixpanpajul Parque Natural

NATURE PRESERVE | FAMILY | Ixpanpajul
Parque Natural is a private nature reserve
sitting on a large stand of primary rain
forest. Hiking the suspended bridges of
the skyway will give you a bird's-eye view
of the indigenous flora and fauna that
make the rain forest the most biodiverse
ecosystem on the planet. The park also
offers myriad adventure opportunities,
from nighttime ATV tours to horseback
rides and mountain-bike excursions, and
the Tarzán Canopy Tour zipline. Camping and rental cabanas are available. A
restaurant has a limited menu averaging
around Q70 (US$9). ✉ Km 468, via Rio
Dulce ✛ 6 miles (10 km) south of Santa
Elena between Santa Elena and Tikal
Park ☎ 502/2336–0576, 502/4062–9812
in park ⊕ www.ixpanpajul.com.

El Remate

GETTING HERE AND AROUND

El Remate is about a half hour from
Flores by car.

TIMING

Most visitors use El Remate as a base
for visits to Tikal and other nearby Mayan
sites, so the length of stay depends
on how much time you want to spend
seeing ruins.

Sights

Biotopo Cerro Cahuí

NATURE PRESERVE | With around 1,500
acres of rain forest, Biotopo Cerro Cahuí
near El Remate is one of the most
accessible wildlife reserves in El Petén.
It protects a portion of a mountain that
extends to the eastern edge of Lago
Petén Itzá, so there are plenty of opportunities for hiking. Two trails put you in
proximity of birds like ocellated turkeys,
toucans, and parrots. As for mammals,

look up to spot the long-armed spider monkeys or down to see squat rodents called *tepezcuintles.* Tzu'unte, a 4-mile (6-km) trail, leads to two lookouts with views of nearby lakes. The upper lookout, Mirador Moreletii, is known by locals as Crocodile Hill, because from the other side of the lake it looks like the eye of a half-submerged crocodile. Los Ujuxtes, a 3-mile (5-km) trail, offers a panoramic view of three lakes. Both hikes begin at a ranger station (with toilets), where English-speaking guides are sporadically available. Some robberies and attacks on tourists have taken place in the reserve, so ask locally in El Remate about safety conditions before you explore on your own. ✉ *West of El Remate* 🎫 *Q40.*

Hotels

Hotel Gringo Perdito

$$ | **HOTEL** | The half mile of beach on the lake and the five private docks with hammocks (and a swing) are the stars of this property, along with the kayaks, stand-up paddleboards, and tubes for use. **Pros:** beautiful lakefront location; relaxed atmosphere; great bargain with breakfast and dinner included. **Cons:** rooms are basic; linens could use an update; can be buggy. [$] *Rooms from: Q384* ✉ *Main Road in the direction of San Andres 3* ☎ *5804–8639* 🌐 *www.hotelgringoperdido.com* 🛏 *16 rooms* 🍴 *Free breakfast.*

★ La Casa de Don David

$$ | **HOTEL** | Don David Kuhn has lived in the area for 40 years and is a great source for Tikal travel tips, while his lakeside hotel, an institution in Petén, also offers much to the visitor. **Pros:** gardens of a four-star resort; knowledgeable hosts; good restaurant. **Cons:** not a lot of frills; limited hot water; could use some maintenance. [$] *Rooms from: Q553* ✉ *On road to Biotopo Cerro Cahuí, near El Remate* ☎ *502/5306–2190, 502/5949–2164* 🌐 *www.lacasadedondavid.com* 🛏 *13 rooms* 🍴 *Some meals.*

La Mansión del Pájaro Serpiente

$ | **HOTEL** | **FAMILY** | Perched on a hillside in El Remate, the aged and charming Mansión del Pájaro Serpiente has some of the prettiest accommodations in El Petén. **Pros:** lakeview cabins; larger rooms have canopied beds and oversize windows; swimming pool carved from stone. **Cons:** not for visitors who can't walk up and down steep hills; credit cards not accepted; not on the lake. [$] *Rooms from: Q352* ✉ *On main hwy. south of El Remate* ☎ *502/5967–9816 in English or Spanish* 🌐 *www.30minutesfromtikal.com* 💳 *No credit cards* 🛏 *11 rooms* 🍴 *Free breakfast.*

Shopping

Although most souvenirs here are similar to those found elsewhere in Guatemala, the beautiful wood carvings are unique to El Petén. More than 70 families in this small town dedicate themselves to this craft. Their wares are on display on the side of the highway right before the turnoff for the Camino Real and La Lancha hotels on the road to Tikal, and also in small shops in El Remate.

North Shore, Lake Petén Itzá, and Quexil Lagoon

8 miles (13 km) west of El Remate.

The small villages of San Pedro, San José, and San Andrés, on the northwest shore of Lake Petén Itzá, have beautiful vistas of the sparkling lake. Several upscale lodges and hotels have opened here or on nearby Quexil Lagoon, and the area is accessible via bus or car on an improved (but bumpy) dirt road from El Remate or Santa Elena, or in the clockwise direction from San Benito.

Hotels

★ Bolontiku Boutique Hotel & Spa
$$$$ | **HOTEL** | A private boat transports you to this posh hideaway, where you're given five-star service in the jungle. **Pros:** exquisite, spacious, lakeview rooms; enticing pool and lakefront; excellent service; boat service will take you to Flores and back. **Cons:** remote location; very limited dining options; may be too relaxing for some. [$] *Rooms from: Q1,920* ✉ *Punta de Piedra Nitum Frente a la Isla De Flores, El Remate* ☎ *7963–0909* 🌐 *www.bolontikuhotel.com* 🛏 *15 rooms* 🍴 *Free breakfast.*

★ La Lancha
$$$$ | **RESORT** | Francis Ford Coppola's Guatemalan lodging is decorated in exquisite taste, with rich textures and all casitas glimpsing Lake Petén Itzá. **Pros:** lovely lake views; excellent restaurant; a/c in rooms; frequent specials. **Cons:** expensive (for Guatemala); somewhat remote; lots of steep steps; you can hear your neighbors in the cheaper duplex units. [$] *Rooms from: Q2,069* ✉ *8 miles (13 km) west of El Remate, San José* ☎ *502/7928–8331, 800/611–9774 in U.S. and Canada* 🌐 *www.coppolaresorts.com/lalancha* 🛏 *10 rooms* 🍴 *Free breakfast.*

Las Lagunas
$$$$ | **RESORT** | **FAMILY** | Las Lagunas' storied founder had a passion for hunting trophy game; now his resort brings a hunting lodge aesthetic to lagoon-side luxury, on the expansive grounds of a nature reserve with spider monkey acrobats giving frequent shows. **Pros:** 200-acre jungle preserve; well-oiled luxury with howler monkey wake-up calls; great attention to detail. **Cons:** rates are sky-high, especially for Guatemala; remote enough that pricey on-site dining is your main option; secluded. [$] *Rooms from: Q2,319* ✉ *Desarrollo de Tayasal, Flores* ✣ *Left off Km 1.5, Carretera a San Miguel* ☎ *502/7790–0300* 🌐 *www.laslagunashotel.com* 🛏 *19 rooms* 🍴 *Free breakfast.*

El Mirador

Sights

El Mirador
ARCHAEOLOGICAL SITE | El Mirador, once equal in size and splendor to Tikal, may eventually equal Tikal as a must-see Mayan ruin. It's just now being explored, but elaborate plans are being laid to establish a huge park four times the size of Tikal. Dr. Richard D. Hansen of the University of Utah is director for the Mirador Basin Project, sponsored by the Foundation for Anthropological Research and Environmental Studies (FARES). The Mirador Basin contains the El Mirador site itself, four other known Mayan cities that probably were as large as Tikal (Nakbé, El Tintal, Xulnal, and Wakná), and many smaller but important sites—perhaps as many as 80 to 100 cities. The Mirador Basin is home to an incredible diversity of plant and animal life, including 200 species of birds, 40 kinds of animals (including several endangered ones, such as jaguars), 300 kinds of trees, and 2,000 different species of flora. It has been nominated as a UNESCO World Heritage Site. Currently, fewer than 2,500 visitors get to El Mirador annually, as it's a difficult trek requiring four to six days of hiking (round-trip). The jumping-off point for the trek is Carmelita Village, about 50 miles (84 km) north of Flores. There are no hotels in the Mirador Basin and no roads except for dirt paths. Local tour companies such as Martsam Tours in Flores and elsewhere can arrange treks. For those with the budget, like actor Mel Gibson, you can visit by helicopter. ✉ *40 miles (66 km) northwest of Tikal* 🌐 *www.miradorbasin.com.*

Index

Photo Credits

Front Cover: Matteo Colombo [Description: Aerial of the Blue Hole, Belize.]. **Back cover, from left to right:** QArts/Shutterstock, Ondrej Prosicky/Shutterstock, Aleksandar Todorovic/Shutterstock. **Spine:** Mark Yarchoan/Shutterstock. **Interior, from left to right:** Mehdi Kasumov/Shutterstock (1). Pedro Hélder da Costa Pinheiro/iStockphoto (2). **Chapter 1: Experience Belize:** Kevin Wells Photography/Shutterstock (6-7). Mr. JK/Shutterstock (8). SimonDannhauer/Dreamstimes (9). WitR/Shutterstock (9). Michael Conlin/iStockphoto (10). Simon Dannhauer/Shutterstock (10). Belize Tourism Board (10). Belize Tourism Board (11). Duarte Dellarole/Dreamstime (11). Kevin Wells/iStockphoto (12). Lucie Petrikova/Shutterstock (12). Gundolf Pfotenhauer (12). Milosk50/Dreamstime (12). Dena Burnett (13). Roijoy/iStockphoto (13). Belize Tourism Board (13). Belize Tourism Board (13). The Placencia (14). Belize Tourism Board (14). Belize Tourism Board (14). ThoseLittleWings/Shutterstock (15). Ethan Daniels/Shutterstock (16). TreeLangdon/Shutterstock (16). Danita Delmont/Shutterstock (16). Pete Niesen/Shutterstock (17). MamoruCordoba/Shutterstock (17). Mehdi Kasumov/Shutterstock (18). Belize Tourism Board (18). Belize Tourism Board (18). Belize Hub (18). Belize Tourism Board (19). shootanywhere/iStockphoto (20). carlosrojas20/iStockphoto (21). **Chapter 3: Belize City:** Roxbur-Photography/Shutterstock (59). Leonid Andronov/Shutterstock (73). **Chapter 4: The Cayes and Atolls:** Duarte Dellarole/Shutterstock (83). Carolyn Bingham/Dreamstime (97). Jacqueline Cabral/Glover's Atoll Resort (138). **Chapter 5: Northern Belize:** Wollertz/Dreamstime (141). Wollertz/Shutterstock (154). Jennifer Williams/Wikimedia (169). **Chapter 6: The Cayo:** Suzi Pratt/Shutterstock (171). Johanna Veldstra/Shutterstock (183). Mehdi Kasumov/Shutterstock (208). **Chapter 7: The Southern Coast:** Matyas Rehak/Shutterstock (211). Matyas Rehak/Dreamstime (221). Roi Brooks/Shutterstock (227). Callum Lee101/Shutterstock (238). **Chapter 8: The Deep South:** Daniel Andis/Shutterstock (247). Kevin Wells Photography/Shutterstock (260). **Chapter 9: Side Trip to Guatemala:** JORGE SEGOVIA VILCHEZ/Shutterstock (269). Simon Dannhauer/Shutterstock (277). Indigoai/iStockphoto (286). **About Our Writers:** All photos are courtesy of the writers.

Every effort has been made to trace the copyright holders, and we apologize in advance for any accidental errors. We would be happy to apply the corrections in the following edition of this publication.

Notes

Notes

Notes

Notes

Notes

Notes

Notes

Notes